MW00617700

Resurrection and the Restoration of Israel

JON D. LEVENSON

Resurrection and the Restoration of Israel

THE ULTIMATE VICTORY OF THE GOD OF LIFE

Yale University Press
New Haven &
London

Quotations from the Hebrew Bible are (unless otherwise noted) reprinted from *Tanakh: The Holy Scriptures,* © 1985, published by The Jewish Publication Society, with the permission of the publisher.

The Scripture quotations from the New Testament contained herein are from the New Revised Standard Version Bible, copyright © 1989 by the Division of Christian Education of the National Council of Churches in the U.S.A., and are used by permission. All rights reserved.

Parts of this book were originally published as the following articles and appear here in substantially reworked form:
"The Fact of Death and the Promise of Life in Israelite Religion," in *The Papers of the Henry Luce III Fellows in Theology,* vol. VI, ed. Christopher I. Wilkins (2003), pp. 139–54. Reprinted with permission of the Henry R. Luce III Fellows Program and the Association of Theological Schools.
"Resurrection in the Torah: A Second Look," *CTI Reflections* 6 (2002): 2–29. Reprinted with permission of the Center of Theological Inquiry.
"The Resurrection of the Dead and the Construction of Personal Identity in Ancient Israel," in *Congress Volume: Basel 2001,* ed. A. Lemaire (2002), pp. 305–22. Reprinted with permission of Koninklijke Brill N.V.

Set in Sabon Roman types by Keystone Typesetting, Inc., Orwigsburg, Pennsylvania.
Printed in the United States of America by Sheridan Books, Chelsea, Michigan.

The Library of Congress has cataloged the hardcover edition as follows:

Levenson, Jon Douglas.
Resurrection and the restoration of Israel: the ultimate victory of the God of life /
Jon D. Levenson.
p. cm.
Includes bibliographical references and index.
ISBN-13: 978-0-300-11735-6 (hardcover)
ISBN-10: 0-300-11735-3 (hardcover)
1. Resurrection (Jewish theology) 2. Jews — Restoration. 3. Bible. O.T. — Criticism, interpretation, etc. I. Title.
BM645.R47L48 2006
296.3'3 — dc22   2006003113

ISBN 978-0-300-13635-7 (pbk. : alk. paper)

A catalogue record for this book is available from the British Library.

The paper in this book meets the guidelines for permanence and durability of the Committee on Production Guidelines for Book Longevity of the Council on Library Resources.

10 9 8 7 6 5 4 3 2 1

To the memory of my mother, Ethyl S. Levenson

"The LORD guards the loyal [*ĕmûnîm*]." This is the people Israel, who recite, "Blessed be He who revives the dead," and answer "Amen" [*ʾāmēn*] with complete trust [*ĕmûnâ*], for they trust [*maʾămînîm*] with all their strength in the Holy One (blessed be He!) that He will revive the dead, even though the resurrection of the dead has not yet come about. They recite, "who redeems Israel," even though they have not yet been redeemed, and "Blessed is He who rebuilds Jerusalem," even though it has not yet been rebuilt. Said the Holy One (blessed be He!): "They were redeemed only for a short time and then they were once again subjugated, yet they trust [*maʾămînîm*] in Me that I will redeem them in the future." Hence, "The LORD guards the loyal [*ĕmûnîm*]."
— *Midrash Tehillim* to Psalm 31:24

Contents

Preface

The study that follows centers on a central belief in rabbinic Judaism to which precious little attention has been given in modern times. This is the belief that at the end of history, God will resurrect the dead and restore them to full bodily existence. Often mistaken for belief in the immortality of the soul — an affirmation with which, to be sure, resurrection can and does readily coexist — resurrection is too often thought by the less learned to be a Christian innovation and by the more learned to be at best tangential to Judaism. This misperception derives much of its strength from the consensus view among specialists in the Hebrew Bible or postbiblical Judaism and informed non-specialists alike. I can paraphrase the consensus thus:

> The resurrection of the dead has no early roots or sources in the Hebrew Bible, which offers a vision of life and death and the relationship between them that is strikingly different from those that underlie a belief in resurrection. In the Hebrew Bible (except for passages that are very few and very late), death is an altogether unproblematic part of God's plan, and there is neither an expectation nor even a hope to transcend it. Indeed, death is there deemed to be part of God's creation and thus presents no theological scandal at all. When people died, they were thought to descend without exception to the dreary netherworld known as Sheol, from which there was no chance of return. Only very late in the period of the Second Temple, as the last books in

the Hebrew Bible were being written, did an alternative position appear. This came about because of the insult to the notion of a just God delivered by the death of the martyrs, that is, the undeserved demise of individuals whose death was owing precisely to their fidelity to God and his revelation. The hope for resurrection developed because of the need to compensate the martyrs for their demise, proving God just after all. A major source of this radically new expectation lay in Zoroastrianism, an Iranian religious tradition that had long voiced a hope for the resurrection of the dead. The Jewish doctrine of resurrection was thus not only unprecedented in the Hebrew Bible; it was also in large measure a foreign importation devised to solve a new and embarrassing theological crisis. Though the resurrection of the dead survived in the Judaism of the ancient rabbis, it was not deeply rooted therein and was, in fact, a minor and dispensable item in the theological repertory of classical Judaism.

I have long regarded each statement in the paragraph above as erroneous and argue so in the course of this book. In chapters 1, 2, and (in a different way) 14, I argue that the expectation of the resurrection of the dead was a weight-bearing beam in the edifice of rabbinic Judaism. It was central to two major and inseparable elements of rabbinic Judaism, the rabbis' vision of redemption and their understanding of Jewish peoplehood. Without the restoration of the people Israel, a flesh-and-blood people, God's promises to them remained unfulfilled, and the world remained unredeemed. Those who classify the Jewish expectation of resurrection under more universal and individualistic rubrics, such as "life after death," miss the promissory character of the expectation and its inextricable connection to a natural family, the Jews. Modern individualism has, in fact, been a major impediment to the proper understanding of resurrection in Judaism, somewhat the way the focus on the nature of the soul was in earlier periods of Western thought. When the programmatic question is defined as "Will I have life after death?" the discussion has already gotten off on the wrong foot.

It is too often forgotten that the classical Jewish doctrine of resurrection does not represent a belief that death can be avoided, averted, or minimized. All to the contrary, it takes the gravity and tragedy of death with full seriousness and represents a belief that death will be — miraculously, supernaturally, graciously — *overcome*. Resurrection finds its place within a larger vision not of the continuation of the world but of its redemption.

In chapter 2, I argue that within their own theological universe and their understanding of biblical interpretation, the rabbis had good reason to find resurrection in the Torah itself and, in doing so, they exposed some important aspects of biblical thought largely overlooked by modern scholars. Chief among these aspects is the fact that in the Torah, promises can be fulfilled even after those to whom they have been promised have died. This is not, as the rabbis would (sometimes) have it, because the recipients of the promise will be resurrected and thus experience the fulfillment of the promise after all. Rather, it is because in the Hebrew Bible, the lives of ancestors and descendants were inextricably connected in ways that modern people have enormous problems imagining.

In chapters 3 and 4, I investigate the nature of Sheol and argue that in the Hebrew Bible Sheol was not generally thought to be the universal destination of the departed, nor was it universally assumed that it was impossible to return therefrom. Rather, we must take seriously the theology that underlies the biblical reports of individuals who die blessed and contented, and we must thus distinguish between fortunate deaths and unfortunate deaths. When we do so, we uncover a tension between a long-standing belief that everyone eventually comes to Sheol, on the one hand, and a newer affirmation of the unlimited power of the God of Israel to deliver faithful worshipers from even the harshest adversity, on the other. This key tension is never resolved but does gesture toward the later expectation of resurrection, in which both the inevitability of death and the power of God to deliver from it are assumed. Chapter 5 offers an investigation of the images of individual immortality that appear principally in Israelite devotional literature and offers a new definition of the immortality for which the authors longed, one closer to the idea of resurrection but also truer to the sources in the Hebrew Bible themselves. This is the immortality that results from God's gracious rescue of his worshipers from death and issues in new or renewed intimacy between the worshipers and God. It is, in fact, quite different from immortality that is based on the belief that the human self possesses an indestructible core — a soul, spirit, consciousness, or the like — that survives death naturally. That the Hebrew Bible does not portray such immortality as realized in actual fact must not be taken to excuse neglect of the longing for it.

Chapter 6 advances the notion that the dominant biblical idea of the people Israel has profound affinities with the later doctrine of resurrection that previous scholarship has utterly missed. The ancient Israelite sources on which I focus in that chapter see Israel's origin and preservation as due to their God's miraculous intervention in bringing them into existence in the first place and rescuing them from certain death afterward. This is, once again, not to claim that the most ancient sources display any belief in individual resurrection. Rather, it is to point out the functional equivalence of infertility with death and, correlatively, of miraculous conception or the restoration of the lost child with resurrection.

Chapter 7 presents an analysis of the most extensive narrative account of resurrection in the Hebrew Bible and challenges (as do other sections of the book) the notion that God's resurrecting the dead was an altogether alien notion until very late in Israelite history. The resurrection that the miracle-working prophet Elisha performs is not, of course, the general resurrection that Judaism later expected at the end-time, but it does demonstrate a firm faith in God's power over death, a key point in the later expectation that is often mistakenly thought to be an innovation in the late sources. Chapter 8 explores the relevance of certain old Canaanite literature to our subject and, in particular, to the theme of the lost and restored children that figures so prominently in chapters 6 and 7.

The way that same theme becomes a paradigm of national restoration will occupy our attention in chapter 9, which concentrates on prophetic visions of the restored Israel as a widow bereaved of her children, who nonetheless miraculously return. In chapter 10, I then connect the themes of national restoration with the longest vision of resurrection in the Hebrew Bible, Ezekiel's vision in the valley of the dry bones. In this symbolic representation of national recovery, restoration comes about not through miraculous fertility or the return of lost children but, significantly, through the resurrection of dead and despondent Israel from their graves, to return to the land God has indefeasibly promised them.

Chapter 11 challenges the conventional notion that death was thought to be theologically unproblematic until very late and argues, to the contrary, that there had always been a tension between the hymnic affirmations that God has power over life and death and prefers life, on the one hand, and the brute fact of human mortality, on the other. Chapter 12 then examines in detail the first clear and explicit canonical affirmation of the expectation of resurrection, Dan 12:1–3, arguing that its language and imagery have deeper roots in previous tradition than most scholars have noticed and that the resurrection of the dead in Judaism cannot be separated from the long-standing faith in the eventual restoration of the people Israel that is its main subject. Chapter 13 explores the Canaanite and older Israelite roots of the notion of the restoration of life and fertility, showing how these powerful themes have been adapted to the vision of resurrection that appears in late Second Temple Judaism, catalyzed by apocalyptic expectation. The healing of nature (including nature's worst infirmity, death) had long played a major role in Canaanite and Israelite theology; Jewish apocalyptic focused the expectation of such a miraculous reversal on the expected end-time, bringing us to the verge of the central rabbinic doctrine of the resurrection of the dead.

Nothing indicates the centrality of the resurrection of the dead to rabbinic Judaism more strikingly than the fact that the rabbis imagine a resurrection to have occurred already at Sinai, when the Torah was given. Chapter 14 outlines the place of resurrection within the moral and theological universe of the ancient rabbis and shows why it was indispensable to their vision of divine revelation and human redemption and renewal alike.

The question of how Judaism came to exhibit an expectation of general resurrection (and, ultimately, to require it) is inevitably pertinent to our discussion. This is not, however, a book primarily about the origin of the doctrine, for in my judgment the quest for a single point of origin and a single cause for the belief in resurrection is fruitless and misguided. Although the immediate catalyst was the apocalyptic expectation of a thoroughgoing reversal of the order of things when God finally secures his reign, the expectation of resurrection linked up with a number of other aspects of Judaism already ancient when Jewish apocalyptic first appeared. My principal focus lies on those multiple linkages, those points of connection, between the new and highly controversial teaching and the long-standing tradition in which it took shape and which it ultimately reshaped.

My argument, then, is that the resurrection of the dead did not appear as a jarring innovation in Second Temple Judaism but instead developed slowly and unevenly over the preceding centuries. Growing out of the convergence of a number of biblical themes, it drew, most centrally, on the long-standing conviction that God would yet again prove faithful to his promises of life for his people and that he had the stupendous might it would take to do so. That there was no historical inevitability to this development is easily seen in the simple fact that when the expectation of resurrection finally appeared in full clarity, it was opposed by some Jews, most famously the Sadducees but hardly them alone. Although my focus here lies on the antecedents of the normative rabbinic belief in the resurrection of the dead, no one should underestimate the diversity of prerabbinic and nonrabbinic Judaism on the subject. The claim that only the opponents of resurrection had biblical tradition on their side, however, is simplistic and shortsighted. It misses both the diversity and dynamism of biblical thinking on death and life and the organic connections between earlier and later visions of redemption.

Acknowledgments

My initial research for this volume began when I was a Henry R. Luce III Senior Fellow in Theology in 1999 and 2000. Hearty appreciation is owed to the Henry Luce Foundation and to the Association of Theological Schools, which administers the fellowship, for their support and generosity.

Four scholars were kind enough to read part or all of my manuscript at various stages in its preparation, Professors Gary A. Anderson, Richard J. Clifford, and Kevin Madigan and Dr. Suzanne Smith. Needless to say, I owe them all a great debt of gratitude for their help, and equally needless to say, they must all be exonerated from any wrongheadedness that remains.

Two eagle-eyed doctoral students, each with extraordinary editorial skills, saved me from much embarrassment. I thank J. Randall Short and Mark A. Nussberger for their good work, and Harvard Divinity School for allowing me to employ them as research assistants over the years.

Two fine typists, Erin McGrath and Sarah Lefebvre, bore the brunt of my increasingly illegible handwriting over the years. I thank them not only for their typing but also for their assistance on the several occasions when my computer skills needed a resurrection of their own.

Quotations from the Hebrew Bible are taken from *Tanakh* (Philadelphia: Jewish Publication Society, 5746/1985), unless otherwise indicated. In the notes, I refer to this translation as NJPS (for New Jewish Publication Society version). As in the NJPS, the enumeration of chapters and verses follows the Hebrew, not the English, where there is a divergence.

I have rendered the tetragrammaton without vowels, even when quoting authors who have inserted vowels, and indicated the difference by putting the term in brackets: [YHWH].

Abbreviations

Hebrew Bible

1 Chr	1 Chronicles
2 Chr	2 Chronicles
Dan	Daniel
Deut	Deuteronomy
Exod	Exodus
Ezek	Ezekiel
Gen	Genesis
Hos	Hosea
Isa	Isaiah
Jer	Jeremiah
Jon	Jonah
Josh	Joshua
Judg	Judges
1 Kgs	1 Kings
2 Kgs	2 Kings
Lev	Leviticus
Neh	Nehemiah
Num	Numbers
Prov	Proverbs
Ps	Psalms

Qoh	Qoheleth
1 Sam	1 Samuel
2 Sam	2 Samuel
Song	Song of Songs
Zech	Zechariah

| MT | Masoretic Text |

Rabbinic Literature

Abod. Zara	*Abodah Zarah*
Abot R. Nat.	*Abot de Rabbi Nathan*
b.	*Babylonian Talmud*
B. Bat.	*Baba Batra*
Ber.	*Berakhot*
Ket.	*Ketubbot*
Lam. Rab.	*Lamentations Rabbah*
Lev. Rab.	*Leviticus Rabbah*
m.	*Mishnah*
Ma'as Sh.	*Ma'aser Sheni*
Meg.	*Megillah*
Mek.	*Mekilta de-Rabbi Ishmael*
Men.	*Menahot*
Mo'ed Qaṭ.	*Mo'ed Qaṭan*
Num. Rab.	*Numbers Rabbah*
Pes. R. Kah.	*Pesikta de-Rab Kahana*
Qidd.	*Qiddushin*
Qoh. Rabb.	*Qoheleth Rabbah*
Sanh.	*Sanhedrin*
Shabb.	*Shabbat*
Sifre Deut.	*Sifre Deuteronomy*
Suk.	*Sukkah*
t.	*Tosefta*
Tam.	*Tamid*

Other Ancient Jewish Literature

Ant	*Jewish Antiquities*
Jdt	Judith
Jub	Jubilees
1QIs[a]	An Isaiah scroll from Qumran, Cave 1
Sir	Wisdom of Joshua ben Sira
Wis	Wisdom of Solomon

New Testament

Acts	Acts of the Apostles
1 Cor	1 Corinthians
Matt	Gospel of Matthew

Scholarly Publications

AB	Anchor Bible
ABD	*The Anchor Bible Dictionary*
AfO	*Archiv für Orientforschung*
ANET	*Ancient Near Eastern Texts Relating to the Old Testament*
AOAT	Alter Orient und Altes Testament
BA	*Biblical Archaeologist*
BBB	Bonner biblische Beiträge
BDB	*The Brown-Driver-Briggs Hebrew and English Lexicon*
BHS	*Biblia Hebraica Stuttgartensia*
BJRL	*Bulletin of the John Rylands University Library of Manchester*
BN	*Biblische Notizen*
BO	Biblica et orientalia
CBOTS	Coniectanea biblica, Old Testament Series
CBQ	*Catholic Biblical Quarterly*
CBQMS	Catholic Biblical Quarterly Monograph Series
FAT	*Forschungen zum Alten Testament*
HNT	Handbuch zum Neuen Testament
HSM	Harvard Semitic Monographs
HSS	Harvard Semitic Studies
HTS	Harvard Theological Studies
HUCA	*Hebrew Union College Annual*
JBL	*Journal of Biblical Literature*
JSOTSS	Journal for the Study of the Old Testament Supplement Series
JSQ	*Jewish Studies Quarterly*
JTS	*Journal of Theological Studies*
NJPS	New Jewish Publication Society translation (*Tanakh*)
OBT	Overtures to Biblical Theology
OTL	Old Testament Library
PAAJR	*Proceedings of the American Academy for Jewish Research*
RBL	*Review of Biblical Literature*
SBLSS	Society of Biblical Literature Symposium Series
ST	*Studia theologica*
TS	*Theological Studies*
VT	*Vetus Testamentum*

Resurrection and the Restoration of Israel

The Modern Jewish Preference for Immortality

We consider ourselves no longer a nation but a religious community.

We reassert the doctrine of Judaism, that the soul of man is immortal, grounding this belief on the divine nature of the human spirit.
— Pittsburgh Platform (Reform Judaism), 1885

That classical Judaism firmly believed in the resurrection of the dead — indeed, insisted upon it as a defining tenet of the community — today comes as a shock to most Jews and Christians alike. The reasons are not hard to find. *The American Heritage Dictionary* gives as the first meaning of "resurrection" (lowercase) "a rising from the dead or returning to life" but soon defines "Resurrection" (uppercase) as "the rising again of Christ on the third day after the Crucifixion." The latter meaning, which has historically stood at the very center of the Church's proclamation of its gospel, has deeply colored the perception of resurrection (lowercase) throughout Christendom. As a result, Christians often hold the opinion that the absence in Judaism of a belief in the Resurrection of Jesus indicates the absence of all notions of resurrection in Judaism.[1] Given the structure of classical Christian doctrine, this misperception is hardly surprising. For therein the Resurrection of Jesus is the basis for all human hope to be raised from the dead and to have life eternal. It is interesting, however, that this misperception, bolstered by the ostensible absence of any notion of resurrection in the Torah, is not unwelcome among modern Jews. Consider the Jews who are eager to differentiate their tradition from its major rival among the world religions but are also uninformed about their own religion. For them, it is enormously useful to present Judaism as this-worldly and uninterested in, or even positively skeptical about, the return from death and the World-to-Come. Indeed, wellinformed expositors of the Jewish tradition have felt compelled so to present it themselves.

Abba Hillel Silver, a learned Reform rabbi in the mid-twentieth century and one of the most important figures in American Judaism in his time, is a case in point. In his influential volume *Where Judaism Differed: An Inquiry into the Distinctiveness of Judaism,* Silver presents the resurrection of the dead as a late and degraded development in Jewish thought, a borrowing from foreign sources "to which the Jews added nothing original." The real cause of it is, in fact, nothing more than "the inability of [ancient Jewish] leaders further to withstand popular pressure." In this case, the difference and distinctiveness that is the subject of the book not only involves a contrast with the other ancient Near Eastern and Mediterranean religions from which he thinks Judaism assimilated the ideas in question. It is also very much a difference from Christianity, for which "the doctrine of resurrection . . . is the chief cornerstone of the entire edifice of its faith."[2] Silver's implication is clear: when Jews believe in resurrection, they lose their distinctiveness and assimilate to the dominant mode of religiousness of antiquity and modernity alike — a mode in sharp contrast to the univocal this-worldliness of authentic Judaism.

What this misses, however, is that in modern Western culture, the cognitive pressure on Jews and Christians alike militates against the classical Jewish and Christian doctrines of resurrection. The emphasis on the ultimacy of this world and on ethical striving that pervades Silver's theology is itself thus a reflection of assimilation — assimilation to the naturalism and scientism of the times. By revising the Jewish tradition in the direction that Silver takes, one can claim to be a good Jew while at the same time adhering to a modern materialist sense of human existence and destiny of the sort that dismisses resurrection as an embarrassing relic of the childhood of humanity, a groundless fantasy. Christianity, by way of contrast, founded on the proclamation of Jesus' Resurrection, thus appears not only as incompatible with modern thought but as a deviation from the teaching of the Scriptures that Jews and Christians hold in common to boot. The true, mature, and genuinely biblical religion had no such idea. In the context of Jewish-Christian disputation, the denial of resurrection can therefore be a potent weapon in the armamentarium

of the Jewish disputants. It provides them with an element of religious justification for their own continued existence in the face of the extraordinarily
powerful pressures to assimilate to the Christian host culture: the Christians,
vulnerable to a crude superstition about a god-man who came back from the
dead, have perverted the Hebrew Bible by introducing something altogether
foreign into it. In contrast, the Jews, by adhering to their Bible's belief in the
naturalness of death, are the true and exclusive heirs to the Scriptures and,
what is more, exemplars of a position altogether in line with modern scientific
thinking. By excluding the resurrection of the dead from Judaism, modern
Jews can appear to the world and, more important, to themselves as simultaneously adhering to a way of thinking that is as old and particular as the
Hebrew Bible and as new and universal as modern science.

Substantial as the inducement to redefine Judaism without its historical
commitment to resurrection has been, the obstacle to doing so that the traditional prayer book poses has been at least as formidable. A highly liturgical
religion, whose forms of worship are regulated by religious law, rabbinic Judaism early on gave the doctrine of resurrection a central place in its daily
worship. Consider the second benediction in the prayer known variously as
the *Amidah* ("The Standing Prayer"), the *Tefilla* ("The Prayer," par excellence), or the *Shemoneh Esreh* ("The Eighteen Benedictions"):

> You are mighty forever, my Lord. You are the one who revives the dead,
> powerful to save.
> (You make the wind blow and the rain fall.)[3]
> He sustains the living with kindness and revives the dead with great mercy,
> supports the falling, heals the sick, releases captives, and keeps faith with
> those who sleep in the dust.[4]
> Who is like You, Lord of power? And who can compare to You, O King
> who brings about death and restores life and makes salvation sprout?
> Faithful You are to revive the dead. Blessed are You, O Lord, who revive
> the dead.[5]

According to rabbinic law, this ancient prayer is to be said three times each
weekday, four times on Sabbaths, New Moons, and Festivals, and five times
on the Day of Atonement. There is never a day — never a morning, never an
afternoon, never an evening — without it. The prayer is thus as authoritative
an epitome of rabbinic theology as one can find, and its second benediction
endorses the idea of resurrection repeatedly and emphatically: "revives the
dead" (four times), "keeps faith with those who sleep in the dust," "brings
about death and restores life." Known as *Gevurot* ("Power"), the benediction
sees in God's revival of the dead the outstanding and incomparable instance of

his insuperable might. The other affirmations of his assistance to those in need — his support of the falling, his healing of the sick, and his release of prisoners — are enclosed within an envelope-like structure that begins and ends with an address to the God of Israel as the one who resurrects.

When precisely the resurrection takes place the benediction does not specify. The mention of God's power "to save" and especially the phrase "makes salvation sprout" (*maṣmîaḥ yĕšûʿâ*) suggests that the miraculous revival forms part of an eschatological scenario. Later on, following long-standing biblical precedent, the fifteenth benediction of the same prayer will use the language of "sprouting" (*ṣemaḥ/taṣmîaḥ*) to refer to the expected messianic king, "the Branch of David"[6] — an unmistakable allusion to the end-time restoration of the people Israel after their long degradation. We cannot say for sure, how-ever, whether Gevurot asserts that God's assistance to the falling, ailing, and imprisoned is a constant and reliable reality in the present order of things. Surely its authors, like the authors of the scriptural texts from which they draw their language, knew that some who fall do not rise, illnesses are often progres-sively debilitating and ultimately fatal, and many who are incarcerated will never leave prison alive. The likelihood, therefore, is that the atemporal lan-guage of the benediction (which speaks in participles rather than finite verbs) affirms that God's deliverance may occasionally be witnessed in the present dispensation but will become fully manifest and unassailable only at or after the messianic consummation. What it affirms, in other words, is not that we can rely upon God to *prevent* our falling, illness, imprisonment, and death but that he has the power to *reverse* these painful conditions and will eventually prove faithful to his promise to do so. That he has indeed made a promise to the dead and can be trusted to keep it becomes evident from the two instances of the root *ʾāmēn* in the benediction. The first, reflecting the language of the eschatological resurrection predicted in Dan 12:1–3 (a text to which we shall devote much attention),[7] speaks of God's "faith with those who sleep in the dust." What is new here, over against the scriptural base, is the affirmation of God's faithfulness (*ʾĕmûnātô*). Here, the pronominal suffix is not objective but subjective. It refers not to the believer's faith in God but to God's faithfulness to raise to life those who, as Dan 12:2 puts it, "sleep in the dust of the earth." The same idea appears in the penultimate affirmation that "Faithful [*neʾĕmān*] You are to revive the dead." Here again, the persons praying are only indi-rectly affirming their own faith that the omnipotent Deity will perform an act of resurrection. That which they directly affirm is God's fidelity or faithfulness to do so. God can be trusted to keep faith even with the dead.

In sum, Gevurot, the second benediction of the Amidah, affirms simultane-ously the cold, hard, unavoidable reality of death and the unshakable trust that

God will revive the dead in the eschatological future. It thus stands among the multitude of texts in the Hebrew Bible (whose language it continually adopts) that maintain that although bad things do indeed happen to good people, they are not the last word. The last word, rather, is a good thing, in this case God's miraculous intervention into history to grant the dead of all generations new life as he finally secures his triumph over evil and suffering and establishes on earth the kingdom over which he already reigns in the higher realm.[8]

In this view of things, death does not lose its reality or its grimness, only its finality. Its continued existence constitutes a standing reproach to the God who "keeps faith with those who sleep in the dust" and yet allows them to do so, having (to all appearances) quite forgotten his promise to revive them. In this way, death must be seen as an opponent of the living God whose faithfulness to his promises will not be perspicuous until death is vanquished and eliminated. Yet the theology that underlies Gevurot is far from dualistic. For the same God who is "powerful to save" and "faithful to revive the dead" is also the "king who brings about death," in other words, death's own author, the One who gives life but also withdraws it. Whatever overtones of ancient myth may still be heard behind this text — myth that, as we shall see, is very much alive in some biblical materials — death is not a force independent of the divine king and outside his control before the final victory is won. Death, no less than life, is part of God's plan, but it is — or can be made into — only one stage of the plan, and not the last. The gracious king who gives and withdraws life will give it again.

Gevurot leaves open a question that readily occurs to us. What is the fate of the dead before they are resurrected? The identification of them as "those who sleep in the dust" tempts us to say that they are not really dead at all but only asleep, enfolded in God's protective grace until they are at last revived. The temptation is best resisted. For neither in the Hebrew Bible nor in rabbinic literature is sleep generally seen as such a benign state. It is more than occasionally associated with death, as it is here, just as waking up is associated (in both literatures) with resurrection.[9] And "dust," not a pleasant place to sleep under the best of circumstances, recalls the LORD's sentence upon Adam that he shall:

> . . . return to the ground —
> For from it you were taken.
> For dust you are,
> And to dust you shall return. (Gen 3:19)

But neither should we say that the Gevurot benediction relegates the dead to oblivion until the day of their restoration into life. For they do still exist at least in the mind of the God who faithfully remembers his promises to them and will bring about their redemption. Nor should Gevurot be taken to imply that the dead lack souls that survive the demise of their bodies. As James Barr has argued, the dichotomy between the resurrection of the dead and the immortality of the soul, though still common in the scholarly literature, is overdone and bears reexamination.[10] A firm belief in the resurrection of the dead does not at all entail a disbelief in the immortality of some aspect of the person or in the notion that the departed righteous even now enjoy a blissful communion with God. The point, rather, is that, whatever notions of the soul circulated in ancient Judaism (and there were several), in the Amidah God was not thought to have fulfilled his promises until the *whole* person returned, body included.[11] Like death, a disembodied existence was deemed to be other than the last word, for the person is not "the ghost in the machine" (that is, the body) but rather a psychophysical unity. Even the familiar language of "body and soul," with its implicitly dualistic associations, cannot do full justice to the Jewish view under discussion.

As the very term *Gevurot* ("power") implies, the resurrection of the dead in this benediction serves as a definitive manifestation of God's might. By reviving those who have gone the way of all flesh, God shows his power to be greater even than the power of nature (itself his own creation). Like creation, resurrection is a preeminently *super*natural act, a miraculous reversal of the course of nature. Through it, God thus transforms death, nature's last word, into a prelude to his own new act of creation, the re-creation of human beings in a form that is bodily yet immune to the vulnerabilities and ravages of biological life. So conceived, resurrection thus recapitulates but also transcends the creation of humanity. The miracle of the end-time restores the miracle of the beginning.

It is this inextricable association of resurrection with supernatural intervention that sticks most persistently in the craw of many modern Jews and Christians.[12] As Milton Steinberg puts it, "Jewish modernists accept less [than the traditional idea of resurrection]" and "abandon the doctrine[] of the Resurrection of the body, at least in any literal sense," though they do "retain faith in the deathlessness of man's spirit not only in its naturalistic connotations but also in its beyond-this-life significance as well."[13] What remains to be explored is the character of this nonliteral doctrine of the resurrection of the body. Obviously, a body that has been revived from true death (and not merely some near-death experience) and raised into eternal life is not literally the body human beings inhabit in the current order of things.[14] Rather, resurrection is one key element in a whole panorama of redemptive and re-creative events that characterize the rabbinic vision of the end of history. These events derive from the visions of the biblical prophets and apocalyptic seers, visions communicated, as they must be, in mythopoetic language. Seen this way, the resurrection of the dead belongs with the other elements of Jewish eschatological expectation, such as the liberation of the Jews from subjugation to Gentile rule, the ingathering of the exile to the Land of Israel, the enthronement of the God of Israel, the reconstruction of Jerusalem as God's dwelling, and the coming of the messianic king. All of these are requested and envisioned in the Amidah, and all are to some degree continuous with ordinary life but also wondrously, scandalously discontinuous with it. Once we have recognized this dimension of discontinuity, we become more chary of speaking of a "literal" doctrine of the resurrection of the body — whether in affirmation or in negation. For to literalize is to prosaize, and to prosaize a mythopoetic vision is to traduce it.

The history of the translation of Gevurot in non-Orthodox prayer books demonstrates that Steinberg's "Jewish modernists" object to more about resurrection than simply the literalism with which some may hold it. His reference to their "faith in the deathlessness of man's spirit . . . also in its beyond-this-life significance"[15] is the key to understanding the transformation that Gevurot undergoes when the resurrection of the dead, even in a nonliteral sense, is no longer deemed credible. Eschatology, in a word, collapses into creation, God's supernatural act turns into humanity's God-given nature, memory takes the place of redemption, and the resurrection of the dead is quietly but eventfully redefined as the immortality of the individual soul.[16]

To those who subscribe to this transformation, the wording of the Gevurot benediction of the Amidah is, of course, a major challenge. Neil Gillman identifies "three possible [Jewish] strategies for handling a liturgy that no longer reflects your theology: replace the Hebrew with a more palatable alternative; keep the Hebrew text and shade the translation to accommodate your new interpretation of the doctrine; or provide options which allow the worshipper to choose a text that reflects his or her particular belief."[17] Gillman points out that the great scholar and early exponent of Reform Judaism Abraham Geiger (1810–74) explicitly wrote that the concepts of afterlife appropriate to modern Jews "should not be expressed in terms which suggest a future revival, a resurrection of the body; rather they must stress the immortality of the human soul" — a view widely held in his time.[18] In consequence, Geiger's own German translation of the close of Gevurot rendered it as "*der Leben spendet hier und dort*," literally, "who bestows life here and there" — "a vaguely-worded promise of eternal life," as Gillman puts it,[19] and hardly an affirmation of resurrection.

Later Reform prayer books have tended to follow the lead of another important figure in early Reform Judaism, David Einhorn (1809–79), who served the movement first in Germany and then in the United States. Advocating the "replac[ement of] the doctrine of resurrection with 'the idea of a purely spiritual immortality,'" Einhorn closed his Hebrew version of Gevurot not with the classical expression "[You] who revive the dead" but with another traditional liturgical affirmation phrase, the benediction one recites after being called to the Torah, "Who has planted immortal life within us."[20] This both removes the scandal of resurrection and transfers the focus of immortality from Torah to something ostensibly more universal, creation itself.[21] This upholds God's miraculous power — for what could be more miraculous than "immortal life"? — but it relegates the miracle safely to the primordial past and removes any expectation that something analogous to it will occur in the eschatological future.

The best-known and longest-lasting Reform prayer book, *The Union Prayerbook* (1895), pursues several strategies to affirm the continued existence of the dead while sidestepping the rabbinic expectation that they will be miraculously revived. "Only the body has died and has been laid in the dust," reads one prayer. "The spirit lives in the shelter of God's love and mercy." Here immortality of the soul is affirmed along with the implication that the body will stay in the dust. "Our loved ones continue," the prayer goes on,

> also, in the remembrance of those to whom they were precious. Their deeds of lovingkindness, the true and beautiful words they spoke are treasured up as incentives to conduct by which the living honor the dead.[22]

Here, all mention of God is dropped, and afterlife is redefined as the memory that the living have of the dead and the positive influence that the departed have on those who survive them. Not only is resurrection nowhere to be found, but even immortality has, in comparison with the classical rabbinic ideas, been massively redefined and drastically curtailed. The affirmation that takes the place of these two traditional doctrines is, however, markedly less optimistic than they are, since it implies that the dead cease to exist when they are forgotten (as nearly all are two or three generations later) or if their deeds and words were other than loving, kind, true, and beautiful. It also excludes a crucial element in the classical vision of God's postmortem involvement with human beings — the element of reward and punishment, which secures in the future life the justice of God so often and so mysteriously absent in this one. In sum, this formulation not only excludes the element of re-creation; it also excludes the exercise of divine mercy and judgment upon the dead. All of these points had been central to the classical rabbinic expectation.

The *Union Prayerbook* follows Einhorn's lead in altering the Hebrew as well as the English translation of resurrection so as to vitiate the unpalatable doctrine without openly negating it. Instead of "You are the one who revives the dead" (*měḥayyēh mētim 'attâ*), for example, it substitutes "Thou preservest all" (*měḥayyēh hakkōl*),[23] thus retaining but also retranslating the Hebrew verb and changing its object as well. The resultant wording leaves open the possibility that God's preservation extends beyond the grave but stops well short of affirming that it does. Even if the traditional possibility is accepted, however, the substitution of "preserve" for "revive, give life to" makes it difficult to conceive the afterlife in question as an instance of God's supernatural intervention to reverse death and establish his longed-for justice. The image, rather, is one of a smooth and uneventful continuation of the this-worldly scenario in which God "sustains the living." Death really does not make much difference. Things continue almost as if it had not happened. In fact, the two movements evident in this text from the *Union Prayerbook* are implications of each other. Since death is no great source of grief—divine sustenance continues whether it happens or not—its reversal in the joy of resurrection or immortality can be safely minimized as well.

Gillman points out that the successor to the *Union Prayerbook*, the *Gates of Prayer* (5735/1975), "adopts the more recent practice of providing several options for the evening and morning service," only one of which, however, retains the traditional Hebrew formulation, *měḥayyēh mētim*, "Who revive the dead." Even this it renders, however, in a very strange way indeed:

> We pray . . . for love through which we may all blossom into persons who have gained power over our own lives.

This wording subordinates the traditional affirmation of resurrection at the beginning of Gevurot to the affirmation immediately preceding it that God "sustains the living with kindness." The objectionable Hebrew phrase, though retained, is now reinterpreted to refer to God's role in aiding human self-empowerment. The dead have disappeared altogether, and resurrection has been redefined as "power over [one's] own life." The inversion is striking: an ancient acclamation of divine power in the face of ultimate and unavoidable human defeat has been transformed into a thoroughly modern prayer for enhanced personal autonomy. At the end of the same blessing, the blurring of the Hebrew is even more thoroughgoing:

> Praised be the God whose gift is life, whose cleansing rains let parched men and women flower toward the sun.[24]

This metaphor views the dead as vegetation in need of watering, resurrection as rainfall, and the new life that follows as a flowering in the presence not of

God but of the sun. Whatever poetic resonance this English prayer possesses or lacks, it continues the old Reform strategy of evading the affirmation of the resurrection of the dead, though in the more moderate form that retains the very Hebrew that the English evades. In this case, however, the English does not seem to substitute immortality, as earlier Reform translations did, but defines God's action in strictly this-worldly terms — as directed toward human self-empowerment and refreshment, metaphorically conveyed by reference to the revival of plants that are not really dead at all.

The strategy that retains the Hebrew but gives it a radically new meaning seems to accommodate both traditionalists and modernists, as Steinberg calls the two groups. It allows the former to affirm the classical teaching and the latter to restrict themselves to an identification of God as the giver of life without subscribing to the ancient (and related) notion that he is also the vanquisher of death. The implication of this liturgical pluralism is to define Judaism in the aggregate as agnostic on the question of the resurrection of the dead. One can affirm it or one can deny it, without loss. The choice is one of personal preference. And in this, the liturgical pluralism shows itself to be anything but neutral in the conflict between the traditionalist and modernist theologies. For the rabbinic tradition, as we shall see in the next chapter, views the resurrection of the dead as a normative and defining doctrine, not simply as one option among many that a Jew may or may not elect without destroying the central claims of Judaism. To the rabbis who formulated or canonized Gevurot, the resurrection of the dead was not dispensable.

A similar equivocation to those in the Reform prayer books can be found in the versions associated with the Conservative Movement. Speaking of one influential volume, Gillman (himself an exponent of Conservative Judaism), notes the "predilection for the second strategy for handling troublesome liturgical passages: wherever possible, retain the Hebrew but shade the English translation to reflect a more modern sensibility." Thus, the *Sabbath and Festival Prayer Book* (1946), which dominated Conservative worship for nearly four decades, defends its translation this way: "The rendering of the phrase *mehayyai hameitem* 'who calls the dead to life everlasting' is linguistically sound and rich in meaning for those who cherish the faith in human immortality, as much as for those who maintain the belief in resurrection."[25] *Siddur Sim Shalom,* which replaced the *Sabbath and Festival Prayer Book* and is now widely used in Conservative services, follows a similar tack when it renders the closing words of Gevurot as "Master of [or over] life and death."[26] "Puzzling enough," Gillman remarks, "the phrase immediately preceding the closing benediction is translated as 'Faithful are You in bringing the dead to life again,' or as 'Faithful are You in giving life to the dead.' "[27] The solution to the puzzle most likely lies in two places, either a genuine ambivalence in the translators themselves or a disagreement among them. The course of least resistance is to allow both options to stand. There is, of course, a price for this avoidance of controversy. For it once again renders Judaism in the aggregate agnostic on the issue of whether the mode of existence in the afterlife is one of a disembodied spirituality or of a resurrection of the full person, body and soul. What had been a central affirmation and defining doctrine of the community is now again a personal option, as in Reform Judaism. Although the *Gates of Prayer* (Reform) separates the different affirmations better than *Siddur Sim Shalom* (Conservative) does and exhibits less ambivalence, each evidences deep-seated reservations about the traditional doctrine of resurrection and an eagerness to conflate it with the immortality of the soul, however defined. Neither looks forward with any eagerness to an event at the end of days that restores and consummates creation.

The doubt about resurrection that one sees in non-Orthodox Judaism is an index of the difference between the ancient Judaism in which Gevurot originated and the theological assumptions of most modern Jews.[28] As an unlikely and inexplicable reversal of a universal event of nature, resurrection surely qualifies as a miracle and thus becomes glaringly vulnerable to the powerful critique that has been leveled against the very idea of miracles over the past three and a half centuries. Resurrection, in brief, violates the laws of nature, and it has never been reproduced under laboratory conditions. Add to this the suspicion of psychologists, learned and popular alike, that the source of all belief in an afterlife lies in the fear of death and the fantasy that death is only a temporary condition, and it begins to look as though the resurrection of the dead must itself be consigned to the dead-letter office of religious doctrine, never to be revived.

In addition, the extraordinary advances that have been made in the life sciences in recent decades have given further impetus to the impression that human beings are ultimately machines — highly complex and sophisticated machines, to be sure, but machines nonetheless, and thus unable to transcend their physical base.[29] In his fascinating philosophical examination of eating, Leon Kass observes:

> Modern biochemists have made great strides in identifying the pathways of intermediary metabolism and biosynthesis, in defining the chemical fates of all absorbed nutrients, in describing the structure and mechanisms of action of the enzymes that catalyze bioorganic reactions, and in working out the genetically controlled regulatory mechanisms that keep the process running smoothly. Physiologists have analyzed the numerous elements of digestion and absorption and have defined the autonomic nervous system's control of

these processes. And neurobiologists are presently searching out the "chemical basis" of appetite. In short the whole is treated in terms of its "parts" and the activities of the living being in terms of the motions of inanimate matter, of that underlying stuff more durable, long lasting, and regular than any living thing it frequents. The great successes of our analytic and reductive biology seem to most scientists to vindicate their mechanistic and materialistic presuppositions, not only as heuristic but as ontological hypotheses. Most biologists are, tacitly if not by explicit profession of faith, philosophical (as well as methodological) corporealists, firmly believing in the primacy of the material. Understood in this sense, "You are what you eat" might well be their motto.[30]

On the corporealist assumptions that Kass describes, the resurrection of the dead is even more absurd than other miracles. For surely that "inanimate matter, . . . that underlying stuff more durable, long lasting, and regular than any living thing it frequents," will never be reassembled as the unique "living being" it once constituted. And if, against all odds, it were, the person thus reconstituted would again be vulnerable to the chemical processes that inexorably drive all living things toward death, and the unlikely resurrection thus accomplished would itself be only temporary.

It must be borne in mind that an embrace of corporealism is incompatible with human consciousness and free will. For if "the activities of the living being [are understood only] in terms of the motions of inanimate matter," then the experience of subjectivity and moral choice is an illusion. The decisions people make, the very consciousness they experience, and the perceptions of transcendence that they have are all in that case really only reconfigurations of the underlying matter to which their being reduces. Reflecting on a kindred form of materialistic determinism, the economic materialism of Karl Marx, Reinhold Niebuhr helpfully points out the self-defeating character of the position. "Marxist political polemic," he writes, " . . . constantly implies a denial of this definition of completely unconscious rationalization by treating the ideologies of the foe with a moral scorn which only conscious wrongdoing deserves."[31] Stephen M. Barr, a physicist, makes a similar observation about the efforts of some contemporary scientists to prove that "all mental phenomena will be explained in physical terms," that "we humans," as Francis Crick, a Nobel laureate in biology, puts it, are " 'nothing but a pack of neurons' ":

> The concept "neuron" itself, in fact, is on this account nothing other than a certain pattern of neurons firing in the brain. Is there not something here to make us vaguely uneasy? Is not the snake of scientific theory eating its own tail—or rather its own head? Traditionally, we explained the physical world, including the brain, using concepts. Now we are to explain the concepts themselves as being mere physical events in brains. In fact, this whole theory

according to which the mind and all conceptual understanding are nothing but electro-chemical discharges of nerve cells is *itself,* by its own account, nothing but a discharging of nerve cells. This makes it, as far as I can see, no more significant or interesting than a toothache. We should listen to great scientific minds because they *are* great scientific minds. However, when they begin to tell us that they really have no minds at all, we are entitled to ignore them.[32]

On the one hand, modern religious thinkers cannot deny the extraordinary advances that science has made in identifying the physical components of life. On the other hand, the very basis of their religious commitment — indeed, of moral judgment itself — collapses if they identify life wholly with its physical components. The wording of the *Union Prayerbook* (Reform Judaism) reflects the simplest solution: "Only the body has died and has been laid in the dust. The spirit lives in the shelter of God's love and mercy."[33] Only the body, in other words, is defined by the corporealist's "motions of inanimate matter, of that underlying stuff more durable, long lasting, and regular than any living thing it frequents," as Kass puts it. The other dimension of human existence, here termed "the spirit," survives the body (which it always transcended) and lives on in the protection of the ultimate incorporeal being or spirit, God himself. In sum, a sharp dichotomy of body and spirit, or (as it is more commonly known) body and soul, solves the dilemma.

Another solution would have been to affirm that persons *transcend* their material dimension — that is, the spirit or the soul transcends the body — but to deny that any aspect of human existence *survives* physical death. The body, in this interpretation, is necessary for consciousness, the experience of free will, and all other spiritual phenomena, but it cannot account for them. As we shall see at length,[34] by not dichotomizing body and soul, this approach stands closer to the biblical view out of which the resurrection of the dead develops: Body and soul, if they are to be distinguished at all, are born together and they die together. Consider these verses from a psalm that Jewish tradition requires to be recited in houses of mourning:

> [10]Shall he live eternally,
>   and never see the grave?
> [11]For one sees that the wise die,
>   that the foolish and ignorant both perish,
>   leaving their wealth to others.
> [12]Their grave is their eternal home,
>   the dwelling-place for all generations
>   of those once famous on earth.
> [13]Man does not abide in honor;
>   he is like the beasts that perish. (Ps 49:10–13)[35]

The psalmist leaves no hint of the idea that some portion of the self survives the grave. Indeed, even "the wise die," proof that the mind is no more immortal than the body.[36] As many modern scholars would have it, this notion of the inevitability and irreversibility of death is the *only* position of the Hebrew Bible/Old Testament on the subject.

Consolation in that set of Scriptures, so goes this line of thought, lies solely in the continuity of the family over the generations: having descendants is the functional equivalent of being immortalized, and familial survival plays the role we moderns associate with a personal afterlife (rather like the affirmation in the *Union Prayerbook* that "our loved ones continue, also, in the remembrance of those to whom they were precious").[37] Thus, whereas Utnapishtim, the "Babylonian Noah" of the *Epic of Gilgamesh,* is granted immortality after he survives the great flood,[38] the Israelite Noah receives a covenant that "never again shall all flesh be cut off by the waters of a flood, and never again shall there be a flood to destroy the earth" (Gen 9:11). The permanent continuation of the human race (that is, the descendants of Noah) plays in Genesis the role that Utnapishtim's personal immortality plays in *Gilgamesh,* and the individual's own death — the issue that drives the narrative of *Gilgamesh* — is no issue whatsoever in the biblical flood story. Indeed, there is no hint in Genesis that Noah's own death poses any theological problem whatsoever. His offspring, explicitly included in the covenantal grant (v 9), shall continue forever. With that, God acquits himself of his promise to Noah and demonstrates beyond cavil the full measure of his good will to humanity. In this theology, death is neither a scandal, the inevitable source of a crisis of meaning, nor in any way a necessary impediment to the communion of the faithful with God.[39]

Given the solid biblical precedent for seeing the individual as altogether and properly mortal, why have liturgical innovations in modern Judaism so emphasized the immortality of the soul? Why have they not followed those streams in biblical literature that see the self as unitary and unable to survive its physical demise (that is, without supernatural intervention)? One answer surely lies in the vastly greater concern with the individual in modern thought. The notion, self-evident in much biblical literature, that God's promise to a person can be fully realized in his descendants after his own death rubs against the grain of this characteristically but not uniquely modern attitude. That God's promise to *me* may not be fulfilled in *my* own lifetime but only in that of my descendants or other kinfolk (including my nation) seems unjust today in ways that, for the most part, it did not in biblical times. However much it may offend the materialist orientation of much modern thought, the doctrine of personal immortality at least allows for the relative detachment of the individual from the group in ways with which many moderns feel more comfortable — and more comforted.

One also has to consider the point at which our discussion began, the central role of resurrection in the statutory rabbinic liturgy. The affirmation that God "revives the dead," reiterated repeatedly in a prayer that is to be said multiple times every day without exception, is not easily ignored. It is more easily reworded, retranslated, or reinterpreted as an affirmation of God in his role of life giver. Over against the particular biblical theology that sees human mortality as part of God's creation and not as a fearful disconnection, a consequence of sin, or the like, modern Jewish prayer-book reform betrays the mark of the rabbinic belief in resurrection even when it resolves not to continue it. The traces remain.

Just as the doctrine of immortality has come to serve as a kind of intermediary point between resurrection and an acceptance of the finality of death, so it serves as a midpoint between the ancient belief in miracles and modern naturalism. Kaufmann Kohler, the leading theoretician of Reform Judaism in the generation before World War I, makes the point nicely in his *Jewish Theology*:

> Certainly it is both comforting and convenient to imagine the dead who are laid to rest in the earth as being asleep and to await their reawakening. As the fructifying rain awakens to a new life the seeds within the soil, so that they rise from the depths arrayed in new raiment, so, when touched by the heavenly dew of life, will those who linger in the grave arise to a new existence, clad in new bodies. This is the belief which inspired the pious founders of the synagogal liturgy even before the period of the Maccabees, when they expressed their praise of God's power in that He would send the fertilizing rain upon the vegetation of the earth, and likewise in due time the revivifying dew upon the sleeping world of man. Both appeared to the sages of that age to be evidences of the same wonder-working power of God. Whoever, therefore, still sees God's greatness, as they did, revealed through miracles, that is, through interruptions of the natural order of life, may cling to the traditional belief in resurrection, so comforting in ancient times. On the other hand, he who recognizes the unchangeable will of an all-wise, all-ruling God in the immutable laws of nature must find it impossible to praise God according to the traditional formula as the "Reviver of the dead," but will avail himself instead of the expression used in the Union Prayer Book after the pattern of Einhorn, "He who has implanted within us immortal life."[40]

The operative dichotomy, as Kohler sees it, is between a God whose greatness lies in "interruptions of the natural order of life" and one whose "unchangeable will" has ordained "the immutable laws of nature." Each God is, of course, supernatural, for only one who transcends nature can ordain its "immutable laws." The key difference, rather, is that the supernatural activity of the God of Einhorn, the *Union Prayerbook*, and Kohler himself is restricted to the primordial past and will not be repeated in any eschatological future, or even in an active intervention into history. In ordaining the laws of nature and creating in human beings an immortal spirit that survives death, the God of Israel exhausted his supernatural mission. He is now encountered exclusively in the quiet, lawful continuities of nature and ethics and in the hidden providential guidance of human events, especially as they manifest progress. In this theology, God's supernatural character is not denied but relegated to a vanished past. The vitalities that characterized that past will not recur, for they do not need to. The laws God has devised are so perfect that he will never violate them — even though they lead only and inexorably to the death of embodied persons.

The view of life out of which Kohler's position arises is enormously optimistic. The world in its God-guided development moves, on balance, in a positive direction, and no reversal is necessary or even defensible. The world stands, in other words, in no need of dramatic intervention from above or beyond, for it already proceeds according to "the unchangeable will of an all-wise, all-ruling God." Even death, in fact, poses no serious challenge, for that same unchangeable will "has implanted within us immortal life," allowing us access after death to the same God who has governed us so well in life.

Kohler's rejection of the key rabbinic doctrine of resurrection, then, reflects a belief eminently characteristic of the liberal theology of his time and far from defunct today. It is the belief that history is not characterized by irreconcilable tension, conflict, and inexplicable loss — in a word, by tragedy. Instead, with enough good will and adherence to the self-evident laws of the "all-wise, all-ruling God," human beings can build the messianic kingdom on earth. Those who are not fortunate enough to survive until that happy day, however, are not cut off. They exist forever in the presence of God in the form of disembodied spirits. In short, Kohler's version of the afterlife — and here he is still typical of liberal Judaism nearly a century after he wrote — is one that has purged the classical rabbinic vision of the end-time of its *redemptive* dimension. Redemption, God's reparative, restorative, and triumphant intervention into the tragedy of fleshly, historical life, has been replaced by the ethical striving of individual persons overcoming evil in a world in which the potencies of God's goodness are, happily, already completely actualized:

> At present Christian theologians and even philosophers have recourse to Platonic and Buddhist ideas, that evil is implanted in the world from which humanity must free itself, and they thus present Christianity as the *religion of redemption par excellence*. Over against this, Judaism still maintains that there is no radical or primitive evil in the world. No power exists which is intrinsically hostile to God, and from which man must be redeemed. According to the Jewish conception, the goodness and glory of God fill both heaven

and earth, while holiness penetrates all of life, bringing matter and flesh within the realm of the divine. Evil is but the contrast of good, as shade is but the contrast of light. Evil can be overcome by each individual, as he realizes his own solemn duty and the divine will. Its only existence is in the field of morality, where it is a test of man's freedom and power. Evil is within man, and against it he is to wage the battles of life, until his victory signalizes the triumph of the divine in his own nature.[41]

Having no power of its own, evil is, in fact, but a privation of the good, and human recognition of God's will is all that is needed to eliminate it. When redemption is collapsed into ethics in this way, human beings, in one sense, take the place of God. For their own ethical "victory signalizes the triumph of the divine in [their] own nature." No triumph of the divine *over* human nature itself, or over the tragic circumstances of all history, is necessary. God's original act of creation was too successful to justify the classic rabbinic expectation of a new creation of humanity without the innate inclination to evil and the dying bodies that characterize humanity as a result of the first creation.

Carol Zaleski rightly identifies the type of immortality that this optimistic classical Reform theology produces as "belong[ing] to the Enlightenment religion of reason." "What is eternal in us," according to this vision,

> is our capacity for moral reasoning, which reveals to us the natural law common to all cultures. The elixir of immortality is liberal education that awakens one's powers of critical reason. . . .
>
> In retrospect, it is easy to see why this softening of the demands of traditional eschatology was bound to fail. When the thorns are removed, a lot of the sap runs out with them. . . . When a Jew or Christian rejects belief in resurrection, what remains is an abstraction that resembles [the immortality of the soul, understood as the soul's intrinsic invulnerability to death] only superficially, for it is without *mythos* or *askesis*. It is reduced to a metaphor for the transcendent value of our animating ideals.[42]

Zaleski may be too categorical, however, or at least premature, in her judgment that this version of immortality has failed. The emphasis on "moral reasoning" and "the transcendent value of our animating ideals" has surely declined, but non-Orthodox prayer books, especially those of the Reform Movement, continue to affirm some form of immortality even if they have "soften[ed] the demands of traditional eschatology beyond recognition."

Long before the emergence of Reform Judaism early in the nineteenth century, some Jewish philosophers had already so emphasized immortality as to call their own acceptance of the traditional belief in resurrection into doubt. In the Middle Ages, the clash between what we might call (with all due caution) the

Hebraic and the Hellenic, or the biblical and the philosophical, dimensions of the Jewish heritage became acute. In particular, the great twelfth-century Sephardic philosopher and legal authority Maimonides advanced the idea that the *nepeš* that survives death is the acquired intellect.[43] For only this dimension of the self is not dependent upon the body in any way but instead comes directly from God. In fact, it is only the *nepeš* so understood to which the Torah refers when it relates that God proposed to "make man in our image, after our likeness" (Gen 1:26).[44] The absolutely incorporeal Deity has created an equally incorporeal dimension of the human self that is, or can become, invulnerable to the forces that bring about bodily death. The implications are as clear as they are heterodox: the hereafter is indeed real, but it is a matter of the intellect alone and thus utterly devoid of any bodily dimension:

> In the World-to-Come, there is no body or corporeality, but only the souls of the righteous without bodies, like the ministering angels. Inasmuch as there are no bodies there, there is neither eating nor drinking nor anything else that the bodies of human beings need in this world. . . . Thus, the early sages said, "In the World-to-Come, there is neither eating nor drinking nor sexual relations, but rather the righteous sit with crowns on their heads and enjoy the radiance of the Divine Presence."[45] . . . And when they said "with crowns on their heads," this means that the knowledge that they acquired and on account of which they merited the World-to-Come remains with them. . . . What does it mean when they said, "and enjoy the radiance of the Divine Presence"? That they know and apprehend something of the truth of the Holy One (blessed be He!) that they do not know when they are in their murky and lowly bodies.[46]

Maimonides' handling of his Talmudic proof text betrays his differences with the classical rabbinic view that he is ostensibly upholding. To be sure, that text (in the name of the third-century C.E. sage Rav) certainly does deny the existence of eating, drinking, and procreation (also business transactions, jealousy, hatred, and competition)—ostensibly very much in accordance with Maimonides' own spiritualizing and intellectualistic tendencies. But the "crowns on their heads" that Rav mentions imply some bodily reality even in the World-to-Come, for all its freedom from material need. It is this implication that Maimonides strives to defeat with his allegorizing interpretation: the crowns are knowledge, the only acquisition that "you can take with you," so to speak. Unfortunately for Maimonides, however, it is an implication that appears too consistently for it to have resulted merely from a figurative use of language. One thinks, for example, of the Talmudic statement that "the righteous are destined to rise wearing their clothes," the proof for which comes from a grain of wheat. "If a grain of wheat, which is buried naked, comes forth with many coverings, the righteous who are buried in their clothing, all the more so!"[47] Louis Jacobs points out that the same idea explains rabbinic concern with the garment in which one was to be buried.[48] Whatever its spiritual dimensions — and they are immense — the resurrection of the dead (*tĕḥîyat hammētîm*) to which the rabbis looked forward was very much a bodily event. It is one thing to say that the persons who experience it will be miraculously free of physical needs and vulnerabilities, deriving sustenance from the beatific vision of the divine radiance. It is a very different thing to say, as Maimonides seems to, that they will be altogether disembodied.

Not surprisingly, Maimonides' bold reinterpretation of the Jewish doctrine of the hereafter sparked a controversy that has reverberated into our own time.[49] In the *Treatise on Resurrection,* the response to his critics, Maimonides insisted that they had badly misunderstood him.[50] He had never denied the resurrection of the dead, "for such a denial . . . leads to the denial of all miracles (chronicled in the Bible) and the denial of miracles is equivalent to denying the existence of God and abandonment of our faith."[51] But precisely because resurrection is miraculous — and thus a natural impossibility — those raised cannot endure in God's beautifully ordered cosmos. As Albert D. Friedberg puts it, "The resurrection will presumably last only minutes; just long enough to impress observers and assure them that they are witnessing a miracle."[52] Maimonides' point, then, is that resurrection is only the penultimate stage in the attainment of everlasting felicity. "Those individuals whose souls return to their bodies (after death) will eat and drink and engage in sexual intercourse and sire children and die after an extremely long life like the life that will exist during the days of the Messiah."[53] Those resurrected, in other words, will undergo a second death, from which they will never rise in bodily form. Rather, they will then — and only then — enter into the complete felicity of the World-to-Come, transfigured into angel-like beings capable at last of comprehending divine truths in ways they never could when they were embodied.

The effect of Maimonides' daring doctrine of a second death[54] was to uphold the traditional belief in resurrection while at the same time rendering it superfluous. To be sure, his affirmation is consonant with rabbinic theology on the face of the matter: God resurrects the dead because he promised he would, and anyone who denies that he can accomplish this stupendous miracle doubts the power of God. The problem, however, is that once accomplished, the miracle is undone, as the beneficiaries return eventually to the dust anyway, with only their intellectual faculty surviving for all eternity. This is not only a drastic departure from the traditional rabbinic doctrine, as Maimonides' critics incessantly noted. It is also a contrived and uneconomical scenario that gives the appearance of being devised simply to free its inventor of the suspicion of heresy. Some have even wondered whether Maimonides fully believed it himself.[55]

The differences between Maimonides' preference for immortality and that of modern liberal Judaism are important and revealing. In Maimonides' case, the root of the preference lies, as we have seen, in a principled intellectualism whose origin lies in classical Greek philosophy. What survives death is its victim's intellect and the knowledge that it had amassed, and not the decedent's memory, deeds of lovingkindness, beautiful words, or the like.[56] Indeed, Maimonides' position owes much to a most unmodern distaste for the body and the physicality into which it perforce drags us, whereas modern liberal Judaism, as we have seen, favors a this-worldly understanding of human existence, in which ethical action in this life trumps all else. We should also mention that Maimonides had none of the reservations about the supernatural God and his election of the Jewish people that lie at the base of the rejection of the classical teaching about resurrection of liberal Judaism. He also had no doubt that the Bible supported his position; he did not, in other words, doubt resurrection because he thought it unbiblical, unlike some of the major figures in modern liberal Judaism.[57] But most important of all for our purposes is the fact that Maimonides was forced to recant (with however much conviction) and to find a place for resurrection in his system.[58] That he did so testifies to the power of Talmudic tradition and the liturgical affirmations that it legislated — a power that was rapidly waning when liberal Judaism was born nearly two centuries ago.

To summarize, resurrection and immortality are both to be found in classical rabbinic Judaism, have, to some degree, precedents in the foregoing biblical and late Second Temple heritages, and need not be seen as exclusive of each other. Indeed, they can and did coexist without tension. Nonetheless, resurrection and immortality can be different in critical ways, and it can be profoundly misleading to subsume them under some simplistic master category, such as "afterlife" or "life after death." More careful definitions are essential here. Resurrection we must define as an eschatological event, that is, one that is expected to occur in history but also to transform and redeem history and to open onto a barely imaginable world beyond anything that preceded it. Although we have been calling it a "doctrine," at its source resurrection is actually a prophetic vision relayed by necessity in mythopoetic language. To the visionaries themselves and to those who accepted their visions in faith and reverence, it served as a key element in the expectation that God will redeem the tragedies of history, not just for the few who survive till the end but for all who have lived, or have lived rightly. The expectation of an eschatological resurrection coexists easily with immortality so long as the latter is defined as the state of those who have died and await their restoration into embodiment, that is, into full human existence. It can also coexist easily with immortality understood as the invulnerability to a second death of those who will be raised and rewarded with eternal life.[59] But if immortality is defined in connection with an indestructible core of the self that death cannot threaten (and may even liberate), then resurrection and immortality are at odds. Imported into Judaism, that version of immortality looks not forward to a new creation in a miraculous end-time but backward to the original creation, when God either made humankind deathless or granted it the capacity to reacquire a lost immortality. If immortality, so understood, involves anything miraculous, its miracle is (thankfully to many moderns) strictly in the past, and human beings already have all they need to survive death — a spirit or soul that is immortal or can be made so through the practice of ethics and morality. Whereas history in the classical Jewish vision of resurrection will culminate in God's supernatural triumph over death, this second idea of immortality assumes a very different scenario: individuals at various times and without relationship to each other quietly shed their perishable casings to continue in an unbroken communion with their benevolent creator.

Powerful currents in the modern world work to undercut the Jewish belief in resurrection and to replace it with immortality understood in the second, more problematic sense. The major such current is the motivation to bring religious affirmations into accord with science, which, in this case, means into accord with what Kass calls a "reductive biology [that] seem[s] to most scientists to vindicate their mechanistic and materialistic presuppositions."[60] When those presuppositions collide with the very different ones of classical Judaism with its insistence on resurrection, several possible resolutions arise. One of them is simply to accept the materialistic perspective with respect to the uncompromising biological nature of human existence and consequently to jettison any notion of survival after death as a vestige of prescientific thinking unworthy of the credence of modern adults. Where this move is made but a desire to retain a Jewish religious identity remains, the result is a claim that the essence of Judaism is best conceived as this-worldly anyway and that the practice of Judaism (especially its ethics) can continue just as well without any affirmation of the ancient rabbis' ubiquitous World-to-Come. As I hope to show in our subsequent discussions, this severs practice from theology in ways for which classical Judaism (biblical and rabbinic) offers scant precedent.

Another possible resolution is an affirmation of immortality in the second sense given above. Like the first resolution, this affirmation upholds science (and thus the absoluteness and irreversibility of death) without compromise but only with respect to the body. The difference is that alongside the perishable body, it also posits a dimension of the self that is immaterial (and thus not essential to the body)—a soul, if you will, that God gave in a miracle that he will never repeat or surpass.

It bears mention that this hope for a disembodied mode of survival is, willy-nilly, a hope to shed Jewishness as it is known in this life. For to be a Jew means to be a member of a natural family, the people Israel, the descendants of Abraham, Isaac, and Jacob. It is, in other words, a bodily state and not exclusively a spiritual or intellectual one. Here a point of halakhah (Jewish law) is instructive. According to halakhah, converts to Judaism acquire not only new religious practices and beliefs but also a new ethnic identity; they acquire new parents, Abraham and Sarah, and become members of the unique natural family with a supernatural assignment that is the Jewish people.[61] To live as a disembodied spirit, however, is to live in disconnection from peoplehood.[62] Indeed, precisely this inextricable connection of resurrection to the corporate, ethnic dimension of Jewishness contributed to the eagerness of most early Reform thinkers to divest the tradition of any expectation of resurrection of the dead. Geiger, who was one of the earliest and most brilliant theoreticians of the movement, correctly saw that the hope for national restoration and the hope for resurrection of the dead were actually "united." "The individual," wrote Geiger, "wanted and was entitled to have his share in the future greatness of the nation, a share which he could not enjoy at the present time. This was guaranteed by the belief in the Resurrection of the Dead in the Days of the Messiah."[63] The early Reform replacement of the hope for resurrection with a belief in the inherent (though God-given) immortality of the soul thus goes hand in hand with its rejection of the national dimension of Jewish identity (including, of course, Zionism).[64] With this, the focus shifts dramatically from God's covenantal faithfulness to his people Israel in history and onto the moral strivings of the deracinated, supposedly universal individual.

The classical Jewish doctrine of resurrection is quite different. As we shall have occasion to see at length, to it the natural, familial dimension is critical.[65] Indeed, the classical doctrine expresses the faith that the God who created will also re-create, and the miraculous potentials he activated at the beginning will again be seen at the end, when he restores the flesh-and-blood people Israel to their land and station, renders justice to Jew and Gentile alike, reverses the very real tragedy of death, and ushers in a better world without it.

Resurrection in the Torah?

*No passage lacks the resurrection of the dead, but we lack the capacity
to interpret properly.*
— *Midrash,* Sifre Deuteronomy 306

The objections to the doctrine of resurrection that we explored in our
first chapter arose, as it were, from outside the religious tradition itself. Their
origin lies in rationalistic and scientific thinking that, while not altogether
unprecedented in the premodern world, has risen to its fullest prevalence only
in the past three and a half centuries, in the wake of the scientific revolution. In
essence, these objections are directed at the very idea of a God who interrupts
the course of nature, supervening and contravening the laws that have governed life from its very emergence. In their more extreme form, which is less
prevalent than it once was, these modern objections presuppose atheism and
thus regard nature and its laws as eternal and absolute. In the more moderate
articulations that religious liberals have given them, the modern objections to
resurrection associate God with the alpha point, creation, but disconnect him
from the omega point, the messianic end-time, which, if it is respected at all, is
reformulated as a product only of human beings following moral law and thus
ushering in a perfect world. If the language of miracle is retained at all, it is
retained as a description of that alpha point. The miracle, in other words, is

that the inviolable laws of nature came into existence at all. But inviolable they are, and inviolable they shall remain, even after the Kingdom comes.

Milton Steinberg draws attention to another objection to the traditional idea of the resurrection of the dead, an objection based on the normative sources of the Jewish tradition itself:

> Traditionalists assume these doctrines to have been revealed at Sinai along with the whole body of Jewish conviction. They find them affirmed explicitly and by innuendo at various points in Scripture, including the earliest and most authoritative section, the Torah-Book.
>
> Not so modernists. As they read the Bible, its most ancient portions have only this to say about an afterlife: that the souls of the dead are consigned to a shadowy underworld called *Sheol* where they continue in a vague and only partly conscious existence. The religion of even the great prophets, according to the modernist view, was without any suspicion of either Resurrection or Immortality as these came to be understood.
>
> Only in the days of the Second Temple did these doctrines emerge, partly as a normal unfolding of potentialities latent in Judaism; partly in response to the stimulation of Zoroastrianism with its teachings concerning Resurrection and the Last Judgment, and of Hellenism with its highly developed notion of immortality.
>
> On the basis of this historical construction, some few modernists draw the inference that neither Resurrection nor Immortality is integral to the Jewish religion. Judaism existed for long centuries without them; it can exist without them again.[1]

In taking the position that "Judaism existed for long centuries without [any suspicion of either Resurrection or Immortality]," Steinberg's modernists adopt an opinion that the Mishnah, the great law code of rabbinic Judaism (compiled about 200 C.E.), brands as a heresy:

> All Israelites have a share in the World-to-Come, as it is written:
>
> > And your people, all of them righteous,
> > Shall possess the land for all time;
> > They are the shoot that I planted,
> > My handiwork in which I glory. (Isa 60:21)

> And these are the ones who do not have a share in the World-to-Come: He who says that the resurrection of the dead is not in the Torah, [he who says] that the Torah is not from Heaven, and the skeptic.
>
> Rabbi Akiva says: Also he who reads in the outside books, and he who utters an incantation over a wound, saying, "I will not bring upon you any of the diseases that I brought upon the Egyptians, for I the LORD am your healer." (Exod 15:26)

> Abba Saul says, "Also he who pronounces the Name according to its let-
> ters." (*m. Sanh.* 10:1)

This Mishnah begins on an inclusive note, promising all Jews a place in the
World-to-Come. The proof text, Isa 60:21, is most apposite here, since it
speaks of the people as "all of them righteous" and thus eligible for survival,
and its language of inheriting the land can, in the rabbinic mind, easily suggest
taking rightful possession of the future world.[2] The Mishnah's statement that
"All Israelites have a share in the World-to-Come" is indeed inclusive, but it
must not be taken as an indication that the rabbis affirmed no standards for
admission thereto or failed to link behavior to salvation. Like any genuine
inclusiveness, the position of the Mishnah can be distinguished from relativ-
ism or cheap universalism by its specification of a control on the inclusion.
And certain positions do indeed exclude a Jew from the World-to-Come.
Those listed are the position that denies that the resurrection of the dead can
be found in the Torah; the one that denies that the Torah is of divine origin;
and that of the "skeptic" (*'apîqôrôs*), an umbrella term that seems to indicate
one who denies the fundaments of rabbinic belief, most centrally the belief in
divine providence and justice. To those guilty of these offenses, Rabbi Akiva
adds those who "read the outside books," almost certainly noncanonical Jewish works,[3] and those who use a text from the Torah as a medical incantation.
Abba Saul adds those who pronounce the Tetragrammaton, the four-letter
name of God, according to its written form (which can be transliterated into
English as Yhwh), instead of substituting a euphemism (such as *'ădōnāy,*
"Lord"), as rabbinic law requires.

A Tannaitic (that is, early rabbinic) authority found it eminently fitting that
the first exception to the rule that "all Israelites have a share in the World-to-
Come" should be "he who says that the resurrection of the dead is not in the
Torah":

> And why so much? A Tanna taught: He denied the resurrection of the dead.
> Therefore he shall have no share in the resurrection of the dead. For all the
> measures [of retribution] of the Holy One (blessed be He!) operate on the
> principle that the consequence fits the deed. (*b. Sanh.* 90a)

As phrased in the mishnaic text translated above, however, the heretic in
question did not deny the resurrection of the dead at all, only its presence in
the Torah. In fact, in some versions the words "in the Torah" are missing,[4] and
surely this latter version is the one that the Tanna quoted immediately above
presupposes.

The wording in the version quoted above, which adds the phrase "in the
Torah," has a somewhat different focus. It seems to be directed against two

positions that were associated with the Sadducees, a Jewish group in opposition to the Pharisees, the group out of whose traditions it is widely believed rabbinic Judaism eventually developed. According to the Acts of the Apostles in the New Testament, "the Sadducees say that there is no resurrection, or angel, or spirit; but the Pharisees acknowledge all three" (Acts 23:8). Early rabbinic literature says much the same thing about the Sadducees. One text traces them to a group that wondered about the saying of Antigonos of Soko, who urged his disciples to "be not like servants who serve their master for the sake of compensation; be rather like servants who serve their master with no thought of compensation."[5] "If our ancestors had known that there is another world and that there is the resurrection of the dead," this group reasoned, "they would not have said this."[6] According to the Jewish historian Josephus, writing toward the end of the first century C.E., the Sadducees also rejected all Pharisaic practice "not recorded in the Laws of Moses," observing, that is, only Pentateuchal norms.[7] By branding as heretical anyone who "says that the resurrection of the dead is not in the Torah," the Mishnah challenges the Sadducees (or some later group with the same theology) on their own turf. The argument thus rests not on oral tradition but on the text of the Torah.

By adding the requirement that a Jew in good standing believe that the Torah itself says the dead will rise, the Mishnah takes a position that is in some ways more exclusive and in some ways more inclusive than would otherwise have been the case. It excludes Jews who either disbelieve in resurrection or believe in it because of some non-Pentateuchal reference to it. But by rooting the belief in the Torah, to which all Jews (in various ways and with varying interpretations) held allegiance, rather than in the peculiarly rabbinic notion of oral tradition, the rabbis, in fact, cast a wider net. The challenge that remained for them—a formidable challenge indeed—was to find allusions to the resurrection of the dead in the Torah.

One strategy they employed was to give a future interpretation to verses that seem at first glance to speak of past events. The result is, to put it kindly, some highly imaginative exegesis. For example, the preface to the Song at the Sea reads:

> Then (*'āz*) Moses and the Israelites sang (*yāšîr*) this song to the LORD. (Exod 15:1a)

The *Mekilta de-Rabbi Ishmael*, an early midrash collection on parts of Exodus, observing correctly that "sometimes the word 'then' (*'āz*) refers to the past and sometimes to the future age (*'ātîd lābō'*)," places our verse in the former category: at that moment, having crossed the sea, Moses and the Israelites sang the ensuing celebratory hymn. Rabbi Judah the Patriarch, redactor of the Mishnah, dissents:

"Then Moses sang (*šār*)" is not written here, but rather "Then Moses will sing (*yāšîr*)." Thus we are instructed that the resurrection of the dead can be derived from the Torah. (*Mek.*, Shirta 1)[8]

Rabbi Judah the Patriarch's dissent is premised upon an understanding of a particular point of Hebrew grammar, one that changed in the transition from the biblical language to the rabbinic. In rabbinic Hebrew, the prefix conjugation of verbs is nearly always future in meaning. In biblical Hebrew, in contrast, the matter is more complicated, and after certain words, such as *'āz* ("then") or *ṭerem* ("not yet"), the prefix conjugation often (but not always) refers to the past.[9] The rabbi's point is that if the Torah wanted us to understand Moses' singing as having already occurred, it would have used the suffix conjugation (*šār*), which in rabbinic Hebrew (but not biblical) is the regular form for past-tense narration. Hence, the singing in question must refer to the future — to a time, that is, after Moses has already died and, if the verse is to be proven true, resurrected as well.

This interpretation makes for exceedingly bad philology, to be sure, but also for rich and powerful theology. For it places the celebratory hymn in the eschatological future, and in so doing, it presents the resurrection of the dead as a radical reversal of the sort attested in the other verses that use "then" (*'āz*) in an eschatological sense listed in the *Mekilta*. These verses speak of Israel seeing and "glowing" as the wealth of nations passes to them and their temple (Isa 60:5); of the light of redemption bursting upon them, as the LORD comes to their rescue and their vindication (58:8); of the lame leaping like a deer (35:6); of the eyes of the blind being opened and the ears of the deaf unstopped (35:5); of maidens dancing gaily when God has turned "mourning to joy" (Jer 31:13); and of Israel's mouth being filled with laughter and the nations saying, "The LORD has done great things for them" (Ps 126:2). Rabbi Judah the Patriarch's interpretation, in short, places the resurrection of the dead squarely in the context of the restoration of Israel in the end-time. Whereas a plain-sense reading of the Song at the Sea views it as a celebration of Israel's redemption from Egypt, vindication over their oppressors, and miraculous passage through the sea, in his reading it celebrates an even greater redemption, an even greater vindication, and an even greater and more miraculous passage: the redemption of the dead, the vindication of the righteous, and the passage from death to life. The exodus has become a prototype of ultimate redemption, and historical liberation has become a partial, proleptic experience of eschatological liberation, a token, perhaps *the* token, of things to come. The full activation of God's potential in the foundational past has been transformed into a sign of the still greater activation of his potential in the future consummation — a consummation that moves the Jews not merely from slavery to freedom but quite literally from death to life as well. Beneath this last transformation lies a conviction that so long as human beings are subject to death, they are not altogether free: resurrection is the ultimate and final liberation.

To moderns given to historical thinking, Rabbi Judah the Patriarch's reading of Exod 15:1a represents a profound reinterpretation and recontextualization of the biblical text and testifies to the sea change that the introduction of the doctrine of resurrection eventually brought about in Judaism. It is, in other words, a marvelous example of the "rewritten Bible" of ancient Judaism.[10] To the rabbi himself, however, his reading involves no reinterpretation or recontextualization, and no recognition of historical development. The grammar of the verse, he claims, supports his interpretation of it as proof of the resurrection of the dead from the Torah itself. This example, connecting as it does with several deep themes in Jewish thought, involves more theological profundity than most, but it is only one of several attempts in rabbinic literature to show that the Torah endorses resurrection, or, to put it differently, that resurrection is not a sectarian tenet of the rabbinic party but an intrinsic element of the Mosaic legacy of the whole House of Israel.

The Talmud, too, asks the question, "How do we know that the resurrection of the dead can be derived from the Torah?" One answer:

> From the verse, "and from them you shall bring the gift for the LORD to Aaron the priest" (Num 18:28). Did Aaron exist forever? Was it not the case that he never entered the Land of Israel; and yet the gift should be rendered to him? Rather, it teaches that he will be resurrected and Israel will give him the gift. Hence, resurrection of the dead can be derived from the Torah. (*b. Sanh.* 90b)

Here the point is simply that an enduring commandment to bring sacrificial offerings to Aaron makes no sense after Aaron's death, which took place even before the Temple was built. Thus, the text in Numbers must predict his return from the dead. Of course, this leaves unacceptably open the question of just who is to receive those gifts in the interim. Thus, it is not surprising that immediately after this proof we find the comment of the School of Rabbi Ishmael that " 'to Aaron' means 'like Aaron,' " that is, to a priest with certain qualifications, of whom Aaron, the ancestor of all priests, is the Torah's paradigm. The same objection can be raised against another Tannaitic proof:

> Rabbi Simai says: How do we know that the resurrection of the dead can be derived from the Torah? From the verse, "I also established My covenant with them [that is, Abraham, Isaac, and Jacob], to give them the land of Canaan" (Exod 6:4). "To you" is not written but "to them." Hence, resurrection of the dead can be derived from the Torah. (*b. Sanh.* 90b)

How can God fulfill his covenantal promise to give the land to the patriarchs if they have already died? Only, Rabbi Simai maintains, by raising them from the dead. Here the exegesis is vulnerable to the same point that the School of Rabbi Ishmael scored about the use of "Aaron" in Num 18:28. The covenantal promise was made to Abraham, Isaac, and Jacob but will be fulfilled only to those who are like them, that is, to their descendants, who bear their name and continue their identity. This interpretation, in fact, accords well with the original promise of land to Abraham in Genesis: "I will assign this land to your offspring" (Gen 12:7). The distinction between Abraham and his descendants as the recipient of the promise is quite foreign to biblical thought.

In silently presuming a sharp division between a man and his descendants, Rabbi Simai, for all his rooting in ancient exegetical practice, is thus in one important way more modern than biblical. For the Hebrew Bible is comfortable in describing national history as biography in ways that are baffling to the modern mind (including even some modern religious traditionalists). To give one prominent example, Jacob (or Israel, as he comes to be called), is both a person and a people, both eponymous ancestor of the promised nation and an individual who pre-enacts the destiny of his descendants. "He went down to Egypt with meager numbers and sojourned there; but there he became a great and very populous nation" (Deut 26:5). A man metamorphoses into a nation? As an individual, Jacob is embedded in, indeed, indistinguishable from, his family in ways that we who are heirs to the more atomistic, individualistic cast of mind of the modern West find exceedingly difficult to fathom but that the Hebrew Bible, in the main, finds quite unexceptionable. This same factor accounts for what is, to the modern mind (and to some ancient minds as well), one of the most repulsive features of biblical thought: God's visiting the sin of the fathers upon the children, an idea enshrined in no less central a text than the Decalogue itself (Exod 20:5). Here, too, rabbinic theology, following some prophetic objections (e.g., Jer 31:29–30; Ezek 18:1–4), broke with the dominant biblical thinking and insisted that the children are punished for their fathers' sins only if they continue them.[11] In the dominant biblical thinking—even, in fact, in the thinking of the very prophets who voice dissent on the inheritability of guilt and punishment—the children are not discrete individuals over against their parents, nor are the parents discrete individuals ontologically disconnected from their descendants, their ancestors, and the whole nation in which they have their being.

Given this biblical concept of the self (which we shall examine in more detail in chapter 6), Rabbi Simai's logic fails. God can indeed give the promised land to Abraham, Isaac, and Jacob after they are dead without resurrecting them, for the people that carries their blood, bears their name, and reenacts their experience (in part) still lives and is still able to experience the fulfillment of the promise. On a deeper level, however, Rabbi Simai's observation points us toward a profound truth: the deaths of the patriarchs of Genesis do not have the finality that we (and he) associate with death. Rather, Abraham, Isaac, and Jacob continue to exist after they have died, not, it should be underscored, as disembodied spirits but as the people whose fathers they will always be. That death represents an absolute terminus, as it does to the modern mind, is not a foregone conclusion in biblical thought. In biblical thinking, it is possible to continue even after death, and without either resurrection or immortality in the sense of survival as a bodiless soul. Not everyone does, of course. Some die cut off from kith and kin and from the worshiping community that enjoys God's radiant, life-giving presence. But it is possible, in biblical thought, to die what the non-Israelite prophet Balaam enviously calls "the death of the upright" (Num 23:10), to die like Abraham, "old and contented . . . gathered to his kin" (Gen 25:8). Among the several ways to understand the doctrine of the resurrection of the dead is to view it as a way to preserve that possibility when biblical notions of identity have eroded and a more individualistic conception of the self has come to the fore. Or, to put it differently, if we hold a more individualistic conception of the self than one finds in most of the Hebrew Bible, one must either accept a notion of the resurrection of the dead or concede that the biblical promise fell void, never to be fulfilled. From the standpoint of the biblical sources in question, the first option introduces a novelty; the second, a theological scandal. In one sense, then, resurrection is a new idea, and it is hardly surprising that prerabbinic and nonrabbinic Jews held a variety of other ideas about ultimate human destiny. In another sense, however, it is a tradition-preserving reaction to new thinking that threatened the older biblical idea that existence in an embodied, communal form could continue after death, through a gracious God's fidelity to his promise.

How shall we take the rabbinic insistence that a doctrine of general resurrection appears in the Torah itself? Or, to put the question differently, how univocally did the rabbis who interpreted various Pentateuchal verses in this way intend their interpretations to be taken? Certainty in cases like this is not possible, for we cannot know whether Rabbi Judah the Patriarch, Rabbi Simai, or others who propounded such interpretations intended their readings to be exhaustive and exclusive. It is difficult to imagine, for example, that Rabbi Judah the Patriarch thought that the Song at the Sea had actually not been sung after the miraculous crossing at all but would *only* be sung after Moses and the Israelites of his generation were resurrected at the end of time. The likelier interpretation is that he understood and accepted the plain-sense reading of Exod 15:1a (that is, the reading that accords with the biblical verbal system) but saw in the verb *yāšîr* a hint of another, more encompassing meaning, one focused on the future rather than the past redemption. The plain-sense interpretation proved less worthy of comment, not only for the obvious reason that it is the plain sense but also for the more important reason that it lacked the capacity to advance the rabbinic case in the argument against the Sadducees or others who thought like them. In sum, an incidental feature of one word could be pressed into service in support of a whole theology, but without necessarily denying the literal sense of the word. Or, to put the point in the terminology of medieval Jewish biblical commentary, Rabbi Judah the Patriarch may have meant his *derash* (his imaginative, midrashic interpretation) to augment, but not to dislodge, the *peshat* (the plain sense) of Exod 15:1a.

Some evidence for this, as a general principle though not in the specific case of the rabbis under discussion, can be found in ancient Jewish translations, especially those associated with the rabbinic movement. Thus, Targum Onkelos, an Aramaic translation known for its literalism (in the main), renders the key verb in the past, not future. Interestingly, the same is true of Targum Pseudo-Jonathan, a periphrastic, midrashic Aramaic translation. Although the latter targum introduces a moralizing thought in this verse — pointing out that God punishes *everybody* who, like Pharaoh, arrogantly exalts himself against him — it still renders *yāšîr* as a past-tense verb. And this seems to be the case across the gamut of ancient translations, Rabbi Judah the Patriarch's *derash* notwithstanding. The same holds for Rabbi Simai's eschatological reading of Exod 6:4, which the ancient Jewish translations in Aramaic (and Greek as well) render without betraying any awareness of his point about the verse.

It bears underscoring that the recognition of the plain sense of these key verses in the ancient translations does not imply that the rabbis thought of the resurrection of the dead as an innovation of their own (or of their post-Mosaic forebears) or as some esoteric dimension of the text that ordinary people could not detect. For the more periphrastic translations do find the resurrection of the dead in other verses in which we do not, and thus give evidence of midrashim that reinterpreted these verses, too, in the light of the key rabbinic doctrine under investigation here. Consider Gen 3:19, which forms part of God's sentence on Adam for humanity's first disobedience:

By the sweat of your brow
Shall you get bread to eat,
Until you return to the ground —
For from it you were taken.
For dust you are,
And to dust you shall return. (Gen 3:19)

Onkelos renders this literally, but Pseudo-Jonathan reads instead:

> By the labor of your hand
> You shall get food to eat,
> Until you return to the dust —
> For from it you were created.
> For dust you are,
> And to dust you shall return.
> For from the dust you are destined to rise,
> To give a reckoning of all you have done,
> On the great Judgment Day.[12]

Genesis 3:19 is often taken as an etiology of death: people die because of Adam's sin. It is unclear, however, whether God had ever intended Adam to be immortal. Indeed, the reason given in 3:22 for the latter's eviction from the Garden of Eden is precisely that he might *become* deathless, having now acquired the knowledge of good and evil and thus the intellectual capacity to taste of the Tree of Life as well and live forever. In short, it may be that Genesis 3 sees in the disobedience of the primal parents the origins not of the loss of immortality itself but of the *chance to acquire immortality*.[13] In that case, v 19 is better taken as an etiology not of death but of burial: Adam as the prototypical human (*'ādām*) ends where he began, in the ground (*'ădāmâ*), returning to the dust from which he was fashioned (2:7). The irony (and the punishment) is that in the interim between his emergence from the dust and his return thereto, he is to be a slave to the ground, toiling for his bread. This stands in glaring contradiction to the lordly charge to humanity in 1:29, in which God grants humanity seeds and fruit as food, without any mention of agriculture whatsoever. Working the land is a burden in Genesis 3, one that comes to an end only when the land reabsorbs the farmer at death. The land wins. The earth (*'ădāmâ*) triumphs over the earthling (*'ādām*).

Of the two interpretations of Gen 3:19, the first, which sees in the verse a punishment of death, is likelier to underlie the "translation" attested in Targum Pseudo-Jonathan. The idea that the sin of Adam (or Adam and Eve) is the cause of human mortality, arguably absent in the Hebrew Bible, became widespread in Second Temple Judaism,[14] displacing the older biblical concept (by no means universal in the Hebrew Bible) that death was God's preferred plan for every human being from the beginning, "the way of all the earth" (Josh 23:14). The notion that God's last word to the human race is a death sentence, however, did not sit well with certain elements of Second Temple culture (just as it had not sat well with the biblical culture that saw in progeny not simply a consolation for death but the survival and continuation of the person who has passed away). After all, the Torah itself records God's dramatic offer to Israel to choose between "life and death, blessing and curse" and his instruction, immediately ensuing, to "choose life . . . by loving the LORD your God, heeding His commands, and holding fast to Him" (Deut 30:19–20). Surely the ground cannot simply reabsorb one who has obeyed that instruction and tried his best to live the life of Torah. Add to this the expectation of a final judgment, increasingly dominant in Jewish apocalyptic thought but not without precedent in the Hebrew Bible, and you have all the ingredients of Pseudo-Jonathan's addition to Gen 3:19 — "To give a reckoning of all you have done, / On the great Judgment Day."

In passages like this, and many similar ones in the Targumim and Greek translations,[15] the goal is different from that of the midrashim spun by Rabbi Judah the Patriarch and Rabbi Simai examined earlier. For the objective here is not to prove the resurrection of the dead from Pentateuchal verses but rather to present the latter the way the translators actually and unself-consciously saw them — as reflecting the structure of Judaism as they affirmed it in their own time. This was a Judaism that confidently expected the justice of God some day to triumph in the lives of all who have ever lived, whether they will have survived to that end-point of history or not. Translations like this demonstrate how thoroughly the expectation of a general resurrection and a last judgment had pervaded the theological world of rabbinic Judaism and how central it had become to their Jewish spirituality. The rabbis, in short, were eminently capable of understanding the plain sense of passages that might be pressed into midrashic service in support of the idea of a general resurrection. But they also found the denial of resurrection to be a negation of the Torah's own promises and of the highest hopes of the Jewish people.

Resurrection in the Torah? The question turns out to be considerably more complicated than it first appears. The rabbinic effort to find allusions to a doctrine of a general resurrection of the dead at the end of history founders, to be sure, on the plain sense of the scriptural verses in question. This is not only the judgment of modern criticism but also a point sometimes made in the rabbinic literature itself. It is also the assumption of ancient and traditional translations that render the verses according to their plain sense, and it conforms to the interpretation given by most medieval commentators. The forced nature of the exegeses in question testifies to the gap between the religious culture of the rabbis, on the one hand, and that of their scriptural sources, on the other. Their exegeses mediate the difference by assimilating the Pentateuch to the pattern of religion of the rabbinic expositors themselves. They are, in a word, *derash*, the product of midrashic interpretation and not historico-grammatical exegesis.

There is a huge gap, however, between the recognition that these interpretations are midrashic and the claim that in the Torah, and the Jewish Bible generally, death was deemed to be good, altogether in accordance with God's will, and irreversible. The critique of that claim and the advancement of a more nuanced counterposition will occupy our attention from here on. We do not pretend to validate the rabbinic interpretations of the verses we have examined in this chapter, but we do hope to show that the rabbis' expectation of resurrection has far more continuities with their biblical predecessors' thinking than has heretofore been recognized.

3

Up from Sheol

The LORD deals death and gives life,
Casts down into Sheol and raises up.
— 1 Samuel 2:6

In the field of biblical studies, renowned for its deficit of basic agreement and the depth of its controversies, one cannot but be impressed by the longevity and breadth of the consensus about the early Israelite notion of life after death. The consensus, to be brief, is that there was none, that "everyone who dies goes to Sheol," as Johannes Pedersen put it about eighty years ago, "just as he, if everything happens in the normal way, is put into the grave."[1] To be sure, Pedersen's fascinating description of Sheol makes it clear that he does not believe that the dead cease to exist altogether when they lie there, only that their existence is then altogether negative. "Firmness, joy, strength, blessing belong to the world of light; slackness, sorrow, exhaustion, curses belong to the realm of the dead."[2] About half a century after Pedersen, John Gray reiterated this still uncontroversial view of Israelite thinking as it stood before the emergence of a doctrine of resurrection late in the Second Temple period. Commenting on the dying David's grim instruction to his heir designate, soon to be King Solomon, to do in David's old and once-trusted commander, Joab, making sure "that his white hair does not go down to Sheol in peace"

(1 Kgs 2:6), Gray explains the destination of the doomed general. "Sheol," he writes, "is the shadowy, insubstantial underworld, the destination of all, good and bad without discrimination, where existence is wholly undesirable. The Hebrews in the classical period had no comfortable prospect of the hereafter."[3] On this reading, the punishment lies not in Joab's consignment to Sheol, for that is "the destination of all," but only in his being deprived of the chance to experience the full measure of his old age. Solomon is to exact retribution upon him for the evil of "shedding blood of war in peacetime" (v 5), but the retribution itself consists simply of a descent sooner rather than later into the realm that consumes "good and bad without discrimination."

So described, the Israelite Sheol recalls numerous accounts of the netherworld from far-flung cultures, not least the related cultures of the ancient Near Eastern and Mediterranean worlds. One thinks, for example, of a fragmentary Akkadian tablet in which the famous hero Gilgamesh and his departed friend Enkidu are, however briefly, eerily reunited:

> "Tell me, my friend, tell me, my friend,
> Tell me the order of the nether world which thou hast seen."
> "I shall not tell thee, I shall not tell thee!
> (But) if I tell thee the order of the nether world
> which I have seen,
> Sit thou down and weep!"
> "[. . .] I will sit down and weep."
> "[*My body* . . .], which thou didst touch as thy heart rejoiced
> Vermin devour [as though] an old garment.
> [. . .] is filled with dust."
> He cried "[Woe]" and threw himself [in the dust],
> [Gilgamesh] cried, "[Woe!]" and threw himself in the dust.[4]

Or consider this description of the "Land of No Return" from the Akkadian poem about the Mesopotamian goddess Ishtar's descent into the netherworld:

> To the house which none leave who have entered it,
> To the world from which there is no way back,
> To the house wherein the entrants are bereft of li[ght],
> Where dust is their fare and clay their food,
> (Where) they see no light, residing in darkness,
> (Where) they are clothed like birds, with wings for garments,
> (And where) over door and bolt is spread dust.[5]

Texts like these profoundly reinforce the summary judgment of one scholar of ancient Mesopotamia that "the orthodox vision of the netherworld and existence there can be expressed in a simple word: gloom."[6] The same English term is revealingly prominent in classical Greek accounts of the netherworld, "this gloom at the world's end," as one translator of the *Odyssey* memorably renders the Homeric language.[7] In both Mesopotamia and Greece, Pedersen's observation about the ancient Israelite netherworld would seem apt: "Life is the opposite of misery, identical with joy."[8] And from this the inference may justly have been drawn that the dead have existence without life — an existence of unqualified and interminable unhappiness, unqualified and interminable hopelessness. The aspect of hopelessness, nicely captured in the Akkadian term, "Land of No Return," again appears as well in Israelite texts. Job's meditation on the frailty and impermanence of human life, for example, makes the same point:

> [7]Consider that my life is but wind;
> I shall never see happiness again.
> [8]The eye that gazes on me will not see me;
> Your eye will seek me, but I shall be gone.
> [9]As a cloud fades away,
> So whoever goes down to Sheol does not come up;
> [10]He returns no more to his home;
> His place does not know him. (Job 7:7–10)

But just what and where is Sheol? This is a question that has long occupied the minds and pens of scholars.[9] The beginning of wisdom in answering the question is to avoid literalism, especially the variety that imagines that elements in the ancient Israelite worldview have close equivalents in ours. We are, in other words, confronting not just the formidable challenge of linguistic translation but also — and more important — the even more difficult one of cultural translation. Complicating the task is the obvious fact that the range of conditions that the Hebrew Bible groups under the rubric of "death" includes many that we designate otherwise. A kindred statement can be made about Sheol. Nicholas J. Tromp points out that "those endangered feel that they are in Sheol already, they become rigid in the grip of the enemy."[10] To understand the condition of those dispatched to Sheol (for in our next chapter we shall argue that not all the dead were), it will be useful to get a sense of the predominant metaphors by which the Hebrew Bible conveys the character of the grim abode of these dead.

Pedersen observes that "the ideas of the grave and of Sheol cannot be separated," since the dead are in both at the same time, "not in two different places."[11] A common synonym for the grave in this pejorative sense and therefore for Sheol as well is "Pit."[12] Thus can the author of one of the most plangent of psalms describe himself as consigned not only to the grave, but to the realm of the dead in Sheol / the Pit, sated with God's fury and his fellows' contempt:

> [2]O Lord, God of my deliverance,
>> by day and by night I cry out before You,
>> [3]let my prayer reach You;
>> incline Your ear to my cry.
> [4]For I am sated with misfortune;
>> I am at the brink of Sheol.
> [5]I am numbered with those who go down to the Pit;
>> I am a helpless man
>> [6]abandoned among the dead,
>> like bodies lying in the grave
>> of whom You are mindful no more,
>> and who are cut off from Your care.
> [7]You have put me at the bottom of the Pit,
>> in the darkest places, in the depths.
> [8]Your fury lies heavy upon me;
>> You afflict me with all Your breakers.   *Selah.*
> [9]You make my companions shun me;
>> You make me abhorrent to them;
>> I am shut in and do not go out.
> [10]My eyes pine away from affliction;
>> I call to You, O Lord, each day;
>> I stretch out my hands to You. (Ps 88:2–10)[13]

Although the author of these verses is surely not yet dead in our sense, in his own view he already dwells — one hesitates to say "lives" — in the realm of the dead. In this, Philip S. Johnston finds a contradiction. He finds it impossible to understand "how an experience of death can be real but partial" — if, that is, "death necessarily entails total deprivation of life and irreversible separation from [Yhwh]." As he puts it, "The psalmist who can still pray is clearly not dead."[14] The answer to Johnston's objection lies in the Israelite conception of death and its difference from others, especially ours. Whereas we think of a person who is gravely ill, under lethal assault, or sentenced to capital punishment as still alive, the Israelites were quite capable of seeing such an individual as dead. Or, to be more precise, they could do so in their poetic literature without, it seems to me, implying that in a more prosaic genre (like historiography or religious law) they would make the same categorization. In other words, for us death is radically discontinuous with life, a quantum leap, as it were, lying between the two. For the psalmists, by contrast, the discontinuity lay between a healthy and successful life and one marked by adversity, in physical health or otherwise.[15] The diagram below illustrates the difference:

   a. Life → illness ‖ death
   b. Life ‖ → illness → death

We are predisposed to think that ancient Israelites conceived of death as involving two stages, one characterized by intense affliction but capable of reversal and another permanent and irreversible, like death as modern secular thought conceives it (figure a). In fact, they saw illness as continuous with death and thought of the reversal of illness as so miraculous as to be in the nature of a resurrection (figure b). To answer Johnston's logical perplexity, consider this as an analogous modern statement: "He was cured of a lethal illness." If he was cured, the illness was, of course, never lethal, but to the person making the statement — and all the more so to the person about whom it is made — the logical correction misses the speaker's subjective experience of the gravity of the situation.

The speaker of the verses from Psalm 88 quoted above differs from the permanent residents of Sheol in harboring the hope that God might still emancipate him from it. Indeed, the affirmation that God has done so is central to several of the psalms of thanksgiving.[16] This being the case, we are compelled to qualify our judgment that Sheol is a Land of No Return. That idea, easily inferred from the Mesopotamian and Joban texts quoted above, does indeed define Sheol in its most horrific mode, a mode that always threatens.[17] But, in the minds of some in ancient Israel, God's miraculous intervention can avert this fate and turn around the failing fortunes of the doomed. As one psalmist puts it:

> He lifted me out of the miry pit,
>   the slimy clay,
>   and set my feet on a rock,
>   steadied my legs. (Ps 40:3)

Nothing in the nature of death, however, guarantees this happy reversal. No one moves naturally up from Sheol. When such a movement occurs, it does so because of God's surprising grace and in defiance of the way of all flesh, in defiance of death, in defiance of Sheol. Indeed, were rescue from the netherworld the norm — were it, that is, a likely event — Sheol would lose its sting, and the grave of the God-forsaken (the "Pit") would never know victory. It is thus imperative to be clear about the theology that underlies the belief in the individual's return from the netherworld in the Hebrew Bible (whether in the form of a plea or an experience). What these texts affirm is neither a belief in the immortality of the soul nor a doctrine of resurrection (both of which will, as we have seen, develop later, in Second Temple Judaism and then in its daughter religions). If the speakers in these poems were certain they possessed an immortal and indestructible soul, they would hardly be so terrified of death. If they expected resurrection, they would not try so hard to persuade God of the horrors of Sheol; indeed, they would, if deemed worthy, never find themselves suffering there at all and, if deemed unworthy, would never escape therefrom. In short, these texts evidence a belief in two possibilities that stand in a painfully tensive relationship. The first possibility—a very real one—is that death will lead to an irreversible state of misery, the grave of the godless or the God-forsaken, the miry pit that is Sheol. The second is that God will offer rescue from death, restoring its erstwhile victim to life as this literature understands it. The former possibility, which has, as we have seen, deep roots and affinities in the ancient Near Eastern world, is rightly to be feared. But sometimes the extraordinary happens, psalms like this one tell us, and he who once found himself in the miry pit now stands on a rock, with steadied legs and a mouth full of praise for the God who performed the unlikely act of deliverance. Was "the Pit" the final destination, or did people consigned to it return to life? No yes-or-no answer can be given without proving false to the spiritual experience of the speaker in poems like Psalm 40. No static, propositional account of the ancient Israelite understanding of postmortal existence can do justice to the dynamism they inscribe.

The imagery of grave and pit with which we began our discussion of Sheol is only one component of the overlapping symbolic renderings of the netherworld in the Hebrew Bible. Some scholars, noticing that Ugaritic, a language closely related to Hebrew, lacks the word *Sheol* but uses *arṣ* ("land") for the netherworld, draw attention to biblical texts in which the Hebrew cognate *’ereṣ* seems to have a similar meaning.[18] In the case of Korah and his faction of rebels against Moses and Aaron, for example, the book of Numbers reports that

> [32] the earth [*hā’āreṣ*] opened its mouth and swallowed them up. . . . [33]They went down alive into Sheol, with all that belonged to them; the earth [*hā’āreṣ*] closed over them and they vanished from the midst of the congregation. [34]All Israel around them fled at their shrieks, for they said, "The earth [*hā’āreṣ*] might swallow us!" (Num 16:32–34)

For some scholars, the rich mythological resonance of this image of "the earth" opening up its mouth to "swallow" the malefactors constitutes potent evidence that we are dealing with more than the ground as we might conceive it and must instead think of it in terms of Sheol.[19] The case is not airtight, of course, and it is possible to see here nothing more than "the solid earth through which the rebels descend to Sheol," as Johnston puts it.[20] But an image so graphic and anthropomorphic, together with the threefold repetition of *hā’āreṣ* suggests that the term refers, if not to Sheol, then at least to its horrific and irresistible orifice in the terrestrial world.

Another highly memorable attestation of the earth's "swallowing" malefactors occurs in the Song at the Sea in Exodus 15, when such is the fate of

Pharaoh's army (v 12). Interestingly, Sheol is not mentioned there at all, and this gives added weight to the possibility that *'ereṣ* can be used as its synonym. The Hebrew word for "ground" (*'ădāmâ*) can have the same meaning, as in Moses' prediction of Korah's miraculous demise: "The ground [*hā'ădāmâ*] opens its mouth and swallows them up" (Num 16:30).[21] Here, the earth or ground is entirely under God's control and serves as the agent of his righteous will. But there is still room to suspect that the highly anthropomorphic or theriomorphic language ("opens its mouth and swallows") indicates that Sheol is animate, a malevolent being, that is, rather than merely a place or a fate. In this regard, a case like Psalm 61 is especially suggestive:

> [2]Hear my cry, O God,
>   heed my prayer.
> [3]From the end of the earth I call to You;
>   when my heart is faint,
>   You lead me to a rock that is high above me.
> [4]For You have been my refuge,
>   a tower of strength against the enemy.
> [5]O that I might dwell in Your tent forever,
>   take refuge under Your protecting wings. (Ps 61:2–5)

In these lines, Tromp detects "a clear antithesis between the unsteady mire of the netherworld and the safe rock." "The end of the earth [*hā'āreṣ*]," in other words, is not some distant terrestrial spot to which the psalmist has been driven; it is the deepest pocket of the netherworld, the outer reaches of Sheol. And to Tromp, the unnamed "enemy" from whom God has rescued the psalmist is none other than "the arch-enemy, Death, himself," a "rapacious monster," well known from Ugaritic mythology.[22] Whether the psalm really reflects so much living mythology is open to doubt,[23] but Tromp's point about "the end of the earth" seems likely. The psalmist is calling upon God to bring him back from the underworld.

Along with the language of grave and of earth/ground, the terminology of water is prominent in the description of the mortal threat that biblical psalmists hope to surmount (or claim to have already surmounted) by the grace of God. Here follows one poet's description of the challenges he faced:[24]

> [5]For the breakers of Death encompassed me,
> The torrents of Belial terrified me;
> [6]The snares of Sheol encircled me,
> The toils of Death engulfed me. (2 Sam 22:5–6)[25]

"Breakers" and "torrents" here serve as names for the chaotic and death-dealing rivers of the netherworld.[26] A poem with a similar thrust has been put into the mouth of the fugitive prophet Jonah, adding a cosmic dimension to his three-day plight in the belly of the fish by reference to these old mythic motifs:

> ³He said:
> In my trouble I called to the LORD,
> And He answered me;
> From the belly of Sheol I cried out,
> And You heard my voice.
> ⁴You cast me into the depths,
> Into the heart of the sea,
> The floods engulfed me;
> All Your breakers and billows
> Swept over me.
> ⁵I thought I was driven away
> Out of Your sight:
> Would I ever gaze again
> Upon Your holy Temple?
> ⁶The waters closed in over me,
> The deep engulfed me.
> Weeds twined around my head.
> ⁷I sank to the base of the mountains;
> The bars of the earth [*hā'āreṣ*] closed upon me forever.
> Yet You brought my life up from the pit,
> O LORD my God!
> ⁸When my life was ebbing away,
> I called the LORD to mind;
> And my prayer came before You,
> Into Your holy Temple. (Jon 2:3–8)²⁷

In keeping with the comic character of the Book of Jonah, God commands the enormous fish to vomit the swallowed prophet, thus restoring him to divine service willy-nilly (Jon 2:11).

In the case of the psalmist of 2 Samuel 22, rescue from the overpowering waters of Sheol comes in loftier imagery, viz., the imagery of the divine warrior as he marches forth to combat his fearsome foe:

> ⁸Then the earth rocked and quaked,
> The foundations of heaven shook—
> Rocked by His indignation.
> ⁹Smoke went up from His nostrils,
> From His mouth came devouring fire;
> Live coals blazed forth from Him.
> ¹⁰He bent the sky and came down,
> Thick cloud beneath His feet.

[11]He mounted a cherub and flew;
He flew on the wings of the wind.
[12]He made pavilions of darkness about Him,
Dripping clouds, huge thunderheads;
[13]In the brilliance before Him
Blazed fiery coals.
[14]The LORD thundered forth from heaven,
The Most High sent forth His voice;
[15]He let loose bolts, and scattered them;
Lightning, and put them to rout.
[16]The bed of the sea was exposed,
The foundations of the world were laid bare
By the mighty roaring of the LORD,
At the blast of the breath of His nostrils.
[17]He reached down from on high, He took me,
Drew me out of the mighty waters;
[18]He rescued me from my enemy so strong,
From foes too mighty for me.
[19]They attacked me on my day of calamity,
But the LORD was my stay. (2 Sam 22:8–19)[28]

The LORD's exposure of the seabed in v 16 is especially illuminating. It recalls the account in Genesis 1 of God's first creating the sky to divide the primordial waters and then draining the terrestrial waters into pools that he called "seas" so that the dry land could be seen (Gen 1:6–7, 9–10). More directly, it recalls the great act of deliverance he performed for the Israelites escaping Egypt: "The LORD drove back the sea with a strong east wind all that night, and turned the sea into dry ground" until his chosen had crossed, only then ordaining that "the waters may come back upon the Egyptians and upon their chariots and upon their horsemen," drowning the murderous foe (Exod 14:21, 26). In the rather different poetic version of these events in Exodus 15 (an older text), it is again the blast of God's wind that does the arrogant enemy in. Here, however, as we have seen, an expression resonant of the netherworld characterizes their disappearing into the sea: "The sea covered them" and "the earth ['āreṣ] swallowed them" (Exod 15:10, 12).[29] In 2 Samuel 22, this ancient cosmogonic imagery is applied to an individual's song of thanksgiving, and God's rescue of the miraculously delivered speaker from his formidable enemies is a rescue from Sheol seen as "the mighty waters" (vv 5–6, 17–18). The defeat of the terrifying foe is the defeat of an overreaching netherworld but also and equally the drying up of the chaotic waters that characterize it and threaten divine order and human life alike.[30] Here again, deliverance is both individual and cosmic. On the individual level, it involves the embattled psalmist's escape from the netherworld and restoration to life. On the cosmic level, it reflects the reestablishment of the divine authority that enables a life-enhancing world order to endure in the face of the ever-formidable forces associated with violent or unjust death.

Other metaphors of Sheol can be treated more briefly. The expression "the gates of death" suggests a city in which Death—perhaps conceived as the Canaanite god of the same name (*Môt*)—reigns supreme, in all his grisly majesty.[31] If so, the contrast underlying Ps 9:14–15 is especially suggestive:

> [14]Have mercy on me, O LORD;
>   see my affliction at the hands of my foes,
>   You who lift me from the gates of death,
>   [15]so that in the gates of Fair Zion
>   I might tell all Your praise,
>   I might exult in Your deliverance.

The energizing contrast here lies between "the gates [*ša'ărê*] of Death" and "the gates [*ša'ărê*] of Zion," between the lowest and highest points in the universe, as it were.[32] In the former, the foe reigns, afflicting the innocent speaker grievously and at will. In the latter, the LORD reigns, having "set up His throne for judgment" (v 8), and receives the grateful praise of the faithful he has delivered from death, yet again giving conclusive evidence of his own incomparability. "Gates of death" may refer not only to a subterranean city where evil works its will but also and equally to Sheol as a prison.[33] Consider the rich and reinforcing symbolism of these verses from another psalm:

> [10]Some lived in deepest darkness,
>   bound in cruel irons,
>   [11]because they defied the word of God,
>   spurned the counsel of the Most High.
>   [12]He humbled their hearts through suffering;
>   they stumbled with no one to help.
>   [13]In their adversity they cried to the LORD,
>   and He rescued them from their troubles.
>   [14]He brought them out of deepest darkness,
>   broke their bonds asunder.
>   [15]Let them praise the LORD for His steadfast love,
>   His wondrous deeds for mankind,
>   [16]For He shattered gates of bronze,
>   He broke their iron bars.
>   [17]There were fools who suffered for their sinful way,
>   and for their iniquities.
>   [18]All food was loathsome to them;
>   they reached the gates of death.

¹⁹In their adversity they cried to the LORD
    and He saved them from their troubles.
²⁰He gave an order and healed them;
    He delivered them from the pits.
²¹Let them praise the LORD for His steadfast love,
    His wondrous deeds for mankind.
²²Let them offer thanksgiving sacrifices,
    and tell His deeds in joyful song. (Ps 107:10–22)

Much of the power of this stanza derives from its overlay of several dominant metaphors of Sheol, and we should be most unwise to attempt to unravel and separate them. The "pits" from which the LORD rescued the rebels humbled in suffering (v 20) recalls the language of the grave, as we saw above. The twice-mentioned "deepest darkness" (vv 10, 14) again suggests the grave, but also the primordial darkness and water that God triumphantly overcomes in the act of creation in Genesis 1.³⁴ The Hebrew word *ṣalmāwet*, best known as the "shadow of death" in the King James Version of the twenty-third psalm (v 4), surely suggests death to the attentive hearer, even if that etymology is unscientific, as many scholars now believe.³⁵ The "gates of death" suggests a city, as we have seen, specifically, the subterranean city that is the diametric opposite of the lofty city atop Mount Zion, in which the life-giving LORD reigns supreme and inviolable. But the references to "cruel irons," "gates of bronze," and "iron bars" depict something far more ghastly than a mere city, even one that is heavily fortified. They depict, in fact, a prison, and in so doing, they interpret the rescue/healing of the afflicted penitents as an act of liberation. That, in turn, draws in its train a large number of biblical parallels, most memorably Joseph, whom his brothers first resolved to murder and subsequently threw into a pit from which he was rescued, only to be enslaved and later imprisoned in Egypt—but then redeemed from these fates no less (Gen 37:18–28, 36; 39:20; 41:14). In this, of course, Joseph pre-enacts the experience of the people Israel a few generations later when they become the target first of Pharaoh's enslavement, then of his genocidal decree (Exod 1:8–22), only to survive both of these and then to march proudly out of the house of bondage (Exod 13:27–14:31). Both of these cases—the one cast as biography, the other as national history—are narrative realizations of the liberation and deliverance celebrated in the verses we have quoted from Psalm 107.

Our examination of various images of Sheol in the Tanakh reinforces the point made earlier that literalistic efforts to locate the abode of the dead in space are misconceived. Grave, pit, underworld, utmost bounds of the earth, engulfing waters, subterranean city, prison—all these metaphors communicate a mode of existence, one that, in fact, characterizes people who have not "died" in our sense of the term at all. As one scholar aptly puts it, "those endangered feel that they are in Sheol already" because they live lives of weakness, defeat, depression, vulnerability, and the like.[36] In passages that deal with the biblical netherworld, the difference between being dead and being almost dead — can *we* imagine a larger difference than that? — often evaporates before our very eyes. Thus can the despondent speaker in Psalm 88 say, "I am at the brink of Sheol" (literally, "my life has reached Sheol") and then three verses later tell the LORD, "You have put me at the bottom of the Pit, / in the darkest places, in the depths" (vv 4, 7). It is not the case that in the intervening two verses he has passed away or somehow changed his locale from the edge of Sheol to its deepest pit. Rather, his condition — agonizing misfortune infinitely compounded by God-forsakenness — is very much the condition of Sheol. Without God's intervention ("cut off from Your care," v 6), he is dead. And, remarkably, for the speaking voice of Psalm 88, unlike most of the comparable psalmists (especially the author of Psalm 107), God never intervenes. This poet remains "a helpless man, abandoned among the dead" (vv 5–6).[37] All that differentiates him from them is his ability to call out to God to save him from Sheol. Unanswered (as he is), he is as good as dead.

We have been concentrating on psalms of thanksgiving and on laments because it is in them that one finds the largest number of references to Sheol. (Given how widespread the belief is that there is no return from Sheol, is it not ironic how much of our information about it comes from those who thank God for redeeming them from it or who petition him to do so?) Since a prime objective of these related genres is to persuade God to reverse the speaker's fatal misfortune, it is hardly surprising to find in them abundant references to the isolation of the dead not only from God but from his (living) fellows as well. As Psalm 88 puts it, "You have put friend and neighbor far from me / and my companions out of my sight" (v 19).[38] To judge by this literature, the land of the living and the abode of the dead are not at all in communication.

A number of biblical passages, however, augmented by archaeological studies, have emboldened some contemporary scholars to suggest an alternative view of the netherworld in Israelite thought. According to this view, the living were believed to be able to affect the dead (especially for the better), and the dead were deemed able, under certain ritual conditions and to some degree, to communicate with the living. These scholars, in other words, evoke a world in which the two realms are not nearly so separate as they appear in the psalms of lament, and death was not so final or so tragic as it appears in them. Those poems, they in fact argue, do not reflect the whole reality of the Israelite construction of death. In particular, it has been conjectured that a cult of the dead had been long and widely practiced in ancient Israel, as in other ancient

Near Eastern and Mediterranean societies, before various biblical sources finally acted to proscribe it.[39] Especially potent fuel for the conjecture comes from the confession that, according to Deuteronomy, an Israelite farmer is to make after depositing his tithe at the central sanctuary:

> [12]When you have set aside in full the tenth part of your yield — in the third year, the year of the tithe — and have given it to the Levite, the stranger, the fatherless, and the widow, that they may eat their fill in your settlements, [13]you shall declare before the LORD your God: "I have cleared out the consecrated portion from the house; and I have given it to the Levite, the stranger, the fatherless, and the widow, just as You commanded me; I have neither transgressed nor neglected any of Your commandments: [14]I have not eaten of it while in mourning, I have not cleared out any of it while I was unclean, and I have not deposited any of it with the dead. I have obeyed the LORD my God; I have done just as You commanded me. [15]Look down from Your holy abode, from heaven, and bless Your people Israel and the soil You have given us, a land flowing with milk and honey, as You swore to our fathers." (Deut 26:12–15)

The traditional Jewish interpretation of the affirmation central to our concern (v 14) is that the farmer has not eaten of the tithed crop while in a state of mourning (those in the initial stage of mourning being thus forbidden to make the affirmation) nor used it to provide a casket or shroud for the deceased.[40] Whatever other strengths this interpretation may have, the understanding it affords of the clause "I have not deposited any of it with the dead" is forced, to say the least, and we should not be surprised that an alternative reading has been proposed.

In light of the practice of feeding the dead to sustain them in the netherworld known from many cultures, some scholars have read v 14 to forbid this only when the food is to be tithed: either it is tithed and thus set aside for the needy or it is offered to the dead, but not both.[41] On this reading, as one of them puts it, "the Torah does not forbid this practice, but because contact with the dead is ritually defiling, it prohibits the tithe for it."[42] Or, to state the matter positively, under ordinary circumstances feeding the dead had long been altogether unobjectionable.[43] Indeed, Joseph Blenkinsopp thinks that the social structure of ancient Israel made this inevitable and that the burden of proof must therefore lie on those who argue that the cult of the dead was an aberration and not the norm of ancient Israelite culture (at least in its earlier periods):

> We can only claim, on the basis of numerous analogies, that solidarity between the living and the dead is what we expect in societies organized by patrilinear descent, and we have no reason to believe that the situation was different in Israel. We note too that the social life of the kinship group (including its

assemblies) and its persistence through time were inextricably bound up with ownership of a parcel of land which also served as a burial plot.[44]

This tight connection between the kinship group, understood as embracing the departed ancestors, and its patrimonial land has been invoked to explain a more particular aspect of the last point Blenkinsopp raises, the importance of burial within the confines of the family. The archaeologist Rachel S. Hallote makes the connection explicit:

> As families grew and shifted the space in the house was relocated. Occasionally additions were made, but in many cases floor plans remained identical for a century at a time. The older generations especially would move from room to room each time there was a new marriage or new birth. When a member of the oldest generation died, he would simply be given another space within the house — this time beneath its floors. His final resting-place kept him within the family unit in the most literal sense and allowed him to continue to participate in the life of the family and the household, even after death.[45]

Given this incorporation and participation of the dead in the life of the family, it stands to reason that Hallote sees in Deut 26:13–14 evidence that "the Israelite desire to appease and please the dead by giving them the best food available was irresistible."[46] Indeed, some scholars find evidence for this in any text that links eating and mourning and thus interpret the meal in question as sacrificial and the recipients of the sacrifice, in turn, as the deceased.[47] On that reading, the departed are not so much dead (in our sense) as deified. However negatively the later biblical and postbiblical traditions were to judge the phenomenon (and they judged it very negatively indeed), the cult of the dead would thus have been a major element of Israelite devotion beforehand.

Among scholars who adhere to this position, it is not uncommon to find in the enigmatic *marzēaḥ* a major locus of the putative cult of the dead.[48] Unfortunately, the nature of the marzēaḥ remains unclear, as is the translation of the term itself, and whether the marzēaḥ necessarily had a funerary dimension at all is a matter of ongoing controversy. The word itself is attested widely in the ancient northwest Semitic world, from the late third millennium B.C.E. through rabbinic Judaism and beyond. But it is the discovery (in 1929) and processing of a trove of texts from Ugarit, a kingdom on the Syrian coast in the second millennium B.C.E., that has caused so much attention to be fixed on the biblical marzēaḥ. It was this new information that energized the view that the term refers to a funerary feast in which the dead participate along with those celebrating their passing. Here, too, however, we should be well advised to bear in mind the point recently made by Johnston that the Ugaritic marzēaḥ, though "a significant social institution," gives no indication of a "generally

cultic or specifically funerary aspect." "Perhaps the nearest modern equivalents," he writes, "are the Masonic Lodges, Rotary Clubs and Gentlemen's
Clubs, with their various religious, social and economic elements." As for
the specific Ugaritic version of the marzēaḥ of which so much has been made,
note the conclusion of another recent and more detailed study: "None of the
data from Ugarit justifies a connection between the *marziḫu* and the mortuary cult."[49]

The evidence of the Hebrew Bible does not do much to cement the connection, either. In light of the amount of ink that biblical scholars have devoted to
the marzēaḥ in recent decades, it may come as a surprise that the term occurs
only twice in that set of books, and never in narrative or law (whether to
regulate or to proscribe it). The first attestation, Amos 6:7, comes at the close
of a fierce oracle against those "who are at ease in Zion," lying "on ivory
beds," feasting on lambs and calves, drinking wine, "anoint[ing] themselves
with the choicest oils," singing and listening to music, and thus eminently
oblivious to the approaching judgment — "not concerned about the ruin of
Joseph," that is, the northern kingdom, in which Amos prophesied (Amos
6:1–6). The prophet concludes his fiery oracle against this sybaritic and self-
indulgent lifestyle thus:

> Assuredly, right soon
> They shall head the column of exiles;
> They shall loll no more at festive meals. (Amos 6:7)

Nothing in the entire oracle gives the slightest reason to suspect that the
carousing so effectively portrayed had a funerary character, still less that it
involved a full-fledged cult of the dead. Some scholars, eager to assimilate the
biblical to the Ugaritic marzēaḥ (in its supposedly funerary mode), connect
Amos 6:1–7 to vv 9–10, which speak of widespread death in the impending
reckoning. But Johnston is surely right that the two oracles "are quite distinct"
and "separated both by the clear conclusion to the earlier oracle (v 7, beginning 'therefore' [*lākēn,* here rendered 'assuredly'] and by an independent
divine oath (v 8)."[50]

The only other clear biblical allusion to the *marzēaḥ* presents a rather different picture:

> [5]For thus said the LORD:
> Do not enter a house of mourning,
> Do not go to lament and to condole with them;
> For I have withdrawn My favor from that people
>   — declares the LORD —
> My kindness and compassion.

> 6Great and small alike shall die in this land,
> They shall not be buried; men shall not lament them,
> Nor gash and tonsure themselves for them.
> 7They shall not break bread for a mourner
> To comfort him for a bereavement,
> Nor offer one a cup of consolation
> For the loss of his father or mother.
> 8Nor shall you enter a house of feasting,
> To sit down with them to eat and drink.
>
> 9For thus said the LORD of Hosts, the God of Israel: I am going to banish from this place, in your days and before your eyes, the sound of mirth and gladness, the voice of bridegroom and bride. (Jer 16:5–9)[51]

The specific references to lamentation, condolence, burial, and mourning rituals in this oracle render the translation of *bêt marzēaḥ* in v 5 as "house of mourning" highly probable. If the "house of feasting" (*bêt mišteh*) of v 8 is the same institution, then we are naturally led to think of the bacchanalian feast Amos savaged in 6:1–7 and thus to suspect that the latter, too, had a funerary or mortuary connection.[52] An alternative and more probable interpretation, however, is the one reflected in the translation above: the prohibition on entering the "house of mourning" is distinct from that on entering the "house of feasting," even though the two prohibitions derive from the same catastrophe that the LORD is about to bring on. Adding to the likelihood that the two houses are different is the rationale for the prohibition on entering the "house of feasting" given in the ensuing verse (v 9), which deals only with weddings and not in any way with mourning, still less a cult of the dead.[53]

The impression that Jer 16:5–9 leaves is that the *bêt marzēaḥ* was a locus for comforting mourners, rather like the "*shiva* house" at which Jews to this day pay respects to the nearest of kin for a week after the burial of a family member. Whether it was the mourners' own home (like the shiva house) or another building is unknown, though the comparative evidence may suggest the latter. What precisely went on in this "house of mourning" is also less than apparent, though it is highly likely that ritual weeping and verbal condolences were prominent features of the institution. The "cup of consolation" in v 7 (unattested elsewhere) suggests that a portion of the comfort may have derived from alcohol. As an analogy to this latter dimension, one might cite the *sĕ'ûdat ḥabrā'â*, the "meal of recovery" readied for Jewish mourners upon their return from interment. Even if wine was prominently featured in Jeremiah's "house of mourning" (unlike today's shiva house), there is no reason to assume that the atmosphere was one of self-indulgence and shallow joy, like that of Amos' marzēaḥ. In any event, it is more likely that only the mourners consumed the "cup of consolation," and the mood remained somber and sorrowful. It is too easily missed but essential to understand nonetheless that the LORD forbids Jeremiah to enter this bêt marzēaḥ not because the occasion was festive and bacchanalian, but because, in light of the impending national catastrophe, he can have no consolation to offer.

We have been at pains to argue against the assumption that the Israelite marzēaḥ was a funeral feast connected to a cult of the dead. Of the two attestations of the term in the Hebrew Bible, one (Amos 6:7) has no funerary association at all. The other (Jer 16:5), focusing on comforting mourners, implies no cult of the dead—a very different thing—and gives no indication that the participants were feeding, sacrificing to, or communicating with the deceased in any way.[54] And even if we assume a high degree of continuity between the highly enigmatic biblical marzēaḥ and the only slightly less enigmatic Ugaritic marzēaḥ and imagine both to focus on death and carousing (both assumptions are highly doubtful), we are still not entitled to the further assumption that the theology of death was the same in the two institutions. The term offers support for a cult of the dead in ancient Israel only to those committed on other grounds to finding one. That there are other grounds is surely the case, as we have seen in connection with Deut 26:14, but this should not cause us to lose sight of the paucity of references to a cult of the dead within the Hebrew Bible itself. Indeed, the Hebrew Bible displays fairly consistently a very different conception of death and the dead, and this critical fact can easily be missed if we reinterpret the biblical data with the reconstructed cult of the dead as our hermeneutical key.

The subject of necromancy, the verbal communication between the dead and the living, is more promising for those who think the dead figured prominently and actively in the lives of the Israelite living.[55] In this case, though the practice came to be strictly proscribed and attributed to foreign influence (e.g., Lev 19:31; 20:27; Deut 18:9–14), a number of texts suggest that it was once widely practiced and, according to some scholars, not viewed as an offense to the God of Israel until relatively late. Thus, a prophetic oracle that predicts a terrifying siege of Jerusalem arranged by God himself likens the victims to ghosts:

> [1]"Ah, Ariel, Ariel,
> City where David camped!
> Add year to year,
> Let festivals come in their cycles!
> [2]And I will harass Ariel,
> And there shall be sorrow and sighing.
> She shall be to Me like Ariel.

> ³And I will camp against you like David;
> I will lay siege to you with a mound,
> And I will set up siegeworks against you.
> ⁴And you shall speak from lower than the ground,
> Your speech shall be humbler than the sod;
> Your speech shall sound like a ghost's ['ôb] from the ground,
> Your voice shall chirp from the sod.
> ⁵And like fine dust shall be
> The multitude of your haughty people;
> And like flying chaff,
> The multitude of tyrants." (Isa 29:1–5)⁵⁶

The image of the dead evoked in v 4 is hardly that of individuals who have passed into oblivion and are no more. Rather, the impression conveyed is that the dead have been humiliated, reduced not to silence but to a humble speech, barely detectable yet real.⁵⁷ To be sure, the verse passes no judgment on those who might be tempted to consult these ghosts, except perhaps indirectly in the unflattering description of the latter, who are likened to those besieged. In this, we may see more continuity with the Pentateuchal proscriptions than first meets the eye. For legal materials do not at all deny the possibility that the dead may endure in some unspecified condition or even that they may have valid insights to communicate. Rather, where a rationale for the prohibition on necromancy appears at all (as in Deut 18:9–14), it is grounded in the assumption that the practice characterizes the wicked and idolatrous Canaanites and thus, if observed by Israel, compromises the chosen people's wholehearted trust in, and loyalty to, their covenanting God. When such consultation is *not* at issue (as it is not in the oracle at hand), the continued existence of the dead and their capacity to communicate a message to the living can be openly (if indirectly) acknowledged.⁵⁸

Things are very different in the most developed and extensive account of necromancy in the Hebrew Bible, the story of Saul's desperate — yet successful — attempt to consult the departed Samuel (1 Sam 28:3–25) on the eve of his own demise.⁵⁹ Here the tone is one of unrelieved tragedy.

> ⁴The Philistines mustered and they marched to Shunem and encamped; and Saul gathered all Israel, and they encamped at Gilboa. ⁵When Saul saw the Philistine force, his heart trembled with fear. ⁶And Saul inquired of the LORD, but the LORD did not answer him, either by dreams or by Urim or by prophets. ⁷Then Saul said to his courtiers, "Find me a woman who consults ghosts, so that I can go to her and inquire through her." And his courtiers told him that there was a woman in En-dor who consulted ghosts. (1 Sam 28:4–7)

In seeking out a necromancer, the king was violating his own decree, for "Saul had forbidden [*hēsîr*] [recourse to] ghosts and familiar spirits in the land" (v 3). The LORD's abandonment of his once chosen king is so thoroughgoing and so irreversible that he even denies him the media that properly replace the forbidden practice — divinely inspired dreams, Urim-divination,[60] and prophecy. Indeed, it is precisely the failure of the legitimate media that motivates Saul to seek a séance with the prophet of the LORD who had anointed him king in the first place but also deposed him (1 Sam 15:1–34; 9:1–10:16).

> Samuel said to Saul, "Why have you disturbed me[61] and brought me up?" And Saul answered, "I am in great trouble. The Philistines are attacking me and God has turned away [*sār*] from me; He no longer answers me, either by prophets or in dreams. So I have called you to tell me what I am to do." (1 Sam 28:15)

Consequently, it is a bit simplistic to say that Saul reverted to the necromancy that he had forbidden (*hēsîr*, v 3). Rather, in response to YHWH's turning away (*sār*, v 15) from him, he sought (and received) a séance with the YHWHistic prophet who had been the agent of his enthronement — and not with any other ghost.[62] And, from one point of view, the séance succeeds: the departed Samuel does indeed impart an oracle. Yet here, too, the note of tragedy is unbroken, for the oracle reiterates the desperate king's deposition from the throne and then adds the chilling message, "Tomorrow your sons and you will be with me," as a result of the impending and unstoppable Philistine victory (v 19). The evaluation of necromancy implied in this passage is too complex to be classified as either fraudulent or legitimate. Necromancy is here both efficacious and forbidden. It yields a valid oracle, but the dead man who gives it is a YHWHistic prophet who simply reiterates the prophetic pronouncement he rendered while alive. The procedure fails to reconnect the rejected supplicant with the God who has renounced him. It provides, in sum, no valuable new knowledge and no deliverance.

The eerie meeting of Saul and Samuel — the rendezvous of the doomed and the deceased — contributes further evidence that in ancient Israel the dead were not always thought to have passed into oblivion. In 1 Samuel 28, the prophet and his message still exist, but only the message — the oracle of the LORD — survives in full force. The messenger himself is simply "an old man . . . wrapped in a robe," upset that he has been disturbed (vv 14–15), whose only special claim is his status as a prophet of the LORD while he yet lived. Whatever the character of Samuel's subterranean abode (it is never actually called Sheol), the higher and more substantial reality lies not there but above, in the realm of the living, where God's unfathomable will works itself out in history. That alone is the realm to which the oracle is addressed. The wisdom of the dead prophet turns out to be essentially a reiteration of the final message he delivered to the king: the LORD has taken the kingship from Saul and given it to David (v 17). The only new information Samuel conveys is that the sinful and rejected king will die the next day (v 19). In 1 Samuel 28, the dead have no special wisdom, no mysteries to reveal, and no new prophecies to make. They do not in the least benefit the one who consults them.

We are reminded by 1 Samuel 28, however, that the patterns of religion generally regarded as normative in the Hebrew Bible reflect only a segment of the ancient Israelite population, many of whom doubtless once engaged without scruple in the very rites therein designated as deviant. Societies do not forbid practices that no one would think to perform. That being the case, the question before us is not whether some Israelites in some periods thought that there could be access to the dead. It is clear that they did (though whether they believed in deified ancestors, benevolent and all-knowing deceased, and the like is considerably less certain). Our question, rather, involves the extent to which the biblical texts assume or approve of that belief and the corollary issue of the rough date at which the belief and its associated practices came to be seen as deviant and disloyal to the God of Israel. The difference between the dominant biblical view and the alternative is well stated by Karel van der Toorn, a scholar thoroughly convinced of the pervasiveness of the cult of the dead until a fairly late date in ancient Israel's history:

> The religious scholars responsible for the collection, selection and editing of the biblical books were not particularly happy with references and allusions to the veneration of the dead in which their forefathers had indulged. They therefore endeavoured to eliminate or disarm any hints of a positive appreciation of the cult of the dead. . . . The biblical texts as we have them are intended to suggest that most of the Israelites looked upon the dead as bleak shadows without power or influence. The impression conveyed by the authorized version of Israel's past is inconsistent, however, with the prominence of the ancestor cult.[63]

One interesting piece of evidence that van der Toorn adduces in support of his conviction is the presence, indeed ubiquity, of personal names that he thinks attest to a belief in the survival and continuing power of the deceased ancestors. On the basis of names like Abida (Gen 25:4), which can be parsed to mean "My Father Knows," he concludes that "deified ancestors . . . 'know' their descendants." Abiezer (Josh 17:2, "My Father is Help") and Ahiezer (Num 1:12, "My Brother is Help") show that they "are ready to 'help' them," just as names like Abishua (1 Chr 5:30, "My Father is Deliverance") indicate that they "are ready . . . to 'come to their rescue.' " "Their help," claims van der Toorn, consists in "support," as demonstrated by the name Ahisamach (Exod 31:6, understood as "My Brother Offers Support") or in "kind judgement," as indicated by a name like Abidan (Num 2:22, meaning "My Father Gives Judgment"). He derives an important point from names like Abiasaph (Exod 6:24), which he understands to mean "The Father Has Added (a Child to the Family)" and Jokneam (Josh 12:22), which he translates as "May the Ancestor create (scil. offspring)." All these he takes to "refer to the multiplication of descendants and the extension of the family by the deified ancestors."[64]

On the basis of these names and others like them, van der Toorn concludes that

> dead kin were regarded as kind and benevolent. Ancestors were not vengeful beings that had to be kept at bay by all means. . . . The dead were believed to take care of their descendants from beyond the grave. Having reached a preternatural state, they used their powers for the good of their family. Not only did they symbolize the identity of that family; in the final analysis, they were also responsible for its continuing growth and welfare.[65]

Van der Toorn's conclusion depends rather heavily on his conviction that "the Israelites were usually aware of the religious significance of their personal names."[66] There is room to wonder, however, how general this awareness was and how long it survived. How many speakers of English name their sons "Christopher" in the hope that the child will be one who "bears Christ," in conformity with the Greek and Latin etymologies of the name? And how many Jews who name their daughters "Esther" intend thereby to do honor to the goddess Ishtar, from which the name probably derives (as even a Talmudic authority recognized)?[67] Whether ancient Israelite parents parsed names as we would is a matter of doubt; the biblical evidence suggests considerable creativity on the part of the ancients[68] and thus urges comparable caution on our part, especially when facing the temptation to build wide-ranging reconstructions of Israelite religion on such evidence. Even if the knowing father or rescuing brother whom the name first honored had been a deceased and deified ancestor, the name may well have been understood differently by the ancient Israelites who later bore or recorded it. In van der Toorn's view, "If the cult of the ancestors had been condemned by the population during the First Temple Period, it might be expected that the theophoric use of kinship names would have been abandoned [along with names derived from those of foreign deities]."[69] Perhaps, but this is to ignore another logical option, that the names were reinterpreted or continued without concern for the meaning they would have if they were parsed as sentences. Indeed, van der Toorn's own reasoning would seem to require that precisely this second logical option did indeed take place. However early Israelites understood names like Ahiezer, Ahisamach, and Abidan, the relatively late Priestly source (P) in which they now occur surely did not believe that the names invoked a deceased but divine ancestor! And the same can be asserted with at least equal certainty about the Chronicler, the very late biblical author who dutifully records the name Abishua, for example. Indeed, Abidan appears as the name of a figure in late Tannaitic Judaism (early third century C.E.).[70] Are we to imagine his name was understood to refer to a deified ancestor who gave judgment for his descendants?

The issue is thus not *whether* the names lost their theophoric denotations (assuming they ever had them) but *when*. The mere existence of names that can be construed to refer to divinized ancestors does not demonstrate in the least that Israelites throughout the First Temple period (ca. 1000–586 B.C.E.) generally and without condemnation worshiped dead ancestors.

One has to reckon also with the possibility that some of these names were already traditional before the emergence of Israel and do not necessarily reflect the dominant Israelite thinking in any period. Jokneam, for example, is a Canaanite town, ruled by a king that Joshua is reported to have defeated (Josh 12:22). That the town retained the old name (whatever it means) when it passed into Israelite control and was assigned to the Levites (Josh 21:34) may not tell us anything at all about the religious beliefs of the Israelites living there.

That names of the sort van der Toorn and others adduce might have referred to deified ancestors at some period is thus quite possible, but far from certain. One can imagine that Israelite and even Canaanite parents would wish to honor their own knowing, helpful, or rescuing kinsmen by the names they give their children, quite without intending to ascribe divinity to their beloved departed. Some names, however, do indeed have explicit theophoric elements in them, such as Ammiel (Num 13:12) and Eliam (2 Sam 11:3), which van der Toorn interprets as "My ancestor is god" and "My god, the Ancestor," respectively.[71] There is a world of difference between "God is a kinsman/father/ancestor," on the one hand, and "My ancestor is a god," on the other. Even accepting the latter interpretation, one cannot discount the possibility that the element "El" refers to the Canaanite father god whose name, and some of whose characteristics, later came to apply to the national God of Israel. If so, then Ammiel would mean "El is my kinsman," and Eliam, "My God is a kinsman," or the like; neither would refer to any departed ancestor at all. A similar point can be made about the name Ammishaddai (Num 1:12), which van der Toorn thinks "proclaims the ancestor to be one of the Šadday gods, chthonic deities that were credited with powers of protection."[72] On the assumption that the religion of Israel emerged only late, having previously been indistinguishable from that of its immediate neighbors, this is surely defensible. But we must not overlook the use of Šadday in connection with YHWH, who is anything but a chthonic deity (e.g., Gen 17:1; Gen 6:2–3; Ruth 2:21).[73] And in each of these cases, even if the parsing I have suggested is not original, there is no reason that it could not have come into existence as a folk etymology or that the name ceased to be understood as a sentence at all.

In support of the theory of the deified dead in ancient Israel, much might be made of the use of the term *ʾĕlōhîm* to describe the being(s) that the necromancer sees "coming up from the earth" in 1 Sam 28:13.[74] Usually translated in other contexts as "God" or "gods," the term might, maximally, indeed be taken as evidence for the deification of the dead. The minimalist interpretation, however, accords much better with Israelite religion so far as the latter can be reconstructed. On this reading, *ʾĕlōhîm* functions like the English word *spirit,* which can denote anything from God to an angel, a demon, a ghost, a tone of an organization, or an alcoholic beverage. The word, in short, has a wide semantic range, and the connotations of one of its usages cannot be legitimately extended to the others. That the dead were *ʾĕlōhîm* in some biblical texts does not in the least imply that they were divine in the same way YHWH was, or even his mythological rivals (Baal, for example) were thought to be, or that they were the recipients of sacrifice, the addressees of prayers, benefactors of their worshipers, or anything of the kind.[75] Terms like "the deified dead" or "divine ancestors," which obscure these key distinctions, can be profoundly misleading.[76]

If we resist the powerful temptation to assimilate the evidence about Israelite religion that the Hebrew Bible provides uncritically to the patterns of the antecedent and neighboring cultures (patterns that are themselves more various and less clear than we might wish), we can avoid the more extreme speculations about the role of the dead in the lives of their kin that have abounded among biblical scholars in recent years. We shall, for example, have to remain unpersuaded by the argument that *ʾĕlōhê ʾābîw* means not "God of his father," as it is usually translated, but rather "divine ancestors [who] continued as vital entities in Judahite religion and society as long as the kingdom existed."[77] We shall have to be skeptical as well of the lack of evidence to support another scholar's claim that the commandment to "honor your father and your mother" (Exod 20:12; Deut 5:16) relates to "the respect shown for parents *after their death.*"[78] Similarly, we shall have to render the Scottish verdict of "not proven" on the claim that David's clan sacrifice in 1 Samuel 20 involved the ritual invocation of the names of deceased ancestors[79] — an element utterly unattested in the passage, whatever the evidence for it in non-Israelite religion. Or, to give one last example, we shall need much more evidence than has been provided before we accept still another scholar's claim that Jacob's mourning for Joseph, and David's for Bathsheba's firstborn (Gen 37:35; 2 Sam 12:15–23), represent "a description of a ritual descent into the netherworld" in an effort (at least in David's case) "to try to bring his son back from the clutches of death."[80] That Jacob mourned Joseph's ostensible death and David hoped his actions would help his baby recover cannot be gainsaid, but in neither case is there a descent into the netherworld, ritual or other. That such a ritual descent existed as an item in ancient Israelite religion is arguable; that it appears in these biblical texts is highly improbable.

Just as biblical exegetes need to remember that Israelite religion was a larger and more variegated phenomenon than the Hebrew Bible authorizes, so scholars of ancient Near Eastern religion need to remember that the biblical authors make a selection out of a larger repertory of religious forms, have criteria of their own for so doing, and, most important, in the process propound patterns of religious belief and practice that have an integrity of their own. Undue harmonization can move in either direction.

One thing that remains unclear is the historical reality of Israelite religion as regards the dead and their abode. As we have just been at pains to stress, the Hebrew Bible and the religion of Israel are not equivalent. Biblical sources, to reiterate, proscribe necromancy (e.g., Deut 18:9–14), deliver prophetic indictments of those who engage in it (Isa 8:19–22), and express contempt for "sacrifices offered to the dead" (Ps 106:28–31), to give just three typical examples. The general (but not universal) tendency in the Bible is to classify such things as imitations of "the abhorrent practices of those nations" (Deut 18:9) whom Israel was to supplant in Canaan or as foreign in some other, less specific way. In other words, Israelites who engage in such practices betray not only their God but also their own national tradition, defecting to the environing idolatry. How those thus indicted interpreted their own actions and their motivations remains unknown. For these people are understandably given no voice of their own in the Bible, and the archaeological remains are mute and, like personal names, patient of more than one interpretation, even when those who have left the remains can be convincingly identified as Israelite (which is not always the case). That a person is buried under the floor of the family home may or may not imply that such an arrangement "allowed him to continue to participate in the life of the family and the household, even after death," to cite again the claim of one archaeologist.[81] But even if it does, surely we must take note of the fact that the Israelites do *not* engage in that practice but instead bury outside the community,[82] and thus reject the same archaeologist's sweeping conclusion that "the Israelites, whether they originated from the midst of the Canaanites, came out of the southern desert, or a combination of both, followed the Canaanite Cult of the Dead to the letter."[83] So to claim is not only to misinterpret the archaeological evidence; it is also to underestimate drastically the degree to which the larger theology of a culture can change even when specific externals (the bailiwick of archaeology) do not. Consider as an illustration the fourth-century Christian adoption of the date of the pagan Roman celebration of the birth of the Unconquered Sun (*Sol Invictus*) as the date of Jesus' birth, or the way that the new holiday absorbed aspects of the Saturnalia that it in some ways replaced, or for that matter, consider the transformation of a Germanic pagan symbol into the familiar "Christmas tree." The relative objectivity and solidity of archaeological data can obscure the critical point that realia are an exceedingly insecure basis on which to rest a reconstruction of myth and theology.[84]

In the absence of reliable data about the cult of the dead in ancient Israel, many scholars simply follow the biblical lead and assume that Israelites practiced a religion indistinguishable on such matters from that of their Canaanite neighbors (the latter phenomenon is, of course, itself highly unclear and a subject of unending scholarly controversy).[85] With that as the guiding methodology, it is hardly a matter for surprise that the conclusion they reach casts doubt on the whole idea of a distinctive Israelite theology of the sort reflected in the Hebrew Bible, suggesting instead that the biblical pattern derives either from a late period very different from antecedent tradition or, alternatively, from a particular social elite with an agenda at odds with that of most of the populace.

The most interesting and creative argument along these lines is that of Baruch Halpern.[86] Using archaeological, epigraphic, and biblical evidence, Halpern mounts a formidable case that King Hezekiah, in the face of a powerful Assyrian advance in the late eighth century B.C.E., engineered a massive shift in settlement patterns throughout his Judahite realm. The result, he conjectures, was "a population herded into fortresses" and thus radically and irreversibly cut off from their ancestral lands and traditional village culture. This could not but profoundly undermine the old—and until then unobjectionable—cult of the dead.[87] "Resettlement, after all, severed the physical links to the ancestors, the material token of that old, pervasive community," and brought forth Isaiah's "fierce polemic against the ancestral cult."[88] In Halpern's view, the new thinking is reflected in burial practices as well, specifically in the "marked shift" from "the old multi-chambered Israelite rock-hewn tombs with several burial benches in each chamber . . . toward single-chambered rock-hewn tombs." This, in turn, reflects the movement toward "smaller [familial] units" and the heightened "integrity of the individual against the claim of traditional bonds."[89] Blenkinsopp, who adheres to the same theory, summarizes the conflict of the new arrangement with the old practice well. "Since the ancestor cult was an essential integrative element of a social system based on lineage," he writes, "it was opposed by a centralized state cult which claimed the exclusive allegiance of those living within the confines of the state."[90]

It will be recalled that Blenkinsopp also observes "that solidarity between the living and the dead is what we expect in societies organized by patrilinear descent, and we have no reason to believe that the situation was different in Israel."[91] Without gainsaying the value of comparative evidence, we must again be alert to the danger of missing the distinctive character of the cultures brought into the comparison. In the case at hand, that of ancient Israel, we do indeed have reason to believe the situation was different, and the source of the countervailing evidence is readily available: the Hebrew Bible.

Let us imagine what the narratives and laws of the Hebrew Bible would look like if they reflected a segment of ancient Israelite culture in which such phenomena as ancestor worship and necromancy actually had long been deemed acceptable and been practiced widely, so that, for example, "the Israelite desire to appease and please the dead by giving them the best food available was irresistible."[92] Consider as our first illustration Isaac, when he has confronted the death of his father Abraham and his own appointment to continue the patriarchal line (Gen 26:1–5). Here, if anywhere, "the Israelite desire to appease and please the dead" through food offerings and other sacrifice would surely be "irresistible." So would the son and heir's desire to receive his father's counsel as he attempted to step into the latter's shoes and faced strikingly similar challenges, like the threat of a potentially lecherous king eager to absorb his wife into the harem (Gen 12:10–20; 20; 26:6–11). In this case, no less than in that of Saul on the eve of the battle that would take his life, Isaac would surely have felt an irresistible urge to make use of a necromancer to raise the shade of the departed and thus to secure the intervention of the knowing, helping, rescuing, and judging god that his father had become upon death. Indeed, given the exquisite narrative artistry of the storytellers of Genesis, one can imagine without much difficulty a heartbreaking rendezvous between Isaac and Abraham, like that of Homer's Odysseus with his mother, asking for information about his long-missed father.[93] Or—a better analogy still—one can picture an Israelite equivalent of the scene in the *Aeneid* in which Aeneas, under the guidance of the Cumaean Sybil, at long last meets with his beloved father Anchises in the netherworld. Just at that moment, Vergil tells us, the old man was "surveying the souls of those imprisoned yet destined to go to the upper light and reviewing, by chance, the whole multitude of his own people and his beloved descendants, their fates and fortunes, their ways and works." In response to Aeneas' gentle questioning, he reveals his son's destiny as the founder of Rome, despite the heroic suffering that Aeneas has undergone and will undergo yet again. Anchises also speaks of the destiny of Rome even to the time of Augustus, when Vergil wrote the epic and the prophesied glory had come to pass.[94] The Israelite authors did not write Homeric or Vergilian epic, of course, but if consultation with the dead were a widespread and acceptable part of their religious heritage, would they not have devised a roughly equivalent rendezvous of Abraham and Isaac, or at least something that anticipates it, however dimly? And if "the invocation of the dead as a part of an ancestor cult" were a widely accepted Israelite practice,[95] then surely we should expect it to appear here if anywhere.

The same can be asked of the next generation in the patriarchal line of Israel, of Jacob when his father Isaac dies (Gen 35:28–29).[96] Had all outstanding issues in the immensely complicated relationship of the two been resolved while the father yet lived? Would Jacob not have still wished more than most sons to "appease and please" the father he had once deceived grievously, plunging him into uncontrollable trembling (Gen 27:1–45)? Would he not have set forth rich fare at the latter's grave — if not out of guilt, then certainly out of a desire to treat his father's ghost as any good Canaanite/Israelite son would be expected to? And would Jacob not have wanted to secure Isaac's blessing once more, this time when it would perhaps be all the stronger, coming from the realm of the divinized dead? If so, then surely he, too, would have sought out the appropriate practitioner to raise his father's shade and perform the requisite and, at that period, thoroughly unobjectionable rites.

Since the initial infertility of the matriarch is an important issue in each of the three patriarchal generations (e.g., Gen 15:1–6; 25:20–21; 29:31; 30:1–2), as well as in the stories of Samson (Judg 13:2), Hannah (1 Sam 1:4–11), and Naomi (Ruth 1:11–13), one would expect to find many remnants of the appeal to the divine ancestor who is responsible for "the multiplication of descendants and the extension of the family by the deified ancestors."[97] Here, too, should we not expect to read that the proper sacrifices and libations were offered, the appropriate necromancer enlisted, and the hoped-for blessing of fertility thus extended?

The same questions could be asked about Joshua, the successor of Moses, whose charisma he has assumed (Num 27:20), or about Rehoboam, the son of King Solomon, whose harshness and intransigence lost him the major part of his father's realm (1 Kgs 12:1–24)—indeed, about dozens of biblical characters in need of appeasing, pleasing, consulting, and benefiting from their ancestors, too many to list here.

Yet the actual literary evidence is stunning. For not a single such narrative exists, and our thought experiment remains, alas, purely theoretical. To be sure, the Hebrew Bible records a variety of burial practices, from the humble Moses' interment in an unknown grave (Deut 34:5–6) to the proud Absalom's erection of a monument to keep his memory alive in the absence of a son (2 Sam 18:18).[98] Biblical authors were also willing to record practices very much at odds with the continuing Israelite tradition, such as the forty days of embalming for Jacob in Egypt and the subsequent seventy days in which the Egyptians mourned the eponymous patriarch of Israel (Gen 50:2–3). More important, the narratives speak unabashedly of esteemed ancestors' engaging in practices that were later fiercely opposed, even anathematized. Consider Abraham's willingness to perform a child sacrifice (Gen 22:1–19; cf. Lev 20:2–5; Deut 12:29–31)[99] or Jacob's marriage to two sisters (Gen 29:21–30; cf. Lev 18:18). Or, again, consider the lack of embarrassment or apologetic about the patriarchs' consecrating sanctuaries outside the one central sanctuary that later came to be seen as exclusively legitimate (e.g., Gen 12:7–8; 21:33; 28:18–19; cf. Deut 12:1–27). Yet nowhere do we find a narrative describing the allegedly "irresistible" and altogether legitimate feeding of the dead or sacrificing to the "divine ancestors [who some think] continued as vital entities in Judahite religion and society as long as the kingdom existed."[100] Similarly, other than Saul's unproductive consultation with Samuel at En-dor, we find no explicit narrative about a consultation with the departed, though this, too, some scholars now think to have been practiced without objection until it ran afoul of royal ambition relatively late in Israel's history, in the time of the Judahite King Hezekiah around 700 B.C.E.

Alas, biblical law offers no more support than narrative for this hypothesis. To be sure, as we have seen, Deut 26:14 can be plausibly construed to imply (and it is at best only an implication) that food deposited with the dead is a problem only if it is then offered for the tithe. But if this is so—in a text that almost surely postdates Hezekiah's reform—why, again, is there no attestation of the practice of feeding the dead in biblical narrative, and why no other law similarly restricting but not prohibiting this putatively "irresistible" practice? I can imagine, for instance, that the firstborn of flock and herd to which YHWH lays claim, according to more than one Pentateuchal source (e.g., Exod 13:11–13; 22:28–29; 34:19–20), would, for the same reason, be ineligible to feed the dead, and the farmer would be sternly cautioned against thinking otherwise. Similarly, laws that regulate freewill offerings (e.g., Lev 7:16–18) might warn against the designation for this purpose of meat left for the dead, or, in forbidding such sacrifices to be eaten after the morrow, might include offering them to the deceased in the same prohibition. But, once more, this is not the case, and the evidence in the legal corpora for this supposedly wide-spread and long-legitimate practice remains limited to exactly one clause in Deuteronomy.

Necromancy, on the other hand, is indeed prohibited, though explicitly only in relatively late law codes (Lev 19:31; 20:27; Deut 18:9–14). An argument from silence could thus suggest that necromancy had been thought quite legitimate early on and was prohibited only in the wake of Hezekiah and the centralizing, royalist party that he championed. This requires us, of course, to discount the report that "Saul had forbidden [recourse to] ghosts and familiar spirits in the land" (1 Sam 28:3). As we have seen, that report heightens the literary impact of the story. Having forbidden (*hēsîr*) such recourse, the king resorts to it himself when YHWH has turned away (*sār*) from him, severing all acceptable modes of communication with the king he once commissioned. Whether literary artistry *generated* the report is, of course, another matter and impossible to determine. If it did not, it is difficult to see why the narrator would want to portray Saul this way in the absence of a historical tradition to that effect. For Israel's first king is (to understate drastically) not generally depicted as foreshadowing the admired reforming monarchs Hezekiah and Josiah, who are, in fact, descended from the man in favor of whom he was deposed, King David. That Saul is depicted as engaging in necromancy is indeed an important piece of evidence for the reconstruction of this aspect of the religion of Israel, but so is the fact that he is reported to have proscribed necromancy three centuries before Hezekiah's centralization.

It is also unclear whether the relatively early legal collection of Exodus 21–23 really is silent on the issue of necromancy.[101] There is ample room to wonder, for example, just what services were performed by the "sorceress" (*mĕkaššēpâ*) whom Exod 22:17 requires to be killed, in an enigmatic verse of a mere three Hebrew words. Could she, too, have been "a woman who consults ghosts" (*'ešet ba'ălat 'ôb*), like the one Saul consulted in violation of his own decree (1 Sam 28:7)?[102] If so, then even the Book of the Covenant, universally classified as the earliest of Israel's collections of law, forbids necromancy, and the prohibition does not originate in the late Judahite monarchy at all. Saul's prohibition of the practice may have been part of a much wider campaign against the cult of the dead in early Israel. In any event, it was hardly a retrojection from late in the First Temple period.

The conclusion to which these factors impel us is that for the ancient Israelites who produced the Hebrew Bible, Sheol seems generally to have remained as lifeless, as remote, and as inaccessible as the psalms of thanksgiving and of lament portray it. Those who entered it were thought to be cut off from the land of the living, from the intimacy of kith and kin, and from the life-giving participation in the worship of YHWH, whom the dead do not praise.[103] They were not thought to play a continuing, active role in the household, and they were not generally regarded as divine or powerful. The archaeological evidence does indicate, however, that the dead were on occasion offered food, though it is unclear for how long and how often this was done or whether the practice reflects the strength or the weakness of the departed.[104] The literary evidence in the form of the Hebrew Bible gives scant indication that the practice existed at all and expresses no explicit approval of it in any period. That there were sectors of Israelite society that thought otherwise, or periods in which the alternative evaluation of feeding the dead prevailed, need not be denied. But neither should it be denied that these were not the sectors or the periods whose views are commonly reflected in the Hebrew Bible, in any of the periods of its composition.

More evidence exists in the case of necromancy. As we have seen, one narrative (1 Sam 28:3–25) purports to describe an early example of the practice, which became a target of prophetic preaching much later, in the late eighth century. Johnston summarizes the distribution well:

> Necromancy is mentioned at the beginning and end of the monarchy, but is unrecorded in other historical narrative, whether of the wilderness wanderings, the judges period, the bulk of the monarchy, or the exile and after. It is mentioned in only one prophetic book [Isaiah], and only occasionally, and is absent from the whole range of psalmody and wisdom. On this evidence, necromancy was not a major problem in Israel.[105]

The combination of Isaiah's preaching and the explicit prohibitions in Leviticus and Deuteronomy suggest, to be sure, a change from the situation that Johnston describes, as Halpern and others rightly insist. It would seem that necromancy did indeed become "a major problem in Israel" (or, to be more precise, in Judah) late in the monarchy. There is no evidence, however, that it had been either widespread or generally deemed legitimate in YHWHistic circles beforehand.[106] There remains, of course, the logical option that narratives and laws centering on necromancy and kindred practices of the sort we have imagined once existed but were expunged when the practices were outlawed late in the Judahite monarchy.[107] In that case, the absence of mention is evidence not of the peripheral character of these things, as Johnston argues, but rather of the thoroughness with which the later authors revised their earlier sources according to their own new-born orthodoxy. But that line of reasoning

is forced and verges on circularity, for it is precisely the lateness of the orthodoxy that stands in need of demonstration. Sometimes an absence is just an
absence, and if most Israelites before the eighth century held a view of necromancy other than that dominant in the Hebrew Bible (the latter view being
that it may establish communication with the dead but is never legitimate),
they have left us no convincing evidence of their view. If the positive view of
necromancy really was once widespread (for the absence of evidence prevents
certainty in both directions), we have no reason to believe that the predominant biblical view arose de novo late in the eighth century. And here we must
question the reductionist assumptions on which the political interpretation of
the supposed reform rests. For no matter how committed to self-interest the
kings were, their reforming agenda would have been unlikely to succeed and
to last without some cultural preparation, some widespread basis in the traditions of the people affected. For surely few projects have less chance of taking
hold than a concerted effort, dictated by the palace, to uproot practices of venerable antiquity, inextricably based in the most fundamental social structures
of the culture, and hitherto without objection. Minimally, then, we should
think of a clash not between palace and people but between sectors of the
population holding different religious views, with some more sympathetic
to food offerings for the dead, necromancy, and the like, and others highly
averse. The assumption that the latter group was the innovator is very much
open to doubt. It may well be that on this point Hezekiah and Josiah were
actually traditionalists, harking back to older patterns of Israelite religion —
precisely as the biblical narratives about them insist (2 Kgs 18:1–8; 22:1–2;
23:19–25).

One of the more remarkable aspects of Sheol is how little we actually know of
it. As we shall see in the next chapter, references to it are far less numerous
than one might think and are clustered in particular genres. One reason that so
many scholars have felt constrained to turn to Ugaritic and other non-Israelite
sources to fill in the picture of the abode of the dead is precisely the disinterest
of the Hebrew Bible in such matters. My contrary claim is that it is misguided
to seek to overcome that disinterest, importing this or that Canaanite or Mesopotamian item into Israel and even into the Hebrew Bible on the slenderest of
textual or archaeological evidence. Instead, we should *respect* the disinterest,
viewing it as characteristic of the nature of Israelite religion as reflected in the
Hebrew Bible and, to some degree, outside it as well. For the focus of that
book is not on the world of the dead but on that of the living, specifically, on
the people Israel and their complicated relationship with their God in history.[108] That historical focus perforce leads to a continual glance backward

toward the ancestors like the patriarchs of Genesis, Moses, and King David, but not because they have become gods or are possessed of wisdom to offer to those who consult them, or because they offer deliverance to the descendants who pray and sacrifice to them, or because they might disrupt those who fail to feed or otherwise honor them. Rather, in the religion of Israel as it is reflected in the Hebrew Bible, the ancestors matter because it was to them that the promise was believed to have been first given, to them that the norms of the God-pleasing life were revealed (whether they succeeded in living up to them or not), and in dealing with them that God made known his ways. They are not gods who, from some other world to which they went at death, now rescue, bless, and instruct. They are altogether mortal and altogether fallible human beings whom God rescued, blessed, and instructed in their lifetimes, in this very world. If the focus of life in the history of Israelite religion was ever on the dead and the esoteric power or wisdom that some believed they possessed, it is all the more significant that in the Hebrew Bible itself, the focus lies principally in two very different places. It lies in this life and the ever-present possibility of obedience to God's known will established in public revelation.[109] And it lies in the indefeasible promises that God made to the national and dynastic founders. If those individuals had ever been conceived as deified ancestors who are sources of rescue, blessing, or instruction, in the Hebrew Bible they have become recipients of promises from the true God, promises that even death ultimately could not defeat.[110]

Are Abraham, Moses, and Job in Sheol?

May I die the death of the upright,
May my fate be like theirs!
    —Numbers 23:10

In the first half of the fourth century C.E., the Babylonian sage Rava raised a grave doubt about Job, the paradigmatic innocent sufferer of the Bible. "Job denied the resurrection of the dead," the rabbi pronounced, thus placing the revered biblical figure among the heretics.[1] The rabbi's proof text is of a kind with the assertions of the hopelessness of Sheol that we have examined:

> As a cloud fades away,
> So whoever goes down to Sheol does not come up. (Job 7:9)

Rashi, the revered eleventh-century commentator from northern France, seconds this view in his comment on these words of Job's two verses earlier:

> Consider that my life is but wind;
> I shall never see happiness again. (Job 7:7)

The happiness that Job would never see again is "after death," Rashi tells us, and with that the once-righteous sufferer "denied the resurrection of the dead."² Needless to say, this depiction of Job as a heretic provoked counter-arguments in behalf of his orthodoxy. One, for example, came from Rashi's own grandson, Rabbi Jacob ben Meir (Rabbenu Tam), who classified Job's words as parabolic and thus not to be taken literally.³ Another came from Rashi's contemporary and compatriot, Rabbi Joseph Kara, who sought to rebut Rava's prooftext. "Whoever goes down to Sheol does not come up again" means that "he will not come up from Sheol for a long time," the eschatological events lying, of course, far in the future. It does not mean that the dead shall never rise at all.⁴

Any student of the Bible who is mindful of historical change will be tempted to dismiss this debate from late antiquity and the Middle Ages as founded on an anachronism, specifically, the assumption that the cardinal Jewish doctrine of an eschatological resurrection already existed in the time of Job. The historical point is obviously valid, but the dismissal of the theological debate is much too hasty. For we can both grant that the rabbinic doctrine did not exist at the time of the book of Job and still find in the debate an insight into one of the key points at issue between the sufferer and his friends. In fact, the deeper truth in the disagreement among the rabbinic commentators involves a theological point that is very much at issue in the biblical book itself and thus hardly an imposition of the Talmudic sages upon it. The question is, can Job legitimately rely on God's much-acclaimed faithfulness to rescue from Sheol—not at the end of days, to be sure, but in his own time of lethal torment? Consider, for example, this exchange between the sufferer and one of his increasingly unsympathetic comforters. First, Job:

> ¹⁰But all of you, come back now;
> I shall not find a wise man among you.
> ¹¹My days are done, my tendons severed,
> The strings of my heart.
> ¹²They say that night is day,
> That light is here—in the face of darkness.
> ¹³If I must look forward to Sheol as my home,
> And make my bed in the dark place,
> ¹⁴Say to the Pit, "You are my father,"
> To the maggots, "Mother," "Sister"—
> ¹⁵Where, then, is my hope?
> Who can see hope for me?
> ¹⁶Will it descend to Sheol?
> Shall we go down together to the dust? (Job 17:10–16)

Were there any doubt about what is missing in Job's vision of his postmortal existence (this having already begun), the word repeated in v 15 would resolve it: "hope."[5] This is very much the same vision of the netherworld as the typical Mesopotamian one that we examined in chapter 3, a vision that, it has been observed, "can be expressed in a single word: gloom."[6] Too often overlooked, however, is the rebuttal from the lips of Bildad the Shuhite:

> [5]Indeed, the light of the wicked fails;
> The flame of his fire does not shine.
> [6]The light in his tent darkens;
> His lamp fails him.
> [7]His iniquitous strides are hobbled;
> His own schemes trip him up.
> [8]He is led by his feet into the net;
> He walks onto the toils.
> [9]The trap seizes his heel;
> The noose tightens on him.
> [10]The rope for him lies hidden on the ground;
> His snare, on the path.
> [11]Terrors assault him on all sides
> And send his feet flying.
> [12]His progeny hunger;
> Disaster awaits his wife.
> [13]The tendons under his skin are consumed;
> Death's first-born consumes his tendons.
> [14]He is torn from the safety of his tent;
> The King of Terrors marches him away.
> [15]It lodges in his desolate tent;
> Sulfur is strewn upon his home.
> [16]His roots below dry up,
> And above, his branches wither.
> [17]All mention of him vanishes from the earth;
> He has no name abroad.
> [18]He is thrust from light to darkness,
> Driven from the world.
> [19]He has no seed or breed among his people,
> No survivor where he once lived.
> [20]Generations to come will be appalled at his fate,
> As the previous ones are seized with horror.
> [21]"These were the haunts of the wicked;
> Here was the place of him who knew not God." (Job 18:5–21)[7]

Bildad's vision is as grim, as gloomy, and as hopeless as Job's, but for one key qualification: it is a vision of the fate of the *wicked* only, "him who knew not God" (v 21). It is not a vision of the future of the righteous, those who know

God and seek his grace. As Job's same friend puts it earlier, sounding a note that his confreres reiterate frequently, God's justice and his protection are sure and reliable, and for those who act as God desires, a hope-filled future lies ahead:

> ³Will God pervert the right?
> Will the Almighty pervert justice?
> ⁴If your sons sinned against Him,
> He dispatched them for their transgression.
> ⁵But if you seek God
> And supplicate the Almighty,
> ⁶If you are blameless and upright,
> He will protect you,
> And grant well-being to your righteous home.
> ⁷Though your beginning be small,
> In the end you will grow very great. (Job 8:3–7)

And within the context of the Book of Job as it has come down to us, Bildad's last point is surely right. Job's end is indeed greater than his beginning, for as the conclusion to the book reports, "the LORD blessed the latter years of Job's life more than the former" and restored seven sons and three daughters to him (Job 42:12–13). (Whether this justifies his protracted pain, physical and emotional, and whether his children died "for their transgression," as Bildad would have it, are quite another question.) The point is that Job's friends — and, I would think, the authors/redactors of the book — do not regard his vision of hopelessness and gloom as the universal human destiny or God as unable or temperamentally unwilling to reverse it. Not everyone is sentenced to Sheol for all eternity. Not all who go to the grave end their lives in misery.

The reversal Job's friends have in mind is not (I must reiterate) an eschatological resurrection of the dead along the lines of the Second Temple and rabbinic doctrine that emerged centuries later; it is not a resurrection of the dead at all. But it is a reversal nonetheless, the replacement of despair with hope, of gloom with shining light. It was such a reversal in the same direction, a restoration in the same direction, that the rabbis (along with their Pharisaic antecedents and Christian contemporaries) expected in the future resurrection of the dead. And this is where Rava and Rashi were right. Had the belief in the resurrection of the dead been a live option in the time of the book of Job, the innocent sufferer of the speeches would surely have denied it, soundly and angrily — and in the end he would just as surely have been proven wrong. For, within the structure of the book of Job in its canonical form, though the paragon of righteousness did indeed experience the horrors associated with death, he was wrong to have doubted that a blessed future could lie beyond them. Job's lapse lay not in a sin that occasioned his suffering—for there was none—but in his failure to see that the hellish suffering of his deathlike condition was not God's last word, that current affliction is no disproof of future redemption. His friends' charge that he deserved his misery proves false, but so does Job's own despair of ultimate restoration. His ostensibly terminal plight turns out not to have been hopeless after all.

Job's view in the speeches we have quoted is actually quite conservative; it harks back to Near Eastern notions of postmortal existence as unrelieved gloom, a fate that none escapes.[8] His comforters, for all their breathtaking insensitivity and shortsightedness on other issues, represent a view that became almost ubiquitous in Israel, the view that the LORD is a reliable and steadfast source of deliverance from the grim fate that Job fears and, indeed, already experiences.[9] For Job, God is fully capable of reversing his undeserved fate but—unjustly, irrationally, maddeningly—does not do so. For his interlocutors, if Job is worthy, repentant, and appropriately submissive, God will surely restore him—as indeed he does in the epilogue to the book as it has come down to us (Job 42:7–17).

But what if Johannes Pedersen was correct in his observation that "everyone who dies goes to Sheol," so that the netherworld is, as John Gray puts it, "the destination of all, good and bad without discrimination, where existence is wholly undesirable."[10] If this is so (and it remains the consensus among scholars), then Job's restoration at the very end of the book that bears his name is ephemeral, and the last word lies with death—a miserable one at that—after all. And if this is the case, then the belief in the resurrection of the dead, when it finally comes into existence, brings about at least two related and monumental changes. The first, of course, is the notion that death is not final, that some of the dead return to life. The second represents the overthrow of Gray's point, for no longer is it the case, as Qohelet (Ecclesiastes) would later put it, that "the same fate is in store for all" (Qoh 9:2), namely, death and the "wholly undesirable" existence that goes with it. Rather, of the departed who awake, some do so, in the words of a late Second Temple apocalyptic vision (Dan 12:2), "to eternal life, others to reproaches, to everlasting abhorrence." In short, resurrection would then represent the extension of God's retributive justice (a major item of belief in the Hebrew Bible, especially among the prophets) beyond the grave. The good could now reliably hope for an ultimate destiny distinct from the misery of Sheol. Whatever felicity the righteous have had would not end at the grave, as it must if Sheol is the universal human destiny.

One should not, however, minimize what is at stake here. If the conventional view is correct, and Sheol was thought to be the abode of the wicked and righteous alike, then the ubiquitous biblical belief in the ultimate justice of God is thrown into severe doubt, as indeed it was by Job in his despair. In that case, Sheol houses not only Hitlerian tyrants like the Babylonian king whose delicious arrival there the book of Isaiah mockingly envisions (14:3–21) or the pharaoh whose descent thereto Ezekiel similarly but more graphically foretells (Ezek 32:17–32). Rather, it perforce also houses Abraham, though he died "old and contented" (Gen 25:8), Moses, whose "eyes were undimmed and his vigor unabated" even at death (Deut 34:7), and, as we have seen, even Job himself, who survived unspeakable suffering to find his life restored, dying like Abraham "old and contented" (Job 42:17). For, if Sheol is the destiny of all, these three must (in the minds of those who wrote and heard about them) even now be enduring a "wholly undesirable" existence, no less than the self-deifying but doomed Babylonian and Egyptian oppressors of Israel whom prophets taunt.

There is, however, ample room to wonder whether in Israelite thought before the idea of resurrection appears Sheol really was always assumed to be the universal destination. Were that the case, one might reasonably expect the term itself to occur with a high frequency, indeed, to be mentioned nearly as often as death itself. In point of fact, it occurs fewer than seventy times (as opposed to one thousand times for the root *mwt*, "die/death," for example), and, as Philip Johnston points out, its distribution is illuminating:

> The term occurs mostly in psalmodic, reflective and prophetic literature, where authors are personally involved in their work. By contrast, it appears only rarely in descriptive narrative, and then almost entirely in direct speech. In particular, "Sheol" never occurs in the many narrative accounts of death, whether of patriarchs, kings, prophets, priests or ordinary people, whether of Israelite or foreigner, of righteous or wicked. Also, "Sheol" is entirely absent from legal material, including the many laws which prescribe capital punishment or proscribe necromancy. This means that "Sheol" is very clearly a term of personal engagement.[11]

The "personal engagement" that Sheol reflects is the struggle against the power-ful and malignant forces that negate life and deprive it of meaning. It is tempt-ing, but fundamentally wrongheaded, to classify death (in the modern, bio-logistic sense of a cessation of animation) as one of these forces. For in the Hebrew Bible, death is malign only to the extent that it expresses punishment or otherwise communicates a negative judgment on the life that is ending. As Ruth Rosenberg puts it, "There was no turning back from natural death, and the grave, as a human destination, is conspicuously devoid of negative connota-tions in the Bible, and often contemplated with composure."[12] Thus, however much Sheol may be conceived in the imagery of the grave, "in the Bible the concept of the grave and Sheol or its semantic equivalents were consistently kept apart."[13] When the psalmist says to the LORD, "You will not abandon me to Sheol, / or let Your faithful one see the Pit [*šaḥat*]" (Ps 16:10), he is therefore not asserting the absurd notion that God will forever spare him from death. Rather, Rosenberg argues, he is expressing his faith that, "You [God] will not let your faithful servant die an untimely, evil death."[14]

Rosenberg casts this critical but usually overlooked distribution in terms of the dichotomy of natural and unnatural. "Whenever death is due to unnatural causes, Sheol is mentioned," she writes; "whenever death occurs in the course of nature, Sheol does not appear."[15] The distinction is not, however, native to the Israelite worldview, though it can easily be replaced by one that is — namely, the ubiquitous distinction between God's anger and his favor.[16] If the circumstances of death do not suggest divine anger, then death (whether today we judge it to be natural or unnatural) need not be feared, and "personal engagement" to avert it is utterly unnecessary. Sheol, in sum, very often has to do with punishment, and those who die in God's good graces, their lives fulfilled through his blessings, therefore have no reason to think that they will be dispatched to Gray's "wholly undesirable" existence in the dark, dank netherworld.[17] Poets who believe that their existential adversity has brought them into the shadow of death have good reason to plead that God spare them Sheol and to thank him for doing so when the lethal adversity subsides. But the texts about the demise of Abraham, Moses, and Job, whose end is undeniably beatified by God's providential intervention, give no hint that at that moment they fear Sheol, for their impending death does not negate God's evident and abundant favor. They die with lives fulfilled and certainly seem to face no future terrors or miseries whatsoever.[18]

A major focus of that favor — especially important, as we are about to see, in the case of Abraham and Job — is family, particularly the continuation of one's lineage through descendants alive at one's death. Many expressions, some of them idiomatic, communicate this essential mode of divine favor. The idiom "He was gathered to his kin" or "to his fathers" (*wayyēʾāsēp ʾel-ʿammāyw / ʾăbōtāyw*), may originally have derived from burial practices, but it does not literally refer to interment in the family grave or to secondary burial any longer, since it is used, for example, of Abraham (Gen 25:8), whose deceased blood relatives all lay in Mesopotamia.[19] "More likely," writes Johnston, it "indicates joining one's ancestors in the afterlife," presumably, according to "most scholars . . . in Sheol, even if Sheol is never mentioned in this context."[20] This last concession, however, is devastating to the widespread presumption to which Johnston alludes. For Sheol is anything but a locus of familial reunion. Those who go down to it are said to feel isolated and abandoned, and the absence of kin in the descriptions of the group imprisoned there is striking. Ezekiel's elaborate depiction (Ezek 32:17–32), for example, portrays once-mighty warriors, some still in "their battle gear" (v 27), now reduced to powerlessness in the face of the great leveler. Like soldiers in wartime, they are far from parents, wives, and children. If being "gathered to one's kin/fathers" refers to the afterlife, it is not an afterlife in Sheol.

Similar points can be made about another idiom for dying in the Hebrew Bible, "He slept/lay [*šākab*] with his fathers."[21] If the verb is translated as "slept," it fits with the identification of death with sleep evident elsewhere in the Hebrew Bible (and beyond). Note, for example, that the prophet Elisha revives the Shunammite lady's son, "laid out [*muškāb*] dead on his couch," after his aide Gehazi's failed attempt to bring him back and the consequent report that "the boy has not awakened [*hēqîṣ*]" (2 Kgs 4:31–32).[22] Similarly, when an expectation of general resurrection appears, it comes in the same language: "Many of those that sleep [*yāšēn*] in the dust of the earth will awake [*hēqîṣ*], some to eternal life, others to reproaches, to everlasting abhorrence" (Dan 12:2).[23] To this day, the traditional Jewish liturgy includes an affirmation that God will eventually take away one's soul but also restore it in the eschatological future ('*ātîd lābô*'). The benediction in which these words appear (which is said soon after awakening) concludes by applying to God the title "Who restores souls to dead bodies." If one recalls that in rabbinic thinking sleep is conceived as a kind of miniature or temporary death, we shall not find this surprising. As one saying in the Talmud puts it, "Sleep is one-sixtieth of death."[24]

Translated as "he lay [with his fathers]," *šākab* again recalls the burial practices in which the deceased remains with his or her kin, whether in the house or in hewn niches. Though this is probably the origin of the expression, the idiom does not now refer exclusively to family burial, since it is used (to give but one example) of Moses, whose ancestors presumably lay in Egypt when he was placed to rest in a grave that "no one knows . . . to this day" (Deut 31:16; 34:6). With very few exceptions (themselves anomalous in other ways), the expression is used for those who died peacefully, whereas "he died," for example, is most characteristically used of kings (whether judged good or wicked) who perished violently.[25] On either translation, the expression itself gives no grounds whatsoever for assuming that one who "slept/lay with his fathers" did so in Sheol, which is, as we have seen, almost always the destination of those who die violently, unjustly, in punishment, or with a broken heart.

I say "almost always" because, despite the arguments I have just developed, there are a handful of passages that affirm that Sheol is the end point for everyone. Especially unambiguous is Ps 89:49:

> What man can live and not see death,
> can save himself from the clutches of Sheol?

Note the equivalence here of death and Sheol, with the clear implication that individuals, no matter how they have died, cannot escape the dreary netherworld. Rosenberg makes a valiant effort to accommodate this and similar passages within her thesis that only those who die because of "unnatural causes" find themselves there, but in some cases her exegesis is strained.[26] The wiser course is to confront the contradiction between those passages that assert that Sheol is indeed the destination of all human beings and those more numerous passages that affirm the possibility of a fortunate end to life. That the former passages are so few and that the differentiation of terminology is so thoroughgoing is remarkable and suggests that the inconsistency is best seen as a tension between two competing theologies. The one that sees Sheol as the universal destination comports well with ancient Mesopotamian and Canaanite notions of human destiny as finally one of pure gloom.[27] This conception survives in the Hebrew Bible, especially in Wisdom literature, the category to which most of those exceptional passages belong. But it is very much at odds with most of the relevant texts, which instead assume a distinction between those who go to Sheol and those who die blessed, like Abraham, Moses, and Job. Another way to state this is to say that the Hebrew Bible displays a tension between an older notion of Sheol as the ultimate destination of all mankind, on the one hand, and a bold and younger affirmation of the LORD as savior, on the other. This second assertion eventually culminated in a proclamation of the God of Israel as the one who is powerful even over the gloomy netherworld and the forces that impel people toward it. But the development toward that point was neither inevitable nor linear, and the remnants of the older view remained, even in relatively late texts.[28]

What exactly was the fate of those fortunate enough to avoid the netherworld? Where, if not Sheol, did the ancient Israelites who wrote of their lives and heard their tales believe *them* to have gone? On this, the Hebrew Bible is strikingly silent and forces us into conjecture. As for actual practice (as opposed to the biblical ideals), it is not hard to imagine that the deposits of food for the dead that we discussed in the previous chapter were intended to nourish the deceased in another place, where (with the proper assistance of the living) their experience would be very different from the torments of Sheol that psalmists pray God to spare them or thank him for so doing. Perhaps the food and similar gestures of attention of the living were thought to mitigate the misery of Sheol. Or perhaps a place other than Sheol was thought to house the dead who did not go there, something like the Garden of Eden (to put it into rabbinic language)[29] in contradistinction to the Gehinnom (or Gehenna) that was Sheol, or, in the familiar Christian terms, heaven as opposed to hell. But even if this is so, it is highly instructive that the Hebrew Bible is so severely reticent about describing it, and there is, as we have seen, room for disagreement about how significant a role such a belief played in ancient Israelite religion.[30]

A better course is to examine the narratives about the end of the lives of those who die blessed. If we do so, we see that a principal source of their survival lies in their lineage (including, in some cases, the larger lineage that is the whole people of Israel). Thus Abraham dies after arranging the marriage of his favored son Isaac and begetting, in addition to the firstborn Ishmael, six other sons, some of them (like Isaac and Ishmael) destined to beget great nations in fulfillment of God's explicit promise to the founding patriarch (Gen 25:1–18; cf. Gen 12:2; 17:20; 21:18; 28:3–4). And so, too, Job lives "to see four generations of sons and grandsons" (Job 42:16). This, in turn, is strikingly reminiscent of the dying Jacob, who tells his son Joseph, "I never expected to see you again, and here God has let me see your children as well," or of Joseph himself, who "lived to see children of the third generation of [his son] Ephraim" (Gen 48:11; 50:23). These instances of the viewing of the future lineage are hardly coincidental or irrelevant to our topic. For, in all these cases, the individual dies fulfilled, the divine promises richly (and unexpectedly) realized at the end of a stormy life, long marked by infertility or other intergenerational problems.[31] The viewing of the distant descendants so prominent in the cases of Job, Jacob, and Joseph establishes the felicity of the individual's destiny at the time of his death. Dying within the blessing of God, the patriarch faces his final destiny with composure, altogether unlike those who, dying outside the blessing of God, face the misery of Sheol, with justified trepidation and despondency. The fulfillment of the blessed individual's life survives him and continues to testify to his final felicity — and to his God's steadfast faithfulness to his pledged word.

In the case of Moses, the matter is only somewhat different. His death notice (Deuteronomy 34), to be sure, mentions nothing of his descendants, of whom little is known in any case.[32] But the promises made to and through Moses never centered on his own personal lineage at all. Indeed, in the episode of the Golden Calf, Moses declines the LORD's offer to make an Abrahamic "great nation" of him in replacement of the sinning Israelites:

⁹The LORD further said to Moses, "I see that this is a stiffnecked peo-ple.¹⁰Now, let Me be, that My anger may blaze forth against them and that I may destroy them, and make of you a great nation." ¹¹But Moses implored the LORD his God, saying, "Let not Your anger, O LORD, blaze forth against Your people, whom You delivered from the land of Egypt with great power and with a mighty hand. ¹²Let not the Egyptians say, 'It was with evil intent that He delivered them, only to kill them off in the mountains and annihilate them from the face of the earth.' Turn from Your blazing anger, and renounce the plan to punish Your people. ¹³Remember Your servants, Abraham, Isaac, and Israel, how You swore to them by Your Self and said to them: I will make your offspring as numerous as the stars of heaven, and I will give to your offspring this whole land of which I spoke, to possess forever." ¹⁴And the LORD renounced the punishment He had planned to bring upon His people. (Exod 32:9–14)

Could it be clearer that the Mosaic promises center on the lineage of Abraham, Isaac, and Jacob, that is, the whole Israelite nation, and not on Moses' own progeny? Thus, when "the LORD showed him the whole land" (Deut 34:1) just before Moses died and the Israelites began to take possession of it, the scene is remarkably reminiscent of Jacob's, Joseph's, and Job's viewing several genera-tions of descendants just before their own deaths. In the Deuteronomic theol-ogy, the fulfillment of Moses' life continues and remains real, visible, and powerful after his death. It takes the form of Israel's dwelling in the promised land and living in deliberate obedience to the Torah book he bequeathed them, for all their generations (e.g., Deut 31:9–13; Josh 1:6–8). In Deuteronomy, all Israel has become, in a sense, the progeny of Moses.

Nothing distorts the proper understanding of the biblical Sheol more than the traditional Jewish and Christian understanding of the afterlife as a locus for reward or punishment. On the analogy of the dichotomies of the Garden of Eden and Gehinnom (Gehenna), or heaven and hell, one instinctively looks for a positive counterpart to the dank, dreary netherworld whose residents endure cut off from God and unable to praise him. Sheol, though an unhappy place, is not Gehenna, as we have now seen.[33] As one scholar, commenting on the Ugaritic epics, puts it, "The infernal world may be gloomy and wet; but it is a far cry from burning Hell,"[34] and the same must be said of the netherworld of ancient Israel. Rather, Sheol is best conceived as a kind of continuation of the end of the deceased's life. If the deceased has died prematurely, violently, bereft of children, rejected by God, or brokenhearted, he faces Sheol (and, as we noted in chapter 3, can experience it even on this side of the grave). Thus, Jacob, having (so far as he knows) lost to the jaws of a wild beast his beloved

Joseph, the son of his old age, "refused to be comforted, saying, 'No, I will go down mourning to my son in Sheol' " (Gen 37:35). It would be a capital error to interpret either Joseph's or Jacob's anticipated presence in Sheol as punitive. Joseph's is owing to his having died a violent and premature death that is not followed by a proper burial or mitigated by the continuation that comes from having children. Each of these conditions alone could bring him to Sheol. Cumulatively, they make his presence there close to certain. As for Jacob's own anticipation of joining him, here the operative factor is his broken heart, the unending ache caused by the loss of his favorite child. In each case, that of the (ostensibly) mauled son and that of the inconsolable father, Sheol is not a punishment from God or any other agent. It does not come in response to some sin or another; it is the continuation of the gloomy circumstances of the individual's death.

Were Sheol the universal destination, we should expect to find many similar statements to Jacob's in the mouths of others whose deaths, or anticipated deaths, are mentioned. But as Johnston astutely observes, this is not at all the case, and one cannot equate dying with going to Sheol.[35] In those accustomed to the familiar Jewish and Christian duality — Garden of Eden/Gehinnom, heaven/hell — this instinctively raises the question of where those go who die a fortunate death — a peaceful death, that is, one that takes place at a ripe old age, the decedent having lived to see a multitude of thriving descendants and possessing the assurance of a decent burial. Deriving from the question of where we go after we die, the question is, in fact, misconceived when posed to the Hebrew Bible. For the Hebrew Bible displays very little interest in that question. It is much more likely to focus on the question of whether God's blessing (especially the blessing of children) was or was not realized in the decedent's life. If it was, then death can be, in Rosenberg's words, "contemplated with composure."[36] The decedent's life has come to fulfillment; there are no lasting deficits, no unresolved issues to impede its fortunate completion. If the blessing was not realized, however, then the decedent is in the domain of Sheol. The binary opposite of Sheol in the Hebrew Bible is not some Israelite version of the Garden of Eden or heaven. It is, rather, a life that is enveloped in the blessing of God and gives persuasive testimony to that blessing.

In sum, the biblical Sheol is the prolongation of the unfulfilled life. There is no equivalent prolongation of the fulfilled life precisely because it is fulfilled. The prolongation of those who die fulfilled comes, rather, not in the form of residence in a place, the joyful antipode to the miserable Sheol, but in the form of descendants, such as those three or four generations that Jacob, Joseph, and Job are privileged to behold just before they die. It also comes in the form of the survival of the decedent's "name" (*šēm*). As one scholar observes, the "name" can express the immortal dimension of the self: "Quite unlike the body, a person's 'name' in this sense is altogether immune to the inroads of time. A name — in this abstract sense of the sum total of all a person's deeds — is immutable, so that eventually that name is all that remains of our earthly existence; years, centuries after our death, the name — in this abstract sense — is what we are, what our life amounted to."[37] To this, we should add that the "name" sometimes seems to affect things even after death:

> The memory (*zēker*) of the righteous is a source of blessing,
> But the name of the wicked rots away. (Prov 10:7)[38]

The "name" or the "memory," in short, survives the person or, to put it more precisely, the person survives in the name as in the descendants. There is scant reason to think that the righteous whose memory is a source of blessing were thought to endure the miseries of Sheol, nonetheless.

If the Jewish and Christian theologies of postmortem reward and punishment cause us to misunderstand Sheol in one way, a hasty harmonization to the patterns inferred (not without uncertainty) from Mesopotamian and Canaanite texts induces a misunderstanding in the other direction. For this can mislead us into thinking that without exception all who die — which is to say, all who live — end up in that gloomy place.[39] On this reading, the biblical texts that speak of the life fulfilled by the promise of God cannot be taken seriously, or must at least be relegated to the penultimate stage, for the dreary, Godless existence in the netherworld is the end that awaits everyone. If this is the case, then, one must understand the book of Job, for example, not to end, as it actually does:

> [11]All his brothers and sisters and all his former friends came to him and had a meal with him in his house. They consoled and comforted him for all the misfortune that the LORD had brought upon him. Each gave him one *kesitah* and each one gold ring. [12]Thus the LORD blessed the latter years of Job's life more than the former. He had fourteen thousand sheep, six thousand camels, one thousand yoke of oxen, and one thousand she-asses. [13]He also had seven sons and three daughters. [14]The first he named Jemimah, the second Keziah, and the third Keren-happuch. [15]Nowhere in the land were women as beautiful as Job's daughters to be found. Their father gave them estates together with their brothers. [16]Afterward, Job lived one hundred and forty years to see four generations of sons and grandsons. [17]So Job died old and contented. (Job 42:11–17)

Rather, we should be obliged to presume that Job's restoration from affliction was temporary, so that the fuller and more accurate account of his end would read:

[11]All his brothers and sisters and all his former friends came to him and had a meal with him in his house. They consoled and comforted him for all the misfortune that the LORD had brought upon him. Each gave him one *kesitah* and each one gold ring. [12]Thus the LORD blessed the latter years of Job's life more than the former. He had fourteen thousand sheep, six thousand camels, one thousand yoke of oxen, and one thousand she-asses. [13]He also had seven sons and three daughters. [14]The first he named Jemimah, the second Keziah, and the third Keren-happuch. [15]Nowhere in the land were women as beautiful as Job's daughters to be found. Their father gave them estates together with their brothers. [16]Afterward, Job lived one hundred and forty years to see four generations of sons and grandsons. [17]So Job died old and contented. [18]Then he went down to Sheol, to the land of slackness, sorrow, exhaustion, and curse, where there is no firmness, joy, strength, or blessing, to the dark pit in which the abandoned lie and in which no one praises the LORD and all are forever cut off from His care and from which no one returns.[40]

It is patently evident that v 18 above radically changes the whole meaning not only of the passage to which it has been appended but of the book as a whole. It transforms a happy ending into a sad one (the same can be said about the ends of the stories of Abraham, Jacob, Joseph, Moses, and many others as well). Fortunately, v 18 does not exist, and to concoct such a spurious closing is to miss one of the most salient features of the ancient Israelite understanding of death and life. The conclusion to the book of Job and kindred happy endings entail a very different understanding of death from the one in which the gloomy underworld is the universal destination. They advance, rather, a theology that robs death of any necessary connection with the dreariness of the netherworld and offers instead the possibility of a happy ending to individual existence. To imagine that all go eventually to Sheol, never to be redeemed therefrom, is thus to fail to reckon sufficiently with the redemptive dynamics of many biblical narratives, as if the authors of those conclusions wrote with their fingers crossed behind their backs. Unfortunately, this is a widespread failure among scholars of the Hebrew Bible, secular and religious alike. Happy endings are sometimes the hardest to accept.

As we have seen, however, some vestiges linger of the older view, the view that all who die end up in Sheol. Qohelet (to cite an extreme example) appeals to the universality of the unfortunate death and thus the unfulfilled life to bolster his overall skepticism about the redeeming God (Qoh 9:2). But, on balance, the Hebrew Bible is remarkably consistent in speaking of the opposite, the possibility of a meaningful life ending in a fortunate death, and of redemption after unspeakable tragedy.

What has happened with the biblical Sheol, it seems to me, is that the affirmation of faith in the omnipotent and rescuing God of Israel, against whom not even the most formidable of enemies can stand, has collided with the brute fact of death, with all the negative denotations that death generally had in Mesopotamia and Canaan. Something had to give. What gave was not the faith in the limitless power of the Rock of Israel and their redeemer. What gave was death. The result, however, was neither that death disappeared, as if humans were rendered immortal, nor (at this point) that the dead rose in judgment, with the worthy among them then awarded eternal life. Rather, to adapt Hosea, death gave up its plagues, and Sheol, its pestilence.[41] Death would remain universal, but not everyone who died would experience it as a plague. Sheol would remain pestilential, but not everyone who died would go there. There is thus a duality to the general view of death in the Hebrew Bible that is different from the duality of those resurrected to "eternal life" and those resurrected to "everlasting abhorrence" known from later Jewish tradition (Dan 12:2), to be sure, but that also anticipates the later pattern in an important way. The pattern predominant in the Hebrew Bible is the duality of the death that closes a fortunate life, one blessed by God, and the death that prolongs an unfortunate life, one lived, for whatever reason, outside the blessing of God.[42]

We have argued that in the Hebrew Bible there is no antipode to Sheol in the sense of a heavenly locale to which the blessed go after death. This should not, however, be taken to mean that there is no spatial antipode to Sheol available in this life. As we have seen and shall see again in detail in the next chapter, the temple in Jerusalem was conceived as just such a paradise-like place where God, for all his purity and holiness, is available on earth and his blessing is abundant. Now we can add that there is also another antipode to Sheol, another heavenly state available in this world, though one that, like descendants or the "name"/"memory," cannot be located in space so readily. It lies in the history of redemption, which centers on the establishment or restoration of familial and national continuity through the efficacious word of the LORD. At the individual level, the redemption through the acquisition of descendants (or a good name) is available to all, from the humble but God-fearing midwives for whom God "established households" (Exod 1:21) to the great non-Israelite patriarch Job, whom God enabled to reestablish his household after unspeakable tragedy. At the communal level, however, the redemption is manifested in the history of redemption that came to constitute the prime self-identification of the people Israel, the people whose liturgical life continually proclaimed that the God who was their rock and their redeemer could, in the end, overcome even the horrors and terrors of death.

Intimations of Immortality

Whoever utters a psalm in this world will merit to utter it in the World-to-Come, as it is said, "Happy are those who dwell in Your house / they will praise you forever."

— *Babylonian Talmud*, Sanhedrin 91b

In the previous chapter, I argued against the preponderant opinion among scholars that until the emergence of an expectation of resurrection, Sheol was the routine destination of all who died. Instead, I defended the minority position that sees that dark, dreary netherworld as "a term of personal engagement," as Phillip Johnston puts it,[1] generally employed to designate only a negative death, that is, a death that is marked by violence, punishment, prematurity, or a broken heart. The biblical Sheol is not, it must be stressed, the same thing as the Christian hell or the rabbinic Gehinnom (Gehenna), the condign postmortem destination (whether permanent or temporary) of sinners, but there are some analogies and some elements of continuity. Most important, although it is not always their sins that send the denizens of Sheol to that unhappy destination, they have for one reason or another died outside the blessing of God.

The analogy with hell and Gehinnom (which are not quite equivalent) raises the question whether there was also an ancient Israelite analogy to the Christian heaven or the rabbinic Garden of Eden (or World-to-Come). What was the destination of those who died within the blessing of God, like Abraham and Job, who both passed away "old and contented" (Gen 25:8; Job 42:17)? In the preceding chapter, I advanced the claim that the postmortem felicity of such figures inhered to an important degree in the fact that their deepest identities were inextricably embedded in continuing familial structures. The death of an individual has a different valence in a culture that constructs the self in familial and thus transgenerational terms more than we do. It is no coincidence that the report of Abraham's death is sandwiched between two sets of genealogies of his descendants and that the account of Job's follows the report that he "lived . . . to see four generations of sons and grandsons" (Job 42:16). To be sure, a few scholars have devoted their philological creativity to finding references to what one of them calls the "beatific afterlife" in the Hebrew Bible, thus claiming that there was indeed a heaven opposite Sheol. The textual basis for this and the use made of Canaanite parallels to bolster it are highly unpersuasive, however, as a number of scholars have, in turn, shown.[2]

This leaves us, then, with an asymmetrical structure that the analogies with heaven and hell, or with the Garden of Eden and Gehinnom, can only obscure. In the Hebrew Bible, there is no place that serves as the binary opposite of Sheol in the sense that the blessed go there to enjoy a beatific afterlife that is the reverse of the miserable existence in the God-forsaken netherworld. For the most part, the postmortem fulfillment of those who die in a state of blessing is realized in the form of the happy continuation of the family of which they were, and forever remain, a generational link. The casual reader of the Bible in a Christian or post-Christian context can perhaps be excused for thinking that in the worldview of that book the Garden of Eden has disappeared, only to be restored in the fullness of time, when resurrection reverses the death sentence on Adam (Gen 3:22–24). This is, after all, the foundation of a central Christological claim from the time of the apostle Paul on.[3] Within the context of the Hebrew Bible, however — and all the more so in rabbinic Judaism — this view is highly misleading; it has done great damage to the efforts of scholars and laypersons alike to understand the issues. We have already seen one exception to this interpretation, that of the Wisdom tradition, which could, in fact, identify its goal with the Tree of Life and see the Tree of Life as still eminently accessible:

> She [that is, Wisdom] is a tree of life to those who grasp her,
> And whoever holds on to her is happy. (Prov 3:18)

In the rabbinic tradition, Wisdom having long beforehand been equated to Torah, the Torah then became the Tree of Life through which God, in the words of the familiar blessing, "planted eternal life within us."[4] This is not to say that either Jewish Wisdom literature or the rabbinic tradition held that those who practice and study Wisdom or Torah never die — a palpable absurdity. It does suggest, rather, that Wisdom and Torah were thought to retard or mitigate death in some sense that we need not explore here. The point is that in that framework of Wisdom/Torah, the Edenic condition is not so lost at present as the familiar Christian reading claims.

Another, more widely attested and symbolically resonant concept of Eden appears in passages like the following:

> [11]The word of the LORD came to me: [12]O mortal, intone a dirge over the king of Tyre and say to him: Thus said the Lord GOD:
>
> You were the seal of perfection,
> Full of wisdom and flawless in beauty.
> [13]You were in Eden, the garden of God;
> Every precious stone was your adornment:
> Carnelian, chrysolite, and amethyst;
> Beryl, lapis lazuli, and jasper;
> Sapphire, turquoise, and emerald;
> And gold beautifully wrought for you,
> Mined for you, prepared the day you were created.
> [14]I created you as a cherub
> With outstretched shielding wings;
> And you resided on God's holy mountain;
> You walked among stones of fire.
> [15]You were blameless in your ways,
> From the day you were created
> Until wrongdoing was found in you.
> [16]By your far-flung commerce
> You were filled with lawlessness
> And you sinned.
> So I have struck you down
> From the mountain of God,
> And I have destroyed you, O shielding cherub,
> From among the stones of fire.
> [17]You grew haughty because of your beauty,
> You debased your wisdom for the sake of your splendor;
> I have cast you to the ground,
> I have made you an object for kings to stare at.
> [18]By the greatness of your guilt,
> Through the dishonesty of your trading,
> You desecrated your sanctuaries.

So I made a fire issue from you,
And it has devoured you;
I have reduced you to ashes on the ground,
In the sight of all who behold you.
¹⁹All who knew you among the peoples
Are appalled at your doom.
You have become a horror
And have ceased to be forever. (Ezek 28:11–19)[5]

Here, the prophet Ezekiel (early sixth century B.C.E.) predicts and justifies the downfall of the Phoenician city-state Tyre, as the mighty forces of the neo-Babylonian empire sweep to the west and south. As is often the case in the ancient Near East, the kingdom is identified with its ruler, but it is the further identification of the king of Tyre that attracts our attention. For underlying Ezekiel's oracle is a variant of the story of Eden so much better known from the version in Genesis 3. A blameless creature inhabiting "Eden, the garden of God," grows arrogant, attracts God's wrath, and, cast to the ground, has "ceased to be, forever." The differences, however, are illuminating and warn against the facile assumption that Ezekiel knows of the version in Genesis.[6] For one, whereas Adam is childlike, lacking the knowledge of good and evil, the mythic figure with whom the king of Tyre is identified is "full of wisdom"(Ezek 28:12). A second difference is that Adam is very much a human being, formed "from the dust of the earth" (Gen 2:7), whereas Ezekiel's primal man is a cherub, a God-like being who dwells not on the earth that Adam is bidden to till and to tend as a garden (Gen 2:15) but "on God's holy mountain," that is to say, the capital from which God exercises sovereignty over his cosmic domain. It is this last point that may account for the high degree of overlap between the precious stones found in Eden in Ezek 28:13 with those on the breastplate of the Israelite high priest in Exod 28:17–20. The primal man in Ezekiel is the special attendant of God, dwelling in the latter's Temple, the palace of the ruler of the world, in intimate association with him.

The most revealing aspect of Ezekiel's oracle for our purposes is its identification of the Temple on "God's holy mountain" with "Eden, the garden of God" (Ezek 28:13–14). This builds, in turn, upon the conception of the Temple as paradise—the world in its ideal state, the world as its creator hoped it would be—which has deep and wide resonance not only in Israel but throughout the ancient Near East as well.[7]

The eminent biblical archaeologist Lawrence E. Stager notes, for example, an Assyrian text that speaks of the performance of the sacred ritual of the *akītu,* or New Year's festival, in a "Garden of Plenty," the semantic equivalent of the Israelite "Garden of Eden." In Babylonia and Egypt as well, monarchs went to great lengths to procure exotic botanical specimens for their capital gardens with the goal to "signif[y] the ecumenic sovereignty of the ruler." It is in this tradition that Stager places the report that Solomon, king of Judah and Israel and builder of the great Temple of Jerusalem, "discoursed about trees, from the cedar in Lebanon to the hyssop that grows out of the wall" (1 Kgs 5:13). "Since cedars do not grow beyond the Lebanon and the Amanus [that is, far to the north of Jerusalem], they could have been transplanted and cultivated in Jerusalem only under the most propitious conditions, such as irrigated gardens secluded behind stone or brick walls might provide."[8] The psalms offer evidence that the Temple was the focus of at least some of Solomon's horticultural initiatives:

> [13]The righteous bloom like a date-palm;
> they thrive like a cedar in Lebanon;
> [14]planted in the house of the LORD,
> they flourish in the courts of our God.
> [15]In old age they still produce fruit;
> they are full of sap and freshness,
> [16]attesting that the LORD is upright,
> my rock, in whom there is no wrong. (Ps 92:13–16)

In Stager's understanding, given the geographical limits in which wild cedars are found, *šĕtûlîm* in v 14 must be translated not as "planted" but as "transplanted." Solomon, or some comparable royal patron, has brought fruitful date palms and exotic, majestic cedars into the Temple itself, reinforcing its divine owner's "ecumenic sovereignty" and the paradisiac character of his palace as well. (In this latter connection, note also the prominence of cedars in the description of the Garden of Eden in Ezek 31:2–9.) Stager makes a similar point about Ps 52:10, in which the speaker compares himself to another tree (this one native to Judah) flourishing, once again, in the Temple:[9]

> But I am like a thriving olive tree in God's house;
> I trust in the faithfulness of God forever and ever.

In each of these two cases, one might, of course, counter that it is only the persons, and not the trees to which they are likened, who are found in the Temple. This interpretation, however, is also uncertain and contradicts other evidence, such as Josh 24:26, which clearly speaks of "the oak in the sacred precinct of the LORD" in Shechem.

In sum, in the ancient Near East, gardens, especially royal gardens, are not simply decorative. They are symbolic, and their religious message is very much involved with that of the Temple in or near which they are not infrequently found. Gardens present and preserve natural things in a form that is so unnatural that it is free from chaos, decay, and death. Like temples, they are walled off from quotidian reality, with all its instability and irregularity and the threats these pose, and thus they readily convey an intimation of immortality.[10]

In the case of the great temple city of Jerusalem, there is a connection with the Garden of Eden that is more specific — and highly revealing. Genesis 2 speaks of four streams that branch off from the river that "issues from Eden to water the garden" (vv 10–14), of which two are readily identified as the major rivers of Mesopotamia, the Tigris and the Euphrates. Another, the Pishon, is unknown. But the remaining stream, the Gihon (whose name seems to mean "Gusher"), bears the name of the spring below the City of David whose waters flow eastward to the Kidron Valley, where, as Stager points out, they "irrigated the gardens and parks planted . . . by kings of the Davidic dynasty." It is, in fact, to this very spring that David orders his son and designated successor Solomon transported on the royal mule to be anointed king (1 Kgs 1:32–40). The Gihon is also the source of the "gently flowing waters of Siloam" that possessed such significance for Isaiah, the great prophet of Judah in the eighth century B.C.E. For Isaiah, these waters symbolized the quiet trust characteristic of authentic faith in the God of Israel, in contrast to the "mighty, massive waters of the Euphrates" that symbolized the king of Assyria and his military forces (Isa 8:5–8). As Stager puts it, "These quiet, cosmic waters emanating from the primordial deep signified the orderliness and tranquility of God's creation on which humans should rely."[11]

The paradisiac character of the Gihon thus draws upon a rich store of mythic materials deeply connected to the ancient Near Eastern theology of temples. Especially in the Zion theology of Judah, the Temple is not only the capital building of the universe but also the place where God's protective care is manifest, tangible, and inviolable:[12]

> [6]O Lord, Your faithfulness reaches to heaven;
>   Your steadfastness to the sky;
> [7]Your beneficence is like the mountains of El;
>   Your justice like the great deep;
>   man and beast You deliver, O Lord.
> [8]How precious is Your faithful care, O God!
>   Mankind shelters in the shadow of Your wings.
> [9]They feast on the rich fare of Your house;
>   You let them drink at Your refreshing stream.
> [10]With You is the fountain of life;
>   by Your light do we see light.
> [11]Bestow Your faithful care on those devoted to You,
>   and Your beneficence on upright men. (Ps 36:6–11)[13]

In this extraordinarily artful psalm about God's succor and protection of the faithful and just, the mythic connections are patent. "Mountains of El" in v 7 alludes to the abode of the Canaanite high god with whom the Israelite deity was frequently identified to one degree or another. The mention of "the great deep" (*těhôm rabbâ*) in the next clause is not surprising, since the abode of the Canaanite El had, as one scholar puts it, both "mountainous and aqueous features" and was located "in the midst of the pools of the Double-Deep" (*thmtm*).[14] In our psalm, however, this particular aspect of the Canaanite heritage lies at best in the background, the "deep" here serving only as a simile for the LORD's boundless justice. On the other hand, the reference to "Your house" (v 9) establishes that the locus of the latter's succor and protection is indeed the Temple. The "refreshing stream" from which he gives his faithful to drink and, even more, the "fountain of life" (v 10) evoke again the mythos of the waters of Jerusalem that we have been discussing. In this connection, we must not overlook the fact that the phrase rendered "refreshing stream" (*naḥal 'ădāneykā*) includes the plural of Eden (*'ēden*) and might be translated more accurately (if less poetically) as "Your stream of delights / the stream of Your delights." Presumably, the source of this Edenic stream lies in the "fountain of life" whose terrestrial manifestation is the Gihon spring.

This, in turn, raises the question of how the "fountain" is related to "life." Unfortunately, Psalm 36 never tells us directly. A practical answer does come to mind, however. That people "feast on the rich fare" in the Temple (v 9) may be taken for a poetic reference to their consuming the sacrificial offerings. The drink mentioned in the same verse would then refer simply to the accompanying beverage, and the "fountain of life" would designate the source of this liquid sustenance, and no more. The practical answer, though probably accurate on one level, is excessively prosaic for so poetic and so intense a meditation on the part of our psalmist and fails to reckon with the density of mythological allusion that we have seen in his poem. A better, or at least fuller, explanation of the fountain of life appears in the vision of the future Temple in Ezekiel:

> He led me back to the entrance of the Temple, and I found that water was issuing from below the platform of the Temple — eastward, since the Temple faced east — but the water was running out at the south of the altar, under the south wall of the Temple. [2]Then he led me out by way of the northern gate and led me around to the outside of the outer gate that faces in the direction of the east; and I found that water was gushing from [under] the south wall. [3]As the man went on eastward with a measuring line in his hand, he measured off a thousand cubits and led me across the water; the water was ankle deep. [4]Then he measured off another thousand and led me across the water; the water was

knee deep. He measured off a further thousand and led me across the water; the water was up to the waist. ⁵When he measured yet another thousand, it was a stream I could not cross; for the water had swollen into a stream that could not be crossed except by swimming. ⁶"Do you see, O mortal?" he said to me; and he led me back to the bank of the stream.

⁷As I came back, I saw trees in great profusion on both banks of the stream. ⁸"This water," he told me, "runs out to the eastern region, and flows into the Arabah; and when it comes into the sea, into the sea of foul waters, the water will become wholesome. ⁹Every living creature that swarms will be able to live wherever this stream goes; the fish will be very abundant once these waters have reached there. It will be wholesome, and everything will live wherever this stream goes. ¹⁰Fishermen shall stand beside it all the way from En-gedi to En-eglaim; it shall be a place for drying nets; and the fish will be of various kinds [and] most plentiful, like the fish of the Great Sea. ¹¹But its swamps and marshes shall not become wholesome; they will serve to [supply] salt. ¹²All kinds of trees for food will grow up on both banks of the stream. Their leaves will not wither nor their fruit fail; they will yield new fruit every month, because the water for them flows from the Temple. Their fruit will serve for food and their leaves for healing." (Ezek 47:1–12)¹⁵

In this strange, and strangely detailed, vision, waters arise from under the Jerusalem Temple itself and, like those of the Gihon, flow down to the east. In this case, however, they flow not merely to the nearby Kidron Valley but much farther, ever deepening as they go, until they reach the Dead Sea. That body of water derives its English name from the fact that it is so saline that fish and plants cannot survive in it; in Hebrew, it is the "Salt Sea." In this vision, its lethal, saline character, however, is miraculously undone, and "the water will become wholesome," or, more literally, "will be healed" (Ezek 47:8). The result is that the once-dead sea will swarm with living things, fish will become as abundant as they are in the Mediterranean (the "Great Sea" of v 10), and fruit trees will grow on its once-arid and forbidding banks. These will not be ordinary trees, to be sure. For their leaves will not wither, nor their fruit give out; rather, they will be renewed every month — all "because the water for them flows from the Temple." Indeed, just as these supernatural trees will result from the healing effects of the Temple waters, so will their leaves, in turn, serve as medicine to cure the ailing (v 12). The trees will serve as agents of the healing and revivification that originates in the Temple of Jerusalem. They will be an antidote to the poison of disease and death.

The Temple vision in Ezekiel 40–48 results, then, in more than simply a reconstructed Temple and a reconstituted Israelite polity centered upon it. It results as well in a vision of the redeemed life that has striking points in common with notions of paradise that appear (inter alia) in the story of the Garden of Eden in Genesis 2–3. The trees whose leaves never wither and whose fruit never fails present us with the tantalizing temptation to draw a connection to the Tree of Life, which, had Adam been permitted to taste it, would have rendered him immune to death (Gen 3:22–24). Perhaps the Tree of Life was analogous to a fountain of youth, protecting not only against death but also against the age-related withering and failing that usually precede it. In light of the source of those trees in the Temple, one is at least equally inclined to connect them with the description of the righteous transplanted into the House of the LORD at the end of Psalm 92 (vv 13–16). In the psalm, as we saw, the righteous or the trees to which they are likened do reach "old age," but even so they "still produce fruit" and even retain the physical appearance of youth.

The implication of the imagery of healing waters and ever-fruitful trees is clear. The Temple serves, among many other things, as a survival of the primal paradise lost to the "profane" world, the world outside the sanctuary (Latin, *fanum*) and as a prototype of the redeemed world envisioned by some to lie ahead. It connects the protological and the eschatological, the primal and the final, preserving Eden and providing a taste of the World-to-Come.

We have now sketched out a chain of associations consisting of the miraculous spring in the Temple, the healing and rejuvenating waters it puts forth, the supernatural trees and other new life that it miraculously and unexpectedly produces, and of course the mode of being of the righteous and faithful in the Temple at which the chain begins. It is this last link that, in turn, brings us back to the question of the "fountain of life" in Ps 36:10. The evidence suggests that the Temple, too — properly approached and respected — was thought to be an antidote to death, giving a kind of immortality to those who dwell there in innocence, purity, and trust.

This notion of the Temple as the locus or source of immortality may, in fact, be the point of the conclusion to the enigmatic little poem that is Psalm 133:

A song of ascents. Of David.

How good and how pleasant it is
   that brothers dwell together.
²It is like fine oil on the head
   running down onto the beard,
   the beard of Aaron,
   that comes down over the collar of his robe;
³like the dew of Hermon
   that falls upon the mountains of Zion.
   There the LORD ordained blessing,
     everlasting life.

Here, fraternal unity (or perhaps reunion after schism) is likened to the oil that anoints the high priest.[16] This, in turn, evokes a further simile, to the dew that falls on Hermon, a mountain in ancient Israel's far north that, reaching an altitude of more than 9,200 feet, readily collects the precipitation that is all too rare throughout most of that arid land. In our psalm, the point is not that the precipitation descends on Hermon but rather that it (or Hermon-like dew in general) then falls upon the parched lands around Jerusalem. "Mountains of Zion" appears nowhere else in the Tanakh in the plural, but "Mount Zion" is, of course, well-known as the name of the Temple Mount. In the Judahite Temple theology, Zion possesses a mystique that one would never suspect from its mere physical reality. In another psalm, for example, it is described as "fair-crested, joy of all the earth . . . summit of Zaphon" (Ps 48:3), the last term designating the mountain, also in the north, that Canaanite tradition identified as the royal residence of the god Baal.[17] Given these old mythic connections, we must not waste time trying to figure out how the dew of Hermon can descend upon the mountains of Zion 120 miles to the south. The geography maps out spiritual, not terrestrial, realities.

That the specific manifestation of divine bounty is dew, however, is highly significant. In chapter 13, we shall have occasion to note that it is dew that effects the resurrection of the dead envisioned in Isa 26:19. In that sense, dew is a good analogy to the healing waters that issue from the Temple on Zion in Ezekiel 47. In our psalm, too, Zion is the place from which "the LORD ordained blessing, / everlasting life" (Ps 133:3). What precisely that last phrase means is, of course, a huge question. Most likely, it denotes the goodness of life in fraternal concord that the psalm begins by extolling. If so, the point is that this blessing rests upon a divine promise akin to or associated with the promises centering on the priestly service in the Temple and on God's promise of protection for his holy mountain, Zion, the spiritual center of the Israelite-Judahite brotherhood. The term "everlasting life" does not connote individual immortality or the result of a collective resurrection like that effected by the dew in Isa 26:19, to be sure. But it still adds an important note. Individual Israelites die and do not rise from the grave, but the collective promise of life to the people Israel that emanates from Zion shall endure forever. Here, as often, Zion serves as a spatial image of the liberation from the ravages of time and decay that characterize ordinary human life.

If we formulate the matter in this way, Psalm 133 seems to support the common view that the Hebrew Bible knows nothing of immortality as we understand it today, except as something placed out of our reach by man's first disobedience in the Garden of Eden. I want to argue, however, that the formulation in question, while not altogether erroneous, is incomplete in significant ways and thus misleading. For it fails to reckon with the Edenic character of the Temple itself, in particular, with the fact that death is as alien to the Temple, indeed, as repugnant to the Temple, as it is to Eden.[18] No one in the Hebrew Bible longs to die in the Temple or to be buried there, and for good reason: a dead body is a prime source of ritual contamination (Lev 21:1–4; Numbers 19). That is why Jewish law to this day forbids *kōhănîm* (men of priestly descent from the line of Aaron) to approach a dead body, except to attend to the nearest of kin. Holiness and death are at odds; there is something on the order of a magnetic repulsion between them. In Psalm 133, the Temple Mount is the place at which God ordained the blessing of eternal life; no thought is given to the brute reality — so evident to us — that those who visit there will ultimately die, the promise of eternal life notwithstanding. That consideration is as alien to the psalm as a corpse is to the Temple or disobedience is to the Garden of Eden.

The implication of the paradisiac character of the Temple that we have been developing is that the paradigm of Genesis 3 must not be overgeneralized, as it usually has been because of the role that chapter plays in the Christian drama of salvation. The familiar Christian use of Genesis 3 is temporal: the opportunity for immortality lay in the past and is unavailable now. Psalm 133 and its kindred literature offer a paradigm that is spatial: death is the norm outside Zion and cannot be reversed, but within the temple city, death is unknown, for there God has ordained the blessing of eternal life. To journey to the Temple is to move toward redemption, to leave the parched land of wasting and death for the fountain of life and the revival and rejuvenation it dispenses.

This conception of the Temple as paradise, the place rendered inviolable by the pervasive presence of God, explains one of the more striking features of Temple-oriented devotion in the Hebrew Bible. I am referring to the longing to remain in the Temple so often expressed by psalmists, their desire to spend their lives there, the reluctance to leave for the more familiar world marked by the murderous designs of the enemy and kindred menaces. Some of this can probably be explained by the status of sanctuaries in Israelite law, where they served as places of asylum for those unjustly accused and fearful of retaliation.[19] Thus, Adonijah, whose campaign for the throne has failed and whose younger brother Solomon has become king instead, refuses to let go of the horns of the altar until the new king swears not to put him to death (1 Kgs 1:50–53; cf. Exod 21:12–14). In this, sanctuaries or altars served a legal function similar to that of the "cities of refuge" to which someone who has committed homicide without malice aforethought could escape the vengeance of his victim's blood-avenger (Num 35:9–34; Deut 19:1–13). That the six cities of refuge are also Levitical towns and thus dedicated to the priestly tribe bears additional witness to the protective functions of holy places in

Israelite thinking (Num 35:6; Josh 20:1–21, 40). Within the sanctuary lies life; outside it lurks death.

Within the Temple also lies innocence. Although worshipers experience therein the rich bounty of a gracious God, they do not enter *sola gratia*. Their lives must qualify them for admittance and residence, as demonstrated by compositions like this psalm:

> A psalm of David.

> LORD, who may sojourn in Your tent,
>   who may dwell on Your holy mountain?
> ²He who lives without blame,
>   who does what is right,
>   and in his heart acknowledges the truth;
> ³whose tongue is not given to evil;
>   who has never done harm to his fellow,
>   or borne reproach for [his acts toward] his neighbor;
> ⁴for whom a contemptible man is abhorrent,
>   but who honors those who fear the LORD;
>   who stands by his oath even to his hurt;
> ⁵who has never lent money at interest,
>   or accepted a bribe against the innocent.
> The man who acts thus shall never be shaken. (Psalm 15)

Many scholars classify poems like this one as "entrance liturgies," on the assumption that their origins lay in ceremonies in which priests guarding the entrance to the Temple precincts set forth the moral prerequisites for admission. Alternatively, Egyptian parallels suggest that the prerequisites may have actually been inscribed on the lintels or doorposts of the Temple as a warning or a self-curse to protect against unauthorized entrance.[20] In either case, the didactic affirmation with which Psalm 15 closes goes further. It ascribes the inviolability of the Temple Mount to the exemplary person who is ethically qualified to dwell there. Those whom the "entrance liturgy" qualifies for admittance become like the eternal and impregnable sanctuary into which they then come. They "shall never be shaken" (*lōʾ yimmôṭ*, v 5). Psalm 125 extends the same assurance to those who trust in the LORD, whatever their location:

> Those who trust in the LORD
>   are like Mount Zion
>   that cannot be moved (*lōʾ - yimmôṭ*),
>   enduring forever.
> ²Jerusalem, hills enfold it,
>   and the LORD enfolds His people
>   now and forever. (Ps 125:1–2)

The Temple in Jerusalem is the objective correlative of the secure and protected life of those who trust in God and strive to live the morally upright life
he demands.

The converse of the Edenic life within the Temple precincts is the danger
that awaits without. The author of the celebrated Twenty-third Psalm tells us
that God "spread[s] a table for me in full view of my enemies." No wonder the
thought appeals to him that he will "dwell in the house of the LORD / for many
long years" (vv 5–6). And no wonder the author of Psalm 84 proclaims, in a
verse that the rabbis have prefixed to Psalm 145 to make the *'ašrê* prayer:

> Happy are those who dwell in Your house;
>   they forever praise You. (Ps 84:5)

At the conclusion of the same poem, the author draws together a number of
themes that we have been developing — God's grace and bounty, the moral
innocence of those who trust in him, and his reliable protection of them — in a
similar paean to life in the holy shrine:

> [11]Better one day in Your courts than a thousand [anywhere else];
>   I would rather stand at the threshold of God's house
>   than dwell in the tents of the wicked.
> [12]For the LORD God is sun and shield;
>   the LORD bestows grace and glory;
>   He does not withhold His bounty from those who live without blame.
> [13]O LORD of hosts,
>   happy is the man who trusts in You. (Ps 84:11–13)

Poems such as those we have been examining attest to the sense of transcendence that the worshipers in the temple experienced. There they rejoiced to
find a world that is a sign of contradiction to the nastier and more familiar
world of everyday life. Or, to be more precise, they rejoiced over the Temple
reality with a keen awareness of the mundane reality from which they had
been rescued. In the Temple, instead of want, they found surfeit; instead of
abandonment, care; instead of pollution, purity; instead of victimization, justice; instead of threat, security; instead of vulnerability, inviolability; instead of
change, fixity; and instead of temporality, eternity. If this sounds like the
World-to-Come or the Garden of Eden of rabbinic tradition, or the heaven of
Christianity, that is surely no coincidence, for the Temple is the source of much
of the imagery out of which those ideas grew. The outstanding difference, of
course, is that the experience of the worshipers in the Temple lies on this side
of death. To the extent that it anticipates the World-to-Come or heaven, it is
exactly that — an anticipation, a pre-enactment, a proleptic experience of what
Judaism and Christianity (but not the Hebrew Bible) promise lies on the far

side of death for those privileged to have it. Some will say that these spiritual experiences are, in the last analysis, this-worldly and thus irrelevant to our topic. I disagree. They are very much experiences of another world, fleetingly available to those granted the ecstasy of worship in the House of the LORD. Were it not for the jarring contradiction of the term itself, we might call this an experience of "temporary immortality." We must remember that the temporariness, though much on our minds, is not, however, on the minds of the worshipers themselves. They, rather, are praising God forever (Ps 84:5), in marked contrast to "the dead [who] cannot praise the LORD / Nor any who go down into silence" (Ps 115:17).[21] The Temple is the antipode of Sheol, as life is the opposite of death, and praise is the opposite of oblivion. If so, it would again be proper to use Wordsworth's term "intimations of immortality" to describe this striking perception of the higher and better world beyond the perceptions available in ordinary time and ordinary experience.

It is not only because of its duration that the term *immortality* must be qualified when it is applied to the experience of total divine protection in the Temple. For surely we are not dealing here with some ancient Israelite analogy to the immortality of the soul as that idea is expressed in Greek philosophical sources (later, of course, to find a home as well in Jewish, Christian, and Muslim theology). Those who shelter in the House of the LORD do not survive death as indestructible disembodied spirits, their bodies alone having passed away. Rather, they survive the very real threat of death — the utter demise of the entire person — because of the special intervention of God, and they survive in bodily form. Were it not for God's just and gracious rescue, they would have been destroyed. Those delivered from death to live in the Temple depend on their relationship with their God for their very lives; they cannot rely on any inherently immortal dimension of the self to withstand the fate he has graciously spared them. In this, the escape from death that they experience exhibits stronger affinities with resurrection than with immortality in the Hellenic mode.

Since the Temple serves as the antipode to Sheol, the locus of life against the God-forsaken realm of the dead, it stands to reason that longing for the Temple can also represent a longing for immortality. The parade example of this is the Psalm of Jonah:

> [3]He said:
> In my trouble I called to the LORD,
> And He answered me;
> From the belly of Sheol I cried out,
> And You heard my voice.
> [4]You cast me into the depths,

Into the heart of the sea,
The floods engulfed me;
All Your breakers and billows
Swept over me.
⁵I thought I was driven away
Out of Your sight:
Would I ever gaze again
Upon Your holy Temple?
⁶The waters closed in over me,
The deep engulfed me.
Weeds twined around my head.
⁷I sank to the base of the mountains;
The bars of the earth closed upon me forever.
Yet You brought my life up from the pit,
O Lord my God!
⁸When my life was ebbing away,
I called the Lord to mind;
And my prayer came before You,
Into Your holy Temple.
⁹They who cling to empty folly
Forsake their own welfare,
¹⁰But I, with loud thanksgiving,
Will sacrifice to You;
What I have vowed I will perform.
Deliverance is the Lord's! (Jon 2:3–10)

The poem itself is actually a "pastiche of different verses taken from Psalms."²² Its placement in the mouth of Jonah, though not without considerable literary and theological significance, is discordant, since the fugitive prophet recites it from the belly of the fish but praises the Lord for having already rescued him from the netherworld. Presumably, within the context of the redacted book, we are to think of the Lord's provision of "a huge fish to swallow Jonah" (Jon 2:1) as the act that rescued the drowning prophet from death, lifting him out of Sheol.

For our purposes, the most interesting feature of the Psalm of Jonah is its geography. Sheol (or "the pit") is the farthest point down. It lies at "the base of the mountains" (Jon 2:7). At the other extreme — presumably up high, though the text never specifies its direction — stands the "holy Temple," and it is there to which the dying prophet's prayer arrives, to precipitate his miraculous deliverance (cf. Ps 18:5–7). It is instructive that the most painful thought Jonah has as he descends into Sheol is that he will never again gaze upon the Temple (Jon 2:5). More than anything else, that is the feature that represents the utter reality, the utter finality, of his death. Fortunately, things never reach that point. Although "there is no praise of You among the dead; / in Sheol, who can acclaim You?" (as Ps 6:6 puts it), Jonah can at least *remember* the LORD in Sheol and call upon him to rescue him from there. The rescue comes to its fulfillment in the place that the prophet thought he would never glimpse again and at which his prayer from the netherworld arrived—the Temple, and it is there that he will praise his deliverer, offering thanksgiving sacrifices (Jon 2:8–10). To move from Sheol to the Temple is to move from death to life. To long to gaze upon the Temple is to long for life itself.

The connection of the Temple with the Garden of Eden that we have been examining survived the destruction of the Temple itself and can still be detected in rabbinic literature. It underlies, for example, a striking midrashic observation about the expulsion of Adam (*Gen. Rab.* 21:8). This happened, it will be recalled, because of the LORD's anxiety that humanity might become immortal:

> ²²And the LORD God said, "Now that the man has become like one of us, knowing good and bad, what if he should stretch out his hand and take also from the tree of life and eat, and live forever!" ²³So the LORD God banished him from the garden of Eden, to till the soil from which he was taken. ²⁴He drove the man out [*waygāreš*], and stationed east of the garden of Eden the cherubim and the fiery ever-turning sword, to guard the way to the tree of life. (Gen 3:22–24)

The midrash interprets "drove out" (*waygāreš*) as *wayyagrēs* ("broke," "crushed"), thus connecting the expulsion from Eden to a verse from Lamentations:

> He has broken [*wayyagrēs*] my teeth on gravel,
> Has ground me into the dust. (Lam 3:16)²³

Lamentations, it will be recalled, is a book about the agony of Fair Zion. It commemorates the destruction of Jerusalem and its Temple and for that reason is chanted in synagogues to this day on the evening of Tish'ah Be'Av, the fast day that tradition associates with the destruction. On the basis of the *waygāreš/wayyagrēs* wordplay, then, our midrash tells us that when God "drove the man out" of the Garden of Eden, "he showed him the destruction of the Temple." It is not simply that the two catastrophes (each involving an expulsion into exile) are similar. Nor is it simply the case that the primal, universal catastrophe anticipates (and is perhaps even repeated in) the historical, national catastrophe generations later. Rather, the two events—the loss of potential for immortality and the destruction of the Edenic refuge from death—are deeply interconnected and draw upon the same elements in the symbolic universe of ancient Israel. The Temple concretizes and re-presents Eden, with its potential for immortality, and the loss of the Temple is the loss not only of tangible, material intimacy with God but also of the life that is inextricably associated with such a spiritual relationship.

Conversely, the image of redemption from exile and rehabilitation of the Promised Land can draw upon the imagery of Eden restored:

> [33]Thus said the Lord GOD: When I have cleansed you of all your iniquities, I will people your settlements, and the ruined places shall be rebuilt; [34]and the desolate land, after lying waste in the sight of every passerby, shall again be tilled. [35]And men shall say, "That land, once desolate, has become like the garden of Eden; and the cities, once ruined, desolate, and ravaged, are now populated and fortified." [36]And the nations that are left around you shall know that I the LORD have rebuilt the ravaged places and replanted the desolate land. I the LORD have spoken and will act. (Ezek 36:33–36)

The destruction of the Temple that the midrash imagines Adam to have foreseen as he was being driven out of Eden is not the last word, either for Ezekiel in the oracle above or for the rabbis. In each case, an astonishing restoration reverses the tragedy, real and wrenching though the latter is. The loss of Eden, like the loss of the Land of Israel, proves to be temporary when God acts to close the tragic parenthesis in history that these cataclysmic events represent.

We have seen that the intimations of immortality in the Temple are only that— intimations and not the confident expectation that the experience of protection afforded in it will forever be the empirical reality. To be sure, the literature of Temple devotion that we have been examining knows nothing of a departure from the inviolable precincts into the world of the raging enemy—except, of course, in the form of prayers that the protection continue and such a departure never occur. In that sense, and that sense alone, we can say that the worshipers dwell in a world without death. But we know, and they occasionally feel, that the sanctuary they have been granted will come to an end, that they will eventually be turned out of their Edenic asylum and, separated from the source of life, will surely die. Although the rhetoric of Temple devotion is indeed one of life and not death, of eternity and not temporality, we are entitled nonetheless to point out that death comes even to those who find refuge in the Temple.

In the Hebrew Bible, and perhaps outside it as well, there are hints of another ancient Israelite perspective, however, one that seems to look forward to a continuation of divine protection even after death. The prime case in point

is an inscription on an amulet found in a burial cave near Jerusalem. Unfortunately, the silver amulet has suffered from severe oxidation over the centuries,
and the reading of the inscription is open to considerable doubt and continuing debate. Dating most likely to the sixth century B.C.E. (and thus predating
the emergence of a belief in resurrection in Second Temple Judaism), it has
attracted attention primarily because of the variant of the priestly benediction
(Num 6:24–26) that appears on it.[24] Just before the lines that offer that famous parallel, we find words that some scholars have read and translated thus:

> For in him is redemption; for YHWH
> Will bring us back light.[25]

In the opinion of two scholars who have studied the matter, the amulet on
which the inscription (so interpreted) appears is specifically intended for the
dead. If this be so, they write, these lines would constitute "eloquent testimony
that a blessing [of YHWH], already in the pre-exilic period, could result in more
than just social prestige, namely nothing short of a hope for the dead who are
incapable of having any further success."[26] The implication, as one of those
scholars puts it, is that in the sixth century B.C.E., YHWH "seems to be on the
point of integrating the world of the dead into his area of competence" — surely
a major development in the history of Israelite religion.[27] In that case, it seems
to me that the dead person for whom the blessing is intended cannot be
destined for Sheol, the dark netherworld where the LORD blesses no one, keeps
no one, and never makes his face shine upon anyone confined there. On the
other hand, this blessing on the dead is too explicit and too individual to consist simply of the hope for familial or national continuation after the person for
whom it is intended has passed away. Rather, if the interpretation of its words
quoted above is correct, it would seem that the Ketef Hinnom amulet inscription indeed attests to a hope for survival after death, a hope intimately and
inextricably involved with the theme of God's gracious protection that dominates the Temple-centered devotional literature we have examined. Where the
dead go in the event that the blessing in the inscription is realized and how,
precisely, they benefit from their new location remain shrouded in mystery.

The same frustrating lack of clarity confronts us when we consider the few
passages in the Hebrew Bible that seem to speak of individuals whose earthly
lives end without death. The best known of these describes the departure of
the prophet Elijah after the commissioning of his successor, Elisha:

> When the LORD was about to take Elijah up to heaven in a whirlwind,
> Elijah and Elisha had set out from Gilgal. ²Elijah said to Elisha, "Stay here, for
> the LORD has sent me on to Bethel." "As the LORD lives and as you live," said
> Elisha, "I will not leave you." So they went down to Bethel. ³Disciples of the

prophets at Bethel came out to Elisha and said to him, "Do you know that the LORD will take your master away from you today?" He replied, "I know it, too; be silent."

⁴Then Elijah said to him, "Elisha, stay here, for the LORD has sent me on to Jericho." "As the LORD lives and as you live," said Elisha, "I will not leave you." So they went on to Jericho. ⁵The disciples of the prophets who were at Jericho came over to Elisha and said to him, "Do you know that the LORD will take [*lōqēaḥ*] your master away from you today?" He replied, "I know it, too; be silent."

⁶Elijah said to him, "Stay here, for the LORD has sent me on to the Jordan." "As the LORD lives and as you live, I will not leave you," he said, and the two of them went on. ⁷Fifty men of the disciples of the prophets followed and stood by at a distance from them as the two of them stopped at the Jordan. ⁸Thereupon Elijah took his mantle and, rolling it up, he struck the water; it divided to the right and left, so that the two of them crossed over on dry land. ⁹As they were crossing, Elijah said to Elisha, "Tell me, what can I do for you before I am taken [*'ellāqaḥ*] from you?" Elisha answered, "Let a double portion of your spirit pass on to me." ¹⁰"You have asked a difficult thing," he said. "If you see me as I am being taken [*luqqāḥ*] from you, this will be granted to you; if not, it will not." ¹¹As they kept on walking and talking, a fiery chariot with fiery horses suddenly appeared and separated one from the other; and Elijah went up to heaven in a whirlwind. ¹²Elisha saw it, and he cried out, "Oh, father, father! Israel's chariots and horsemen!" When he could no longer see him, he grasped his garments and rent them in two. (2 Kgs 2:1–12)

As is generally the case in the stories of Elijah and Elisha, the major emphasis lies on the defiance of nature characteristic of these wonder-working itinerant prophets.²⁸ Elijah's parting of the Jordan, reenacting both Moses' splitting of the Sea of Reeds and Joshua's stopping the waters of the Jordan (Exod 14:21–31; Josh 3:9–4:24), confirms anew his supernatural authority and more important, the limitless power of the God who grants it. Here, the question of authority is especially apposite, since Elijah is about to commission a successor. The miracle of Elijah's ascent into the sky in a whirlwind validates the "difficult thing" that Elisha has requested, a "double portion" of the prophet's spirit. The language recalls the law that specifies the "double portion" as the firstborn son's inheritance (Deut 21:17) and thus underscores Elisha's status as the sole successor to the man he calls "father" (2 Kgs 2:12). From now on, it will be Elisha who serves as the head of the "disciples" (literally, "sons," *běnê*) of the prophets" (2 Kgs 2:15; cf. 1 Sam 10:12).

Where was Elijah after he "went up to heaven in a whirlwind" (2 Kgs 2:11)? The Hebrew word *šāmāyim* is better rendered "sky" than "heaven," since the latter term suggests a paradisiac abode unknown in the Hebrew Bible. One should therefore guard against the impression that our passage describes an ancient Israelite counterpart to the Christian belief in the Assumption, or Dormition, of the Virgin Mary, for example. For there is no reason to think that Elijah is here assumed into heavenly glory, rewarded for his service, or brought into the company of other righteous servants of God. Rather, the God of Israel, whose throne is in the sky,[29] whisks his servant Elijah away from the earth and toward his own mysterious and unapproachable abode. The storm or "whirlwind" (*sĕ'ārâ*, 2 Kgs 2:11) through which he does this contributes a sense of awesome violence, intensifying our perception of the unpredictable, unnatural, indeed, otherworldly character of the event. The same word is used for the "tempest" from which God suddenly thunders out his reply to the protesting sufferer in Job 38:1.

That Elijah should leave the earth in this eerie fashion is altogether congruent with the presentation of him elsewhere in Kings. Unlike most prophets, for example, we know nothing of his paternity; no father's name is given. His introduction into the narrative also sounds the notes of numinous power and abrupt appearance that resound throughout the narrative, until his abrupt disappearance after parting the Jordan that we have just seen:

> Elijah the Tishbite, an inhabitant of Gilead, said to Ahab, "As the LORD lives, the God of Israel whom I serve, there will be no dew or rain except at my bidding." (1 Kgs 17:1)

The mysterious closeness to God, manifest in the awesome display of divine power at the end of Elijah's earthly life, accounts for his eerie transport into the sky. To speculate about his destination is as fruitless as speculating about his origin or the way in which he acquired those miraculous powers. Indeed, so little is known about his destination that we cannot safely say even that he never died. Perhaps 2 Kings wants us to think that death followed his miraculous disappearance in the very sight of his prophetic successor.

Jewish tradition, beginning perhaps as early as the late prophet Malachi (Mal 3:23–24), sees the matter differently. It conceives Elijah as a prophet who never died and thus continually stands ready to serve as the messenger or human agent of heavenly reconciliation.[30] To this day, the Jewish liturgy voices the petition that God send Elijah to announce the good news of comfort and deliverance. But where the Tishbite resides in the interim (if, that is, he did not die) is something the biblical sources never address. The story of Elijah's translation into the sky testifies to the power of God over death but says nothing about the nature of immortality.

The other passage about an earthly life that seemingly ends without death is equally mystifying but even more cryptic:

> [21]When Enoch had lived 65 years, he begot Methuselah. [22]After the birth of Methuselah, Enoch walked with God 300 years; and he begot sons and daughters. [23]All the days of Enoch came to 365 years. [24]Enoch walked with God; then he was no more, for God took [*lāqaḥ*] him. (Gen 5:21–24)

The seventh figure in the Priestly (P) antediluvian genealogy, Enoch has the shortest longevity — only 365 years. The number recalls the solar year and has suggested a connection to "the Mesopotamian Enmeduranna, who is the seventh king before the Flood" and whose "capital city was the ancient center of the sun god."[31] One has the sense that there was once a much larger and richer account of Enoch's premature disappearance, heavily mythological in character, that has been lost. Perhaps something of that material lies behind the massive amount of Enoch literature that Jews wrote between the third century B.C.E. and (roughly) the sixth C.E.[32] What is beyond dispute, however, is that P has (quite characteristically) suppressed whatever myth had circulated, leaving commentators guessing ever since about the cause of Enoch's early disappearance. Rashi (eleventh century), for example, thought that "God took him" prematurely in order to prevent him from sinning, presumably in the pandemic corruption that resulted in the great flood.[33]

It is less clear whether the "taking" in question signified something other than death. As ibn Ezra (twelfth century)[34] and others point out, the same verb (*lāqaḥ*) appears in Jonah's death wish (4:3) and in the LORD's announcement of Ezekiel's wife's impending death. The latter passage is especially germane, since God is the subject of the verb:

> [15]The word of the LORD came to me: [16]O mortal, I am about to take away [*lōqēaḥ*] the delight of your eyes from you through pestilence; but you shall not lament or weep or let your tears flow. [17]Moan softly; observe no mourning for the dead: Put on your turban and put your sandals on your feet; do not cover over your upper lip, and do not eat the bread of comforters."
>
> [18]In the evening my wife died, and in the morning I did as I had been commanded. (Ezek 24:15–18a)

The assumption, by no means secure, that God's taking Enoch was of the same order as his taking Ezekiel's wife would compel us to interpret Enoch's earthly end simply as death. In that case, the absence of the verb *to die* in Gen 5:24 (in contrast to Jon 4:3 and Ezek 24:18) in favor of the softer and more ambiguous term "was no more" (*'ênennû*) may suggest a tenderer attitude on God's part, as befits the innocent man whose end the verse reports — but nothing more. Consider the telling contrast the Targum Onkelos (an ancient Aramaic translation of the Torah) makes merely with the addition of these words: "for the LORD had caused him to die."

This rabbinic insistence that Enoch's body indeed died (whatever God did with his soul) may well originate in reaction to the Jewish Enoch literature already mentioned. The book of Jubilees (second century B.C.E.) gives this account:

> 22. . . And Enoch bore witness against all of them. 23And he was taken from among the children of men, and we led him to the garden of Eden for greatness and honor. And behold, he is there writing condemnation and judgment of the world, and all of the evils of the children of men. 24And because of him none of the water of the Flood came upon the whole land of Eden, for he was put there for a sign and so that he might bear witness against all of the children of men so that he might relate all of the deeds of the generations until the day of judgment. 25And he offered the incense which is acceptable before the LORD in the evening (at) the holy place on Mount Qater. (Jub 4:22–25)[35]

Here we see a striking adumbration of the rabbinic notion that the destiny of the righteous lies in the Garden of Eden. But we also hear an echo of the more ancient identification of that magic place with the Temple. Enoch is not simply rewarded by being whisked off to paradise. Offering sacrificial incense, he also serves there as a priest. Most likely, the sweet savor of the incense corresponds to the rectitude of his own earthly life, which must have brought a kindred pleasure to God. The life he has after "he was taken from among the children of men" not only rewards but also continues and even enhances the direction of his life beforehand. He enacts symbolically in ritual the ethical character of his godly conduct.

Finally, we must consider passages from two psalms that seem also to speak of a future life for the upright after they have died. The first appears in Psalm 49:

> 15Sheeplike they head for Sheol,
>   with Death as their shepherd.
> The upright shall rule over them at daybreak,
>   and their form shall waste away in Sheol
>   till its nobility be gone.
> 16But God will redeem my life from the clutches of Sheol,
>   for He will take me [*yiqqāḥēnî*]. (Ps 49:15–16)

The first verse is so obscure and grammatically difficult that one should not dispute one commentator's judgment that "the restoration of the seriously corrupt text is hopeless."[36] The translation quoted above, however, comports well with the overall theme of the poem, the futility of wealth and social status in the face of inevitable death. If "Death" (v 15) refers to the Canaanite god of that name (Mot),[37] then we are to see a contrast between those whom Death leads to Sheol and the psalmist himself, whom God redeems and "takes." If so, Death/Mot has now been assigned a *moral* function in God's world: it/he leads those who are arrogant, self-satisfied, and materialistic to the miserable netherworld to which they have condemned themselves, but he has no authority over those who humbly trust in God. Verse 16, as clear textually as its predecessor is opaque, nonetheless admits of some semantic ambiguity. Does it affirm that God will not allow the psalmist to remain in Sheol when he has died or that he will prevent him from descending thereto in the first place?[38] Either way, the same ambiguity as to the destination that we saw in connection with Elijah and Enoch remains, signaled by the presence of the same verb, "to take" (*lāqaḥ*). Where does God take the life of the faithful servant who relies on him, rather than on wealth and status, for his ultimate felicity? We again find no answer.

The other passage in Psalms, though textually more secure than Ps 49:15, presents at least the same degree of ambiguity as v 16:

> [23]Yet I was always with You,
>   You held my right hand;
> [24]You guided me by Your counsel
>   and will receive me [*tiqqāḥēnî*] with glory.
> [25]Whom else have I in heaven?
>   And having You, I want no one on earth.
> [26]My body and mind fail;
>   but God is the stay of my mind, my portion forever.
> [27]Those who keep far from You perish;
>   You annihilate all who are untrue to You.
> [28]As for me, nearness to God is good;
>   I have made the Lord GOD my refuge,
>   That I may recount all Your works. (Ps 73:23–28)[39]

The main uncertainty lies with v 24b. The rendering above understands *'aḥar* to be a preposition meaning "with," a rare usage, to be sure, but one for which there is persuasive evidence.[40] The future tense ("will receive") seems called for, since the psalmist is speaking of the decline of his own "body and mind," which, in striking contrast to the demise of those far from God, does not sever his relationship with God. If it was generally thought that "they who descend into the Pit / [do not] Hope for Your grace" (Isa 38:18), it is all the more striking that this psalmist continues emphatically to regard God as his rock and his refuge even in the face of death.

To be sure, it is possible to read the psalmist's words as expressing confidence in God only despite death and not after it. But to do so is to vitiate the force of the contrast between those distant from God and untrue to him, whom God "annihilates" so that they "perish," on the one hand, and the speaker himself ("As for me . . ."), on the other (vv 27–28). The psalm resolves the problem of the wicked who prosper and the innocent who suffer the way the Hebrew Bible usually resolves it — not with an intellectual insight but with confidence that God will dramatically turn the tables, righting the wrong that has caused the psalmist such grief.[41] In Psalm 73, the turning of the tables involves the annihilation of the unfaithful, whereas the psalmist has God as his "portion forever." The prosperity of the wicked is transient; the felicity of the faithful, eternal.[42]

As in the cases of Enoch, Elijah, and Psalm 49, we cannot say where it is that God will receive/take the speaker of Psalm 73 with glory. Since Klaas Spronk is surely correct that "the accent is on YHWH and not on the afterlife itself,"[43] we shall already have distorted the message of the psalm if we focus on the place (if there *is* a place) in which its author enjoys his unending closeness to God. Rather, it would seem that all of these texts that speak of the enigmatic "taking" are expressing a belief that whether spatial or not, it is in God's power to provide an antipode to the misery of Sheol.[44] Although some — perhaps most — are "sent down" to Sheol (e.g., 1 Kgs 2:9), others God "takes" himself, continuing even at or beyond death his reliable protection of those who find refuge in him. As Spronk puts it in reference to Psalm 73, what we see here is "the trust that the communion of the faithful with God shall last forever."[45] It is a trust that has itself lasted millennia.

The conclusion we drew about the intimations of immortality in the House of the LORD applies no less to the texts about Elijah, Enoch, and the psalmists that we have just examined. Here, too, if God's "taking" involves survival after death or disappearance, the analogy with resurrection is stronger than that with immortality of the soul as the term has usually been understood. For these four texts do not speak of any indestructible core of the self that endures in a disembodied state even after the flesh and bones have rotted away. Rather, they speak of an active intervention (*lāqaḥ*) of God, snatching up to the sky the person found worthy (Elijah), taking him before his time and still in his innocence (Enoch), redeeming him from the power of Sheol (Psalm 49), or receiving him with glory, in contrast to the wicked whom God annihilates (Psalm 73).

In all these cases, one must not miss the powerful theme of special grace. In each instance, the person might have died as others do, with as much or as little hope for the future as they have. In the cases of Enoch and especially the two psalmists, there is also an important note of judgment. Presumably, it is because "Enoch walked with God" that "God took him" (Gen 5:24). One psalmist's confidence that "He will take me" (Ps 49:16) stands in pointed contrast with the dreary fate of those who foolishly trust in their wealth. The other psalmist's expectation that God will receive him "with glory" (Ps 73:24) is the correlative of his confidence that the wicked, though at present thriving, shall nonetheless be overthrown ("How suddenly are they ruined," v 19). In these two psalms, it is not too much to speak of an eschatological dimension, so long as we bear in mind that the final judgment comes not at the end of history but at the end of the psalmist's own experience, that is, at the end of his life. His death is his eschatological moment. It attests to the long-delayed justice of God. As we shall see,[46] the same must be said for the resurrection of the dead, when it at last develops.

It would be simplistic, then, to polarize immortality and resurrection. For one thing, doing so obscures the critical point that there is a version of immortality that is quite close to resurrection. To be sure, this is not the version on which philosophers from Plato to Kant (and beyond) have focused — the version that posits an immaterial and imperishable soul. Rather, the version of immortality of which this biblical literature speaks concentrates on almost the diametric opposite — a painfully vulnerable "life" (*nepeš*, as in Ps 49:16) that God will "take" or redeem — or so its possessor hopes — whereas others less worthy will descend into Sheol without hope. Second, even when a full-blown expectation of resurrection develops, one should not assume that those who hold it thought that people simply do not exist between death and resurrection. "Many of those that sleep in the dust of the earth shall awake," one reads in Daniel 12:2, in language that suggests inactivity ("that sleep") rather than nonexistence or the miserable fate of those dispatched to Sheol. As N. T. Wright observes with regard to the Wisdom of Solomon (a Hellenistic Jewish text), this is "an immortality which would ultimately consist not in a disembodied soul but in a renewed bodily life, when at last the soul is given a body to match it."[47] Later, the survival of the deceased even before their resurrection becomes a staple of rabbinic thought. In one particularly touching account, God is said to devote a quarter of each day to teaching Torah to little children who had died.[48]

Finally, the aspiration to immortality that we have been exploring exhibits another connection to resurrection, and this lies in the fact that when the expectation of resurrection arises, resurrection is still only the prelude to something greater and more permanent. This is "eternal life," as the book of Daniel puts it (12:2), or, to use the familiar rabbinic expression, life in the World-to-Come. Since this new life is thought to follow upon resurrection, it perforce entails embodiedness: people come back in the flesh. But the flesh in which they come back is necessarily different from the kind they knew in their mortal life, for now they have become immune to death and the bodily infirmities associated with it. There is no second death for those granted eternal life. Once raised from the dead, they are granted immortality, and the flesh in which they are raised can only be analogous, and not identical, to the sort of flesh that characterized them beforehand. Their new life is thus not a mere continuation of the old but rather a radical transformation of it, a perfecting of the self in a world distinguished from this one by its perfection.[49]

Although the longing for immortality that we have been exploring in this chapter does not envision resurrection, neither does it envision life in a disembodied state. Rather it tends to imagine embodied persons immune to the ravages of disease, death, scarcity, injustice, and enmity, living forever in a perfected world, the world symbolized, most commonly, by the Temple. That Jews believing in resurrection continued to cherish the old literature that so vividly expressed this longing for immortality is hardly surprising.

Individual Mortality and Familial Resurrection

Thus said the LORD,
Who established the sun for light by day,
The laws of moon and stars for light by night,
Who stirs up the sea into roaring waves,
Whose name is LORD of Hosts:
If these laws should ever be annulled by Me
    — declares the LORD —
Only then would the offspring of Israel cease
To be a nation before Me for all time.
          — Jeremiah 31:35–36

In our second chapter, we discussed one of the prime warrants often adduced either for the rejection of resurrection (by better-informed individuals) or for its alleged absence, and the alleged absence of any notion of the afterlife, in Judaism (by less informed individuals). That warrant is the finality of death in the Hebrew Bible, or at least in most of it, and certainly in what is from a Jewish point of view its most important subsection, the first five books. For no resurrections take place therein, and predictions of a general resurrection at the end of time can be found in the written Torah only through ingenious *derash* of the sort that the rabbinic tradition itself does not univocally endorse or replicate in its translations. In the same chapter, we also identified one difficulty with this notion that the Pentateuch exhibits no possibility of an afterlife but supports, instead, the absolute finality of death, and to this point we must now return. I am speaking of the difficulty of separating individuals from their families (including the extended family that is the nation). If, in fact, individuals are fundamentally and inextricably embedded within their families, then their own deaths, however terrifying in prospect, will lack the finality that death carries with it in a culture with a more individualistic, atomistic understanding of the self. What I am saying here is something more radical than the truism that in the Hebrew Bible, parents draw consolation from the thought that their descendants will survive them (e.g., Gen 48:11), just as, conversely, the parents are plunged into a paralyzing grief at the thought that their progeny have perished (e.g., Gen 37:33–35; Jer 31:15). This is, of course, the case, and probably more so in the ancient world, where children were the support of one's old age, than in modern societies, where the state and the pension fund fill many roles previously concentrated in the family. That to which I am pointing, rather, is that the self of an individual in ancient Israel was entwined with the self of his or her family in ways that are foreign to the modern West, and became foreign to some degree already long ago.

Let us take as an example the passage in which Jacob is granted "the blessing of Abraham," his grandfather, according to the prayer of Isaac, his father, to "possess the land where you are sojourning, which God assigned to Abraham" (Gen 28:1–4). The blessing on Abraham, as we have seen, can be altogether and satisfactorily fulfilled in Abraham's descendants. Thus, too, can Ezekiel envision the appointment of "a single shepherd over [Israel] to tend them — My servant David," who had passed away many generations before (Ezek 34:23). Can we, without *derash,* see in this a prediction that David, king of Judah and Israel, will be raised from the dead? To do so is to move outside the language of the text and the culture of Israel at the time of Ezekiel, which does not speak of the resurrections of individuals at all. But to say, as the School of Rabbi Ishmael said about "to Aaron" in Num 18:28,[1] that Ezekiel means only one who is "like David" — a humble shepherd boy who comes to triumph in battle and rises to royal estate, vindicating his nation and making it secure and just — is not quite the whole truth, either. For biblical Hebrew is quite capable of saying that one person is "like" another or descends from another's lineage (e.g., Deut 18:15; 2 Kgs 22:2; Isa 11:1) without implying identity of some sort. The more likely interpretation, rather, is that Ezekiel here predicts the miraculous appearance of a royal figure who is not only *like* David but also *of* David, a person of Davidic lineage, that is, who functions as David redivivus. This is not the resurrection of a dead man, to be sure, but neither is it the appearance of some unrelated person who only acts like David, or of a descendant who is "a chip off the old block." David is, in one obvious sense, dead and buried (1 Kgs 2:10), and his death is final and irreversible. In another sense, harder for us to grasp, however, his identity survives him and can be manifested again in a descendant who acts as he did (or, to be more precise, as Ezekiel thought he acted) and in whom the promise to David is at long last fulfilled. For David's identity was not restricted to the one man of that name but can reappear to a large measure in kin who share it.

This is obviously not reincarnation. For that term implies that the ancient Israelites believed in something like the later Jewish and Christian "soul" or like the notion (such as one finds in some religions) of a disembodied consciousness that can reappear in another person after its last incarnation has died. In the Hebrew Bible, however, there is nothing of the kind. The best approximation is the *nepeš*, the part of the person that manifests his or her life force or vitality most directly. James Barr defines the nepeš as "a superior controlling centre which accompanies, exposes and directs the existence of that totality [of the personality] and one which, especially, provides the life to the whole."[2] Although the nepeš does exhibit a special relationship to the life of the whole person, it is doubtful that it constitutes "a superior controlling center." As Robert Di Vito points out, "in the OT, human faculties and bodily organs enjoy a measure of independence that is simply difficult to grasp today without dismissing it as merely poetic speech or, even worse, 'primitive thinking.'" Thus, the eye talks or thinks (Job 24:15) and even mocks (Prov 30:17), the ear commends or pronounces blessed (Job 29:11), blood cries out (Gen 4:10), the nepeš (perhaps in the sense of gullet or appetite) labors (Prov 16:26) or pines (Ps 84:3), kidneys rejoice and lips speak (Prov 23:16), hands shed blood (Deut 21:7), the heart and flesh sing (Ps 84:3), all the psalmist's bones say, "LORD, who is like you?" (Ps 35:10), tongue and lips lie or speak the truth (Prov 12:19, 22), hearts are faithful (Neh 9:8) or wayward (Jer 5:23), and so forth.[3] The point is not that the individual is simply an agglomeration of distinct parts. It is, rather, that the nepeš is one part of the self among many and does not control the entirety, as the old translation "soul" might lead us to expect.[4] A similar point might be made about the modern usage of the term *person*.

All of the organs listed above, Di Vito points out, are "susceptible to moral judgment and evaluation."[5] Not only that, parts of the body besides the nepeš can actually experience emotional states. As Aubrey R. Johnson notes, "Despondency, for example, is felt to have a shriveling effect upon the bones . . . just as they are said to decay or become soft with fear or distress, and so may be referred to as being themselves troubled or afraid" (e.g., Ezek 37:11; Hab

3:16; Jer 23:9; Ps 31:11). In other words, "the various members and secretions of the body . . . can all be thought of as revealing psychical properties,"[6] and this is another way of saying that the nepeš does not really correspond to Barr's "superior controlling centre" at all. For many of the functions here attributed to the nepeš are actually distributed across a number of parts of the body. The heart, too, often functions as the "controlling centre," determining, for example, whether Israel will follow God's laws or not (e.g., Ezek 11:19). The nepeš in the sense of the life force of the body is sometimes identified with the blood, rather than with an insensible spiritual essence of the sort that words like "soul" or "person" imply. It is in light of this that we can best understand the Pentateuchal laws that forbid the eating of blood on the grounds that it is the equivalent of eating life itself, eating, that is, an animal that is not altogether dead (Lev 17:11, 14; Deut 12:23; cf. Gen 9:4–5). If the nepeš "provides the life to the whole,"[7] so does the blood, with which laws like these, in fact, equate it. The bones, which, as we have just noted, can experience emotional states, function likewise on occasion. When a dead man is hurriedly thrown into Elisha's grave in 2 Kgs 13:21, it is contact with the wonder-working prophet's *bones* that brings about his resurrection. And when the primal man at long last finds his soul mate, he exclaims not that she (unlike the animals who have just been presented to him) shares a nepeš with him but rather that she "is bone of my bones / And flesh of my flesh" (Gen 2:23).

In sum, even if the nepeš does occasionally function as a "controlling centre" or a provider of life, it does not do so uniquely. The ancient Israelite self is more dynamic and internally complex than such a formulation allows. It should also be noticed that unlike the "soul" in most Western philosophy, the biblical nepeš can die. When the non-Israelite prophet Balaam expresses his wish to "die the death of the upright," it is his nepeš that he hopes will share their fate (Num 23:10), and the same applies to Samson when he voices his desire to die with the Philistines whose temple he then topples upon all (Judg 16:30). Indeed, "to kill the nepeš" functions as a term for homicide in biblical Hebrew, in which context, as elsewhere, it indeed has a meaning like that of the English "person" (e.g., Num 31:19; Ezek 13:19).[8] As Hans Walter Wolff puts it, nepeš "is never given the meaning of an indestructible core of being, in contradistinction to the physical life . . . capable of living when cut off from that life."[9] Like heart, blood, and bones, the nepeš can cease to function. It is not quite correct to say, however, that this is because it is "physical" rather than "spiritual," for the other parts of the self that we consider physical — heart, blood, bones, or whatever — are "spiritual" as well — registering emotions, reacting to situations, prompting behavior, expressing ideas, each in its own way. A more accurate summary statement would be Johnson's: "The

Israelite conception of man [is] as a psycho-physical organism."[10] "For some time at least [after a person's death] he may live on as an individual (apart from his possible survival within the social unit)," observes Johnson, "in such scattered elements of his personality as the bones, the blood and the name."[11] It would seem to follow that if ever he is to return "as a psycho-physical organism," it will have to be not through reincarnation of his soul in some new person but through the resurrection of the body, with *all* its parts reassembled and revitalized. For in the understanding of the Hebrew Bible, a human being is not a spirit, soul, or consciousness that happens to inhabit this body or that — or none at all. Rather, the unity of body and soul (to phrase the point in the unhappy dualistic vocabulary that is still quite removed from the way the Hebrew Bible thought about such things) is basic to the person. It thus follows that however distant the resurrection of the dead may be from the understanding of death and life in ancient Israel, the concept of immortality in the sense of a soul that survives death is even more distant. And whatever the biblical problems with the doctrine of resurrection — and they are formidable — the biblical problems with the immortality that modern Jewish prayer books prefer (as we saw in our first chapter) are even greater.

Di Vito points, however, to an aspect of the construction of the self in ancient Israel that does have some affinities with immortality. This is the thorough embeddedness of that individual within the family and the corollary difficulty in the context of this culture of isolating a self apart from the kin group. Drawing upon Charles Taylor's highly suggestive study *The Sources of the Self*,[12] Di Vito points out that "salient features of modern identity, such as its pronounced individualism, are grounded in modernity's location of the self in the 'inner depths' of one's interiority rather than in one's social role or public relations."[13] Cautioning against the naïve assumption that ancient Israel adhered to the same conception of the self, Di Vito develops four points of contrast between modern Western and ancient Israelite thinking on this point. In the Hebrew Bible,

> the subject (1) is deeply embedded, or engaged, in its social identity, (2) is comparatively decentered and undefined with respect to personal boundaries, (3) is relatively transparent, socialized, and embodied (in other words, is altogether lacking in a sense of "inner depths"), and (4) is "authentic" precisely in its heteronomy, in its obedience to another and dependence upon another.[14]

Although Di Vito's formulation is overstated and too simple — is every biblical figure, even David, presented as "altogether lacking in a sense of 'inner depths' "? — his first and last points are highly instructive and suggest that the familial and social understanding of "life" in the Hebrew Bible is congruent with larger issues in ancient Israelite culture. "Life" and "death" mean different things in a culture like ours, in which the subject is not so "deeply embedded . . . in its social identity" and in which authenticity tends to be associated with cultivation of individual traits at the expense of conformity, and with the attainment of personal autonomy and independence.

The contrast between the biblical and the modern Western constructions of personal identity is glaring when one considers the structure of what Di Vito calls "the patriarchal family." This "system," he tells us, "with strict subordination of individual goals to those of the extended lineal group, is designed to ensure the continuity and survival of the family."[15] In this, of course, such a system stands in marked contrast to liberal political theory that has developed over the past three and a half centuries, which, in fact, virtually assures that people committed to that theory above all else will find the Israelite system oppressive. For the liberal political theory is one that has increasingly envisioned a system in which society is composed of only two entities, the state and individual citizens, all of whom have equal rights quite apart from their familial identities and roles. Whether or not one affirms such an identity or plays the role that comes with it (or any role different from that of other citizens) is thus relegated to the domain of private choice. Individuals are guaranteed the freedom to renounce the goals of "the extended lineal group" and ignore "the continuity and survival of the family," or, increasingly, to redefine "family" according to their own private preferences. In this particular modern type of society, individuals may draw consolation from the thought that their group (however defined) will survive their own deaths. As we have had occasion to remark, there is no reason to doubt that ancient Israelites did so, too. But in a society like ancient Israel, in which "the subject . . . is deeply embedded, or engaged, in its social identity," "with strict subordination of individual goals to those of the extended lineal group," the loss of the subject's own life and the survival of the familial group cannot but have a very different resonance from the one most familiar to us. For even though the subject's death is irreversible — his or her nepeš having died just like the rest of his or her body/soul — his or her fulfillment may yet occur, for identity survives death. God can keep his promise *to* Abraham or his promise to Israel associated with the gift *of* David even after Abraham or David, as an individual subject, has died. Indeed, in light of Di Vito's point that "the subject . . . is comparatively decentered and undefined with respect to personal boundaries," the very distinction between Abraham and the nation whose covenant came through him

(Genesis 15; 17), or between David and the Judean dynasty whom the LORD has pledged never to abandon (2 Sam 7:8–16; Ps 89:20–38), is too facile.

Our examination of personal identity in the earlier literature of the Hebrew Bible thus suggests that the conventional view is too simple: death was not final and irreversible after all, at least not in the way in which *we* are inclined to think of these matters. This is not, however, because individuals were believed to possess an indestructible essence that survived their bodies. On the one hand, the body itself was thought to be animated in ways foreign to modern materialistic and biologistic thinking, but, on the other, even its most spiritual part, its nepeš (life force) or its něšāmâ (breath), was mortal. Rather, the boundary between individual subjects and the familial/ethnic/national group in which they dwelt, to which they were subordinate, and on which they depended was so fluid as to rob death of *some* of the horror it has in more individualistic cultures, influenced by some version of social atomism. In more theological texts, one sees this in the notion that subjects can die a good death, "old and contented . . . and gathered to [their] kin," like Abraham, who lived to see a partial—though only a partial—fulfillment of God's promise of land, progeny, and blessing upon him, or like Job, also "old and contented" after his adversity came to an end and his fortunes—including progeny—were restored (Gen 25:8; Job 42:17). If either of these patriarchal figures still felt terror in the face of his death, even after his afflictions had been reversed, the Bible gives us no hint of it.[16] Death in situations like these is not a punishment, a cause for complaint against God, or the provocation of an existential crisis. But neither is it death as later cultures, including our own, conceive it.

Given this embeddedness in family, there is in Israelite culture, however, a threat that is the functional equivalent to death as we think of it. This is the absence or loss of descendants. It is in this light that we should understand the association the book of Proverbs makes between Sheol and infertility:

> [15]The leech has two daughters, "Give!" and "Give!"
> Three things are insatiable;
> Four never say, "Enough!":
> [16]Sheol, a barren womb,
> Earth that cannot get enough water,
> And fire which never says, "Enough!" (Prov 30:15–16)

The three items analogized here to "a barren womb" are all redolent of death—Sheol (the dark, miserable netherworld), parched earth that cannot sustain life, and a raging fire that consumes everything and everybody in its way. Given such associations, we can better understand why the future patriarch Abraham's childlessness evokes such terror and depression:

[1]Some time later, the word of the LORD came to Abram in a vision. He said,
"Fear not, Abram,
I am a shield to you;
Your reward shall be very great."
[2]But Abram said, "O Lord GOD, what can You give me, seeing that I shall die childless!" (Gen 15:1-2)

All the reward in the world—wealth, longevity, even having God as one's personal protector—cannot compensate for childlessness.[17] And the proof that Abraham truly "fears God," that he places obedience to the divine command above his personal welfare, is that he is willing to sacrifice the promised son when at long last his previously barren and now elderly primary wife has borne him (22:11-12).[18]

Given the central role of children in the identity of parents in ancient Israelite culture, we have a credible clue as to the meaning of the common punishment formula, "that person shall be cut off [*nikrĕtâ*] from his kin" (e.g., Gen 17:14). The rabbinic opinion that this punishment (which the rabbis call *kārēt*) involved both a premature death and childlessness may well be close to the mark in the Hebrew Bible as well.[19] As one biblical scholar puts it, the penalty constitutes "a divine curse of extinction" that entails the death of children and not simply the absence of them.[20] It is akin to the death of one's self; indeed, in the biblical context, I submit, it is a form of the death of one's self.

The book of Job is an instructive case in point. Job's miseries begin not with lack of children, like Abraham's, but with the loss of his children, which provokes suicidal thoughts and an existential and theological crisis that has continued to reverberate through the millennia (Job 1:13-19; Job 3). Here, bereavement of progeny is the functional equivalent of death, and here, too, the patriarch's restoration inevitably entails his recovery of his seven sons and his three daughters (Job 42:13; cf. 1:2). To us, of course, the loss has not been made good, since these are not the same children who died at the onset of the tale. But that very objection only demonstrates the distance between our individualistic and nonfamilial construction of personal identity and the highly collective and familial concept that underlies these ancient Israelite narratives. For the epilogue, which speaks of Job's restoration, gives no indication whatsoever that grief about his deceased first set of children impaired his contentment at the time of his own death. The tragedy of the mortality of individuals cannot but attract the attention of the modern reader. The interest of the ancient narrator lies, rather, in the restoration of Job through the return of his family.

If childlessness is the equivalent of death, what is the equivalent of resurrection here? The stories about Abraham and Job, and of many other figures, male and female, throughout the Hebrew Bible, provide the answer: birth is the reversal of death and thus to a large degree the functional equivalent of resurrection (or of afterlife in general) in later cultures, including our own. The births of his first heir, Ishmael, and then of the promised son, Isaac, render God's promise of a reward to Abraham feasible, just as the birth of Job's new brood in the epilogue is the comic counterpoint to the tragic death of his first set of children in the prologue. In these stories, birth, not death, is God's last word, and the continuance of the family beatifies the patriarch's personal death.

Similarly, in the book of Ruth, one of the great masterpieces of biblical narrative artistry, a tale that begins with famine, expatriation, and death (Ruth 1:1–5) is transformed into one of abundance, return home and integration of the alien, and, most of all, birth (2:14–19; 4:7–15). Naomi, bereft of husband and sons alike, acquires a surrogate daughter in the Moabitess Ruth, who in faithfulness to her Israelite mother-in-law "left [her] father and mother and the land of [her] birth," as Ruth's husband-to-be, Boaz, puts it, "and came to a people [she] had not known before" (2:11). Through Ruth — now married to Boaz and on her way to becoming a matriarch of the House of Judah and even of its royal line — Naomi, herself apparently past her childbearing years, becomes the equivalent of a mother (4:11–12; 1:12–13; 4:16–17).[21] The deaths of her husband and sons, which occasioned her calling herself Mara ("bitter") in place of Naomi (derived from a word for "pleasantness," "sweetness"), have now been reversed, and she is once again "Naomi" (1:19b–21; 4:17). "Shaddai has made my lot very bitter," she had once told the women of Bethlehem, using a rare name of God. "I went away full, and the LORD has brought me back empty" (1:20–21). But by the end of the story, when Ruth has given birth, Naomi, too, has been brought back full. As in Job, so here the tragedies of the first chapter are reversed, and more, in the last. God's last word is not death but life.

The tales of Abraham, Job, and Ruth and Naomi, though much more developed in narrative artistry than most, are hardly unique within the Hebrew Bible. In more rudimentary form (though perhaps epitomizing longer oral formulations), the pattern in which birth reverses death can be found in many other stories. Its earliest attestation (in terms of literary order, whatever the chronology of composition) lies in the folk etymology of Adam and Eve's third son, whom Eve named "Seth [šēt], meaning God has provided [šāt] me with another offspring in place of Abel, for Cain had killed him" (Gen 4:25).[22] Twenty-three generations later, Judah, ancestor of Boaz and thus of the royal line from which David would hail, loses two sons, the second because of a refusal to fulfill the levirate requirement, "to provide offspring for his brother"

(38:9; see Deut 25:5–10). Having refused to release his third son for fear the same fate would befall him, too, and mistaking his widowed daughter-in-law for a prostitute, Judah inadvertently fulfills the requirement himself. In the end of this strange and disquieting tale, full of odd twists and unexpected reversals, the man who lost two sons gains twins, as the widow whose in-laws neglected her gives birth to the boys who will carry on her father-in-law's tribe and her late husband's name.[23] And this, let it not be forgotten, is the tribe from which King David's dynasty would someday spring (Gen 38:27–30; 1 Chr 2:3–15; Ruth 4:18–22).

A few chapters later, Jacob loses (so far as he knows) his beloved son Joseph; the sight of the latter's bloody tunic plunges Jacob into mourning and depression (Gen 37:31–35). As in the story of Naomi and Ruth, so here death is conjoined with famine and expatriation, as the surviving sons of Jacob (minus his other beloved son, Benjamin, Joseph's only full brother) leave the promised land and descend into Egypt in search of grain. When they return without Simeon, who Joseph has demanded be kept as a hostage in lieu of Benjamin, Jacob understandably sees himself bereft of *two* sons, and, to add insult to injury, he now faces the demand to release a third as well:

> Their father Jacob said to them, "It is always me that you bereave: Joseph is no more and Simeon is no more, and now you would take away Benjamin. These things always happen to me!" (Gen 42:36)

Yet it is precisely the release of the third son that eventually restores the other two, saves the family from famine, and reunites it after a long estrangement.[24] The pattern of death and revival that underlies the Joseph story is nicely highlighted by Jacob's response to his sons' report that "Joseph is still alive; yes, he is ruler over the whole land of Egypt." "His heart went numb, for he did not believe them," the narrator reports. "But when they recounted all that Joseph had said to them, and when he saw the wagons that Joseph had sent to transport him, the spirit of their father Jacob revived" (Gen 45:26–27).

Jacob's own apparent death and revival here encapsulates the underlying movement of the entire tale, a tale of the apparent death of children reversed through the providential restoration of them to their grieving father. Since the comic resolution focuses on the same children lost in the tragic opening, the pattern is more reminiscent of the binding of Isaac (Gen 22:1) than of the books of Ruth and Job. For those books close with the birth of *new* children rather than the restoration of those lost in the first chapter of each book. We should not, however, make too much of the difference. For in each case a death—apparent, real, or threatened—is reversed, and a parent gains or retains progeny after death has made its terrifying presence known. In fact, in the case at hand, Jacob, who thought he had lost two sons, acquires two *new* sons, when on his deathbed he adopts Joseph's children as his own (Gen 48:5–7). Birth again qualifies and diminishes the finality of death.

It is crucial to understand that the qualification is not automatic. Death has not lost its sting, even when there is a real possibility that birth might reverse death. For it is only that: a *possibility*. When a divine promise underlies the birth and survival of an heir (in such cases as Abraham's), trust in the promise does not come easily (Gen 15:1–3). In other instances, no such assurance is given, and parents die bereft. In the latter category, one thinks of the priest Eli, who, hearing that his two unworthy sons have died at the hands of the Philistines and the Ark has been captured, falls backward from his chair, suffers a broken neck, and dies. To be sure, his pregnant daughter-in-law, hearing the same news, was "seized with labor pains . . . and gave birth" (1 Sam 4:19), suggesting a striking parallel with the book of Ruth: a person's two sons die, Naomi losing Mahlon and Chilion (Ruth 1:5), Eli losing Hofni and Phinehas (1 Sam 4:17), but in each case the widowed daughter-in-law gives birth nonetheless. The structural parallelism of the situation, however, only underscores the deep and dispiriting contrast between the two episodes, brought out nicely by the comments made at the respective births. Whereas Ruth's delivery causes the women of Bethlehem to exclaim, "A son is born to Naomi!" (Ruth 4:17), Eli's daughter-in-law "named the boy Ichabod, meaning, 'The glory [*kābôd*] has departed from Israel' — referring to the capture of the Ark of God and to [the death of] her father-in-law and her husband." " 'The glory is gone from Israel,' " said this nameless woman in the last we ever hear of her or her son, " 'for the Ark of God has been captured' " (1 Sam 4:21–22). Whereas Naomi has, by the strange workings of the levirate law, become a mother (or at least a grandmother), Eli, unable to control his wicked sons (1 Sam 2:22–25), dies childless, his grandson a byword for God's righteous renunciation of the House of Eli and his temporary abandonment of the House of Israel as well. Birth, in short, *can* qualify the finality of death. It does not *have* to. The character of the parent and the disposition of the Deity are crucial. Absent proper parental conduct and the grace of God, death has very much the last word. Its sting is excruciating, and its finality, readily evident.

Earlier, we saw that the construction of personal identity in biblical Israel renders problematic the conventional claim that the Pentateuch in particular and the Hebrew Bible in general (with the exception of a few late passages) offer no expectation of survival after death. A more accurate generalization is that the hope for survival centers on the family, including (eventually) the extended family that is the nation, the whole House of Israel. If this seems to offer moderns scant consolation in the face of their own inevitable death, as it

indeed does, this is primarily because modern constructions of personal identity perceive higher and more rigid boundaries between the subject and the
social group, especially the involuntary grouping that is the family. When the
emphasis lies on the individual and his or her power of self-determination, as it
generally does in modern Western thought, then the loss of the individual to
death will inevitably seem catastrophic and irreversible (unless, of course,
it can be reversed through resurrection), and the survival of the family through
new births offers nothing more than purely psychological consolation, of
whatever worth. To the modern Western mind of the sort I am describing, it
seems right to say that in the last chapters of the respective books Naomi,
Ruth, and Job recover psychologically from the deaths reported in the first
chapters. They carry on and rebuild. But to imply, as those biblical tales do,
that the births of Ruth's son Obed and Job's seven new sons and three new
daughters *overcome* the deaths of Elimelech, Mahlon, Chilion, and Job's first
set of seven sons and three daughters seems to be missing the point badly. To
us, the shadow of death always overcasts to an appreciable degree the felicity
that the books of Ruth and Job predicate of Naomi and Job at the end of their
travail. We look in vain for some acknowledgment that the newfound or
recovered felicity is not absolute, since death is. The authors of these books
thought otherwise.

The notion that the continuation of the family constitutes the biblical expectation of survival — birth thus serving as the reversal of death — can lead to a
misunderstanding that needs to be confronted immediately. Since the family
carries on after the death of one of its members, it might be thought that the
form of survival to which the biblical pattern best corresponds is immortality:
the core of the indestructible self is simply embedded in a larger unit and thus
survives with that unit, even after the individual subject has indeed and in-
dubitably perished. If that is the case, then death surely has lost its sting. In
fact, it has become inconsequential, and the subject can face it in equanimity
and tranquility, certain of the survival that his continuing family guarantees.

The stories that we have examined suggest, however, a different and far
more pessimistic vision and, with it, a stormier and less complacent mode of
spirituality. For in the stories of Abraham and Judah, of Ruth and Job, death
indeed threatens. It threatens not only individual subjects (though their subjective response to its looming may be unreported and unknown to us) but
also the family itself. In other words, given the construction of personal identity in the Hebrew Bible, infertility and the loss of children serve as the functional equivalent of death. Striking at each generation of the patriarchs of
Genesis, and then at Judah in the next, childlessness in one or both of these
modes threatens to terminate the family, thus evoking the terror that later

generations (including our own) feel in the face of their personal deaths. That individuals in ancient Israel felt that same terror cannot be gainsaid; such fear is in plentiful evidence in the Psalms.[25] Nonetheless, and despite a long tradition of viewing the sin of Adam and Eve (and the mortality thought to go with it) as the most memorable event in Genesis, the great enemy in that book is not death as we think of it at all (still less is it sin) but death in the twin forms of barrenness and the loss of children.

A key idiom for this larger, more encompassing understanding of death involves the notion of the loss of one's "name" (*šēm*), as we have had occasion to note.[26] Here we must revert to the book of Proverbs:

> The memory [*zēker*] of the righteous is a source of blessing,
> But the name of the wicked rots away. (Prov 10:7)[27]

As one commentator on this verse rightly puts it, "The *zēker* or *šēm* is in effect an indirect prolongation of a man's influence and authority beyond death. . . . The contrast is between the beneficent persistence of the righteous man's vitality expressed in his enduring influence on the life of his community, and the process of decay which induces the memory of the wicked to rot away to nothingness."[28] It would seem, however, that the community in which the effect of that "beneficent persistence" is felt is very often the family that hails from the deceased. The "name" is, in fact, closely associated with the patrimonial land of his family.[29] We find prime evidence for this in the plea of the five daughters of Zelophehad to Moses:

> [3]"Our father died in the wilderness. He was not one of the faction, Korah's faction, which banded together against the LORD, but died for his own sin; and he has left no sons. [4]Let not our father's name [*šēm*] be lost to his clan just because he had no son! Give us a holding among our father's kinsmen!" (Num 27:3–4)

Without a son, Zelophehad's name and the real estate with which it was associated are endangered. Fortunately for him and for his daughters, the LORD instructs Moses to allow the hereditary land of a man who dies without sons to pass to his daughters (Num 27:5–8).[30] So long as the dead man's descendants survive on his hereditary holding, his name survives. If he lacks descendants or the land is alienated from his lineage, his name perishes.

The same logic underlies the institution of levirate marriage, which requires the brother of the deceased to marry his widow (Deut 25:5–10). "The first son that she bears shall be accounted to the dead brother, that his name [*šēm*] may not be blotted out in Israel," Deuteronomy tells us (25:6). In this way, the late brother can beget a child even after his death, and one of the most dreaded aspects of his own demise, the extinction of his name through the lack of a son, can be reversed.[31] By a kind of legal fiction, his family brings something of their dead kinsman back to life, birth again reversing death. Levirate marriage is a mode of redemption of the dead.

Finally, mention must be made of David's son Absalom's provision for his own continuance after death:

> Now Absalom, in his lifetime, had taken the pillar which is in the Valley of the King and set it up for himself; for he said, "I have no son to keep my name [*šēm*] alive." He had named [*šēm*] the pillar after himself, and it has been called Absalom's Monument [*yād*] to this day. (2 Sam 18:18)

An interesting Canaanite parallel has led some to suggest that the expression translated above as "keep my name alive" actually refers to cultic invocation of a deified ancestor even in this text.[32] The analogies with Zelophehad's daughters and with levirate marriage, however, argue that the issue is instead one of memorialization and the perpetuation of the name. Absalom takes preemptive action against the threat of extinction that death and childlessness jointly pose.[33] Indeed, the closest parallel to this verse actually lies in the LORD's promise to eunuchs who observe the Sabbath:

> I will give them, in My House
> And within My walls,
> A monument [*yād*] and a name [*šēm*]
> Better than sons or daughters.
> I will give them an everlasting name [*šēm*]
> Which shall not perish. (Isa 56:5)

In this instance, God's promise to the observant eunuchs functions as the equivalent of levirate marriage for those biologically precluded from having children. The name, God assures the eunuchs, is the equivalent of the descendants they cannot engender; it thus guarantees that they will not lack an "everlasting" continuance. God once again arranges things so that death is not final in all its aspects, and something of the deceased survives his physical demise.

The mode of spirituality that befits the view of the world of the texts that we have been discussing is light-years away from untroubled confidence in the survival of an indestructible core, whether of the individual self (the "soul") or of the larger kin group. Rather, it is one that fervently hopes against hope for continuation and the fertility, safety, and memorialization that make it possible. It also seeks divine protection against the death-dealing forces that threaten the family by closing wombs and taking children away. Just as creation in the biblical vision is not a steady state of serenity but rather a precarious order maintained or renewed in the face of potent and malevolent chaos;[34] and just as righteousness is often, perhaps usually, seen as vindication against powerful and successful evildoers and their false accusation (e.g., Jer 15:15–21; Ps 25:18–22, 35); so is the continued life of the family a *triumph* over the forces of death, a *vindication* against evil, and therefore a consequence of *struggle*. It is a turning back of the very real and deadly forces of adversity. In this, it resembles the resurrection of the dead much more than the immortality of the soul.

In the previous chapter and this one, we have examined two antipodes to Sheol, the first focused on worship in the LORD's Temple, and the second on lineage and the miraculous origin and survival of the larger lineage that is the people Israel. Our argument has been that these serve as symbols of continuation and thus call into question the heavy-handed claim that the Hebrew Bible always regards death as inevitable and in accordance with the divine will. These two antipodes are not only symbols, however; they are also the means by which certain types of continuation despite death can be acquired. The two come together strikingly in a psalm that expresses the biblical view of felicity memorably:

> A song of ascents.
>
> Happy are all who fear the LORD,
>   who follow His ways.
> [2]You shall enjoy the fruit of your labors;
>   you shall be happy and you shall prosper.
> [3]Your wife shall be like a fruitful vine within your house;
>   your sons, like olive saplings around your table.
> [4]So shall the man who fears the LORD be blessed.
>
> [5]May the LORD bless you from Zion;
>   may you share the prosperity of Jerusalem
>   all the days of your life,
>   [6]and live to see your children's children.
> May all be well with Israel! (Psalm 128)

Although the psalmist does not affirm or even mention immortality or resurrection, it is very much to be doubted that he thought the felicity of which he sang ended at the grave.

The Man of God Performs a Resurrection

If someone should say to you, "Is it possible the Holy One (blessed be He!) will resurrect the dead?" say to him, "It has already happened. He has already resurrected the dead through Elijah, through Elisha, and through Ezekiel in the Valley of Dura."

—*Midrash*, Leviticus Rabbah 27:4

The intimate connection of infertility with death, and of childbirth and familial survival with resurrection, that we developed in our previous chapter appears nowhere in the Hebrew Bible with greater clarity than in 2 Kgs 4:8–37, the story of the great lady of Shunem and the wonder-working prophet Elisha ben Shaphat. The tale itself is deceptively simple. The wealthy woman, we are told, urges the prophet to stop at her house for a meal, and soon the practice becomes regular whenever the prophet is in town (vv 8–9). After a while, at her suggestion, she and her husband provide him with a furnished apartment in their house as well. In gratitude for her patronage, Elisha has his servant Gehazi summon the woman so that he may ask how he might reciprocate, offering to speak to the commander of the army on her behalf. Her reply stresses her satisfaction with her life as it is and her disinclination to seek special favors: "I live among my own people." "The fact is," Gehazi then observes, ominously, "she has no son, and her husband is old." This prompts the prophet to summon her again and to predict that "next year, you will be embracing a son" — a most unlikely prospect, to be sure, as her incredulous response brings out: "Please, my LORD, man of God, do not delude your maidservant." Yet Elisha's prediction comes true, and soon we hear of the little boy in the fields with his father and the reapers (vv 13–18).

The happy ending proves no ending at all, for death reverses the miraculous fertility of the devout but childless woman and her elderly husband. "Oh, my head, my head!" the boy cries to his father, who instructs a servant to carry the stricken child to his mother. But it is too late: "And the child sat on her lap until noon; and he died" (vv 19–20). Joy has tarried for a few years, but now the wealthy couple are plunged back into the darkness of childlessness from which the wonder-working "man of God" had all too briefly delivered them.

The great lady of Shunem does not, however, give up. Concealing her mission from her husband, she finds Elisha and accosts him, "in bitter distress," as the prophet puts it to Gehazi. "Did I ask my LORD for a son?" she challenges the prophet. "Didn't I say: 'Don't mislead me'?" Perhaps underestimating the gravity of the situation or overestimating his own powers, Elisha dispatches Gehazi with instructions to touch the boy's face with the prophet's staff. But the woman will not accept an underling, and she and the prophet go back together (vv 22–30).

Meanwhile Gehazi, following his instructions, fails in his assignment: "There was no sound or response." The prophet's staff is no substitute for his person, and his assistant lacks the master's charismatic gift. "The boy has not awakened," Gehazi reports to Elisha when the latter has arrived (v 31). Then the prophet, alone with the dead boy in the very room that symbolizes the couple's devotion to God (v 21), first prays to the LORD and then, through the miraculous power of his own body, resuscitates the child. Having instructed Gehazi to summon the woman again, he tells her, "Pick up your son." She prostrates herself at his feet, picks up the resurrected boy, and leaves (vv 32–37).

The reader dependent on a summary like the one just provided is, alas, likely to miss the rich intertextual resonance of the story. The most striking connection is to the stories of the birth and near sacrifice of Isaac (Gen 18:1–15; 22:1–19), where specific points of diction suggest that we may be dealing not merely with a similar theme, deeply rooted in Israelite culture,[1] but with actual literary dependence as well. Both stories begin with a note of extraordinary hospitality, Abraham's to his three angelic (or divine) visitors, and the great lady's to the itinerant prophet (Gen 18:1–8; 2 Kgs 4:8–11).[2] Gehazi's first remark — "she has no son, and her husband is old [*wěʾîšāh zāqēn*]" (2 Kgs 4:14) — recalls Sarah's response to the annunciation of Isaac's conception: "And Sarah laughed to herself, saying, 'Now that I am withered, am I to have fertility—with my husband so old [*wa'dōnî zāqēn*]?'" (Gen 18:12).³ It is unclear whether Sarah's laugh is born of joy or of disbelief, but in the narrative of Genesis 18, the LORD takes it as the latter:

> ¹³Then the LORD said to Abraham, "Why did Sarah laugh, saying, 'Shall I in truth bear a child, old as I am?' ¹⁴Is anything too wondrous for the LORD? I will return to you next year [*kā'ēt ḥayyâ*], and Sarah shall have a son." (Gen 18:13–14)⁴

And in 2 Kings 4, too, the response of the mother-to-be to the announcement of her impending pregnancy is one of disbelief: "She replied, 'Please my Lord, man of God, do not delude your maidservant'" (v 16; cf. v 28). In each case, the mother's incredulity communicates the unnaturalness of what is about to take place—Sarah's conception of Isaac or that of the Shunammite boy (Gen 18:13–14; 2 Kgs 4:28) and the resurrection of the latter from death (2 Kgs 4:34–36).

Living, as we do, in an age that has seen great advancements in the treatment of infertility, we are, of course, inclined to place these events in categories completely different from those of the ancients. The birth of a first child to a childless couple (one or both of whom is old or has always been infertile, to boot) is surely a cause for joy and wonder, we are likely to say, but not an impossibility like the resurrection of a dead person. But the placement of the Shunammite woman's objections suggests that, at least to the author of 2 Kings 4, the two unlikely events were much closer in kind than they appear to us, perhaps even identical. Both the birth of a child to an infertile couple and the resurrection of a dead person testify to the triumph of the wonder-working God (and the validity of his wonder-working prophet, the "man of God") over the cruel course of nature. Each is a humanly inexplicable reversal of the seemingly inevitable sequence of events whose last word is death. Each represents a victory of life over death.

The possibility that Genesis 18 and 2 Kings 4 stand in a genetic relationship is enhanced by the use of the rare and enigmatic construction *kā'ēt ḥayyâ* ("next year") in the two stories. In fact, the term occurs in these texts *alone,* twice in each chapter (Gen 18:10, 14; 2 Kgs 4:16, 17). Robert L. Cohn astutely points out an additional connection in the arrangement of the physical space in which the two annunciation scenes take place. Both Sarah and the Shunammite are standing at an "entrance" or "doorway" (*petaḥ*) when the unbelievable good news comes (Gen 18:10; 2 Kings 4:15).⁵ The unnamed son of the Shunammite woman and her aged husband thus becomes a kind of Isaac redivivus, the promised heir of an otherwise amazingly fortunate couple whom infertility has tragically deprived of a future that extends beyond their individual lives. If so, then the death and resurrection of the unnamed son correspond markedly to the near sacrifice of Isaac (the event known in Jewish tradition as the *aqedah*, or "binding"). Isaac's death is not reversed by a miracle-working prophet, to be sure, but it is miraculously averted by a heavenly being's dramatic intervention.[6] As the messenger of the glad tidings, the "angel of the LORD" (Gen 22:11, 15) is the equivalent of the "man of God" (2 Kgs 4:9, et al.). The former averts a death, the latter reverses a death, but each acts to guarantee that the couple's line survives and that they have descendants, which is to say, continuation after their individual deaths.

In the rabbinic lectionary as it has come down in the Ashkenazic tradition, 2 Kgs 4:1–37 is the prophetic complement (*haftarah*) to the Torah portion that extends from Genesis 18 through 22 (*pārāšat wayyērā'*). It thus corresponds to the section of the Pentateuch that recounts the events with which we have been comparing it, from the annunciation of Isaac's miraculous conception to his equally miraculous rescue from death at the hands of his ever-obedient father.[7] In both the Torah portion and its accompanying *haftarah*, a family confronts two threats to its continuation — sterility and death — and in each case God reverses the ostensibly hopeless situation, defeating the forces of annihilation and granting a future to a lineage that had seemed doomed. The two threats appear very different to us, to be sure, for the Shunammite boy's resurrection seems more miraculous than the sparing of Isaac. Perhaps it seemed so to the ancient audience as well, but it is doubtful that the author of 2 Kgs 4:8–37, if he indeed knew of Genesis 18 and 22, sought to heighten its effect by adding resurrection to birth on the register of miracles. More likely, he wrote his story with that of Isaac in mind, only in the framework of a new institution characteristic of his own time and place, the wonder-working prophet (*'îš 'ĕlōhîm*). The latter, and not God directly or an angel, is the instrument by which God's unlikely promise of life comes about — whether in the face of death or after death. The point is not resurrection per se; it is the mastery of God and his prophet over the death-dealing power of nature.

There is, however, another, more noteworthy difference between Genesis 22 and 2 Kgs 4:8–37. Whereas the binding of Isaac ends with Abraham's return to Beersheba (Gen 22:19), the story of the Shunammite woman ends when, Elisha having worked his resurrection, "She came and fell at his feet and bowed low to the ground; then she picked up her son and left" (2 Kgs 4:37). The aqedah, in other words, terminates with the return of Abraham from his last trial; no mention is made of the boy's mother. Indeed, the original promise of offspring to Abram, which Genesis 22 unmistakably reflects,[8] had never designated any given woman as the matriarch of the "great nation" to stem from him (Gen 12:2–3; cf. 13:14–17; 15:1–6). Sarai's offer of her bondswoman Hagar as a surrogate mother, occasioned by her own sterility (16:1–2), thus violated no aspect of the Abrahamic promise. And God's subsequent annunciation of Isaac's birth by Sarah (to which Sarai's name had been changed) is, as we have remarked, an extraordinary intervention. As such, it elicits laughter from each of the aged parents-to-be (17:17; 18:12).

There is an interesting pattern in the doubled rescue of Abraham and Sarah from the oblivion with which, first, their collective childlessness and, second, their new loss of Isaac threatens them. Preceding both the annunciation of the promised son's conception in Genesis 17–18 and his rescue from death in chapter 22 are stories of Hagar's near loss of her own son—the aqedah of Ishmael, so to speak.[9] In Genesis 16, the slave woman, pregnant with Abraham's first son, flees into the wilderness in hopes of escaping her resentful mistress Sarai's oppression. The hopes, alas, fail, and an angel sends Hagar back to further mistreatment—only with the crucial qualification that she, too, will fall heir to the Abrahamic promise of innumerable progeny and shall bear a powerful son whose very name (meaning "God heeded") testifies to her rescue (vv 9–11). In the variant in Genesis 21, a much more developed and powerfully narrated version, Ishmael undergoes his own aqedah in a more intense way, driven into the wilderness by Sarah's jealousy and God's instruction to Abraham to obey his wife. The rub is that the patriarch has, oddly, ill equipped his secondary wife and infant son (as he is characterized in this text), giving them only "some bread and a skin of water" to sustain them in the desert until they reached their unspecified destination (vv 9–14).

Predictably, the water ran out, and the mother, putting her baby under a bush, "sat down at a distance, a bowshot away; for she thought, 'Let me not look on as the child dies'" and then "burst into tears." Unpredictably—unless, of course, one remembers that Israel's God is no less renowned for rescuing from death than from childlessness[10]—an angel intervenes, announces that "God has heeded the cry of the boy where he is" (vv 16–17) and re-presents the promised son, now delivered from death, to his mother:

> [18]"Come, lift up the boy and hold him by the hand, for I will make a great nation of him." [19]Then God opened her eyes and she saw a well of water. She went and filled the skin with water, and let the boy drink. (Gen 21:18–19)

"Come, lift up the boy" (*qûmî śĕ'î 'et-hanna'ar*) is highly reminiscent of Elisha's parting charge to the Shunammite woman, "Pick up your son" (*śĕ'î bĕnēk*, 2 Kgs 4:36), which in turn reflects her husband's order to the servant when the boy was first stricken, "Carry him to his mother" (*śā'ēhû 'el-'immô*, v 19). The presentation of the revived child to his grieving mother—whether recovered from lethal dehydration like Ishmael or literally resurrected from the dead like the unnamed Shunammite boy — underscores the intimate connection between birth and revival. Or, to state the converse, it draws our attention again both to the connection between the infertility that, in different ways, accounts for each son's birth, and to the death that threatens to rob each mother of her promised child, proving God's word and his reputation for deliverance unreliable and dashing her hopes for continuation beyond her own time.

The placement of the story of Elisha in Shunem in its current literary location sheds further light on the deeper dynamics of life and death that the story unfolds. The tale abuts two stories of miraculous feedings. In the first (2 Kgs 4:1–7), a widow of "one of the disciples of the prophets" has become impoverished, and a creditor is about to seize her two sons as debt slaves. In response, Elisha miraculously manages to fill every vessel in sight with oil, and when the oil has stopped, he instructs her, "Go sell the oil and pay your debt, and you and your children can live on the rest."

The parallels of this brief miracle story with the ensuing story of the childless couple are patent, though at times the relationship is inverted. Whereas Elisha in the first little tale produces food for an impoverished woman, at the beginning of the longer story that follows, a wealthy woman produces food for the prophet (2 Kgs 4:8). Whereas in the first narrative the woman has children but no husband or food, in the second she has husband and food but no children, and this, too, calls for a remedy. In the opening tale, the widow is about to lose her two sons, but Elisha averts this and proclaims that she and they now have the means to "live" (*ḥyh*). In the sequel, Elisha gives the wealthy lady of Shunem one son twice, first by curing her infertility and then by resurrecting the child she has borne and lost. In each case, the survival of the family is threatened, in the first by poverty and enslavement, in the second by sterility and death. And in each case the prophet steps into the breach to ensure that mother and children stay together, that the integrity and continuity of the family be preserved.

By prefacing the story of the childless couple of Shunem with the tale of the destitute widow, the author or redactor of 2 Kings 4 has done more than simply enhance our appreciation of the dynamics of the latter story that we have just mentioned. He has also connected the tale with more distant texts (whether intentionally or not) in ways that further illuminate the underlying concepts of life and death. For to the astute reader of the Bible, the widow's fear that she will lose her two sons cannot but recall other mothers who faced similar threats — Eve, for example, who loses Abel to murder and Cain to exile, and Rebecca, who tells Jacob to flee from Esau's murderous revenge: "Let me not lose you both in one day" (Gen 4:1–16; 27:45).

But the particular conditions that motivate the action, poverty (which in that cultural context means lack of food) and enslavement, suggest that the closest analogy actually lies with events later in Jacob's life, specifically with the famine that takes his sons to Egypt. When Joseph demands that Simeon be held as a hostage until Jacob releases his beloved son Joseph's only full brother, Benjamin, the thematic commonalities become even more striking:

> ³⁶Their father Jacob said to them, "It is always me that you bereave: Joseph is no more and Simeon is no more, and now you would take away Benjamin. These things always happen to me!" ³⁷Then Reuben said to his father, "You may kill my two sons if I do not bring him back to you. Put him in my care, and I will return him to you." ³⁸But he said, "My son must not go down with you, for his brother is dead and he alone is left. If he meets with disaster on the journey you are taking, you will send my white head down to Sheol in grief." (Gen 42:36–38)

It is finally Judah—having already lost two sons of his own, making his daughter-in-law a double widow (Gen 38:6–11)—who, as the famine worsens, secures Benjamin's release from his doting father's grasp (Gen 43:1–14).[11]

In sum, the seven-verse narrative of Elisha and the impoverished widow in 2 Kgs 4:1–7 encapsulates in the context of one little family the dynamics of life and death that engulf the entire nation—itself represented as a man and his twelve sons—in Genesis. Seen in this light, the movement in 2 Kings 4 from the widow's tale to the events in Shunem takes on added resonance. For with it, the threat to familial survival moves from enslavement to infertility to death, and that is also the movement that underlies Pharaoh's assaults upon Israel in Exodus 1.[12] First, the tyrant reduces the special nation to slavery, setting taskmasters over them and putting them to work on the royal store cities. When that fails, he instructs the midwives to destroy all male babies—a decree that, given the patrilineal assumptions of the time, ensures that in another generation no Israelite children will be born and the troublesome nation will become extinct. Finally, the midwives having defied the king's command, Pharaoh orders the boys thrown into the Nile, so that only the girls will live (vv 8–22). As in 2 Kings 4, so in Exodus 1 enslavement has escalated into death. And in Exodus, as in Kings, though the suffering is real and no justification for it is offered, God yet triumphs over it. Neither slavery nor death has the last word.

Now let us turn our attention to the little story that follows the tale of Elisha's resurrection (2 Kgs 4:38–41). Like the more developed tale that precedes it, this one, too, deals with a famine and the prophet's miraculous remedy for it. In this case, the prophet instructs his servant to make a stew, which, given the slim pickings, happened to include as a prime ingredient the gourds of a wild vine. The effect is literally deadly:

> ⁴⁰While they were still eating of the stew, they began to cry out: "O man of God, there is death in the pot!" And they could not eat it. ⁴¹"Fetch some flour," [Elisha] said. He threw it into the pot and said, "Serve it to the people and let them eat." And there was no longer anything harmful in the pot. (2 Kgs 4:40–41)

The odd locution "there is death [*māwet*] in the pot!" connects this little tale of a mere four verses to the longer story of resurrection that it follows. Just as Elisha reversed the death of the Shunammite's son, so does he instantaneously provide an antidote for the poisonous gourds. How, precisely, flour was able to counteract the toxin is unknown; this, too, is probably intended to be viewed as a miracle. Indeed, the very fact that there was flour to be had at all in a time of famine, when the disciples of the prophets were reduced to foraging for foodstuffs, is most likely intended as another example of the prophet's supernatural gifts. The display of those gifts is, in fact, the unifying theme of the entire chapter. Seen in this light, the tale of the resurrection of the Shunammite boy is not only the longest story in the chapter; it also constitutes a refocusing of the theme of the prophet's powers more specifically on the power to reverse death.

Finally, we must deal with the fourth little tale in 2 Kings 4, which brings to a close the chapter that focuses on the story of the resurrection of the Shunammite couple's promised son. Here Elisha proves able to feed a hundred people with but twenty loaves of bread (2 Kgs 4:42–44). Like Sarah and the Shunammite lady, his attendant is skeptical: "How can I set this before a hundred men?" But the prophet, who sees the situation from the divine and not the natural perspective, is adamant: "Give it to the people and let them eat. For thus said the LORD: They shall eat and have some left over." And "as the LORD had said," so it was.

Here, in this shortest narrative of 2 Kings 4, we see the familiar theme that has dominated the previous tales of the chapter, menacing shortage and miraculous provision. The development over the course of the chapter is revealing and suggests connections to the story of the people Israel that dominates the Hebrew Bible. The first tale, of the widow in debt, takes place in the context of a humble nuclear family: a woman without a husband is about to lose her two sons to a creditor. The second tale, the long narrative about Elisha in Shunem, also takes place in the context of family, though one of considerable means: a couple living on their estate without a son lose and then recover the boy with whom God wondrously graces them. The third story, about the lethal stew, takes place in a larger grouping, the prophet and his disciples. This group serves as the prophet's family: Elisha, like his predecessor Elijah and unlike other prophets, seems to have neither wife nor children. Note that his "disciples" are literally "sons of the prophets" (*bĕnê hannĕbî'im*, 2 Kgs 4:38). If so, of course, it is not a natural family but, as it were, a supernatural one, a family founded on the charisma of the master and his ability to provide for his disciples. Finally, in this last tale, the miraculous feeding of the "people" (*'am*, 2 Kgs 4:42–43), we sense the rescue of a larger group, neither a nuclear family nor a prophetic brotherhood but some other "people," whose life depends on the prophet's divine powers to overcome shortage and deliver them from impending starvation.[13] In this, the incident reminds us of the reason given in Deuteronomy for another miraculous provision of food, the manna, supplied "in order to teach you that man does not live on bread alone, but that man may live on anything the LORD decrees" (Deut 8:3). That 2 Kgs 4:42–44, considered as a self-contained narrative, anticipates this more national understanding of the miraculous deliverance from starvation is properly open to doubt. The idea makes eminent sense, however, when the narrative is placed in the larger canon of the Hebrew Bible.

The major threats to well-being in all these tales in 2 Kings 4 — enslavement, infertility, death, and starvation — are, as we have seen, deeply interconnected in biblical narratives with a national focus as well. It is especially instructive that these include the narratives of the birth of the *'am*, the people par excellence Israel, in Genesis. In each of these four narratives, the theological point is the same: God's power to reverse life-threatening adversity is uncanny and absolute, and some of it has been committed into the keeping of a wonder-working prophet.[14] To us, who have seen enslavement, famine, and infertility overcome but no one resurrected, the story of the restoration of the dead boy seems to fall into a category different from that of the other miracles in 2 Kings 4. But there is no reason to think the original audience or readership thought it did, and much reason to believe they saw all these threats to well-being as equally capable of reversal at the hands of a "man of God." Resurrection in 2 Kings 4 is indeed a miracle, but it is precisely the capacity to perform miracles that defines the "man of God," and it is by the miracles of God that the ever-dying, ever-reviving people of Israel lives.

The differences between the striking tale of the resurrection of the Shunammite's son in 2 Kings 4 and the resurrection of the dead as envisioned in Second Temple and rabbinic Judaism must not be minimized. The former is a specific episode of limited scope; its subtle and manifold resonances with the larger story of Israel do not suggest (at least not directly) a context of national restoration, a key ingredient in the Jewish expectation of resurrection. Even less does the tale in 2 Kings 4 imply a worldwide judgment and rectification of injustice. There is, to be sure, a sense that the couple eventually graced with the unexpected child deserved better than their lot in life. They lacked a child, and thus a future beyond their own lifetimes, and the prophet was to some degree repaying them for their hospitality and their generosity to him and, by implication, to the God who sent him. But the two miracles he wrought for them cannot be construed as a moral judgment on their whole lives, and, even were such the case, there is no contrasting judgment against those whose moral records fall short. And, of course, there is every reason to believe that the child whom Elisha resurrects will eventually die a second and irreversible death, unlike those awakened to "eternal life" in Dan 12:2, for example. In short, 2 Kgs 4:8–37 altogether lacks the apocalyptic framework out of which the classic Jewish doctrine grows.

There is, nonetheless, a lesson to be learned from this tale about the expectation of resurrection that will first appear much later. It is simply that long before the apocalyptic framework came into existence, the resurrection of the dead was thought possible—not according to nature, of course, but through the miraculous intervention of the living God. In the arresting little tale about Elisha at Shunem, we see again the collision of the LORD's power to rescue those faithful to him with the hard fact of human mortality, and, significantly, it is again the LORD's power to rescue that triumphs.[15] In the apocalyptic expectation of a general resurrection of the dead at the end of history, the experience of deliverance of the Shunammite couple will become general and irreversible. But some of the lineaments of that new expectation can already be detected when the man of God performs a resurrection in 2 Kings 4.

"Death — Be Broken!"

He will destroy death forever.
My Lord GOD *will wipe the tears away*
From all faces
And will put an end to the reproach of His people
Over all the earth —
For it is the LORD *who has spoken.*
                                        — Isaiah 25:8

We have uncovered a widespread biblical pattern centering on the loss
and restoration of a child, including in one prominent variant the loss of the
very possibility of children because of sterility.[1] The pattern is probably most
familiar from the book of Genesis, since this is the first and best-known narrative book in the Hebrew Bible. There it can first be detected as early as the
story of Adam and Eve, who lose Abel to murder and Cain to exile but gain a
replacement for the former through the birth of Seth (Gen 4:1–16, 25–26). It
is more prominent and much more developed in the tales of Abraham and
Sarah, who struggle with years of infertility that is healed through the same
God who then orders their promised son sacrificially immolated — yet relents
in the nick of time (Gen 11:26–22:18). In still another variant, the pattern of
the near loss and recovery of the child envelops the figure of Hagar, who is

expelled into the desert by her jealous mistress (with the consent of their common husband—and of their God), gives up hope that her infant son can survive, and yet revives him in response to the unexpected intervention of the angel of God (Gen 21:9–21; cf. 16:1–16). Indeed, the pattern of infertility and the loss and recovery of children affects each of the last two patriarchal generations as well, not to mention Judah in the next.[2] But we have also established that the pattern is not restricted to the generations of the first fathers and mothers of Israel. It has much wider resonance and can be found in high relief in the books of Ruth and Job, for instance, as well as in the tales of the wonder-working prophets, the "men of God," of the northern kingdom, Elijah and Elisha. In one of the latter narratives, the story of the Shunammite couple in 2 Kgs 4:8–37, examined in the previous chapter, we saw that the connection of the gift of fertility with the resurrection from the dead is particularly pointed. It occurs in a context that strongly suggests that the great themes of famine and enslavement in Genesis and Exodus belong to the same cluster of ideas.

The wide distribution and striking prominence of the theme of the recovery of the lost child, or the opening of the infertile womb, in the Hebrew Bible tempts us to see in it both a telling characteristic of ancient Israel's self-conception and a point that distinguishes Israel from the nations around her. We must, however, distinguish these two things carefully, for if we do not, all kinds of false claims of distinctiveness will result.[3] It must not be forgotten that a feature can be highly characteristic of a given culture and enormously influential within it but also and simultaneously widespread in the larger world and, thus, in no way unique to any one setting. In the case of the pattern under discussion, the affinities of the Israelite materials with those of ancient Canaan are striking and argue for its deep rooting in the prebiblical Levant. A brief examination of the most immediate parallels throws welcome light on the biblical examples.

One thinks first of two compositions from Ugarit, a Late Bronze Age Canaanite city-state whose literary remains, written in alphabetic cuneiform, shed powerful light on Israelite language and religion. One fragmentary composition, the Story (or Epic) of Kirta, begins with the household of the king by that name in ruins.[4] For the king's rightful wife has disappeared (probably through death), and, what is worse, his descendants have died off in a succession of calamities, some from illness, others at the hands of the plague god (Rashap), still others by the sword or by means of less decipherable but no less fatal disasters. Just as all seems lost, however, the god El (a name employed, significantly, to denote the Israelite deity YHWH as well)[5] appears to Kirta in a dream and offers the bereft monarch a way forward. He instructs him to offer sacrifices and commit to all-out war in pursuit of Lady Hurriya, daughter of Pabil, king of Udm, a city-state seven days' march away. Kirta complies with and even exceeds his divinely revealed instructions. For en route he vows to give great amounts of precious metals to the goddess Asherah, should his life-or-death mission prove successful. It does indeed, and El, taking a goblet in hand, pronounces a blessing over his faithful servant Kirta:

> Kirta, you have taken a wife,
>> you have taken a wife into your house,
>> you have brought a maiden into your court.
> She will bear you seven sons,
>> she will produce eight for you.[6]

And indeed she does:

> Then, after seven years,
>> the sons of Kirta were as many as had been promised;
>> so too were the daughters of Hurriya.[7]

No sooner does Kirta regain his future than a cloud comes over it. For the victorious king, having neglected his vow to Asherah, soon falls deathly ill. In fact, one of his sons is heard to say within earshot of Kirta:

> Our father, we were glad while you seemed to live forever,
>> we rejoiced at your immortality;
> As a dog is removed from your house,
>> a hound from your court,
>> so you too, father, must die like a mortal,
>> and your court become a place of mourning.[8]

The effect on his realm of the king's apparently terminal illness is nothing less than catastrophic: food, wine, and oil give out, and famine worsens. When all the subordinate deities repeatedly prove unable to answer El's question — "Who among the gods can expel illness, / drive out the disease?" — "El the kind, the compassionate" acts on his own, pronouncing an execration on death itself:

> Death — be broken!
>> Shataqat — be strong![9]

And so it is. Death is broken, Shataqat, a goddess of healing, grows strong, and Kirta ascends his throne anew. How the tale ends, however, we do not know, given the fragmentary character of the text. The ending we have speaks of a challenge to Kirta on the part of one of his sons — remarkably reminiscent of Absalom's revolt against his father David (2 Samuel 15) — and Kirta's cursing of his upstart heir.

Given the geographic proximity of Ugarit to ancient Israel, and the close relationship of the Ugaritic language to biblical Hebrew, it is not surprising that a composition like the Story of Kirta should so thoroughly and frequently recall a wide assortment of biblical texts. Leaving aside the fragmentary account of the prince's attempts to supplant his aging father at the end of our preserved text, the overall theme of the composition is strikingly pertinent to the topic of our investigation. For the Story of Kirta is, in the last analysis, the story of how "Death [was] broken" — broken, that is, at the command of the kind and compassionate father god, El. To be sure, death in our modern sense of the word had not yet stricken Kirta; the king, though ailing, was still alive. But death in the ancient Near Eastern understanding, death in the sense of a preternatural power that saps vitality and destroys the capacity for human flourishing, has been at work from the start of the tale.[10] Its first appearance (again given the fragmentary character of the tablets) comes with the literal death of Kirta's wife and children. In this, as is often remarked, we find a parallel to Job, who loses his children and, like Kirta later in the tale, is himself grievously stricken with disease, to boot. But Kirta's loss of his rightful wife also recalls Ruth's loss of Mahlon and Naomi's loss of both her husband and her two sons — in short, the loss (to put it in the native Israelite understanding) of all reasonable expectation for the continuation of the individual's identity after his or her personal death. Kirta's quest for a wife also suggests, in a different way, the barrenness of Sarai, the patriarch-to-be Abram's rightful wife. The Canaanite king's campaign to win Lady Hurriya in order to restart his household and refound his dynasty recalls Abram's marriage to Hagar in the face of his continued childlessness and the challenge this poses to YHWH's covenantal pledge that Abraham shall father a great nation.

The story of Kirta, in sum, is about the loss and recovery of family, about the loss and restoration of children, the healing of terminal illness, the consequent reversal of famine and renewal of foodstuffs — in a word, about how death was broken. It was broken through the intervention of a kind and gracious god who provided a new family to his faithful servant/son and who rescued him from fatal illness and his realm from starvation.

A similar dynamic underlies the Ugaritic poem that has come to be known as *Aqhat*.[11] The opening scene of this story shows a man named Danel[12] engaged in a rite of incubation, followed by six days of sacrifices. The objective soon becomes clear when, on the seventh and climactic day, the god Baal addresses the divine assembly:

> Danel . . . is unhappy . . .
>> he has no son, but his brothers do,
>> no heir, like his cousins;
> unlike his brothers, he has no son,
>> nor an heir, like his cousins. . . .
> So, my father, El the Bull, won't you bless him?
>> Creator of All, won't you show him favor?
> Let him have a son in his home,
>> a descendant inside his palace. . . .[13]

El, the supreme god, obliges, blessing Danel, curing him and his wife of whatever it was that impeded their having the son they so desired:

> Let him go up to his bed:
> when he kisses his wife she'll become pregnant;
>> when he embraces her she'll conceive;
> she will become pregnant, she will give birth, she will conceive;
> and there will be a son in his house,
>> an heir inside his palace. . . .[14]

And indeed, so it is: Lady Danataya gives birth to the promised son, Aqhat the Hero. Soon the craftsman god presents Danel with a special bow and arrows, which the fortunate father gives to his son.

Then the complication comes, one reminiscent of the problem that Asherah brings about for Kirta. When the goddess Anat asks for the bow and arrows, promising young Aqhat exorbitant gifts in exchange — silver, gold, even eternal life — Aqhat refuses her offer, and what is worse, he even mocks her proposal:

> Don't lie to me, Virgin,
>> for with a hero your lies are wasted.
> A mortal — what does he get in the end?
>> What does a mortal finally get? . . .
>
> As every man dies, I will die;
>> yes, I too will surely die.
> And I have something else to tell you:
> bows are for men!
>> Do women ever hunt?[15]

Enraged, the goddess stomps off to the abode of El, threatening even the Creator of All, and soon we see her instructing her henchman Yatpan to assist her in killing the promised son. And so, amid a flock of vultures, Anat and Yatpan swoop down upon Aqhat, pecking his skull until he bleeds to death:

> [Yatpan] struck him twice on the skull,
> > three times over the ear;
> he made his blood run like a slaughterer,
> > run to his knees like a butcher.
> His breath left him like wind,
> > his spirit like a breeze,
> > like smoke from his nostrils. . . .[16]

The long-awaited son, the heir that El promised and provided, is dead. The devout Danel is once again childless.

Though his daughter Pagat, sighting the swooping vultures, senses what has happened, Danel is not informed immediately. Still, Pagat rends her father's clothes in a gesture of mourning, and Danel

> cursed the clouds in the still heat,
> > the rain of the clouds which falls in summer,
> > the dew which drops on the grapes:
> "For seven years let Baal fail,
> > eight, the Rider of the Clouds:
> no dew, no showers,
> > no surging of the two seas,
> > no benefit of Baal's voice.
> For the clothes of Danel . . . have been torn. . . ."[17]

Shattered by the news of his son's death when it does come, the grieving father curses the vultures above, one after another, and, when the god Baal obliges and fells the birds, he inspects the gizzards, but "there was no fat, there was no bone." Finally, however, the fat and bone of his beloved son do appear in the gizzard of "Samal, the mother of the vultures," and weeping, Danel buries the remains of his slain son.

But in *Aqhat,* as in the biblical parallels, tragedy is not the last word. First, Danel curses the vultures again, "if they fly over my son's grave / and wake him from his sleep."[18] Then he pronounces woe upon the cities near which Aqhat was killed. Seven years of national mourning come to an end when Pagat offers to avenge her brother's murder. Danel accepts:

> "Pagat, you will restore my life. . . .
> I will truly live again
> when you have killed your brother's killer,
> put an end to whoever put an end to your mother's son."[19]

As in the case of Jacob (Gen 37:29–35; 44:30–31), here the father's vitality is intimately and inextricably tied with his son's. Whether, as in the case of

Jacob, the father also receives his son anew is, unfortunately, impossible to know, given the fragmentary character of the third tablet of *Aqhat,* the last that has been found. What we do know is that Pagat straps a sword under her feminine garb, arrives at Yatpan's tent, and in a manner reminiscent of Jael in Judges (Judg 4:17–22; 5:24–27) gives him drinks. On the basis of that analogy, and also the much later example of Judith with the drunken Holofernes, whom she beheads (Jdt 12:10–13:10), we can hazard a reasonable speculation. The likelihood is that Pagat did in her brother's killer, thus restoring her family's honor and the condition of justice that Anat and Yatpan had upset by their murder of Aqhat.

Even if this is so, it still remains unclear whether Pagat succeeded as well in reviving her slain brother, in performing, that is, a resurrection somewhat in the manner of Elisha when he raised the Shunammite lady's dead son (2 Kgs 4:8–37). It may be that she did not and Danel (if the tale had a happy ending at all) attained his restoration simply by dint of the vindication of his son's murder. Weighty considerations, however, speak against this. For one, were this the dénouement, Danel would return to the condition in which we meet him when the tale begins, childless and thus lacking one of the indispensable elements in the good life: someone, as the first tablet tells us repeatedly, to set up a stele, "free his spirit from the earth, / guard his footstep from the Slime," crush rebels, assist him when he is drunk, eat his sacrificial offerings, patch his roof, or wash his clothes — the tasks, apparently, of a dutiful Canaanite son.[20] Moreover, from the standpoint of Ugaritic theology, it is surely problematic that Anat's rage and vindictiveness should trump El's kindness and compassion in granting the childless Danel and Danataya a son. For whatever his limitations in comparison with the Israelite YHWH or still later concepts of God in the monotheistic traditions, El is the highest deity in the Ugaritic pantheon, the universal father and creator, and it is no coincidence that it is to him that Baal and Anat herself repair to present their petitions. That his gracious response was irreversibly thwarted seems unlikely.

It is conceivable, of course, that El's gracious intentions for his servant Danel came to fulfillment *after* Aqhat's death through the birth of another son and not through the resurrection of Aqhat himself — after the manner, that is, of Kirta, Job, Ruth, and Naomi, in marked contradistinction to that of the Shunammite couple. The imperfection of the analogy, however, speaks against this. For God never promised Kirta, Job, Ruth, and Naomi the children or spouses they lose, and those whom they *are* promised do not, in their respective stories, die. If Aqhat's death at the hands of Anat and Yatpan is final, Aqhat is, in this respect, unique among the promised sons. More likely, in a fulfillment of his devout father's prayers and a vindication of the great god El's reputation, Aqhat came back from the dead. If so, he (and his father) would more closely resemble another figure from the Hebrew Bible, the people Israel.

The full force of this analogy requires us to bear in mind the frequent assertion in the Hebrew Bible that Israel is the LORD's son. One thinks, for example, about the LORD's instruction to Moses when the latter returns to confront the Egyptian oppressor:

> ²²Then you shall say to Pharaoh, "Thus says the LORD: Israel is My first-born son. ²³I have said to you, 'Let My son go, that he may worship Me,' yet you refuse to let him go. Now I will slay your first-born son." (Exod 4:22–23)

Deuteronomy presents the consecration of the people Israel (with the key behavioral implication that they must avoid the practices of their neighbors) as filiation: "You are children [*bānîm*] of the LORD your God" (Deut 14:1–2). The ultimate origin of this formulation probably lies in tribal conceptions of the Deity as kinsman, but its resonance here in Deuteronomy is thoroughly covenantal in the diplomatic sense: the greater king (the suzerain) becomes the father of the lesser king (the vassal). The vassal must serve his liege lord, and the suzerain must rescue his faithful servant. Thus, Ahaz, a king of Judah in the eighth century B.C.E., sends this message to Tiglath-Pileser III, king of Assyria in a moment of dire threat: "I am your servant and your son; come and deliver me from the hands of the king of Aram and from the hands of the king of Israel, who are attacking me" (2 Kgs 16:7). The legal or diplomatic context, however, must not be allowed to blind us to the affective dimension of either the father's or the son's experience of sonship:[21]

> Truly, Ephraim is a dear son to Me,
> A child that is dandled!
> Whenever I have turned against him,
> My thoughts would dwell on him still.
> That is why My heart yearns for him;
> I will receive him back in love
>   — declares the LORD. (Jer 31:20).

Here, we come to an important difference between the Ugaritic poems that we have been examining and the biblical materials that they illumine. In the latter, YHWH is not only the loving father, grieving at the loss of his son (in whatever form and for whatever cause) and eager to welcome him back; he is also the benign and gracious God whose assistance is essential to bring him back. In other words, YHWH corresponds both to Kirta/Aqhat and to El. He is the bereft father and the omnipotent Deity who aids bereft fathers. In our next chapter, we shall see the way in which some relatively late biblical literature presents its vision of an imminent redemption of the people Israel in the image of the return of lost children and the restoration of the bereft parent. An important image in the Canaanite world long before the Israelite literature that came to make up the Hebrew Bible was written, it became even more important as an image of the restoration of Israel after death and destruction.

9

The Widow Re-Wed, Her Children Restored

He sets the childless woman among her household
  as a happy mother of children.
  — Psalm 113:9

Probably the greatest assault on Israel's existence in biblical times was
the Babylonian capture of Jerusalem in 586 B.C.E., which resulted in the torch-
ing of the Temple (Yhwh's own house), the overthrow of the House of David,
and the exile of a significant segment of the populace of the southern kingdom,
Judah (the northern kingdom, Israel, had fallen to the Assyrians about 135
years earlier). At the end of that exile nearly half a century later, as the Persian conquest of Babylonia and release of the Judahites loomed, an anonymous prophet (whom scholars call Second Isaiah because his writings have
been appended to the book of Isaiah) predicted the restoration of the people Israel to their ancestral land.[1] In soaring poetry, he strove mightily to
awaken their faith after the long years of misery and ostensible abandonment
by their God:

> [1]But now thus said the LORD —
> Who created you, O Jacob,
> Who formed you, O Israel:
> Fear not, for I will redeem you;
> I have singled you out by name,

You are Mine.
²When you pass through water,
I will be with you;
Through streams,
They shall not overwhelm you.
When you walk through fire,
You shall not be scorched;
Through flame,
It shall not burn you.
³For I the LORD am your God,
The Holy One of Israel, your Savior.
I give Egypt as a ransom for you,
Ethiopia and Saba in exchange for you.
⁴Because you are precious to Me,
And honored, and I love you,
I give men in exchange for you
And peoples in your stead.
⁵Fear not, for I am with you:
I will bring your folk from the East,
Will gather you out of the West;
⁶I will say to the North, "Give back!"
And to the South, "Do not withhold!
Bring My sons from afar,
And My daughters from the end of the earth —
⁷All who are linked to My name,
Whom I have created,
Formed, and made for My glory —
⁸Setting free that people,
Blind though it has eyes
And deaf though it has ears." (Isa 43:1–8)

In this oracle, the prophet brings major themes of Israel's miraculous origins and continuing divine promise together with breathtaking concision and poetic power—their origin in the man Jacob/Israel, the LORD's special relationship with them, and his protection of them in life-threatening waters, probably a recollection of the exodus (cf. Exodus 14). As usual with Second Isaiah, the past is prologue, and the ancient paradigm of redemption serves as a model for what the LORD — whose love for Israel perdures despite all (v 4) — is about to do again. At the center of this new redemption, however, lies an element unprecedented in the exodus narrative but well known, as we have seen, from Genesis and 2 Kings 4 and from the Ugaritic literature before them: the return of the lost sons and daughters (v 6). When this occurs, the God of Israel plays the role of Job, Naomi, or, for that matter, King Kirta of the

Ugaritic poem known after his name. He becomes, so to speak, the parent who against all odds recovers his children and the promise for futurity and continuation that they represent.

Elsewhere, essentially the same image of redemption recalls most explicitly the patriarchal promise of posterity, as the desiccated nation of the exile comes back to life, renewing its dedication to the LORD and the service that goes with it.

> ¹But hear, now, O Jacob My servant,
> Israel whom I have chosen!
> ²Thus said the LORD, your Maker,
> Your Creator who has helped you since birth:
> Fear not, My servant Jacob,
> Jeshurun whom I have chosen,
> ³Even as I pour water on thirsty soil,
> And rain upon dry ground,
> So will I pour My spirit on your offspring,
> My blessing upon your posterity.
> ⁴And they shall sprout like grass,
> Like willows by watercourses.
> ⁵One shall say, "I am the LORD's,"
> Another shall use the name of "Jacob,"
> Another shall mark his arm "of the LORD"
> And adopt the name of "Israel." (Isa 44:1–5)
>
>   . . .
>
> ¹⁷Thus said the LORD your Redeemer,
> The Holy One of Israel:
> I the LORD am your God,
> Instructing you for your own benefit.
> Guiding you in the way you should go.
> ¹⁸If only you would heed My commands!
> Then your prosperity would be like a river,
> Your triumph like the waves of the sea.
> ¹⁹Your offspring would be as many as the sand,
> Their issue as many as its grains.
> Their name would never be cut off
> Or obliterated from before Me. (Isa 48:17–19)

Whatever the shape, oral or literary, of the patriarchal traditions to which our nameless prophet had access, the resonances of Genesis in his oracle are still remarkable. The divine blessing on the posterity (or "seed") of the chosen people about to leave Mesopotamia for Canaan recalls the initial oracles to

Abraham as he leaves his homeland, promising to make him a great nation, to bless him abundantly, and then, after he has entered Canaan, to give the land to his posterity or "seed" (Isa 44:3; Gen 12:1–7). Similarly, the promise that "Your offspring would be many as the sand" recalls the LORD's promise to Abraham to "make your offspring as the dust of the earth, so that if one can count the dust of the earth, then your offspring too can be counted" (Isa 48:19; Gen 13:16). But it resembles still more closely the divine promise to his grandson Jacob, eponymous ancestor of the nation, to "make your offspring as the sands of the sea, which are too numerous to count" (Gen 32:13). And the identification of the LORD as Jacob's "Creator . . . since birth" (literally, "from the belly") in Isa 44:2 doubtless derives from the tradition that God had already designated Jacob for greatness in utero (Gen 25:21–23). The revitalization of the downtrodden and despondent people is clearly patterned on the old legends of their having come into being against all odds, historical and natural. Given the social-familial construction of personal identity in ancient Israel that we explored in chapter 6, it is hardly surprising that Israel's renewal or restoration is here phrased in ways that suggest fertility and birth. For fertility and birth constitute the prime model of renewal in ancient Israel, whose literature often affirms that their supernatural mandate depended upon natural replenishment of the lost individuals and that supernatural redemption inevitably involved natural increase.

Alongside the similarities to the patriarchal narratives of Genesis, these images in Second Isaiah exhibit differences that are critical to understanding the exilic and postexilic appropriation of the ancient story of natural origins. We have just examined one nuance of difference in that appropriation, the identification of the community addressed with the patriarch in his anguish, when the promise is still unfulfilled and the existence of the promised great nation still lies in the future. This is not Jacob/Israel in triumph, his hearty brood of tribal ancestors-to-be gathered about him, but Jacob/Israel in distress and fear, comforted with a mere promise of faithful and dedicated posterity yet to be (Isa 44:1–5).

But a more daring appropriation involves a concentration not on the patriarchs (though that endures) but on their barren or bereaved wives:

> [1]Shout, O barren one,
> You who bore no child!
> Shout aloud for joy,
> You who did not travail!
> For the children of the wife forlorn
> Shall outnumber those of the espoused
> — said the LORD.

²Enlarge the site of your tent,
Extend the size of your dwelling,
Do not stint!
Lengthen the ropes, and drive the pegs firm.
³For you shall spread out to the right and the left;
Your offspring shall dispossess nations
And shall people the desolate towns.

⁴Fear not, you shall not be shamed;
Do not cringe, you shall not be disgraced.
For you shall forget
The reproach of your youth,
And remember no more
The shame of your widowhood.
⁵For He who made you will espouse you —
His name is "LORD of Hosts."
The Holy One of Israel will redeem you —
He is called "God of all the Earth."

⁶The LORD has called you back
As a wife forlorn and forsaken.
Can one cast off the wife of his youth?
    — said your God.
⁷For a little while I forsook you,
But with vast love I will bring you back.
⁸In slight anger, for a moment,
I hid My face from you;
But with kindness everlasting
I will take you back in love
    — said the LORD your Redeemer.
⁹For this to Me is like the waters of Noah:
As I swore that the waters of Noah
Nevermore would flood the earth,
So I swear that I will not
Be angry with you or rebuke you.
¹⁰For the mountains may move
And the hills be shaken,
But My loyalty shall never move from you,
Nor My covenant of friendship be shaken
    — said the LORD, who takes you back in love. (Isa 54:1–10)²

The opening address to the "barren one" recalls Sarah's long period of infertility — according to Priestly tradition, she bore Isaac at ninety (Gen 17:17) — as

well as Rebecca's years of barrenness — twenty, according to the same source (Gen 25:20, 26b). But it especially brings to mind Jacob/Israel's more beloved wife Rachel's years of waiting in frustration until God finally opens her womb (Gen 30:1–8, 22–24). Like the text of Genesis itself, however, this oracle of restoration after exile does not make a triumphalistic identification of the nation with the preferred wife but rather offers consolation to the wife who is unloved or bereft. In particular, the prediction that "the children of the wife forlorn [or, desolated] / Shall outnumber those of the espoused" draws on the motif (if not the actual story) of Leah, Rachel's highly fertile older sister, whose very fertility is the LORD's compensation for her lesser appeal in the eyes of Jacob (Gen 29:31). More distantly, the oracle of Isa 54:1–10 brings to mind the story of Elkanah's barren wife Hannah who conceives Samuel at the LORD's initiative, but only after years of taunting by her fertile co-wife, Peninah (1 Sam 1:1–8, 19b–20). As in the case of Joseph, whom Rachel bears, so with Hannah it is the single child of the barren wife, not the many children of the fertile one, who brings about Israel's deliverance.

In this, the stories of Rachel and Hannah resemble the book of Ruth, at least in its current form, in which the child born to Ruth (and, by a legal fiction, to Naomi as well) is identified as the grandfather of David, the founder of the Judahite dynasty and the prototype of the national deliverer (Ruth 4:16–22; see also Mic 5:1–5). In these stories of the unexpected birth of the one who delivers Israel from affliction, we see the conjunction of personal and collective redemption in a particularly poignant statement. In the cases of Rachel and Hannah, two barren women find a personal fulfillment that proves to be the basis of national rescue as well. Rachel's longed-for son, Joseph, rescues Israel from death through famine, just as Samuel, the son for whom Hannah prayed and whom she vowed and dedicated to the LORD, rescues the nation from Philistine attack, among other things, restoring lost territory (1 Sam 7:5–14). And when Joseph has again disappeared — this time not in the form of one young man sold into slavery but as the northern tribes collectively carried into exile — a prophet envisions his mother at first distraught and then comforted:

> ¹⁵Thus said the LORD:
> A cry is heard in Ramah —
> Wailing, bitter weeping —
> Rachel weeping for her children.
> She refuses to be comforted
> For her children, who are gone.
> ¹⁶Thus said the LORD:
> Restrain your voice from weeping,

Your eyes from shedding tears;
For there is a reward for your labor
    —declares the LORD:
They shall return from the enemy's land.
¹⁷And there is hope for your future
    —declares the LORD:
Your children shall return to their country. (Jer 31:15–17)

Here it is the mother, at least as much as the son, in whom the national story is enacted. We are once again confronted with a tale of loss and mourning that gives way to return and restoration. Not surprisingly, therefore, the resonances of the Joseph story in this oracle in Jeremiah 31 are unmistakable. Like Jacob when he learns of Joseph's (apparent) death, Rachel "refuses to be comforted" (*mĕ'ănâ lĕhinnāḥēm*, Jer 31:15; cf. *waymā'ēn lĕhitnaḥēm* in Gen 37:35). Mention of her children "who are gone" recalls the evasive words of Joseph's brothers to him (whom they take for the pharaoh's vizier): "one is no more" (*'ēnennû*, Jer 31:15; Gen 42:13, 32). But in Jeremiah it is not Jacob who is pictured in deep, inconsolable mourning, nor is it his brothers who bear the painful consequence of the brother who "is no more." Rather, it is Rachel, the beloved but barren wife, who mourns for her lost children. And then, like Jacob in Genesis, she, too, receives them anew — after providence has wondrously intervened.

The reference to Noah and the great flood in Isa 54:9–10 ("For this is to Me like the waters of Noah . . .") frames this return of the lost children in the context of cosmic renewal.³ The death-dealing threat has passed, God's righteous anger is spent, and his covenantal love (*ḥesed*) now comes to the fore anew, never totally dislodged, never to be totally dislodged.

Other traditions lie in the background of the identification of the people Israel in its miserable demise and joyful restoration with an afflicted woman whose fortune unexpectedly turns for the better. One of these, of course, is the tradition, already old by the time of Jeremiah and Second Isaiah, which sees Israel as YHWH's wife and the relation between the special people and their God as erotic and marital in its essence.⁴ Probably the oldest attestation of this metaphor in Israelite literature is found in the first two chapters of the book of the eighth-century prophet Hosea. Here, the wife is at first unfaithful and gives birth to children whose ominous names communicate the termination of the marital relationship of YHWH and Israel, Lo-ruhamah ("Unloved, Unpitied") and Lo-ammi ("Not-My-People"). But then the corresponding positive names replace the negative ones, the children rebuke their wayward mother, and she, after a painful period of retribution and reorientation, is restored. YHWH, in fact, woos her tenderly anew, remarries her in righteousness, justice, goodness, and mercy — and this time for good. The result is that a covenant of cosmic peace comes into effect. In Hosea, the remarriage of YHWH and Israel signifies the redemption not just of the people Israel but of nature as well.

There is, however, an essential difference between the governing metaphor of Hosea 1–2 and the use of the motif of Israel as matriarch in Jeremiah and Second Isaiah that we have been examining. In Hosea, the sufferings of Israel as wife and mother are punitive. She deserves her fate because of her meretricious breach of covenant, and her rebetrothal to her divine husband signifies that she has learned her lesson, concluding, in her own words:

> I will go and return
> To my first husband,
> For then I fared better than now. (Hos 2:9)

In Jeremiah and Second Isaiah, on the other hand, the sufferings of Rachel, or of Israel itself, imagined as a barren wife or bereaved mother, are undeserved (or no longer deserved), and no new lesson is cited or resolution to repent given. Rather, this rebetrothal and these new births (or the return of the lost children) are closer in nature to the annunciation to the matriarchs of Genesis or to Hannah or the birth of Obed to Ruth and Naomi: they are an unexpected delight and/or a reward for faithful patience during the time of adversity about to come to a surprising end. This difference makes sense in light of the differing historical circumstance. Hosea prophesies *before* catastrophe, calling for return and renewal. Jeremiah and Second Isaiah prophesy *after* the exile (of the northern and southern tribes, respectively) and announce a new beginning, the rebirth of the deadened nation, the return of the lost children, an unbelievable renewal of national hope after a long and agonizing eclipse. In a word, they prophesy life in place of death.

Another source of the metaphor of the barren or bereaved wife as it appears in Second Isaiah comes from the conception of Zion, the Temple Mount in Jerusalem, as a woman, specifically a princess or matron who has fallen into contempt and ruin, as we find in a lament over its fall:

> Alas!
> Lonely sits the city
> Once great with people!
> She that was great among nations
> Is become like a widow;
> The princess among states
> Is become a thrall. (Lam 1:1)

The Temple Mount becomes a name for the sacred city, the holy see of YHWH, the ruler of the world, and the mountain and the city, in turn, become synonymous with the consecrated people that worship there — or once did — and for their fate in the tides of history:

> [14]Zion says,
> "The LORD has forsaken me,
> My Lord has forgotten me."
> [15]Can a woman forget her baby,
> Or disown the child of her womb?
> Though she might forget,
> I never could forget you.
> [16]See, I have engraved you
> On the palms of My hands,
> Your walls are ever before Me.
> [17]Swiftly your children are coming;
> Those who ravaged and ruined you shall leave you.
> [18]Look up all around you and see:
> They are all assembled, are come to you!
> As I live
>   — declares the LORD —
> You shall don them all like jewels,
> Deck yourself with them like a bride.
> [19]As for your ruins and desolate places
> And your land laid waste —
> You shall soon be crowded with settlers,
> While destroyers stay far from you.
> [20]The children you thought you had lost
> Shall yet say in your hearing,
> "The place is too crowded for me;
> Make room for me to settle."
> [21]And you will say to yourself,
> "Who bore these for me
> When I was bereaved and barren,
> Exiled and disdained —
> By whom, then, were these reared?
> I was left all alone —
> And where have these been?"
> [22]Thus said the Lord GOD:
> I will raise My hand to nations
> And lift up My ensign to peoples;
> And they shall bring your sons in their bosoms,

And carry your daughters on their backs.
²³Kings shall tend your children,
Their queens shall serve you as nurses.
They shall bow to you, face to the ground,
And lick the dust of your feet.
And you shall know that I am the LORD —
Those who trust in Me shall not be shamed.

²⁴Can spoil be taken from a warrior,
Or captives retrieved from a victor?
²⁵Yet thus said the LORD:
Captives shall be taken from a warrior
And spoil shall be retrieved from a tyrant;
For *I* will contend with your adversaries,
And *I* will deliver your children.
²⁶I will make your oppressors eat their own flesh,
They shall be drunk with their own blood as with wine.
And all mankind shall know
That I the LORD am your Savior,
The Mighty One of Jacob, your Redeemer. (Isa 49:14–26)

In this complex oracle, we find a particularly thick weave of the constituent elements of the tradition that we have been exploring — the perduring faithfulness of the God of Israel despite the reality of affliction (vv 14–16, 24–26), the rebetrothal of the disgraced woman (v 18), the return of the lost children (vv 17–20, 22–23), the unexpected birth of children to the forsaken and barren wife (v 21), the divine warrior's reliable rescue of his chosen family (vv 24–26), and — as befits an oracle to Zion — the reconstruction of ruins and the repopulation of the destroyed areas (v 19). Logically, of course, these metaphors are not all consistent one with the other, but strict logic cannot do justice to their surpassing poetic power. The common denominator is the reversal of fate for the better, the victory over the forces of death and destruction, and its corollary, the miraculous appearance of vitality where only recently sterility had held seemingly unassailable sway.[5] The rich interweaving of traditional metaphors for the relationship of God to his people is in the service of the deeper theme of Second Isaiah, God's stupendous revival and restoration of fallen Israel.

One aspect of that reversal of fate for the better is the reappearance of the vanished husband, without whom, of course, the lost children might return but their new replacements could never be born. Oracles like Isa 49:14–26 thus have more in common with "pagan" notions of sexuality than is often recognized. Though literal mating does not take place here, a metaphorical mating does, in the rendezvous of Israel's husband YHWH with the wife he has abandoned, which results in the return/birth of the desired progeny. Indeed, there is perhaps nothing more characteristic of the ancient Israelite vision of redemption than renewed fertility and new life — fertility where there had been sterility, life where there had been death.[6]

Why, precisely, had Israel's divine husband vanished? On occasion, Second Isaiah insists that one obvious possibility, divorce, is not the correct metaphor:

> Thus said the LORD:
> Where is the bill of divorce
> Of your mother whom I dismissed?
> And which of My creditors was it
> To whom I sold you off?
> You were only sold off for your sins,
> And your mother dismissed for your crimes.
> [2]Why, when I came, was no one there,
> Why, when I called, would none respond?
> Is my arm, then, too short to rescue,
> Have I not the power to save?
> With a mere rebuke I dry up the sea,
> And turn rivers into desert.
> Their fish stink from lack of water;
> They lie dead of thirst.
> [3]I clothe the skies in blackness
> And make their raiment sackcloth. (Isa 50:1–3)

This passage recalls another that we have examined, 2 Kgs 4:1–7, in which a widow fears that creditors will seize her children as debt slaves but Elisha miraculously saves them.[7] In Isa 50:1, however, YHWH insists that he has not literally divorced his children's mother or sold them to creditors at all. Rather, he has only punished mother and children for their misdeeds. His "power to save" remains unlimited, and the painful parenthesis in the family relationship caused by the sins of the mother and the sons is not final: it is about to be closed. The afflictions of Israel — in this case, the agonies and humiliations of defeat and exile — are only temporary, and the legal separation of YHWH and his people will soon come to an end, however insuperable the odds against that redemptive resolution may seem. The miraculous rescue from the creditors that Elisha effected on a familial level God now effects on the national level, restoring a damaged and depleted Israel to wholeness.

A more radical metaphor for the disappearance of the divine husband is implied a few chapters later:

[4]Fear not, you shall not be shamed;
Do not cringe, you shall not be disgraced.
For you shall forget
The reproach of your youth,
And remember no more
The shame of your widowhood.
[5]For He who made you will espouse you —
His name is "LORD of Hosts."
The Holy One of Israel will redeem you —
He is called "God of all the Earth."
[6]The LORD has called you back
As a wife forlorn and forsaken.
Can one cast off the wife of his youth?
  — said your God. (Isa 54:4–6)

Here "widowhood" (*'almānût*) serves as the functional equivalent of the temporary separation of the spouses in Isa 50:1 and, as was the case there, the temporary condition is about to come to an end as YHWH espouses his bride anew. But, in this case, between widowhood and remarriage lies the resurrection, as it were, of the husband who has died. The qualification "as it were" is important here, but not because of the offence to traditionalists of the very notion of a God who dies and rises. Rather, the widowhood of Israel, like the bill of divorce of Isa 50:1, is mostly an illusion. YHWH has not renounced Israel with the finality that the term *divorce* implies; rather, he has temporarily withdrawn from her in righteous and retributive anger. And he has not died, either, at least not with all the finality that one associates with death, relegating his wife to the vulnerable status of a widow. Instead, he has but disappeared for a spell, plunging her into justified mourning, before he returns like the loving husband he is. "Can one cast off the wife of his youth?" (Isa 54:6).

The image of YHWH's disappearing in a metaphorical death, only to return in matrimonial faithfulness, bears some analogy to an important Canaanite cycle of poems, the Ugaritic story of the god Baal.[8] There, too, a deity dies, as Mot (Death) devours Baal, and there, too, much of the focus lies on the deity's consort, Anat, who proceeds to exact vengeance on his conqueror and effects his resurrection, renewing the fertility of nature. During the intermediate period, between the devouring and the revival, Baal is surely dead in a sense in which YHWH in Second Isaiah is not. The conclusion is inescapable: the exilic prophet of consolation, following in the footsteps of much earlier Israelite literature, prophetic and other, has reinterpreted YHWH's abandonment of Israel to the Babylonians and his subsequent return to his people in the light of pre-Israelite myths of a dying and rising deity. As they come back to life with the providential overthrow of Babylon by Cyrus, so does he return to his grieving widow and remove the shame of her condition. This is not, to be sure, simply an Israelite version of the story of the god altogether defeated by Mot (Death) but revived through his sister's violent intervention. But neither is it a story of a god whose presence and power are always fully activated and fully available, as if the suffering and death of the innocent that his own disappearance reflects were unreal.[9] Israel's God is, in other words, a God who is vulnerable, as anyone involved in a deeply personal — nay, erotic — relationship is inevitably vulnerable, and the ostensible death of the relationship and of the children are sources of deep pain. Yet this God is at the same time sovereign over all adversity and destined to redeem the people with whom he is eternally in love. Restoration perforce implies that something must genuinely be restored, and the narrative of redemption perforce implies that something must be redeemed, that things are not always in the state celebrated in poems like those of Second Isaiah that we have been examining. The point is not that the fracturing of the relationship is unreal but that it is temporary, not that the death of the offspring is an illusion but that it will in the end be miraculously reversed.

To us, it is natural to describe the language of widowhood and remarriage, of the loss of the divine husband and his miraculous, triumphant return, and of the restoration of the vanished children (or the birth of their replacements) as metaphorical, as I have indeed done above. For Israel or Zion is not literally a wife, their God does not literally die, and the return from exile and repopulation of the Promised Land is not a matter of literal birth. Sometimes, however, this distinction of the literal and the metaphorical can lead us astray, causing us to miss the deep interconnections internal to ancient Israelite culture but foreign to us. The sources in the Hebrew Bible, as we have already seen, have a definition of death and of life broader than ours.[10] That is why they can see exile, for example, as death and repatriation as life, in a sense that seems contrived (to put it negatively) or artful (to put it positively) to us but probably did not seem so to the original authors and audiences. In part, this is because the ancient Israelites, altogether lacking the corporealist penchant of thought so powerful in modernity, did not conceive of death and life as purely and exclusively biological phenomena.[11] These things were, rather, *social* in character and could not, therefore, be disengaged from the historical fate of the subjects of whom they were predicated. Or, to put it differently, death and life in the Hebrew Bible are often best seen as relational events and are for the selfsame reason inseparable from the personal circumstances of those described as living or as dead. To be alive in this frequent biblical sense of the word inevitably entailed more than merely existing in a certain physical state.

It also entailed having one's being within a flourishing and continuing kin group that dwelt in a productive and secure association with its land. Conversely, to be widowed, bereaved of children, or in exile was necessarily to experience death. Indeed, each of these states (even death) and others (notably, health or illness) could serve as a synecdoche for the condition brought about by any of the others. None of them is the master category or bedrock reality for which the other conditions serve as mere metaphors.

To almost all the biblical writers, it was inconceivable that the positive condition (which we, following ubiquitous biblical usage, can term "life") could be other than a gift of God and thus associated with a proper relationship of the community to him. Given the thoroughly social and relational character of life and of death in the Hebrew Bible, the well-being of Israel could never be detached from the relationship of the nation and its subsidiary kin groups to its Deity. For the evolving national traditions increasingly ascribed the very existence of the nation and the gift of the land in which they dwelt to the will of their God. The *natural* state of affairs, that is, did not result in that flourishing kin group living, generation after generation, in a productive and secure association with its land of which we have just spoken. Rather, the death of spouse or children, infertility, exile, famine, and the like were perceived as the common lot from which the God of Israel miraculously and graciously offered redemption. The restorative action of God here is not simply *super*natural; it is *contra*natural. It reverses the pattern of national death and loss by reactivating powers within nature — principally the power to procreate — that had shriveled and virtually disappeared before God's new intervention. This reversal of national death anticipates (but does not yet quite approximate) the end-time resurrection that appears later in Jewish history. In passages like those on which we have concentrated here, the redemption takes, not coincidentally, a form that recalls the formation of the people Israel in the beginning — a miraculous birth by an infertile mother, the wondrous return of the lost children, joy replacing grief, all of them brought about by the intervention of the indomitable divine warrior to rescue and restore the people with whom he has mysteriously fallen in love. The end-time is like the beginning. God's restoration of Israel recalls how he first gave them life.

Israel's Exodus from the Grave

It was taught:
Rabbi Eliezer says: The dead whom Ezekiel resurrected stood up,
*   uttered a song, and died.*
What song did they utter?
"The LORD deals death in righteousness and gives life in mercy."
Rabbi Joshua says: They uttered this song:
"The LORD deals death and gives life,
Casts down into Sheol and raises up."
*   — Babylonian Talmud, Sanhedrin 92b*

We have now discussed at length two important biblical antecedents of the doctrine of the resurrection of the dead, the characteristic embeddedness of the individual in family and nation and the close connection of exile with death. Now we must turn to the text in which these two combine to offer the best known and most stirring example of resurrection in the Hebrew Bible, the prophet Ezekiel's celebrated vision of the valley of the dry bones:

> The hand of the LORD came upon me. He took me out by the spirit of the LORD and set me down in the valley. It was full of bones. ²He led me all around them; there were very many of them spread over the valley, and they

were very dry. ³He said to me, "O mortal, can these bones live again?" I replied, "O Lord GOD, only You know." ⁴And He said to me, "Prophesy over these bones and say to them: O dry bones, hear the word of the LORD! ⁵Thus said the Lord GOD to these bones: I will cause breath to enter you and you shall live again. ⁶I will lay sinews upon you, and cover you with flesh, and form skin over you. And I will put breath into you, and you shall live again. And you shall know that I am the LORD!"

⁷I prophesied as I had been commanded. And while I was prophesying, suddenly there was a sound of rattling, and the bones came together, bone to matching bone. ⁸I looked, and there were sinews on them, and flesh had grown, and skin had formed over them; but there was no breath in them. ⁹Then He said to me, "Prophesy to the breath, prophesy, O mortal! Say to the breath: Thus said the Lord GOD: Come, O breath, from the four winds, and breathe into these slain, that they may live again." ¹⁰I prophesied as He commanded me. The breath entered them, and they came to life and stood up on their feet, a vast multitude.

¹¹And He said to me, "O mortal, these bones are the whole House of Israel. They say, 'Our bones are dried up, our hope is gone; we are doomed.' ¹²Prophesy, therefore, and say to them: Thus said the Lord GOD: I am going to open your graves and lift you out of the graves, O My people, and bring you to the land of Israel. ¹³You shall know, O My people, that I am the LORD, when I have opened your graves and lifted you out of your graves. ¹⁴I will put My breath into you and you shall live again, and I will set you upon your own soil. Then you shall know that I the LORD have spoken and have acted" — declares the LORD. (Ezek 37:1–14)

The last four verses interpret the vision of the first ten. The dead bones are the people Israel, who, living in exile after the great destruction at the beginning of the sixth century B.C.E., have given up hope: "Our bones are dried up, our hope is gone; we are doomed" (v 11). The restoration of those bones to life — the LORD's giving them sinews, then flesh, skin, and finally the breath of life — indicates that God will open the graves of Ezekiel's audience and restore them to the land of Israel, so that they may once again live upon "[their] own soil" (vv 13–14). What Ezek 37:1–14 presents, in short, is a vision of resurrection that is then decoded as a prediction of exceedingly improbable historical events that the God of Israel will soon miraculously unfold.

That Ezekiel's experience begins with a vision of desiccated bones readily suggests a connection to Zoroastrianism, an ancient Iranian religion in which an expectation of a resurrection of the dead figures prominently.[1] Understandably, it has been proposed from time to time that the Israelites borrowed their own expectation from these Iranian sources, and the possibility of Zoroastrian influence remains real. There are, however, some important differences between the Zoroastrian and the Israelite ideas. For our purposes here, the most important of these is that unlike the Israelites, for whom burial was essential, the Zoroastrians exposed the corpses of their deceased. Ezekiel's conclusion that God will lift the Israelites out of their graves thus fits the Iranian model poorly, though his initial vision of the bones scattered across the valley fits it better. Perhaps we are dealing with a somewhat clumsy effort to adapt the Iranian idea to an Israelite context. The historical leaps that even this more modest proposal requires, however, must give the historian pause. For it seems unlikely that there was strong Zoroastrian influence as early as Ezekiel's time (first half of the sixth century B.C.E.) in his venue (Babylonia). In any event, when a fully developed expectation of resurrection appears in Judaism in the second century B.C.E., its idiom and description do not coincide with what we would expect from the Zoroastrian sources.[2]

Have we at last found in Ezekiel 37 incontrovertible evidence that a belief in the resurrection of the dead existed in ancient Israel in the Hebrew Bible long before its undeniable presence in late Second Temple Judaism? Against the facile assumption that we have, one might argue that the resurrection in question occurs only in the prophet's imagination. It is not depicted as something that will ever take place on the plane of history, even providential history. Indeed, it is less than clear that Ezekiel thinks that he was ever literally in the valley of the dry bones, to which he was, it must be noted, taken "by the spirit of the LORD" and not necessarily in his ordinary bodily self.[3] The resurrection, too, is symbolic, as the ensuing decipherment makes clear (vv 12–14) and as a Talmudic tradition already understood when it classified the event as a "parable" (*māšāl*).[4] Ezekiel's prophesying is, then, something akin to a prophetic sign act rather than the literal means by which an actual historical event takes place. In the vision in the valley of the dry bones, in short, resurrection is not an end in itself but stands in service to the prophet's real message — that God will bring his chosen people out of the depths of exile and restore them to their land. Even in the prophet's own mind, it could be argued, the revival of the dead in this famous vision is only a figure.

It is also significant that the visionary resurrection does not occur, as we might have expected, in the form of suddenly reanimated individuals rising from their graves. Rather, it is described in stages, as the dry bones acquire first sinews, then flesh, and finally skin before the climactic moment in which God places "breath" and "spirit" in them, finally making them alive anew (vv 6, 9–10).[5] In a recent study, John F. Kutsko has developed an interesting argument that this picture of Israel in the process of its resurrection owes a debt to Mesopotamian rituals for the consecration and activation of cultic icons.[6] If he is right, then we must detect here a model of the replenishment of a devastated people that is markedly different (at least at the level of imagery) from the model centering on remarriage and procreation that we examined in the last chapter. In any event, the difference between the two models of the restoration of Israel — the one centering on the *replenishment* of population and the return of the lost children, the other on the *resurrection* of the dead nation — must not be minimized. Less naturalistic and more miraculous than those of Second and Third Isaiah, Ezekiel's vision anticipates the later expectation of resurrection much more closely. We seem to be turning a corner.

Kutsko's study also makes the interesting claim that Ezek 37:1–8 "clearly describes the process of revivification using imagery of human creation."[7] He draws attention in particular to the verbal parallels with these verses in Job:

> [8]Your hands shaped and fashioned me. . . .
> [9]Consider that You fashioned me like clay. . . .
> [11]You clothed me with skin and flesh
> and wove me of bones and sinews. (Job 10:8, 9, 11)

The prophet's vision of the reassembling and revivification of the dead thus seems to reflect ancient Israelite notions of the stages through which a baby forms in his or her mother's womb.[8] Kutsko goes on to argue, more specifically, that Ezekiel's vision of Israel resurrected depends on a much more familiar account of creation as well:

> What is more, the imagery of 37:1–8 appears directly to reflect and develop the scene of the creation of man in Genesis 2, using a constellation of imagery that relates re-creation with creation. For example, the description of this valley of dry bones suggests imagery of the parched earth, which no man has yet cultivated. Second, man is formed but becomes a living being only after God breathes life into him (Gen 2:5–7). Third, God plants a garden in Eden and sets [*nwḥ*] the man there (Gen 2:15), just as God promises to set [*nwḥ*] the reformed people back in their land (Ezek 37:14).[9]

The visionary resurrection of Ezek 37:1–14 is, then, a kind of re-creation — the creation of the people Israel in a new mode, a mode that entails their recognition of his power and his action on their behalf (v 14). In a culture in which God's creation of humankind and his gift of life were undisputed, the proposition that he could reassemble his deadened people and bring them back to life was hardly outrageous. Centuries later, a Jew of Talmudic times made the same point in rebuttal of a skeptic's doubt about the doctrine of resurrection: "If those who never existed can come to life, those who once lived — all the more so!"[10]

In its image of redemption as re-creation, Ezek 37:1–14 conforms nicely to the oracles of redemption in the previous chapter, for example:

> ²⁴I will take you from among the nations and gather you from all the coun-
> tries, and I will bring you back to your own land. ²⁵I will sprinkle clean water
> upon you, and you shall be clean: I will cleanse you from all your uncleanness
> and from all your fetishes. ²⁶And I will give you a new heart and put a new
> spirit into you: I will remove the heart of stone from your body and give you a
> heart of flesh; ²⁷And I will put My spirit into you. Thus I will cause you to
> follow My laws and faithfully to observe My rules. ²⁸Then you shall dwell in
> the land which I gave to your fathers, and you shall be My people and I will be
> your God. (Ezek 36:24–28)

The oracle excerpted above reinforces the sense one gets from Ezek 37:1–14
itself (especially its last verse) that the restored and renewed Israel is also a
spiritually and morally transformed Israel. They have become a regenerate
people in both senses of the word. Their regeneration, however, is owing not
to repentance on their part but rather to God's prevenient action, removing
their "heart of stone" and replacing it with a "heart of flesh." They are, in
other words, not simply restored but *re-created,* transformed from a wicked
and idolatrous people into one capable (probably for the first time, in Ezekiel's
thinking) of giving the LORD the obedience that is his by right. The recreation
and transformation in question do not involve a removal from history or from
embodied existence. Still less do they involve any weakening of the familial-
national definition of Israel. Rather, they are bound up with reconsecration of
the people Israel that enables them to fulfill their unchanging mandate of
faithful obedience to the laws of the one who created them in the first place.

As in the Pentateuch, so here, this ideal state is associated with Israel's
restoration to their ancestral and promised land. The verbs that denote God's
lifting them (*heʿĕlâ*) out of their graves and bringing (*hēbîʾ*) them into the land
of Israel immediately recall the promise in Exodus to bring the enslaved Israelites out of the House of Bondage and into the land promised their fathers.
Heʿĕlâ ("to bring up") is a standard and ubiquitous term for God's involvement in the exodus.[11] The use of *hēbîʾ* ("to bring") in connection with the land
promise, together with an emphasis on the recognition of the LORD as Israel's
God in Ezek 37:12–14, is strikingly reminiscent of an oracle to Moses in
Exodus 6:

> ⁶Say, therefore, to the Israelite people: I am the LORD. I will free you from the
> labors of the Egyptians and deliver you from their bondage. I will redeem you
> with an outstretched arm and through extraordinary chastisements. ⁷And I
> will take you to be My people, and I will be your God. And you shall know
> that I, the LORD, am your God who freed you from the labors of the Egyp-
> tians. ⁸I will bring [*wĕhēbēʾtî*] you into the land which I swore to give to
> Abraham, Isaac, and Jacob, and I will give it to you for a possession, I the
> LORD." (Exod 6:6–8)

The next verse reports a situation of hopelessness among the victims of Egyptian bondage that is of the same order as that of Ezekiel's interlocutors in chapter 37, who declared that "our hope is gone; we are doomed" (v 11):

> But when Moses told this to the Israelites, they would not listen to Moses, their spirits crushed by cruel bondage. (Exod 6:9)

Critical scholars generally ascribe the passage in which these verses in Exodus appear to the Priestly source (P) of Pentateuchal tradition, a source whose affinities with Ezekiel are well established. If we assume that P predates Ezekiel, as one scholar has compellingly argued,[12] then it would seem plausible that Ezekiel has reconceived the exodus so as to include death alongside exile and bondage among the conditions from which God redeems Israel—subject, of course, to the limitation of the figurative sense in which the resurrection in Ezekiel 37 functions.

This limitation is, however, actually much less encompassing than it first seems. If resurrection were thought ludicrous, or impossible even for God, then it would be a singularly inappropriate metaphor for the national renewal and restoration that Ezekiel predicts, and the vision in Ezek 37:1–10 could never have succeeded in its goal of overcoming the hopelessness of the audience. "We have as much chance of being restored to our land as dry bones have of being clad in flesh and restored to life," his despondent audience could then have retorted. In short, even as a figure, the vision of resurrection must have carried considerable credibility if it was to do what the prophet intended.

But there is another reason to be leery of categorizing the vision of Ezek 37:1–10 as only figurative. As we noted in the previous chapter, none of the various conditions from which God was thought to redeem Israel served as the master category of which the others were mere tropes. Barrenness, exile, loss of children, abandonment by one's husband (either through divorce or through death), estrangement from God, death—all could function as metaphors for others in the list. To these must be added slavery, of course, which often appears in connection with them, especially with death. Thus, it is revealing, as we have observed,[13] that Joseph's brothers, seething with resentment over their father's rank favoritism, resolve first to kill the boy and then, having given that nefarious plan up, sell him into slavery instead (Gen 37:18–28). This parallels and adumbrates (in reverse order) Pharaoh's efforts to control the rapid growth of Israel's population, which begin with enslavement and graduate to genocide (Exod 1:8–22). It also parallels, and perhaps distantly reflects, the Canaanite tale of the god Baal, who miraculously overcomes the daunting challenges of enslavement to Yamm (Sea) and annihilation by Mot (Death).[14] That Israel, fleeing Pharaoh's enslavement, escapes *death* by a miraculous passage through the *sea* (Exod 14:1–15:21) is thus no coincidence and anything but an arbitrary concatenation of unrelated items.[15] It is, rather, a manifestation in narrative of the deep inner connection between slavery and death that we have been exploring in another genre, the poetic oracles of prophets.

Whether Ezek 37:1–14 presupposes a narrative in which enslavement was the principal affliction of Israel in Egypt is unknown. In chapter 20, the longest and most developed account of Israel's experience in Egypt and in the wilderness afterward outside the Pentateuch itself, the prophet betrays no hint of the idea that the Israelites were ever slaves. There the emphasis falls, first, on Israel's perverse penchant for idolatry, which Ezekiel, interestingly, sees as present already during their Egyptian exile, and, second, on the LORD's subsequent revelation to them of his laws (especially those governing the Sabbath) in the wilderness. As befits an oracle of judgment (and one dated before the great destruction of 586 B.C.E.), the dominant note of Ezekiel 20 is one of disobedience and punishment. The vision of the dry bones resurrected is, by way of contrast, one of the prophet's oracles of restoration and thus appropriately speaks of the people Israel's future obedience to the God who has revived them and restored them to their own land (Ezek 37:13–14). To ask whether he restores them from hopelessness, slavery, exile, estrangement from God and his righteous will, or, rather, from death is excessively academic and misses the way Israel conceives these things. Most seriously, it misses the deep inner connection between the substance of the symbol (resurrection from death) and its decoded message (a return to the land, to the knowledge of God, and to obedience to him). That Israel could be fully alive dwelling outside the promised land and lacking the knowledge of God was inconceivable to Ezekiel. Conversely, given Israel's long-standing pattern of disobedience to God's laws (which, in his mind, brought about their national destruction and exile), their undeserved repatriation was surely an exodus from death to life: no one who knows God and has experienced the fulfillment of his promise, it would seem, is dead.

The vision in the valley of the dry bones in Ezek 37:1–14 is thus the best approximation that we have yet seen to the developed doctrine of a general resurrection that one finds in Second Temple and rabbinic Judaism (and, of course, early Christianity). What it envisions is, nonetheless, different, and not only for the obvious reason that the vision of resurrection is explicitly decoded as a prediction of national restoration. Unlike the later texts, Ezekiel 37 does not connect the envisioned resurrection with a last judgment, such as that in Daniel 12, in which the dead awake "some to eternal life, others to reproaches, to everlasting abhorrence" (v 2). Rather, Ezekiel's is a vision of resurrection *after* judgment has been passed on the nation of Israel and on its gentile tormentors as well. Having no sense that the new life into which the nation rises is a *reward*—his pessimism about Israel's character and his uncompromising theology of divine honor do not allow this self-flattering theology[16]— he does not discriminate between classes of Israelites. The entire nation rises, just as the entire nation fell.

Did Ezekiel think that those resurrected in his symbolic vision rose "to eternal life," like the fortunate group in Dan 12:2, or did he, rather, expect that they would eventually die a second death? In the opinion of Rabbi Eliezer (late first, early second century C.E.), "The dead whom Ezekiel resurrected stood upon their feet, sang a song, and died."[17] The point of the rabbi's statement is not to deny the doctrine of a future resurrection of the dead, which had a venerable history in Judaism and was already normative among the rabbis by the time Rabbi Eliezer taught. The point, rather, is to distinguish between Ezekiel's resurrection, whose effect was only temporary, and the eschatological resurrection, which, as the comments in the Talmud just before his show, would be irreversible. The very question of whether the people in Ezekiel's vision died again or live on betrays, however, the influence of the later doctrine. For, as we have seen, Ezekiel's vision focuses exclusively on the nation and not on the individuals who comprise it in any given generation. There is, therefore, no reason to think that Ezekiel saw the individuals who were resurrected in the valley as now endowed with immortality. What does not die is the people Israel, because God has, despite their grievous failings, honored his indefeasible pledge to their ancestors. *Israelite people* die, like anyone else; the *people Israel* survives and revives because of God's promise, despite the most lethal defeats.

For this reason, although Ezekiel's vision in the valley does not attest to the expectation of resurrection in the later sense, it does constitute a significant step in the direction of the later doctrine. For one thing, its vision of the restored and reconstituted people of Israel differs markedly from visions of the sort we explored in the previous chapter. There, as we have noted, the restoration and reconstitution results in procreation and the return of the lost children, themes already ancient when those oracles were written, as we demonstrated. Here in Ezek 37:1–14, by contrast, the restoration and reconstitution are presented as a resurrection of those long dead. In both cases, we are, of course, dealing with metaphors, but the difference in the metaphors is itself a datum of high significance.

Another fruitful comparison, which also records a striking change, lies with the other highly developed account of a resurrection in the Hebrew Bible, the story of the Shunammite woman and the son whom Elisha revives in 2 Kgs 4:8–37.[18] If we compare these texts, it immediately becomes evident that in the story in Kings, there is no element of deathlessness at all. The prophet simply honors his original promise to the childless woman by resurrecting the child who he promised would be born to her (see esp. v 28). This having been accomplished, the child will eventually go the way of all flesh, though presumably not before he has lived to a respectable age and thus fulfilled his mother's hopes for him. Ezekiel's vision is predicated upon the opposite idea — that the people Israel (as distinguished from the individuals who make it up) will never go the way of all flesh but will endure forever. For, as we have seen, Ezekiel's vision is not one simply of revivification but of transformation and re-creation as well, and the cause of the people Israel's death — their persistent failure to recognize and heed their God — itself finally vanishes. " 'You shall know, O My people, that I am the LORD, when I have opened your graves and lifted you out of your graves. . . . Then you shall know that I the LORD have spoken and have acted' — declares the LORD" (Ezek 37:13–14).

To put the same point differently, the Shunammite woman's fulfillment is a consequence of her immediate situation only. Her pregnancy and the resurrection of the son with whom Elisha has rewarded her are owing to her extraordinary devotion to the "man of God." She attends to his needs first for food, then for shelter, and he responds with the unlikely news of her impending pregnancy (2 Kgs 4:8–10, 16). When the child has died, the prophet makes her whole again — and, not incidentally, demonstrates his own supernatural charisma to all skeptics — by reviving the promised son (vv 32–37). Had the unfortunate mother not demonstrated her devotion, or had she already borne a child at the outset of the tale, the miraculous revival would not have been needed and would never have occurred. Once the resurrection of the lad has taken place, Elisha has discharged his obligation to the Shunammite woman. Although she may be more impressed than ever with his supernatural abilities, there is no sense that she has drawn closer to her God or that the son will have a different spiritual or moral disposition as a result of these events.

The basis for the new resurrection envisioned in Ezek 37:1–14 is, by contrast, the perduring and unshakable promise of God that the people of Israel shall eventually recognize him, dwell in the land he has given them, and serve him there with undivided loyalty. Far from having deserved this stunning reversal of their fate, the people of Israel in exile are the bearers, according to Ezekiel's theology, of a long and unremitting history of rebellion against their God and immoral behavior and perversion of the lowest order.[19] They have been the rankest of idolaters from early on — even in Egypt — yet their God's commitment to restore and repatriate them remains steadfast. Resting, as it thus does, on an unconditional promise of national restoration, the visionary revival of Israel in Ezek 37:1–14 again foreshadows later notions of the eschatological resurrection, and in ways in which the touching story of the childless Shunammite couple does not. For the Jewish expectation of a resurrection of the dead is always and inextricably associated with the restoration of the people Israel; it is not, in the first instance, focused on individual destiny. The question it answers is not, "Will I have life after death?" but rather, "Has God given up on his promises to his people?" Ezekiel's answer to the latter question is a resounding "No!" Even a history of the most hideous disobedience and the most obscene idolatry shall not prevent the dry bones that are the whole House of Israel from living again.

The Fact of Death and the Promise of Life

Let the groans of the prisoners reach You;
reprieve those condemned to death,
as befits Your great strength.
— Psalm 79:11

Having now examined at length the questions of resurrection and immortality in their various permutations before the expectation of a general resurrection emerged, we are now in a good position to revisit the topic of our second chapter, the claim of the rabbis of the Talmudic age that the resurrection of the dead is already in the Torah. The first inclination of a scholar practicing historical criticism is to dismiss the claim as tendentious and anachronistic. For surely the rabbis, like the early Christians and, for that matter, religious people in all communities and times, here simply retrojected their own central and tenaciously held belief in an eschatological resurrection into the Scriptures — Scriptures in which the finality and irreversibility of death is, in fact, everywhere the belief. On this reading, the position of the Hebrew Bible is nicely and exhaustively stated by the wise woman of Tekoa to King David, "We must all die; we are like water that is poured out on the ground and cannot be gathered up" (2 Sam 14:14).

To some modern people, this sad observation may be greeted with a certain joy. Those displaying the characteristic modern skepticism about the traditional doctrines of resurrection, whether in their Jewish or their Christian form, for example, can thus find in the Hebrew Bible a resource for a religious justification for their own naturalism. In this approach, the Hebrew Bible is interpreted to support the idea that death is natural, irreversible, and, most important, altogether in accordance with God's will — until, that is, the idea of resurrection mysteriously appears very late in the biblical period, in Hellenistic times.[1] Lloyd Bailey states the consensus well when he writes, "Mortality as the Creator's design for humans seems to be the basic perspective of the O[ld] T[estament] literature."[2] If so, then the common modern suspicion that resurrection is a vestige of childish, prescientific thinking is not so heterodox after all. For there was a time when the religion of Israel did not know of this now eminently orthodox doctrine. The wise woman of Tekoa was not only wise but ahead of her time as well.

There is, to be sure, a large measure of truth in this, but it is a truth based mostly on the familiar modern phrasing of the question, "Will I have life after death? Will I be resurrected from the grave?" If the question is asked that way, the wise woman's observation constitutes the answer most characteristic of the Hebrew Bible: Death, sadly, is universal and final. It comes to all of us; it is the last word in our existence. There is, however, a problem with this way of posing the question: It misses another equally characteristic feature of the Hebrew Bible, the highly social and familial construction of personal identity that we explored at length in chapter 6. In ancient Israel, identity tends to be at least as much communal as individual. As Robert Di Vito puts it, "ancient Israel is an 'aggregate of groups rather than as a collection of individuals,' and, apart from the family, the individual is scarcely a viable entity — socially, economically, or juridically."[3]

To Di Vito's list of three adverbs, we must surely add another — "religiously." For the idea that their God had promised them national greatness and a land of their own was very ancient among the Israelites, long preceding the late monarchic and exilic articulation of the idea characteristic of the late Pentateuchal sources. The prime enemies of that promise to the collectivity, the lethal threats to Israel's survival, in those sources are the barrenness of its would-be matriarchs and the loss of its promised sons. The story of the threat these realities pose and the way nascent Israel overcomes them suffuses the book of Genesis, and not just its demonstrably late sources; it also reverberates through the rest of the Hebrew Bible.[4] Amazingly, against all odds and the dictates of a cruel nature, these assaults on the promise of life, though real and the source of enormous grief (all of it justified), are turned back, and God grants fertility and restores the doomed son, either literally or through a new birth. In sum, within the familial context death does not have the last word, though it does have a prominent and painful word.[5] Within the familial context, the last word lies, rather, with life restored, with the return of fertility or of the doomed children.

Mention must also be made of the ubiquitous biblical promise of life as a reward for careful and faithful obedience to God and his will. This appears most memorably in the Deuteronomic injunction to Israel, "Choose life—if you and your offspring would live—by loving the Lord your God, heeding His commands, and holding fast to Him" (Deut 30:19–20). Priestly tradition makes an analogous promise: "You shall keep My laws and My rules, by the pursuit of which man shall live: I am the Lord" (Lev 18:5). The theme is especially pronounced in Wisdom literature, for example:

> My son, do not forget my teaching,
> But let your mind retain my commandments;
> [2]For they will bestow on you length of days,
> Years of life and well-being.
>
>   . . .
>
> [13]Happy is the man who finds wisdom,
> The man who attains understanding.
> [14]Her value in trade is better than silver,
> Her yield, greater than gold.
> [15]She is more precious than rubies;
> All of your goods cannot equal her.
> [16]In her right hand is length of days,
> In her left, riches and honor.
> [17]Her ways are pleasant ways,
> And all her paths, peaceful.
> [18]She is a tree of life to those who grasp her,
> And whoever holds on to her is happy. (Prov 3:1–2, 13–18)
>
>   . . .
>
> [20]My son, listen to my speech;
> Incline your ear to my words.
> [21]Do not lose sight of them;
> Keep them in your mind.
> [22]They are life to him who finds them,
> Healing for his whole body. (Prov 4:20–22)

Whether the idiom is Deuteronomic, Priestly, or sapiential, the promise of life to those who observe God's directives suffuses the Hebrew Bible.

Between this promise or offer of life and the equally ubiquitous fact of death, there is, as theologians say, a "tension." How can the same God who creates human beings mortal and decrees their death also promise them life as a consequence of their obedience to his commands, or even as a gracious gift made despite their failure to obey? By way of answer, let it first be noticed that within its ancient Near Eastern context this tension is not so extreme as it seems to us, for "life" has a much wider semantic range in the Hebrew Bible than it does for us. It includes, for example, power, skill, confidence, health, blessing, luck, and joy.[6] Thus can the factitive verb "to bring to life" (*ḥiyyâ*) mean simply "to cure, to make healthy," as we should expect in a culture in which the division between sickness and death was less clear than it seems to us and fewer victims of serious illness survived.[7] And so, when ancient Israelite texts speak of life, they usually mean not deathlessness but a healthy, blessed existence — happiness and "length of days," as the texts from Proverbs quoted above put it. That such an existence must come to its inevitable end in no way implies, therefore, a defeat of God's promise of "life," so understood. The brevity and frailty of human life did, of course, occasion some somber reflections on the human condition and its difference from divinity:

> [3]You return man to dust;
>> You decreed, "Return you mortals!"
> [4]For in Your sight a thousand years
>> are like yesterday that has passed,
>> like a watch of the night. (Ps 90:3–4)[8]
>
> . . .
>
> [6]A voice rings out: "Proclaim!"
> And I asked, "What shall I proclaim?"
> "All flesh is grass,
> All its goodness like flowers of the field:
> [7]Grass withers, flowers fade
> When the breath of the LORD blows on them.
> Indeed, man is but grass;
> [8]Grass withers, flowers fade —
> But the word of our God is always fulfilled!" (Isa 40:6–8)[9]

One's death, or the death of a loved one, was never a happy prospect; there was no dancing on the grave in ancient Israel. But if God grants the wish to "teach us to count our days rightly," as the psalmist quoted above puts it (Ps 90:12), and if the unfailing word of God is favorably fulfilled in one's own life, then one could, like Abraham or Job, die "at a good ripe age, old and contented" (Gen 25:7–8; Job 42:17). Whatever complaints one had against God could be properly relegated to the past, so long as God graced the end of one's life. This, and only this, could rob death of its sting.

The opposite of "life" in this understanding includes not only weakness, disease, depression, and the like, but also a humiliating death, especially one that is violent or premature.[10] This is the kind of end that I earlier termed "an unfortunate death." It is this form of death, and not mortality in general, that King Hezekiah, for example, prays that God spare him (Isa 38:1–3), a death in which, as the king puts it, "I must depart in the middle of my days . . . consigned to the gates of Sheol" (v 10). And when God grants his prayer, Hezekiah quite naturally speaks as one who has been given life and spared "the pit of destruction" to which his sins had doomed him (vv 16–20). That he will still die at the end of his fifteen-year reprieve, symbolized by the miraculous retreat of the shadow on his father's sundial, does not seem to qualify his joy in the least or to suggest to him that his sins were still working their toxic magic after all. Anyone so favored could die "old and contented," and without recrimination that the fact of death — the inevitable return of the shadow on the sundial — had undermined God's ubiquitous promise of life. The question was not whether one died but whether one did so within God's favor or outside it. And *that* is a question very far removed from the thinking of modern naturalism.

Further mitigation of the ostensible tension between the inevitability of death and God's promise of life comes from the highly social and familial construction of personal identity that I have been stressing. In a culture in which identity is so deeply embedded in family structures, life is, as we have seen, largely characterized by the emergence of new generations who stand in continuity and deference to the old. Barrenness is here the functional equivalent of death in more individualistic cultures, and the return of fertility functions like resurrection: it replaces death with life. It is thus not surprising that the blessings and curses of covenant offer abundant fertility to those who observe God's commands but threaten those who violate them with sterility and the death (or loss by other means) of children.[11] Note that the blessings and curses are addressed primarily to the entire nation, not to individuals within it. The individual Israelites will all surely die, but without in the slightest impairing the promise of life and fellowship with him that the LORD has extended to the House of Israel. Here again, the fact of death and the promise of life stand in no great tension, for the two move on different planes, the individual and the national, respectively. In any event, the experience of undeserved adversity did not necessarily impel an ancient Israelite to accuse the Deity of injustice or unfaithfulness to his own pledged word. It could, but it did not have to. For the unfulfilled promise (or threat) might come to fulfillment later, or even in a later generation.[12] In Wisdom literature the failure to recognize the time lag between unjust events and God's inevitable and reliable justice is, in fact, characteristic of the fool (e.g., Ps 92:7–8). The wise person knows that God's justice comes at its own unfathomable pace. It may, in fact, arrive only in a future generation. In the words of an apocalyptic vision placed in the mouth of the ancient wise man Daniel, "Happy the one who waits" (Dan 12:11).

Seen within the universe of ancient Israelite belief, then, the promise of life, so prominent throughout the Hebrew Bible, is generally not inconsistent with the brute fact of human mortality equally prominent therein. The God of Israel can without contradiction both offer life to his faithful and decree that all shall die. Still, even within the cultural universe of ancient Israel, there remains, I submit, a tension between the fact of death and the promise of life. Or, to phrase the same point slightly differently, the arrangement in which both of these are affirmed is inherently unstable, and we should not be surprised to find a different model of simultaneous affirmation appearing in the post-exilic period, as we shall see in the next two chapters.

To understand the tension in the pre-exilic settlement to which I am pointing, let us first revisit our crucial point that "life" (*ḥayyîm*) in biblical Hebrew has a wider semantic range than its English equivalent. If "life" can mean health and well-being, and "to bring to life" (*ḥiyyâ*) can signify simply "to cure, to make healthy," then the biblical promise or offer of life inevitably comes into contact with another ancient Israelite affirmation, also of high frequency and venerable antiquity — the affirmation that the LORD is Israel's healer:

> See, then, that I, I am He;
> There is no god beside Me.
> I deal death and give life;
> I wounded and I will heal:
> None can deliver from My hand. (Deut 32:39)

The early rabbis stated the interpretive problem in this verse with surpassing concision:

> Our Rabbis taught: "I deal death and give life." One might think that death applies to one individual and life to another, as the world goes its course. Therefore the text reads, "I wound and I will heal." Just as the wounding and the healing apply to the same individual, so do death and life apply to the same individual. From this, one can derive a refutation to those who say that the resurrection of the dead is not in the Torah. (*b. Sanh.* 91b)

Within the older, biblical understanding of death and life, however, the position the rabbis want to eliminate has considerable probability. On that understanding, the third line in the poetic excerpt from Deuteronomy 32 ("I deal death and give life," v 39c) would mean simply that the LORD alone is the sole source of both death and life, as he is the sole source of both wounding and healing in the fourth line (v 39d). The linchpin of the rabbinic argument — that the wounding and healing must refer to the same person — is hardly necessary, however. One person may suffer an ailment and never recover, whereas another is healed. In each case, the poem is telling us, the omnipotent and inscrutable God is the source of the person's destiny. And just as he decrees both disease and its remedy, he alone decrees both the end and the beginning of life. "I deal death and give life" (*'ănî 'āmît wa'ăḥayyeh*), in other words, need not imply resurrection, as the wording (especially the word order) might imply to today's reader. It may mean simply that deaths and births are ultimately the LORD's doing, as one generation replaces another, "as the world goes its course."[13]

But note that the same observation cuts the other way as well: if life is somehow equivalent to healing, and death to wounding, then why cannot the sole and unchallengeable Deity who heals lesser wounds also heal the graver malady that is death? To put it differently, if the semantic range of "death" in biblical Hebrew includes both disease and biological cessation, is there any reason — again, strictly within the cultural universe of pre-exilic Israel — to think that God could heal disease but could not reverse death? The question is all the more pressing if we recall Aubrey R. Johnson's observation that "death in the strict sense of the term is for the Israelite the weakest form of life."[14] If death could be seen as the most severe of illnesses and characterized (in this understanding) not by nonexistence but by debilitation and physical fragility, then the possibility arises that God might heal it, too, just as he heals other diseases and wounds.[15] Not that he heals death in every instance, any more than he heals any other ailment in every instance (as if no one were ever sick), but that he could, in an exception so rare as to call forth exuberant praise, reverse death no less than any other condition.

The Song of Hannah (1 Sam 2:1–10) indicates that this possibility is much more than an abstract logical deduction. The main theme of the poem is how God's victory inverts the ordinary realities of the world:

> [4]The bows of the mighty are broken,
> And the faltering are girded with strength.
> [5]Men once sated must hire out for bread;
> The hungry are fattened on food.
> While the barren woman bears seven,
> The mother of many is forlorn. (1 Sam 2:4–5)[16]

The hymn goes on to speak of God's reversing the status of the rich and the poor, lifting up the "needy" to "seats of honor," and guarding those loyal to him while "the wicked perish in darkness" (1 Sam 2:7–9) — establishing, in other words, an order of things quite the reverse of what obtains in the familiar world in which God has not yet won, or not yet definitively won, his great victory.

Our concern lies with a verse in the middle of the poem:

> The LORD deals death and gives life,
> Casts down into Sheol and raises up. (1 Sam 2:6)

The first half-line closely resembles the affirmation of Deut 32:39 that the LORD "deal[s] death and give[s] life"; only the person of the verb varies, with a first person in Deuteronomy and a third in Samuel. The second half-line of the verse from the Song of Hannah, however, does not permit the view that only the LORD's control of the change of generations is affirmed here, as Deuteronomy 32 does. That he "raises up" from Sheol can mean only that he reverses death, resurrecting the denizens of the netherworld just as he reverses other cruel fates in the hymn.[17] The injustice that resulted in the dispatch of some individuals to Sheol will be reversed when the LORD establishes the reign of justice that the hymn celebrates throughout. The Song of Hannah does not regard the netherworld as beyond his power; it suggests that neither does Deuteronomy 32.

If we return to our question of the relationship of the fact of death to the promise of life, we are compelled to say that the Song of Hannah upholds both. God brings death upon all human beings, casting at least some down to Sheol, but he also brings a subset of the latter group — context suggests they are those who arrived there unjustly — up afterward, or will do so when he wins his earth-shaking victory and establishes his reign of justice.

This is not to deny that some biblical texts tacitly assume the accuracy of the wise woman of Tekoa's observation, "We must all die; we are like water that is poured out on the ground and cannot be gathered up" (2 Sam 14:14). The hymnic affirmations that I have been discussing alert us, however, to the presence of another perspective, one in which death, or at least unjust death, will be miraculously reversed. I am thinking of psalms, for example, that praise the LORD for bringing the psalmist up from Sheol (e.g., Ps 30:4).[18] The obvious objection that the psalmists in question were never "really" dead only betrays the modern definition of death of the one who voices the objection. For in the psalmists' mind, the adversity they had experienced — illness, false accusation, enemy attack, or whatever — had truly brought them into the terrifying domain of death, from which their God's faithfulness and justice marvelously rescued them.[19] A major ingredient in the marvel, and in the psalmists' ecstasy, it seems to me, is that such rescues from death are exceedingly rare. For the wise woman of Tekoa's observation being the rule, not the exception, deliverance from death is a miracle and thus defies the regularity of nature. Even rarer are those instances in which someone who is "really" dead returns to life, as do the boys whom Elijah and Elisha resurrect in parallel narratives.[20] Were resurrections not thought to be rare, were they, that is, the ordinary course of things, the mother of the child whom Elijah resurrects would hardly have had occasion to affirm, as she does in the last words of the narrative, "Now I know that you are a man of God and that the word of the LORD is truly in your mouth" (1 Kgs 17:24). Resurrection in the Hebrew Bible, and in Judaism ever after, is miraculous, and miracles, as C. S. Lewis writes, "are, by definition, rarer than other events," and "it is obviously improbable before-hand that one will occur at any given place and time."[21] But this is very different from saying that death is universal, absolute, and irreversible, even at the hands of the God who is acclaimed as healer and deliverer of the afflicted. It is also very different from saying that God was thought to be invariably pleased with the fact that humans are mortal.

This train of reasoning gives us another insight into the relationship between the fact of death, on the one hand, and the promise or offer of life, on the other. We saw above that these are not in logical contradiction in the Hebrew Bible after all, since "life" there can mean simply a long life span or one that ends in peaceful and honorable circumstances, which bespeak God's approval of the person. The association of death with disease suggests another way of understanding the simultaneous acceptance of these two seeming opposites. Death is the ordinary human fate, and it is ordinarily irreversible, just as serious disease in the ancient Near Eastern world was ordinarily incurable. For in a world without antibiotics, steroids, and effective surgery, few victims recovered from illnesses that are today readily curable, or at least controllable. Consider Naaman, the leprous Aramean general whom Elisha, the Israelite man of God, cures in the chapter that appears — instructively — just after the one that tells of the Shunammite resurrection. Surely Naaman had visited the best healers in Damascus in a futile quest of a cure for his affliction. His response when the man of God has healed him is strikingly reminiscent of the response of the mother of the boy whom Elijah resurrected. "Now I know that there is no God in the whole world except in Israel!" (2 Kgs 5:15; cf. 1 Kgs 17:24). Indeed, within the tale of Naaman itself there is a basis to connect healing with resurrection. It lies in the answer of the king of Israel to the letter in which the king of Aram asks that he cure his ailing general: "Am I God, to deal death and give life, that this fellow writes to me to cure a man of leprosy?" (2 Kgs 5:7). The close resemblance here in language and thought to both Deut 32:39 and 1 Sam 2:6 is obvious, as is the implication that to heal the leper would be a miracle on the order of resurrecting the dead. In the ordinary course of events, lepers remain lepers, and the dead remain dead.[22] But the God who "heals all your diseases" and "redeems your life from the Pit," as a psalmist says (Ps 103:3–4), is not constrained by the ordinary course of events, and the exceptional case is still a reality with which to reckon. Indeed, its very status as a rare exception commends it to the Israelite mind as an act of God, a supernatural intervention into the dreary course of nature, marked as it is by incurable disease and irreversible death. It is the reprieve of those condemned to death and an outstanding demonstration of God's great strength.

The pre-exilic worldview of which I am speaking is, to be sure, different from the worldview of those later Jews and Christians who held a doctrine of the resurrection of the dead. It does not, however, do justice to the difference to say, as many do,[23] that in the pre-exilic period death was thought to be irreversible, appropriate, and in accordance with God's will, whereas in the later period (among those who believed in resurrection) God was thought to rescue from death. A better way of stating the point, I maintain, is to say that what had been a rare exception in the early period became the basis for a general expectation in the late one. This is the apocalyptic expectation of a universal resurrection in a coming dispensation in which all of God's potentials would be activated in a grand finale of stupendous miracles very much at odds with the natural course of history. One central aspect of the eschatological inversion is that the previous exception becomes the norm, as even the most formidable opposition to God's saving power melts before his triumphant might — death emphatically included.[24] It is not that human nature becomes invulnerable to death, spontaneously and on its own. Rather, God would at long last grant the rescue from adversity for which Israelites had always prayed, delivering those who, against all hope, had placed their hope in him.

A major contributing factor in this change seems to be the disappearance, at least in some circles, of belief in the possibility of a fortunate death. To those Jews of the Second Temple period who accepted the doctrine of a future resurrection, death was always unfortunate; one should die with more than merely a sense of fulfillment and contentment of the sort that characterized Abraham or Job at the end. Death per se became, in other words, a form of adversity, like severe illness, and one's only hope lay, once more, with the rescuing God.

The burden of the preceding discussions is that there are tensions within the older Israelite notion that the "life" that God offers has to do with longevity and happiness, rather than with deathlessness or resurrection. Happiness, in this older understanding of things, requires and includes health, and the health that is thus promised may result from God's curing a fatal illness. This includes the fatal illness that the ancient Israelites (and we as well) call death and that modern persons instinctively consider final and irreversible in all cases. Similar tensions, only stronger, characterize the other understanding of the promise of "life" in pre-exilic Israel that I developed above. Here I refer again to the collective or national character of that promise in the Hebrew Bible: it is the people of Israel and not individual Israelites who are granted the eternal covenant that, among other things, prevents their annihilation, fertility thus being the rough functional equivalent of resurrection in a more individualistic culture. The promise of a bright future after affliction, whether tendered in Pentateuchal sources or in the prophets, in no way implies that any given individual will have a future beyond his or her appointed life span. The promised future finds its fulfillment in the later generations of the chosen people.

In this instance, the tension inheres in the fact that a sharp distinction between the individual and the group usually cannot be drawn in this literature. When Robert Di Vito, whom I have quoted, writes that in the Hebrew Bible "the subject is deeply embedded, or engaged, in its social identity," it must be noted that he is not denying the existence of a subject. He is, rather, only differentiating the characteristic Israelite construction of personal identity from "salient features of modern identity, such as its pronounced individualism [which is] grounded in modernity's location of the self in the 'inner depths' of one's interiority rather than in one's social role or public relations."[25] The deep involvement of the person in his or her social role explains a number of prominent aspects of ancient Israelite thinking that are as uncontroversial to the ancient Israelites as they are foreign to modern persons, including most modern persons who regard the Hebrew Bible as sacred scripture. I am thinking, for example, of the way national or tribal ancestors can pre-enact the experience of their descendants — a point that modern scholars of various types not infrequently miss.[26] Similarly, the fact that the "Suffering Servant" of Second Isaiah can be both an individual and the nation has not prevented generations of scholars from arguing over which of the two, precisely, he was. Or, to give one last example, one might consider the long-standing dispute among exegetes as to whether the first person singular in the Psalms refers to a lone speaker or to the community personified as such.[27] The very fact that these disputes have gone on so long raises the suspicion that the modern categories are less than ideally appropriate to the culture to which we seek to apply them. It also suggests, however, that promises of felicity that are directed to the nation at large may have been taken on occasion as applicable to individuals within it as well. If so, then the "life" promised the covenanted people may also have been taken on occasion to apply to individuals within it.

An analogy to the process I have in mind can be found in Ezekiel 18, the chapter in which the great prophet of the early exile protests against the notion of inherited guilt, epitomized in the popular saying, "Parents eat sour grapes and their children's teeth are blunted" (v 2). Ezekiel's retort — "The person who sins, only he shall die" (v 4) — is often taken as a denunciation of the idea of collective guilt and a decisive advance for the opposing notion of moral and spiritual individualism.[28] The prophet's focus, however, is not on contemporaneous individuals at all but on *generations,* and his principal point is that the guilt of the ancestors which caused the destruction of the Judahite kingdom and the ensuing exile does not condemn their current descendants to unending misery. A righteous father, one who abstains from abuses like robbery or sexual relations with a menstruous woman, "shall live," the prophet assures us (vv 5–9). Should he have a son who engages in such flagrant sins, however, "He shall not live!" Ezekiel insists. "If he has committed any of these abominations, he shall die; he has forfeited his life" (vv 10–13). But his own son, if he "has taken heed and has not imitated" his father's abuses, "shall not die for the iniquity of his father . . . he shall live!" (vv 14–19). The message is obvious:

> The person who sins, he alone shall die. A child shall not share the burden of a parent's guilt, nor shall a parent share the burden of a child's guilt; the righteousness of the righteous shall be accounted to him alone, and the wickedness of the wicked shall be accounted to him alone. (Ezek 18:20)

The upshot of this would seem to be that in God's moral calculus, each moment carries equal weight. No one generation can condemn their descendants, or acquit them. It bears mention that Ezekiel's preaching is in opposition not only to the popular proverb he cites but also to some sources in the Hebrew Bible itself. The affirmation in the Decalogue that God "visit[s] the guilt of the parents upon the children" (Exod 20:5; Deut 5:9) springs to mind immediately. More relevant to Ezekiel's situation, however, is the claim that the destruction of the Judahite kingdom and the Jerusalem Temple in the prophet's own time is owing to King Manasseh's sin two generations earlier (2 Kgs 21:11–15; 24:3–4).

For our purposes, two points about Ezekiel 18 are especially interesting. One is that the language of God's approval or disapproval of a person's actions is the language of life and death, respectively. The righteous shall live; the wicked shall surely die, even when the misdeeds are not classified as capital offenses in the surviving biblical law codes. What Ezekiel is reporting is not case law or guidance for human courts but God's ultimate verdict — a judgment of life and death, with no intermediate points. How, exactly, that judgment is realized in human affairs and procedures is left vague.

The more important point for our discussion lies in the scenario the prophet sketches after having laid out his scenario of the righteous father with the wicked son and the righteous grandson and stated the conclusion cited above. Now Ezekiel moves away from the problem of generations that has occupied his attention throughout the chapter and speaks, instead, of two moments in the life of one person:

> ²¹Moreover, if the wicked one repents of all the sins that he committed and keeps all My laws and does what is right and just, he shall live; he shall not die. ²²None of the transgressions he committed shall be remembered against him; because of the righteousness he has practiced, he shall live. ²³Is it my desire that a wicked person shall die? — says the Lord GOD. It is rather that he shall turn back from his ways and live. (Ezek 18:21–23)

The reverse, the prophet then goes on to say, is also the case. The treachery a once-righteous person now commits condemns him: "He shall die" (vv 24–25). In each situation, the national has become personal. The two *generations* have been consolidated into two *moments in one life,* a life once imperiled by sin but always graced by God's preference for life and by the availability of repentance. We must not overlook the consequence of this consolidation. The idea that Israel, condemned to a sentence of death, will, by the grace of God, recover in a future generation uncontaminated by the ancestors' violations has been transformed into the notion that an analogous recovery can occur in one individual's lifetime. In a certain sense, the parent and the child have been telescoped into one person, a former sinner who has now repented, and just as the child's status was determinative in the intergenerational scenario, so now it is the new person, the penitent, whose moral status is determinative. The national or familial history has been transformed into biography, and, as a result, the life offered to the innocent new generation applies to the repentant individual as well. The condemned person can escape a death sentence by returning to God and his commandments. One who faced certain death can find life.

But how shall we take that happy verdict, "he shall live" (Ezek 18:28)? Does Ezekiel really believe that the righteous and the repentant will never know death's sting, that returning to God invariably removes the prospect of individual death? Does he not know that eventually there comes a time when even repentance (or good deeds or faith) is powerless to stave off death? It would seem more likely, rather, that Ezekiel 18 understands "life" the way the verses from Proverbs 3 discussed above understand "length of days" — as a prosperous and healthy life that is of normal or above-normal length and ends peacefully and in dignity. Biological cessation terminates such a life but does not constitute "death" in the highly freighted theological and forensic sense that Ezekiel intends when he pronounces the words "he shall die!" We cannot be certain of this, of course, because the whole question of the ultimate fate of individuals, however pressing it is to us, is simply not on Ezekiel's mind. That "the same fate is in store for all," as Qohelet would later put it, "for the righteous, and for the wicked; for the good and the pure, and for the impure" (Qoh 9:2), does not seem to have occurred to the great prophet of the early exile. It is tempting, nonetheless, to speculate on how he would have reacted if it had. Would he have turned away from the apodictic, forensic idiom, "he shall live!" and "he shall die!" that dominates Ezekiel 18 and made it explicit that all he means is "length of days" and premature death, respectively? Or would he have continued to elect the promise of life over the fact of death, upholding without compromise his remarkable insistence that God does not want the wicked to die but only to return to him—and thus to life (Ezek 18:23)? Were the latter the option he chose, Ezekiel would have had to connect repentance with some vision of personal immortality or individual resurrection, thus embarking on the course that develops fully only in a much later form of Judaism and in Christianity and Islam. As it is, he stops short of that, leaving the ambiguities of his rhetoric unresolved.

Let us pose again the question we first asked in chapter 2: Is the notion of a resurrection of the dead to be found in the Hebrew Bible? At one level, the obvious answer is negative. With the exception of a very few special individuals like Elijah and perhaps Enoch, whom God takes directly to himself,[29] death is universal and inevitable in this literature. And with the exception again of a very few individuals—special sons whom Elijah and Elisha revive, the man who comes back to life when his body touches the latter's bones[30]— death is never reversed. This is not just an empirical observation about biblical narrative. Biblical texts articulate the point explicitly and offer theological explanations of how humanity rightly lost the opportunity for the immortality for which they long and how they came to have their life span limited.[31] This being the case, it is no cause for wonderment that those who identify Judaism with the Hebrew Bible are surprised to find that belief in resurrection occupies a prominent and central place in Jewish literature and theology and becomes, in fact, a normative and obligatory aspect of the rabbinic tradition.

But I have been at pains to argue that the inevitability and irreversibility of death in the Hebrew Bible is only part of the story. The other part is the ubiquitous promise of life, sometimes conditional, sometimes not, offered by a God who enjoins his people, in the words of Deut 30:19, to "choose life." Especially in the foundational texts in Genesis and Exodus, the survival of that people is continually under attack by infertility and genocide. And yet just as continually—and often miraculously—new life appears, and God's promise overcomes the power of death that had seemed invincible. That God has the power to heal the most hopeless of diseases and even to bring people up from Sheol, restoring their vitality, is also a well-attested affirmation in the hymnic and lament literature of the Hebrew Bible. The revival of the recently deceased individuals who come into contact with Elijah or Elisha provides suggestive narrative examples of this theology at work. Ezekiel's vision in the valley of the bones (Ezek 37:1–14) comes somewhat closer to the idea of resurrection, however, for the people revived there have long been dead; their bones are dry.

We face, in sum, a more complicated situation than scholars of the Hebrew Bible have usually taken to be the case. Death is universal in the Hebrew Bible and seldom reversed, but God promises, offers, and prefers life and saves his chosen people from annihilation. He even saves some individuals (in extraordinarily rare and therefore especially noteworthy circumstances) from a death that is impending or one that has already occurred. My point is not that a full-fledged doctrine of the resurrection of the dead, when it arrives, changes nothing. It changes much. But it also reflects certain key features of the deep structure of the theology of pre-exilic Israel. For this is a theology in which the fact of death and the promise of life, each of them of capital importance, stand in a relationship of tension. That tension, or more precisely, the eagerness to uphold its two poles, will contribute to the full-fledged expectation of resurrection when it appears. The explicit expectation of a future general resurrection (the subject of the next chapter) does not arise around the early second century B.C.E. solely out of the needs of the moment. Contrary to what is almost always claimed, it is not primarily an answer to the challenge to God's justice that the death of the martyrs of the Seleucid persecution (and the like) posed, though that problem doubtless contributed to its diffusion and acceptance. Indeed, the resurrection of the dead is best seen not as a solution to a problem at all, still less as the way out of a logical embarrassment. It is best seen, rather, as another statement of the continuing Jewish need to uphold both the fact of death and the promise of life, while expecting and celebrating the victory of the God who promises life.

12

"He Keeps Faith with Those Who Sleep in the Dust"

*"[His mercies] are renewed every morning—
Ample is Your grace!"
Rabbi Alexandri said: Because You renew us every morning, we know
that Your grace is ample to bring about the resurrection of the dead.*
— *Midrash,* Lamentations Rabbah *to Lamentations 3:23*

The first transparent and indisputable prediction of the resurrection of the dead in the Hebrew Bible appears in Dan 12:1–3:

> [1]At that time, the great prince, Michael, who stands beside the sons of your people, will appear. It will be a time of trouble, the like of which has never been since the nation came into being. At that time, your people will be rescued, all who are found inscribed in the book. [2]Many of those that sleep in the dust of the earth will awake, some to eternal life, others to reproaches, to everlasting abhorrence. [3]And the wise will be radiant like the bright expanse of sky, and those who lead the many to righteousness will be like the stars forever and ever.[1]

The passage comes toward the end of a long narrative in which an angelic figure ("one who looked like a man," Dan 10:16) gives an exceedingly detailed, and maddeningly opaque, account of future events on the international plane. These events have, of course, vast implications for the Jewish people. The penultimate stage centers on "a contemptible man," a violent king who, in his godlessness and arrogance, will be determined to do harm to "the holy covenant," "desecrate the temple," and "set up the appalling abomination" — an idol in the most sacred place on earth. Contrary to what one might expect, the foreign king's assaults on the traditional order meet with a mixed response in the Jewish community. The angelic figure's own sympathies, however, are hardly divided:

> [32]He will flatter with smooth words those who act wickedly toward the covenant, but the people devoted to their God will stand firm. [33]The wise among the people will make the many understand; and for a while they shall fall by sword and flame, suffer captivity and spoliation. [34]In defeat, they will receive a little help, and many will join them insincerely. [35]Some of the wise will fall, that they may be refined and purged and whitened until the time of the end, for an interval still remains until the appointed time. (Dan 11:32–35)

The split is between "those who act wickedly toward the covenant," on the one hand, and "the people devoted to [*yōdĕʿê*] their God" — here better rendered "who know their God" — on the other. The latter receive their sacred and invaluable knowledge from a smaller group, termed "the wise" (*maśkîlîm*), who impart understanding to the masses (*yābînû lārabbîm*). The wisdom of this group, however, cannot deter death; and some of these "wise" will die, for the consummative moment will not yet have arrived. Interestingly, the prophecy evaluates their death positively. It is purgative, part of a process of purification and refinement whose full meaning will be apparent only at "the appointed time." Here, death remains real and tragic, and no immediate restoration into life, no "presto-magico" reversal, nullifies its reality and its tragedy. But it is, in the mysterious divine economy, also temporary.

Meanwhile, our prophecy tells us, the evil "king will do as he pleases," continuing on his course of unrestrained blasphemy, failing to honor even "the god of his ancestors" (Dan 11:36–37). Finally, after many a victory and having plundered richly, "he will pitch his royal pavilion between the sea and the beautiful holy mountain" — the Temple Mount in Jerusalem — "and he will meet his doom with no one to help him" (v 45). At long last, death will vanquish the victor.

If it had come in an earlier period in the history of ancient Israel, the text could well have stopped there, with the defeat of the arrogant idolater, perhaps with a codicil noting the escape of Israel, or some subset of Israelites, from his clutches.[2] In Daniel, however, a question remains open and the traditional structure cannot adequately answer it. That question is the fate of the "wise" (*maśkîlîm*) who have fallen by "sword and flame" or suffered "captivity and spoliation." Their demise, it will be recalled, is to be but temporary, lasting only "an interval . . . until the appointed time" (Dan 11:33, 35). It is the events at the other end of that painful interval, the events of the eschatological "appointed time," that occupy the first clear and indubitable text about resurrection in the Hebrew Bible.

Central to those events is the figure of Michael, identified earlier in the prophecy as Israel's guardian angel (Dan 10:21). What it means to say that the angel "stands beside [*'ōmēd 'al*] the sons [better, members] of your people" (12:1) is unclear, the verb in question having both military and judicial connotations. In this context, the likelihood is that both are present.[3] For the unprecedented "time of trouble" of which the verse speaks surely involves a continued physical threat that, in the mind of the author of the prophecy at least, only heavenly intervention can overcome. Yet the same verse also speaks of a book in which those to be rescued are already inscribed, and their rescue (vv 2–3 go on to say) entails a division between the worthy who are granted "eternal life" and the unworthy, condemned to the shame of "everlasting abhorrence." This is surely as much judicial as the more physical deliverance of the nation is military. Indeed, the difference between the two dimensions is much more real to our culture than to that of ancient Israel, for whom the LORD's frightening omnipotence was intimately and inextricably connected to his righteousness and justice. As we saw in connection with the Song of Hannah,[4] the march of Israel's Divine Warrior signifies the imminent righting of injustice — demise for oppressors, deliverance for their ostensibly helpless victims.

In Dan 12:1–3, the victims seem to be both the nation as a whole and those individuals within it deemed worthy of resurrection. "Your people will be rescued," the manlike being prophesizes to Daniel, but also — or is it exclusively? — "all who are found inscribed in the book," especially the "wise" (vv 2–3). The national dimension here recalls an earlier prophecy of "a time of trouble" (*'ēt-ṣārâ*) from which the chosen people are likewise delivered:

> [5]Thus said the LORD:
> We have heard cries of panic,
> Terror without relief.
> [6]Ask and see:
> Surely males do not bear young!
> Why then do I see every man
> With his hands on his loins
> Like a woman in labor?
> Why have all faces turned pale?

> [7]Ah, that day is awesome;
> There is none like it!
> It is a time of trouble for Jacob,
> But he shall be delivered from it. (Jer 30:5–7)

In Dan 12:1–3, however, the traditional affirmation that "[the] people will be rescued" and their oppressors doomed is complicated by the aforementioned division between those "who act wickedly toward the covenant," on the one hand, and those who are "devoted to their God," on the other (Dan 11:32). Presumably, only the latter will benefit from the predicted resurrection, as the covenant breakers share the ignominious fate of the foreign invaders with whom they have cast their lot, politically and religiously. How "[the] people will be rescued" when some of them are, in fact, doomed is less mysterious in the cultural world of ancient Judaism than in ours. For membership in the "people" was both ascribed and achieved, a matter of birth but also of behavior, in particular the observance of the moral and ritual norms that one born a Jew was charged to obey. As this passage would have it, those who disobey — especially through rank idolatry — have excluded themselves from the national identity and thus from the expected redemption as well. If so, then "all who are written in the book" (Dan 12:1) do not comprise a subset of "the people." Rather, the term is appositive: the traditionalists *are* the people. The other party has unwisely removed itself from the category of Jews who will participate in the national restoration that their God has promised.

The notion of a "book" in which destinies are inscribed appears only a few times in the Hebrew Bible. Perhaps the most memorable is in Moses' demand upon the LORD in the wake of another great act of defection and idolatry, the episode of the Golden Calf: "Now, if You will forgive their sin [well and good]; but if not, erase me from the record [or "book," Heb. *sēper*] which You have written!" To which the LORD responds in words with a clear affinity to our passage, perhaps even an influence upon it: "He who has sinned against Me, him only will I erase from My record [*sēper*]" (Exod 32:32–33). In short, contrary to what is sometimes said, the idea of a fateful internal division within the chosen people does not originate in the sectarianism characteristic of late Second Temple Judaism. The sectarianism does, however, harden the division, giving it an ideological cast that it did not earlier have.[5]

In Psalm 69, the mysterious book exhibits a name familiar from rabbinic tradition, especially the liturgy of the High Holy Days: "the book of life."[6] In this the psalmist believes the righteous are inscribed but hopes that his sadistic persecutors will not be (v 29). Similarly, in another anticipation of our passage in Daniel, an oracle in Isaiah speaks of a remnant "who are inscribed for life in

Jerusalem" (Isa 4:3).[7] Here, of course, there is every reason to believe that the remnant escape death. They do not undergo it and return to life, as the remnant in Daniel 12 do. Eventually, the remnant in Isaiah 4 will experience a death from which there is no return to life. But as we have observed, a narrow escape from death can be described as being brought up from the underworld or burial pit (e.g., Ps 30:3–4).[8] Here, too, what is to us a clear and decisive difference seems to have been a matter of uneventful continuity in ancient Israel.

One inclined to dispute this is still obligated to acknowledge, it seems to me, that the language and symbolism of resurrection were present and available, perhaps even abundant, long before the literal expectation. Modern historians, researching the origin of the Jewish idea of resurrection, understandably think of it as an innovation and seek a situation of keen discontinuity in which it arose. This is not necessarily wrong, but it does underestimate the verbal particularity and the textual character of its appearance — points of great significance to the ancient Jewish culture itself. Given the rich intertextual connections and dependence in which it is enveloped, the resurrection of the dead in Dan 12:1–3 may have seemed (at least to some sectors) much less innovative than it does to those who, ignoring its linguistic embedding, think of it as an *idea*. Much is lost when the resurrection of the dead is treated as a free-floating concept whose essence remains constant no matter what the culture in which it appears or to which it migrates. For every item in a religious tradition stands in a systemic relation to every other and cannot be detached and examined on its own without grave damage to its organic function (and thus to our capacity to understand its nature). In the case of Judaism from the Second Temple period onward, religious affirmations (even new ones) are so deeply embedded in the particularity of the scriptural language that efforts to disregard the latter in order to penetrate back to a core "idea" only lead us into grave misunderstanding.

Another misunderstanding arises if we think of the resurrection envisioned in Dan 12:1–3 as universal. As one commentator aptly puts it, the author's "concern is focused on the fate of the faithful . . . and their perfidious counterparts," for the phrasing "many of those that sleep in the dust" (v 2) seems to imply that some of the deceased never rise at all.[9] If so, the oddity of a partial resurrection — with only a sample of the Jewish people rising (no Gentiles are mentioned) — does not at all seem to be on the author's mind. It should not be on ours, either, unless we are committed to harmonizing their text anachronistically with more universalistic doctrines that appear later in the history of Judaism, Christianity, and Islam. It is much better at this point to keep the context and setting of our passage in the book of Daniel firmly in mind.

Other than the statement that those destined for resurrection "sleep in the dust of the earth" (Dan 12:2), the text gives no indication of their location, and we should be wise to respect its reticence on that point, too. Texts in the pseudepigraphical book of 1 Enoch evidence a belief that the dead are in the netherworld, though in different chambers in accordance with their different moral characters; not all of them currently dwell in the place of torment to which the wicked will finally be dispatched.[10] In comparison, Daniel 12 is remarkably restrained, giving no indication that those about to be resurrected, whatever their ultimate destinies, are sleeping in Sheol, Gehinnom, or wherever.

The familiar identification of sleep with death that Dan 12:2 makes is by no means universal. It has been pointed out, for example, that the Zoroastrians (from whom the Jews have often been said to have taken the belief in resurrection) did not make the equation.[11] Here again, the book of Daniel exhibits its thoroughgoing indebtedness to the culture and scriptures of what could already in its own time be justly termed "ancient Israel." It will be recalled that when Gehazi fails to restore the Shunammite woman's dead son, he tells Elisha, *lō' hēqîṣ hannā'ar*, "The boy has not awakened" (2 Kgs 4:31).[12] Similarly, Jeremiah predicts that when God exacts his punishment on the murderous Babylonians, who have destroyed Jerusalem and its temple and exiled the Judahites, those punished will "sleep an endless sleep, / Never to awake" (Jer 51:39, 57), using the same two verbs as Dan 12:2a. Perhaps most memorable are Job's sarcastic words in one of his laments over the finality of death:

> So man lies down never to rise;
> He will awake only when the heavens are no more,
> Only then be aroused from his sleep. (Job 14:12)

We must remember that sleep in the Hebrew Bible is not characterized primarily by refreshment and renewal. It can also be a dangerous and liminal state.[13] It is no wonder that momentous events, like the creation of woman and the first prediction of the enslavement in Egypt and the ensuing exodus, occur when the subject is asleep (Gen 2:21; 15:12). Nor is it a wonder that a psalmist likens waking after lying down to the LORD's answering from his sacred mountain when he calls out for aid against the attacks of the foes who outnumber him (Ps 3:6). Sleep, in short, is a mini-death, or, as an anonymous passage in the Talmud puts it, "sleep is one-sixtieth of death."[14] In the Hebrew Bible, however, it would be more precise to say that sleep is a death that is — or one devoutly hopes will be — temporary. Thus, the Christian apostle Paul can write that "Christ has been raised from the dead, the first fruits of those who have fallen asleep" (1 Cor 15:20). And thus, finally, does the daily rabbinic liturgy begin with thanks (recited while still in bed) to God for compassionately returning one's soul. This is not to say that ancient Israel, or its Second Temple, Christian, and rabbinic successors, could not distinguish sleep from death, or waking up from being resurrected. It is to say, however, that the vocabulary in which the belief in resurrection is couched builds on an already ancient perception that sleep is a mortal threat and waking life something miraculous, a testimony to God's special care for his faithful. Israelite literature attests to a belief that God restores the worshiper's soul (or, more precisely, the life force) well before a belief in the general resurrection of the dead appeared. If we bear all this in mind, the novelty of the belief in resurrection will diminish a bit, and we shall feel less urgency to embark on a bootless quest for this or that single, extraordinary factor that can explain the innovation — an unprecedented historical situation, an unexpected foreign influence, or whatever.

One element that truly is novel in Dan 12:1–3 is, however, signaled by an expression that, for all its frequency in later Jewish literature, occurs nowhere else in the Hebrew Bible, *ḥayyê ʿôlām*, "eternal life" (v 2). In it we can detect the outstanding difference between the beneficiaries of this resurrection and those brought back to life in the few places that speak of a similar restoration, such as the fetching tale of Elisha's resurrection of the Shunammite woman's little boy.[15] The difference, in a word, is its finality. Dan 12:1–3 envisions no second death for those resurrected, only "eternal life" for the faithful and "everlasting abhorrence" for the desecrators of the covenant. At long last, the periodic alternation of death and life comes to a dramatic halt. The granting of "eternal life" thus corresponds to — indeed, it is inseparable from — the prediction earlier in Daniel that

> the God of Heaven will establish a kingdom that shall never be destroyed, a kingdom that shall not be transferred to another people. It will crush and wipe out all these kingdoms, but shall itself last forever. (Dan 2:44)

The irreversible triumph of life is, in other words, of a piece with the establishment of the kingdom of heaven and the decisive and definitive victory of justice over the injustice that has, in the author's view, characterized all of human history to date.

The precise identity of the "wise" (*maśkîlîm*) who are the prime beneficiaries of the apocalyptic transformation remains unclear. The term is common in the book of Proverbs and in this context recalls the promise of abundant life and the avoidance of Sheol that Wisdom literature (Proverbs in particular) promises those who tread steadfastly on the path of the wise.[16] But it has long been recognized that the choice of this particular term has been dictated to

some degree by a famous passage about the so-called suffering servant prominent in Isaiah 40–55.[17] This is the first of three influential antecedents of
Dan 12:1–3 that will concern us here. In the process, I hope to show that the
origin and character of the belief in resurrection in Second Temple Judaism are
rather different from the way they are often conceived. The passage from
Isaiah begins:

> [13]"Indeed, My servant shall prosper [*yaśkîl*],
> Be exalted and raised to great heights.
> [14]Just as the many [*rabbîm*] were appalled at him —
> So marred was his appearance, unlike that of man,
> His form, beyond human semblance —
> [15]Just so he shall startle many nations.
> Kings shall be silenced because of him,
> For they shall see what has not been told them,
> Shall behold what they never have heard." (Isa 52:13–15)[18]

The passage goes on to detail the man's humiliation — his ugliness, his suffering and disease, his repudiation and rejection by those who thought themselves his moral superiors but actually fell far short of him. All this he bore
submissively, "like a sheep being led to slaughter," until he was taken away in
defiance of justice, "cut off from the land of the living." As a result, though
he was a man of justice and truth, "his grave was set among the wicked"
(Isa 53:7–9). Not least among the murky questions this exceedingly enigmatic
and ambiguous passage poses is the postmortem fate of the servant. For the
text goes on to say that all this happened, at least in part, so that "he might see
offspring" (Isa 53:10). Shall we, then, add Isa 52:13–53:12 to the small list
of pre-Danielic texts that speak of the resurrection of the dead?[19] This depends, in part, on a more basic and equally murky question, whether the
servant is an individual (in which case the restoration and vindication occur
after his death) or the people Israel (in which case the offspring and long
life that follow his death need not be taken as a resurrection in the later
and more individualistic sense of the term).[20] Either way, of course, the God
of life triumphs dramatically over death in this passage; either way, hope
survives death.

For our purposes, it is thus not necessary to resolve these points of long-
standing contention. For it is clear that whatever Isaiah 53 understands to be
the nature of the servant's vindication, Daniel 12 interprets it to apply to its
own vision of resurrection. As has often been noted, the announcement in Dan
12:3 that "the wise . . . lead the many to righteousness" (*maṣdîqê hārabbîm*)
similarly echoes the prediction that the once suffering and now vindicated

servant "makes the many righteous" (*yaṣdîq lārabbîm*, Isa 53:11).[21] The "wise" have taken on the identity of the servant, afflicted and mocked in life, vindicated and exalted after death.

The language of Dan 12:1–3 thus leaves it beyond doubt that the postmortem fate of the righteous is one of resurrection—the reanimation of corpses rather than vindication in the heavenly realm with a conferral of life (as may be the case in Isaiah 53).[22] But it would be a mistake to imagine that the "eternal life" the deserving receive is simply a restoration to their old quotidian reality, only without the pain and injustice. To "be radiant like the bright expanse of sky" (Dan 12:3) is (if the pun may be pardoned) light years away from having to reinhabit one's old body for all eternity. This is worth noting because scholars often present the issue as if the only alternatives are immortality of the soul, on the one hand, and resurrection of the body, on the other. Doing so is to neglect the key fact that resurrection was thought to yield a transformed and perfected form of bodily existence and thus a state of being both like and unlike any we can know in the flesh. To glance ahead to later historical periods, one thinks, for example, of the Christian apostle Paul's comment on the resurrection of the dead: "It is sown a physical body (*sōma psuchikon*); it is raised a spiritual body (*sōma pneumatikon*)" (1 Cor 15:44).[23] Or, to give a Jewish analogy from a century and a half or so after Paul, the early third-century Talmudic sage Rav contrasts this world and the World-to-Come in these words: "In the World-to-Come, there is neither eating nor drinking nor sexual relations nor business transactions nor jealousy nor hatred nor rivalry. Rather, the righteous sit with their crowns on their heads and enjoy the radiance of the Divine Presence [*zîw haššĕkînâ*]."[24] I do not mean to imply an easy equivalence of Paul's resurrection existence with the rabbinic World-to-Come. Both do, however, imply embodiedness—Rav's righteous have heads on which to put crowns, after all—though in a transfigured mode that is hard to visualize and can be conveyed only symbolically; the convenient modern dichotomy of physical versus spiritual cannot capture it. In both the Pauline and the rabbinic texts at hand, the beneficiaries of the new way of being are not disembodied spirits, but neither are they ordinary human beings who, amazingly, were once dead but have since recovered their lives. In both cases, postmortal existence is a radical transformation, not the indefinite prolongation, of earthly life.

In the case of Dan 12:1–3, the radiance of those rewarded after resurrection is probably connected with what John J. Collins describes as "notions of astral immortality . . . current in the Hellenistic world." He notes a mocking comment of the classical Greek comedian Aristophanes about a belief that "when we die we straightaway turn to stars."[25] In the Jewish and Christian materials that we have been discussing, however, the connections with astral immortality are muted. In the vision in Daniel, "those who lead the many to righteousness will be *like* the stars" (Dan 12:3, emphasis added); they do not *become* stars.[26] The spiritual body (to use Paul's term) with which they will be raised will have the permanence and radiance of astral bodies, but it is not one of them.

The ultimate fate of those unfortunates who, in the words of Dan 12:2, "awake . . . to reproaches, to everlasting abhorrence" is less clear. If we are to take postmortem experience as the opposite of the "eternal life" granted their fortunate counterparts, then perhaps we should imagine a second death following the public humiliation to which they awaken. Alternatively, "eternal life" may refer to quality more than to duration, so that each group survives in perpetuity, the one in blissful vindication, the other in wretched disgrace. If so, then Daniel 12 envisions something more along the lines of the Christian hell. An intermediate position — death that never ends — appears in a passage that also contains the only other attestation of the Hebrew word *dērā'ôn* ("abhorrence") in the Bible, and whose influence on Dan 12:1–3 is patent.

> [22]For as the new heaven and the new earth
> Which I will make
> Shall endure by My will
> — declares the LORD —
> So shall your seed and your name endure.
> [23]And new moon after new moon,
> And sabbath after sabbath,
> All flesh shall come to worship Me
> — said the LORD.
> [24]They shall go out and gaze
> On the corpses of the men who rebelled against Me:
> Their worms shall not die,
> Nor their fire be quenched;
> They shall be a horror [*dērā'ôn*]
> To all flesh. (Isa 66:22–24)[27]

Here, the rebels seem to endure forever, though, to be sure, not in life but in the disgraceful mode of unburied corpses whose putrefaction and consumption in flame will never end. Rather than arguing rationalistically and prosaically for this or that view of the postmortem fate of the condemned in these highly poetic and visionary texts, we should do better to note that in both Daniel 12 and its Isaianic antecedents, the fates of the two groups are linked. The main point in each case is not afterlife; it is *vindication,* the vindication of the just and their God against the rebels or defectors who had of late triumphed over them and disgraced him.[28] In short, in these texts the resurrection of the dead is best conceived as a *reversal,* not so much of death as of condition and status. God intervenes to make the downtrodden and the triumphant change places, in the process vindicating his own honor and sovereignty. Resurrection in this context is thus an implication of the eschatological inversion common in apocalyptic literature (and anticipated in older hymns).[29] In stark contrast to recent experience, the faithful traditionalists will live (and the "wise" among them will shine radiantly), but the desecrators of the covenant will either die or endure an unending ignominy.

One of the most secure and long-lived contributions of historical criticism of the Bible is the dating of Daniel to the time of the Seleucid persecution of 167–164 B.C.E. The "contemptible man" who "rag[es] against the holy covenant" and instigates the desecration of the temple, the abolition of the daily offering, and the setting up of the idolatrous "appalling abomination" in that most sacred precinct (Dan 11:21–31) is thus none other than Antiochus IV, the Hellenistic monarch against whom the Maccabees would rise in resistance and ultimately triumph. Although Jewish traditionalists over the centuries have stereotypically spoken of this confrontation as one of the evil foreign oppressor versus faithful innocent Jews, it is clear that many Jews were more sympathetic to the new Hellenistic culture than to the old ways of their ancestral Torah.[30] The conflict, in other words, was internal and not just external, and it is this split between traditionalists and innovators among Jews that the book of Daniel reflects when it contrasts "those who act wickedly toward the covenant" with "the people devoted to their God" (11:32). More important for our purposes, it reflects the same split when it contrasts those who awake to "eternal life" with those who awake "to reproaches, to everlasting abhorrence" (12:2).

Another commonplace among scholars draws a causal connection between this concern for retributive justice — that all should receive what they deserve — and the emergence of the belief in resurrection itself. Reflecting on the differing fates of the faithful traditionalists and the more cosmopolitan innovators in this period, George Nickelsburg puts it well. "Thus piety caused death, and disobedience led to life," he writes. "Clearly this confounded the standard Israelite canons of justice and retribution. Resurrection to life, on the one hand, and to punishment, on the other, was the answer to this problem."[31] More recently, John Day has articulated the same point in the language of Hegelian dialectic. Proverbs, with its supposed belief in an invariable nexus of deed and consequence, represents the thesis. Job and Qohelet (Ecclesiastes), with their frontal assault on the same doctrine, constitute the antithesis. The synthesis then comes with the notion of afterlife as it develops in Judaism in Greco-Roman times. Those denied justice in their lifetimes shall receive what they deserve afterward; the traditional theology proves true after all.[32]

Whatever theologians or philosophers may think of this common line of reasoning, as an explanation for the emergence of a belief in resurrection it fails, in my judgment, rather drastically. For one thing, the notion that the pious may experience death (even as a consequence of their piety) and the disobedient may experience life (even as a consequence of their disobedience) was hardly a discovery of Second Temple Judaism. Consider, for example, the narrative of Cain and Abel (Gen 4:1–16), already ancient by the time of the book of Daniel. Abel loses his life because God "paid heed to . . . his offering" but not to Cain's (vv 4–5), and Cain, unable to control his jealousy and his rage, commits the first murder, a cold-blooded fratricide at that. Yet Cain is not condemned to death, as Israelite law requires (Exod 21:12). Quite the reverse: "The LORD put a mark on Cain, lest anyone who met him should kill him" (Gen 4:15). In sum, when the tale ends, the innocent victim, whose favor in God's eyes led to his demise, is still dead, and his murderer is still alive, protected by the mysterious grace that had once provoked his lethal rage. This is not to say that the theme of judgment and vindication that we saw behind Dan 12:1–3 is absent here. On the contrary, God confronts Cain directly: "What have you done? Hark, your brother's blood cries out to Me from the ground!" (Gen 4:10). As a consequence, the ground "shall no longer yield its strength to you," and Cain the farmer must become a "restless wanderer on earth" (vv 12, 14). But the indictment of Cain and the vindication of Abel in no way reverse the former's survival or the latter's death. More important, the narrator does not seem bothered by the grave theological problem that modern scholars (and hardly they alone) perceive in this. He feels no need to construct a theodicy with a postmortem vindication.

Similar things can be said for a host of other texts, all of them earlier than Job, Qohelet, or Daniel, and none provoked by the deaths of Jewish martyrs in the second century B.C.E. One thinks, for example, of the murderous assaults of Jezebel and her husband, King Ahab, in the ninth century B.C.E., which resulted in the deaths of many of "the prophets of the LORD" (1 Kgs 18:13) and of the innocent traditionalist Naboth in particular, who refused to cede his ancestral holding to the palace: "The LORD forbid that I should give up to you what I have inherited from my fathers!" (1 Kgs 21:3). Here, too, vindication arrives, when Elijah first discredits and then slaughters Jezebel's prophets of Baal and when, just as the prophet predicted, the queen dies an ignominious death: the horses trample her body and the dogs devour her remains (1 Kgs 18:20–40; 2 Kgs 9:30–37).[33] But here, too, the vindication of the LORD's justice and his prophets takes place purely and exclusively on the plane of history (whether the narrated events happened or not): the innocent victims remain dead, and death in disgrace exhausts the punishment on their murderers. Neither victim nor victimizer awakens to a further judgment.

Consideration of texts like these impels us to but one conclusion: that the innocent die and the guilty continue to live was indeed recognized as a possibility early on and, more important, was not necessarily thought to impugn God's justice. For God's vindication of the oppressed could be realized after the latter's death, quite without objection (however inadequate this may seem to us). The opposing view, that people receive in their own lifetime only and exactly what their deeds warrant, is in the nature of an intellectualistic and schematic formula useful (then as now) for moral exhortation but hardly the unanimous view of the culture. It exerted a profound appeal in certain theologically self-conscious circles,[34] but biblical narratives are generally more subtle, more lifelike, and more cognizant of tragedy. Cases like those of Abel, the prophets of the LORD in Elijah's time, and Naboth all demonstrate that in pre-exilic narratives the righteous will of God could triumph, justice could be done, and the hapless victim vindicated, all without the felt need for the dead to be compensated.

One might retort (in the manner of Day's quasi-Hegelian dialectic) that after the challenge of Job and Qohelet things were different, so that thenceforth a vindication in which the victim remained deceased would inevitably have seemed inadequate, a blot on the glory of the altogether righteous God. In the case of Job, however, it is surely relevant that the restoration occurs before death — or, to be more precise, before Job's own death, since, as we have seen, the seven sons and three daughters who die in the prologue never come back but are only replaced by new children in the same numbers in the epilogue (Job 1; 42:13–15).[35] Surely if the author of the prologue and epilogue or the redactor of the whole book (who may have been the same person) thought that restoration and vindication must reverse the death of the victimized individuals themselves, the book would have had a different conclusion, or, if it did not, it would hardly have reported that Job "died old and contented" (42:17). In general, what Job seems to want, even in the poetic dialogues, is not so much a new lease on life as vindication, a divine act of justice that will clear his record.[36] In this, the underlying assumption is very much of a piece with those of the narratives about Abel and Elijah that we have examined.

The same cannot be said for the book of Qohelet, which casts into grave doubt the belief in a personal and just God who providentially directs the destinies of nations and individuals. For Qohelet, rather, "God" refers to an inexorable and ultimate fate unresponsive to human action (e.g., 9:1–2). That is indeed a frontal assault on the previous thinking, but it should not go missed that Qohelet has a resolution of his own to the problem. What he counsels is not the abandonment of religious norms or a life of unreflective hedonism, as one might have expected. Instead, he thinks that a happy life is possible even with all the limitations that follow from the absence of a personal, intervening deity, including the limitation represented by certain and inexorable death (e.g., 11:9–12:8). We have no real basis on which to claim that Qohelet had an influence on Judaism during the period in which the belief in resurrection was emerging (though it does seem that a later Jewish book, the Wisdom of Solomon, countered Qohelet with a strong claim of immortality).[37] But even if we were to grant, quite without evidence, that the book of Qohelet exerted great influence on the literature of its time, we should still have to wonder why its challenge had to be answered but its own resolution rejected. It seems odd to say that a book was highly influential, on the one hand, but idiosyncratic and without followers, on the other.

Finally, we must note one other logical difficulty with the claim that the theological problem posed by innocent victims and triumphant victimizers is the mother of the belief in resurrection. If the inner logic of Jewish theology necessitated the belief, why did so many Jews at the time not accept it? For example, as is well known, the Sadducees rejected it outright, and early rabbinic Judaism anathematized those who denied it or denied that it would be found in the Torah — obviously a group large enough to draw the anathematization.[38] It is, of course, often difficult in the extreme to reconstruct the thinking of those branded as heretical, since it is their opponents who have usually left the descriptions of them, but it does seem likely that in this case they continued to adhere to the older and supposedly discredited theology. In that theology, God's promises are reliable and his justice sure, but they apply to groups and to history rather than to individuals and personal destinies. One finds no better example of the survival of the older model into the period when an expectation of resurrection is first clearly attested than in the book of Ben Sira (also known as Sirach or Ecclesiasticus), a Jewish composition from the early second century B.C.E. Ben Sira's disbelief in resurrection is so explicit that one might surmise that he was acquainted with the new belief and wanted to refute it:

> [19]When a person is taken away, sorrow is over;
>   but the life of the poor weighs down the heart.
> [20]Do not give your heart to grief;
>   drive it away, and remember your own end.
> [21]Do not forget, there is no coming back;
>   you do the dead no good, and you injure yourself.
> [22]Remember his fate, for yours is like it;
>   yesterday it was his, and today it is yours.

> [23]When the dead is at rest, let his remembrance rest too,
>   and be comforted for him when his spirit has departed.
> (Sir 38:19–23)[39]

Ben Sira simply denies that the theological problem of the death of the innocent exists:

> [26]For it is easy for the Lord on the day of death
>   to reward individuals according to their conduct.
> [27]An hour's misery makes one forget past delights,
>   and at the close of one's life one's deeds are revealed.
> [28]Call no one happy before his death;
>   by how he ends, a person becomes known. (Sir 11:26–28)

Punishment, in other words, surely comes, even if it must tarry till the hour of
one's death. Ben Sira's view, it thus seems, is that we are neither to give up the
expectation of retribution nor to expect it to occur postmortem. At least, this
is the case if we translate the end of v 28 from a surviving Hebrew manuscript.[40] It is interesting, however, that the Greek reads "and through his
children [*kai en tois teknois autou*] a person becomes known." The version
that survives in Greek, in other words, represents the old intergenerational
theory of promise and punishment, still alive and well in the second century
B.C.E. If that reading is to be adopted, we should have to qualify our denial of
postmortem retribution in Ben Sira. For in that case the sage seems to conceive
of the final judgment on the person as extending beyond his irreversible death
and active somehow in his children, very much in accordance with older
biblical teaching.

Given this familial orientation, we should not be surprised to find that for
Ben Sira, retribution is not only for the individual but also for the nation:

> [23]May he give us gladness of heart,
>   and may there be peace in our days
>   in Israel, as in the days of old.
> [24]May he entrust to us his mercy,
>   and may he deliver us in our days! (Sir 50:23–24)

Like the book of Daniel, Ben Sira harbors a hope for the restoration of Israel.
Indeed, the verses that follow express contempt for three traditional enemies
of the Jews (Sir 50:25–26), beginning with the Edomites, whose downfall
has eschatological connotations in the Hebrew Bible (e.g., Obadiah 21). Yet
here, too, there is no sense that God's intervention involves any resurrection
whatsoever.

What cases like Ben Sira indicate is that it is a mistake to attribute the
emergence of an expectation of resurrection to a logical problem that only the

new belief could solve. On the contrary, however incredible the older settlement represented (with some new twists) by Ben Sira may now seem, it continued to hold the allegiance of many. There was nothing inevitable about the rise of the expectation of resurrection. The fact of death and the promise of life continued to exist, with all the old internal tensions, alongside the new eschatology. It is interesting to probe (though we cannot do so here) why some Jews in the Second Temple period came to find it inadequate, while others did not. Surely there are social and cultural factors that are at least as important here as the points of theology that are as often brought to bear on the emergence of an expectation that the dead will rise to judgment.[41] In any event, we must reject the reductive understanding of religion that sees in resurrection "a sort of ideological wood putty employed by engineers of a 'religious system' . . . to repair breaks in its defenses (or to plaster them over) and to restore equilibrium between expectations and observed reality."[42] The development of a belief in resurrection is too deeply and thickly rooted in early Israelite and other ancient Near Eastern tradition for any monocausal explanation to do it justice.

We have been examining the formidable logical obstacles to the idea that the martyrdom of faithful traditionalists under Antiochus IV around 167 B.C.E. accounts for the expectation of resurrection. Had we only Dan 12:1–3, which has been securely dated to that period and reflects its salient events, the explanation would, to be sure, have a certain historical plausibility. Even then, however, one would have to pay attention to the long-standing tradition that the God of Israel is a God of life, not death; nothing historical emerges in a vacuum. When we go outside the current Jewish canon, we find that predictions of resurrection and a last judgment already appear in literature that is generally thought to predate those events. Here I am thinking specifically of the reports of some of the cosmic journeys of the ancient sage and visionary Enoch, such as his journey to the high mountain in which "the spirits of the souls of the dead should assemble . . . until the date of their judgment" (1 Enoch 22:3–4).[43] A few chapters later, Enoch asks, "For what purpose does this blessed land, entirely filled with trees, (have) in its midst this accursed valley?" The answer comes from the angel Uriel:

> "This accursed valley is for those accursed forever; here will gather together all (those) accursed ones, those who speak with their mouth unbecoming words against the Lord and utter hard words concerning his glory. Here shall they be gathered together, and here shall be their judgment, in the last days. There will be upon them the spectacle of the righteous judgment, in the presence of the righteous forever. The merciful will bless the Lord of Glory,

the Eternal King, all the day. In the days of the judgment of (the accursed), the (merciful) shall bless him for the mercy which he had bestowed upon them." (1 Enoch 27:1–4)

As in Daniel, so here in Enoch, the context of resurrection is forensic. It is one of judgment and vindication, in which the wicked and the righteous finally receive their due deserts, of which they were apparently deprived in their lifetimes. Here again, there is continuity between the envisioned resurrection, a relatively new phenomenon, and the older and well-attested concern for a posthumous vindication of the innocent and punishment of the wicked. But in 1 Enoch 27, unlike in Daniel 12, there is no sense that the righteous have died because of their righteousness, or that the wicked have survived and triumphed to date because of their wickedness, whether manifest in the lethal persecution of the righteous or otherwise. In sum, although Dan 12:1–3 was surely the first passage in what is now the canonical Bible to speak of "a double resurrection of the righteous and the wicked and judgment of the dead," the idea was already present in apocalyptic Jewish circles beforehand and cannot be attributed to the immediate situation of the martyrs of the Antiochian persecutions of 167–164 B.C.E.[44]

In the case of Daniel, the "double resurrection" occurs within the framework of the eschatological restoration of Israel: "At that time, your people will be rescued" (Dan 12:1). The doubleness of judgment is not new: that "the LORD watches over all who love Him, / but all the wicked He will destroy" (Ps 145:20) is a principle ubiquitous in biblical literature of various periods and genres. Daniel 12:1–3, in common with much Second Temple literature, applies the same principle to the restoration of Israel. The "people will be rescued," but the wicked among them—those who have not acted as the Jewish people ideally acts—will awaken to disgrace, and not to life everlasting. The double resurrection may be relatively new, but the doubleness of divine judgment is not.[45]

Even the idea of national resurrection is not quite so new in the second century B.C.E. as is often claimed. Apart from Ezekiel's vision of the dry bones,[46] one finds an anticipation of Dan 12:1–3 in a text on which the latter manifestly depends:

Oh, let Your dead revive [*yiḥyû*]!
As a corpse they shall arise [*yĕqûmûn*]!
Awake [*hāqîṣû*] and shout for joy,
You who dwell in the dust [*'āpār*]! —
For Your dew is like the dew on fresh growth;
You make it fall on the land of the shades [*rĕpā'îm*]. (Isa 26:19)[47]

The verse occurs in a section of the book of Isaiah (chaps. 24–27) that is widely and reasonably believed to date from a relatively late period, surely in the time of the Second Temple. The focus of these chapters is thoroughly eschatological, fixed firmly on the frightening yet (for some) joyous events about to dawn. As one contemporary commentator puts it, Isaiah 26 "offers a great variety of conventional forms, but in the end it results in a highly theological presentation directed to the faithful, who testify to the effect of God's victory, yet still experience the full weight of divine and human judgment."[48] Thus, a few verses before ours, the poet can speak of the final, irreversible punishment of masters other than his own, and in language that anticipates our verse. The coming revival of the dead is the mirror image of the fate of the idolatrous lords whom the true LORD has dispatched:[49]

> [13]O LORD our God!
> Lords other than You possessed us,
> But only Your name shall we utter.
> [14]They are dead [*mētîm*], they can never live [*yiḥyû*]
> Shades [*rĕpā'îm*], they can never rise [*yāqūmû*];
> Of a truth, You have dealt with them and wiped them out,
> Have put an end to all mention of them. (Isa 26:13–14)

Yet just afterward, the poet can liken his community to a woman "writhing and screaming in her pangs"; it is "as though we had given birth to wind [and] won no victory on earth" (Isa 26:17–18). As is generally the case in apocalyptic literature, the era of affliction and tribulation — though still in force — is not ultimate. The last word of the God of life is not death and sterility at all but revival and "fresh growth," the awakening of the dead to new life on analogy to the new life that dew brings forth in the fields.[50] The end of the chapter nicely captures the complex temporal situation:

> [20]Go, my people, enter your chambers,
> And lock your doors behind you.
> Hide but a little moment,
> Until the indignation passes.
> [21]For lo!
> The LORD shall come forth from His place
> To punish the dwellers of the earth
> For their iniquity;
> And the earth shall disclose its bloodshed
> And shall no longer conceal its slain. (Isa 26:20–21)

The connections of these three passages in the book of Isaiah to the prediction of resurrection in Dan 12:1–3 are obvious. Isa 26:19, too, speaks about an awakening (*hēqîṣ*) to life (*ḥyh*) of those in the dust (*'āpār*). If one reads the verse in conjunction with Isa 26:13–14, the second passage above, then it, too, depicts a judgment, contrasting those who rise to live again with those whom God has wiped out so that "they can never live." To be sure, Isaiah 26 gives no indication that this latter group will "awake" to punishment, but the notion of contrasting verdicts and a revival of the faithful is prominent there nonetheless.

Whether we may correctly describe that revival as resurrection along the lines of the event envisioned in Dan 12:1–3 has been subjected to considerable doubt. John J. Collins, for example, thinks not. "Isa 26:19 can be read by analogy with Ezekiel 37: Israel was dead in the Exile," he writes, "and its restoration is as miraculous as resurrection." In short, the key verse in the book of Isaiah, for all its undoubted influence on Daniel 12, does not yet speak of an "actual resurrection of dead Israelites."[51] Against this view, however, Robert Martin-Achard makes an astute observation. "The author of Isa 26:19," he writes, "is not, like Ezekiel, envisaging the political revival of the nation; he is not even speaking about an event that would concern all Israel; he is thinking only of certain members of the chosen People, of those to whom 'thy dead' refer."[52] Not readily apparent from the English translation is the fact that the substantive in the phrase "thy dead" (*mētêkā*) is plural in Hebrew and thus somewhat more difficult (though hardly impossible) to read as a reference to the people as a unity. The implication seems to be that some (but not all) of Israel will rise. The verse can thus be profitably contrasted with Ezekiel 37, in which the prophet sees (at first) only bones, not individual corpses, and then learns that "these bones are the whole House of Israel." In other words, the dead individuals are explicitly identified as the nation in its entirety. Indeed, in the same verse, the metaphoric character of the dead is rendered explicit, again in revealing contrast to the Isaiah passage: "They [i.e., the whole House of Israel] say, 'Our bones are dried up, our hope is gone; we are doomed'" (Ezek 37:11). We should also note that in the previous chapter of the Isaianic Apocalypse we see a prophecy that at the time of the definitive victory

> He will destroy death forever.
> My Lord GOD will wipe the tears away
> From all faces
> And will put an end to the reproach of His people
> Over all the earth —
> For it is the LORD who has spoken. (Isa 25:8)

The mention of "the reproach of His people" demonstrates the historically particular circumstance to which the oracle speaks. But that alone does not require us to read the allusion to the destruction of death as only metaphorical. Rather, it would seem that death (which here quite possibly refers to the Canaanite god by that name, Mot)[53] is one of the enemies, or even the ultimate enemy, of the people of God, and no victory of that God can be complete until this lethal foe is finally eliminated. The final victory of the God of life requires the elimination of his great foe, death. Minimally, then, we must conclude that the dead in Isa 26:19 are markedly less metaphorical than the dry bones of Ezekiel 37. Maximally, we may conclude that the verse in Isaiah envisions (or prays for) a resurrection of the dead quite close to that predicted in Dan 12:1–3.

The argument represented by Collins and Martin-Achard, respectively, could be misleading in a way that merits attention. As I have been at pains to note,[54] when personal identity is constructed in corporate terms — when, that is, the subject is profoundly embedded in familial, tribal, and national groupings — some questions natural to modern Westerners become unproductive, even dangerous. In the case at hand, the question of whether it is individuals or the nation, Israelites or Israel, that God revives has about it a certain artificiality that can seriously distort our understanding of the text in question.[55] The classical Jewish belief in the resurrection of the dead is not simply the notion that departed individuals will eventually receive their due. It is the confidence that God will in the end fulfill his outstanding promises to Israel, even to those worthy members of Israel who sleep in the dust. That promise is very much centered on life. Here it is useful to recall a point I made about Ezekiel's celebrated vision of the valley of dry bones in chapter 10. We are tempted to observe that the individual Israelites resurrected in this text will die a second death, their new life proving to be only a temporary reprieve. The text itself, however, makes no such observation, and its author would surely find it odd. For Ezekiel's vision knows only of dry bones changed back into a living people. Its last word lies with life, with the Israelite people risen from their graves at the onset of their long-overdue restoration.

Whether in the vision of national restoration in Ezekiel 37, the ambiguous revival of the dead in Isaiah 26, or the clear prediction of resurrection with judgment in Daniel 12, resurrection does not simply vindicate the justice of God. It also fulfills the promise to Israel of the God of life. And in that, all these texts in their differing ways adumbrate the affirmation that the ancient rabbis ordained that Jews must make every day of their lives — the affirmation that God "keeps faith with those who sleep in the dust."

God's Ultimate Victory

"The miracle of rainfall must be mentioned in the benediction about resurrection." What is the reason? Rabbi Joseph said: Since it is on the same level as the resurrection of the dead, they inserted it into the benediction about the resurrection of the dead.
— *Babylonian Talmud*, Berakhot 33a

We have now established that the first universally acknowledged biblical reference to a general resurrection of the dead (Dan 12:1–3) is itself a passage rich in intertextual resonances. However new the belief may have been in the second century B.C.E. (when that passage was written), its textual articulation looks back to multiple scriptural antecedents of its own. One such antecedent lay in Isa 52:13–53:12, which speaks of the vindication and restoration of the servant of the LORD, so despised in his life, so humiliated in his death. The other lay in the "Isaianic Apocalypse," which speaks of violent changes about to occur, specifically the resurrection of the dead when the season of national affliction finally passes and the yearned-for resurrection comes to be (Isa 26:19). Historians of biblical literature tend to date both these texts to a relatively late period, the end of the Babylonian exile (ca. 540 B.C.E.) or the early Second Temple period (late sixth or early fifth centuries B.C.E.). This can give the impression that the idea of a general resurrection first appeared late in the development of the Hebrew Bible, most likely as an import from abroad.

Lateness, in turn, can suggest inauthenticity, in this case that resurrection emerged as an excrescence unrelated to deeper and long-established currents in the religion of Israel. It is this widespread misperception that I have been seeking to cast into doubt throughout my discussion, and in this chapter I hope to give further demonstration of its shortsightedness. Prophetic predictions of a reversal of death, in fact, long predate their transformation into an expectation of an eschatological resurrection and last judgment of the sort described in Daniel 12. Indeed, the hope that death may be reversed predates the emergence of Israel itself and constitutes an important aspect of the legacy of ancient Canaan. Without this hope, the religion of Israel would have assumed a very different shape.

To demonstrate this, we must push back further than the immediate antecedents of Dan 12:1–3. We must, in other words, trace the antecedents of the antecedents and pay more attention to the surrounding passages of some of the ones we have discussed. In the case of Isa 26:19, the most revealing source lies in Hosea 13–14. John Day has identified fully eight parallels between this verse (or its surroundings in the Isaianic Apocalypse) and these chapters.[1] The first involves Hosea's claim that:

> Only I the LORD have been your God
> Ever since the land of Egypt;
> You have never known a [true] God but Me,
> You have never had a helper other than Me. (Hos 13:4)

To this Day likens Isa 26:13:

> O LORD our God!
> Lords other than You possessed us,
> But only Your name shall we utter.

The Hebrew original underlying the ancient Greek version of this verse is even closer, for between the second and third lines the Greek reads:

> O LORD, apart from You, we know no other.

Were this the only connection, one might write it off as a coincidence. But Day notes similar parallel texts about the "imagery of birthpangs, but the child refuses to be born":

> Pangs of childbirth assail him [i.e., Ephraim]
> —And the babe is not wise—
> At the time when children are born, he would not have survived.
>   (Hos 13:13)[2]

. . .

¹⁷Like a woman with child
Approaching childbirth,
Writhing and screaming in her pangs,
So are we become because of You, O LORD.
¹⁸We were with child, we writhed —
It is as though we had given birth to wind;
We have won no victory on earth;
The inhabitants of the world have not come to life! (Isa 26:17–18)

More to the point of our discussion are the passages in Hosea 13–14 that speak of a redemption from death, such as 13:14:

From Sheol itself I will save them,
Redeem them from very Death.
Where, O Death, are your plagues?
Your pestilence where, O Sheol?
Revenge shall be far from My thoughts.

In idea, though not in wording, this famous verse recalls the affirmation of (or prayer for) resurrection in Isa 26:19, which drew our attention in chapter 12:

Oh, let Your dead revive [*yiḥyû*]!
As a corpse they shall arise [*yĕqûmûn*]!
Awake [*hāqîṣû*] and shout for joy,
You who dwell in the dust [*'āpār*]! —
For Your dew is like the dew on fresh growth;
You make it fall on the land of the shades [*rĕpā'îm*].³

The revivifying role of dew here recalls, in turn, another nearby text in Hosea:

⁵I will heal their affliction,
Generously will I take them back in love;
For my anger has turned away from them.
⁶I will be to Israel like dew;
He shall blossom like the lily,
He shall strike root like a Lebanon tree. (Hos 14:5–6)

The opposite of this healing, life-giving substance is a "blast, a wind of the LORD" that, as Hosea puts it, "[s]hall come blowing up from the wilderness," parching Ephraim's fountain, drying up his spring, and plundering his treasures (Hos 13:15).⁴ Similarly, the Isaianic Apocalypse speaks of "His pitiless blast [that] bore them off / On a day of gale" (Isa 27:8). In each case, Day points out, the imagery of the "destructive east wind [is] symbolic of exile."⁵

The representations of redemption in the two texts also display a remarkable resemblance, in Day's view. For example, the imagery of "Israel blossoming like a vineyard" appears prominently in both (Hos 14:1–8; Isa 27:2–6). Day also sees their denunciations of idolatry as a point in common. In particular, he puts forward the ingenious suggestion that *'ăšûrennû* in Hos 14:9 ("and look to Him") may play on the name of the Canaanite goddess Asherah, which is, in turn, reflected in the reference to "sacred post[s]" (*'ăšērîm*) in Isa 27:9.[6] Similarly, he finds a revealing likeness in the passages in which the two texts speak of "[t]he importance of discernment [and] judgment for the wicked" (Hos 14:10; Isa 27:11).[7]

Of the eight parallels between Hosea 13–14 and Isaiah 26–27 that Day develops, some are surely more compelling than others. The imagery of the destructive east wind or of the flourishing vineyard, for example, is far from unique to these two texts, and the specific language in which the common image is rendered is in any event none too close. Similarly, the condemnation of idolatry is so widespread in the prophets that one should assume the influence of one text upon the other only with the greatest circumspection. Finally, we must note a similar lack of verbal congruence in the commendation of discernment and pronouncement of judgment upon the wicked in the two texts. The use of the frequently attested root for words of discernment (*byn / bwn*) hardly establishes the deep and illuminating connection between Hosea 13–14 and Isaiah 26–27 for which Day argues.

Whatever the weakness of some of Day's parallels taken individually, the sheer density of them in a delimited corpus is highly curious and suggests that Hosea 13–14 has indeed had an influence to one degree or another on Isaiah 26–27. In particular, the case of allusions to unproductive birth pangs followed directly by references to deliverance from the underworld or resurrection of the dead (Hos 13:13–14; Isa 26:17–19) seems unlikely to be coincidental. In fact, that progression from agony and diminished vitality to new life and vigor is characteristic of the underlying movement of each text. It is also critical to the context in which an expectation of resurrection develops.

The theme of death and resurrection, it turns out, is much more prominent in Hosea than these parallels with Isaiah 26–27 would indicate. Day makes a strong case for the influence of two earlier chapters (chaps. 5–6) in Hosea on chapters 13–14, in turn, and these are replete with images of death and resurrection into life. Here are the parallels that he draws:[8]

> No, I will be like a lion to Ephraim,
> Like a great beast to the House of Judah;
> I, I will attack and stride away,
> Carrying the prey that no one can rescue. (Hos 5:14)

. . .

⁷So I am become like a lion to them,
Like a leopard I lurk on the way;
⁸Like a bear robbed of her young I attack them
And rip open the casing of their hearts;
I will devour them there like a lion,
The beasts of the field shall mangle them. (Hos 13:7–8)

. . .

Come, let us turn back to the LORD:
He attacked, and He can heal us. (Hos 6:1)

. . .

Return, O Israel, to the LORD your God,
For you have fallen because of your sin. (Hos 14:2)

. . .

And He will come to us like rain,
Like latter rain that refreshes the earth. (Hos 6:3)⁹

. . .

I will be to Israel like dew;
He shall blossom like the lily,
He shall strike root like a Lebanon tree. (Hos 14:6)

Many scholars have argued, to be sure, that the pertinent texts in Hosea 5–6 refer not to resurrection but only to recovery from illness. God does not revive here; he only heals.[10] If so, then Hosea 13–14, too, cannot easily be placed in a trajectory that eventuates with the Jewish belief in a resurrection at the end of days. In the ancient context, however, the difference between those actions, reviving and healing, is not so great. As we have had occasion to note,[11] death in the ancient Near Eastern world was often conceived as a disease — the most serious disease, to be sure, and seldom if ever, curable — but a disease nonetheless. Michael Barré puts it well: "For the ancient Semites, life and death were not contradictory categories, but simply the opposite ends of a continuum; hence, to bring a dead person back to life would represent only a further step to healing a gravely ill person."[12] In defense of the notion that Hosea 5–6, and therefore chapters 13–14 as well, speak of the healing of death rather than of a lesser disorder, Day draws attention to two key verbs in Hos 6:2:

In two days He will revive us [yĕḥayyēnû]
On the third day He will raise us up [yĕqīmēnû],
And we shall live [niḥyeh] in his presence.[13]

"All the other places in the Old Testament where these two verbs (*ḥyh*, *qwm*) appear as word pairs," he maintains, "the meaning clearly relates to resurrection, not simply healing."[14] Furthermore, the image Hosea uses for God's action in inflicting the malady to be reversed is clearly one of nothing less than killing: "I, I will attack and stride away, / Carrying the prey that no one can rescue"; "[I] have slain them with the words of My mouth" (Hos 5:14; 6:5). In short, the prophet's addressees are dead, and the healing for which they pray and which God ultimately promises to grant them is a restoration into life — deliverance from Sheol, redemption from death.

To us, of course, they are not really dead at all. If they were, how could they say, in Hosea's hearing, that "in two days He will revive us" (Hos 6:2)? Once again we butt up against a key difference between ancient and modern perceptions of the basic categories of life and death. Our modern conception of death as totally discontinuous with life impels us to understand the community's condition as one of grave affliction and debility only, and thus to interpret the unmistakable language of resurrection as thoroughly metaphorical. If so, it is still a metaphor founded on the conviction that the literal referent is, however miraculous, indeed possible in the hands of God nonetheless. What in Hosea's experience could have generated that conviction? Perhaps it stemmed from traditional affirmations of the LORD's unlimited power, which, precisely because it is unlimited, extends to death as to life.[15] Why, after all, should almighty God be able to heal all illnesses but death? Or perhaps Hosea's conviction stemmed from folklore of the sort represented by the three resurrections that came about through his fellow northern prophets, Elijah and Elisha.[16] In truth, we need not choose between these alternatives (and others that can be suggested), for all of them attest to the possibility that death might indeed be reversed, and its victims miraculously revived.

In the larger perspective, the language of death and resurrection so prominent in Hosea seems also to owe much to old Canaanite myths of the god Baal, whom Mot, the god of death, swallows, but who nevertheless revives and assumes his throne anew.[17] In defending this long-established connection, Day concedes that "Hosea, of course, was highly polemical against the cult of Baal," but he makes the important point that "polemic can sometimes involve taking up one's enemies' imagery and reutilizing it for one's own purposes."[18] In the case at hand, the reutilization involves a momentous transformation of the myth of the god who dies and rises, for Hosea's God is not in the least subject to the fluctuations that characterize his great rival's existence. The "living God" (Josh 3:10; Jer 10:10) neither fails nor dies. But we would commit a capital error if we interpreted this to mean that the pattern of dying and rising was relegated to the Canaanite past and altogether foreign to Israelite culture. For dying and rising is amply attested in the Hebrew Bible. Only there, it is his people Israel who manifest that pattern, perishing under the weight of their own sins (ironically, their involvement with Baal in particular) and yet coming back to life when their God raises them up. In losing fertility and natural abundance, Israel manifests the telltale signs of Baal's disappearance in the parched summer when the rain, clouds, wind, and dew fail, and human life fails with them.[19] Yet the God who is lord over death and life is also faithful to them beyond their deserts, bringing them back, as his great rival Baal, too, returned from the realm of the dead, as the life-giving rains return in the autumn. In the process, Hosea insists, the people Israel will recognize that it is the LORD and not Baal who gives them life and sustenance, returning faithfully to the God they shamefully and self-destructively betrayed for his impotent rival.[20]

The claim that Hosea's use of death and resurrection is metaphorical is thus only partly true. For in the prophet's understanding, Israel sinning has indeed died, losing fertility and vitality along with its identity as the loyal covenant partner of the LORD. If the subject is the Israelites as atomized individuals, the language of resurrection is highly metaphorical (though based in the literal resurrection of an individual, Baal). If the subject is the people Israel in their collective, national life on their land, it is less so. And, once again, if death encompasses such phenomena as drought, infertility, famine, and defeat, and life encompasses their opposites, then the language of death and resurrection in the book of Hosea is not metaphorical at all.

The sort of dichotomy associated with Baal dead and Baal alive anew is actually widely attested in the Hebrew Bible. It is not limited to the fortunes of the people Israel, nor is it, of course, attributed to Baal himself. It is best known from a pattern that has come to be called that of the *Divine Warrior*.[21] God marches out to battle against a formidable foe, and, as Frank Moore Cross puts it, "Nature convulses (writhes) and languishes when the Warrior manifests his wrath." When he has won his victory and has been gloriously enthroned on his holy mountain, however, "Nature again responds. The heavens fertilize the earth, animals writhe giving birth, and men and mountains whirl in dancing and festive glee."[22] The natural order, in other words, reflects and manifests the mode of divine activity. When God is angry, it loses its vitality and its fertility, dying for a season, as it were. When God has triumphed and received the glory that is his due as universal king, the natural order again responds, this time with new life, fertility, and luxuriance. Contrary to a common stereotype, the religion of Israel did not effect a radical separation between history and nature or pit the God of history against nature.[23] Quite the opposite: the order that we call "nature" (a term with no counterpart in biblical Hebrew) is closely bound up with God's action in history, and when his kingship, so often challenged in history, is finally secure, nature flourishes richly along with the human community that does his will:

> ¹¹Let the heavens rejoice and the earth exult;
>   let the sea and all within it thunder,
>   ¹²the fields and everything in them exult;
>   then shall all the trees of the forest shout for joy
>   ¹³at the presence of the LORD, for He is coming,
>   for He is coming to rule the earth;
>   He will rule the world justly
>   and its peoples in faithfulness. (Ps 96:11–13)

What we (but not the ancient Israelites) dichotomize as history and nature are simply two dimensions of the same reality, a reality that answers to the mode of divine activity at the moment—the mode of anger and death or the mode of deliverance and life. But in the Divine Warrior these two modes are more closely related, and the inner life of the Deity less dichotomous, than first seems the case. For the anger of the Divine Warrior is often a righteous anger, a reaction, that is, to injustice, and thus a sign of imminent deliverance to its victims.

The term *Divine Warrior* is misunderstood if it first calls to mind the all too familiar world of violent religious fanaticism, in which believers kill for the greater glory of their God (and a better chance to enter paradise). For the focus of the literature about the Divine Warrior in the Hebrew Bible does not lie on the destruction of the infidel. It more often lies on the enthronement of God in righteousness and justice, the longed-for arrival of the one who "will rule the world justly / and its peoples in faithfulness." In the Hebrew Bible, and more generally in the ancient Near East, the just rule of the king is inseparable from his deliverance of the weak and victimized from the stronger hand of the oppressor.[24] In the "festive glee" with which human beings and nature alike respond together to the Divine Warrior's victory, one can thus usually detect a markedly ethical dimension:

> The LORD has become king!
> Let the earth exult,
>   the many islands rejoice!
> ²Dense clouds are around Him,
>   righteousness and justice are the base of His throne.
> ³Fire is His vanguard,
>   burning His foes on every side.
> ⁴His lightnings light up the world;
>   the earth is convulsed at the sight;

⁵mountains melt like wax at the Lord's presence,
　　at the presence of the Lord of all the earth.
⁶The heavens proclaim His righteousness
　　and all peoples see His glory.
⁷All who worship images,
　　who vaunt their idols,
　　are dismayed;
　　all divine beings bow down to Him.
⁸Zion, hearing it, rejoices,
　　the towns of Judah exult,
　　because of Your judgments, O Lord.
⁹For You, Lord, are supreme over all the earth;
　　You are exalted high above all divine beings.

¹⁰O you who love the Lord, hate evil!
He guards the lives of His loyal ones,
　　saving them from the hand of the wicked.
¹¹Light is sown for the righteous,
　　radiance for the upright.
¹²O you righteous, rejoice in the Lord
　　and acclaim His holy name! (Psalm 97)[25]

To be sure, the false gods are discredited here, and their misguided worshipers embarrassed as a consequence (v 7). The latter are not, however, killed (as admittedly idolaters are in some biblical texts). Instead, the Lord's supremacy having become undeniable, the psalmist enjoins all who love him — there is no reason to think this group was restricted to Israelites alone — to practice the ethic of doing right that defines his character, stands at the base of his very throne (vv 2, 10), and wins its decisive victory when, triumphant, he becomes king over all the world. In those instances in which his victory entails the death of his opponents (e.g., Ps 18:26–46), the underlying assumption is that good is not self-enforcing and the power and determination of the forces of evil can be met only with greater power and greater determination.[26] Few things are more characteristic of the Israelite idea of the Divine Warrior than the confidence of his beleaguered and oppressed loyalists that their divine patron will not prove impotent in the face of the challenge and allow his justice and his power to be discredited. When at last he manifests his long-acclaimed power, the effects are felt, as we have seen, not only in the social realm (with the establishment of justice) but also in the natural realm, in which desiccation and languishing yield to revitalization and health.

The same language of desiccation and languishing, on the one hand, and vitality and flourishing, on the other, can be detected in some passages that contrast the faithless and idolatrous person with the opposite, the one who trusts the LORD above all, for example:

> ⁵Thus said the LORD:
> Cursed is he who trusts in man,
> Who makes mere flesh his strength,
> And turns his thoughts from the LORD.
> ⁶He shall be like a bush in the desert,
> Which does not sense the coming of good:
> It is set in the scorched places of the wilderness,
> In a barren land without inhabitant.
> ⁷Blessed is he who trusts in the LORD,
> Whose trust is the LORD alone.
> ⁸He shall be like a tree planted by waters,
> Sending forth its roots by a stream:
> It does not sense the coming of heat,
> Its leaves are ever fresh;
> It has no care in a year of drought,
> It does not cease to yield fruit. (Jer 17:5–8; cf. Psalm 1)

Here we must cite the important observation of Leonard J. Greenspoon:

> The state of the wicked is precisely that of nature at the time the Divine Warrior marches off to combat his foes. The righteous man, on the other hand, is like an ever-verdant tree firmly established and continuously nourished by waters which stand as the source of life against any onslaught that threatens the vitality and growth of nature. . . . The return of the Divine Warrior brought just such fertility and blossoming forth throughout nature.[27]

If so, then we must reckon with a whole set of interlocking dualities: the Divine Warrior challenged / the Divine Warrior victorious; nature dying / nature revitalized; the wicked and faithless individual / the ethical and loyal individual. Inasmuch as the campaign of the Divine Warrior in Israelite religion is, in large part, in the service of justice and righteousness, we should hardly be surprised that those who practice that same God's ethic and put him first in their lives (which are really the same thing) experience the fruits of his victory in their own individual destinies, unfazed by the heat that destroys the faithless.

In Jer 17:5–8, enhanced or diminished vitality—whether one flourishes like a luxuriant tree or atrophies before the force of the elements like a bush in the desert—thus depends upon the quality of one's life. Jeremiah does not, of course, envision "a double resurrection of the righteous and the wicked and a judgment of the dead," to recall a characterization of Dan 12:1–3.[28] But his vision does render different judgments on the worthy and the unworthy, and it is life — "Its leaves are ever fresh" — with which the worthy are rewarded. The biological character of the trope is striking.

For all their similarity, the difference between enhanced vitality or the sort we see in Jeremiah 17 (and many other passages) and the gift of eternal life (as promised in Daniel 12) remains real nonetheless. One difference is that in the implication of perpetual youth, the traditional blessing of enhanced vitality carries with it the correlative implication of deathlessness. The faithful who are likened to a tree whose "leaves are ever fresh" and which "does not cease to yield fruit" (Jer 17:8) do, of course, die; there is no evidence that Jeremiah would have thought otherwise. But the image itself and the poem in which it is embedded do not reckon with that grim fact. In fact, they give the opposite impression, that if the faithful do age, even then they do not cease to bear fruit — or to be immune to the infirmities that fell the faithless.[29] It is as if they have tasted of the Tree of Life.

The idea of resurrection, as it appears in relatively late biblical texts like Dan 12:1–3 and (in my judgment) Isa 26:19, is, in one respect, more realistic than this, for it does not obstruct a reckoning with death but rather requires one. The righteous along with the wicked, the "wise" along with the perfidious, must "sleep in the dust of the earth" before the great awakening at the end of history.

If we take into account the complex of images that has come to be known as the Divine Warrior, this difference between enhanced vitality and resurrection into eternal life (and, for that matter, between diminished vitality and everlasting humiliation) contracts markedly, though it does not disappear. We recall that when the Divine Warrior marches forth in wrath against the oppressive forces of chaos and death, nature languishes, and when he returns enthroned in victory and justice, nature flourishes and luxuriates. A good example of this pattern appears in Isaiah 34–35, where each chapter represents one of these two moments.[30] In chapter 35, which represents the flourishing of nature in response to the LORD's deliverance, we read not only of the blooming of the desert and the like (vv 1–2) but also, and more important for our purposes, of the miraculous reversal of human infirmities:

> [5]Then the eyes of the blind shall be opened,
> And the ears of the deaf shall be unstopped.
> [6]Then the lame shall leap like a deer,
> And the tongue of the dumb shall shout aloud;
> For waters shall burst forth in the desert,
> Streams in the wilderness.
> [7]Torrid earth shall become a pool;

Parched land, fountains of water;
The home of jackals, a pasture;
The abode [of ostriches], reeds and rushes. (Isa 35:5–7)[31]

Here, we see not just the transformation of wild land hostile to human habitation into well-watered farmland but also a kindred and equally miraculous healing of human disabilities. The blind shall see, the deaf hear, the lame leap, and the mute sing. In a world like ours, which has witnessed advances in surgery and medication that would have been classified as science fiction only a few decades ago (think of gene therapy), these transformations doubtless seem less amazing than they did to the prophet's original audience. Similarly, the experience of the past two centuries may cause us to underrate the impact of the transformation of the desert into a blossoming garden and the appearance of a highway in it for the ransomed to traverse on their return to Zion (Isa 35:1–2, 8–10). We can too easily forget that the fertilizers and pesticides that have vastly increased agricultural production, and the explosives and other engineering advances that have enabled mountains to be leveled and huge canals to be built did not exist in the prophet's world. For him and his audience, all these transformations were equally miraculous, equally inconceivable apart from the triumphal advent of God.

What is missing in Isaiah 35 is the healing of another disorder, the greatest of all—death. I term it a "disorder" because, as we have seen and many scholars have remarked,[32] death was conceived as a disease. To us, who have as yet found no way to reverse death, the omission comes as no surprise. Surely that is the one disease that is intractable! It is highly unlikely, however, that the ancient Israelites saw the matter in such a naturalistic manner. To them, all these transformations, whether of deserts or mountains or unjust fates or human disabilities, were equally impossible and equally exceptional. Or, to put the point positively, all of these reversals were equally exceptional: if they were to take place at all, they would have to take place by the special intervention of the Divine Warrior, for whom (so the liturgies affirmed) no obstacle was too great, no exception impossible to accomplish. The ancients saw the blind recovering their sight, the deaf their hearing, the lame their ability to leap like a deer, and the mute their ability to sing, as often as we have seen the dead recover their lives. Such was the state of medicine at the time. All of these reversals were thought to be the rarest of exceptions; to those of little faith, they were doubtless mere fantasies and impossibilities. But within the complex of ideas associated with the Divine Warrior, they were all, I submit, equally to be expected when the omnipotent redeemer at long last comes in justice and victory. If that is so, then the absence of mention of resurrection in Isaiah 35 is not so important, and the presence of resurrection in the related text of Isaiah 24–27 is not so unparalleled, as first seems the case. That the omnipotent God of deliverance "will destroy death forever" and revive the dead (Isa 25:8; 26:19) is readily understandable in the context of the stupendous reversals that characterized the victory of the Divine Warrior. Within that scenario of exceptions, it was hardly exceptional.

Having traced the antecedents of the expectation of a general resurrection of the dead in the form in which it appears in Dan 12:1–3, we are now in a position to summarize the results and draw conclusions. The central concern of Dan 12:1–3 is twofold, the rescue of the Jewish people from their oppression and the vindication of those who held fast to the tradition against those who cast their lot with their foreign tormentors. The notion of a full vindication that takes place after death was already ancient, and in no sense strange, at the time this text appeared. What was new (relatively speaking) is the participation of the deceased righteous in their own posthumous vindication and, correlatively, of the wicked in their posthumous condemnation. Both groups (or representative samples of them) now rise from the dust in which they have been "sleeping" to confront either eternal life or unending disgrace, as befits their conduct while alive. The vindication of righteous individuals no longer takes place only in a historical reversal in which they, now deceased, cannot participate, nor does it come about solely in the lives of their future descendants. Indeed, in the apocalyptic thinking that is the immediate matrix of the belief in resurrection, the old notion of a fortunate death has no place.[33] The condemnation of the wicked no longer involves their simply ceasing to exist or their being dispatched to Sheol, never to rise from there. Now both groups awake from death, but to different verdicts.

Among the immediate antecedents of Dan 12:1–3 is Isa 52:13–53:12, which seems to speak (admittedly with considerable obscurity) not only of the postmortem vindication and exaltation of a faithful but mistreated servant of the LORD but also of his being awarded new life in the process. It is evident that the vision in Daniel identifies the righteous of its own time of persecution with the servant of that text and sees the language of healing and restoration after death therein as references to resurrection. The vindication of the servant takes place against the denigration and mistreatment of him by others, to be sure, but the latter do not rise from death to face any punishment (indeed, their death forms no part of Isa 52:13–53:12 at all). Rather, the servant, like the "wise" of Daniel 12, "makes the many righteous" (Isa 53:11; cf. Dan 12:3), presumably changing their behavior by some unspecified process, perhaps prophetic preaching.

The interaction of individuals and the community is, in fact, essential to the expectation of resurrection as it appears in Daniel 12 and in subsequent Judaism as well. For resurrection is part of a larger scenario of national deliverance in which God at long last makes good on his promises to his people Israel. It is, in short, inherently historical and communal in character, and little or no light is shed on it if it is subsumed under the more familiar question, "How can I (that is, a deracinated individual) attain life after death?" or, "Is there an aspect of the self that death cannot destroy?" This historical and communal dimension appears in bold relief in the dependence of Dan 12:1–3 on passages from the Isaianic Apocalypse (Isaiah 24–27), especially Isa 26:19, which speaks of those "who dwell in the dust" awakening with shouts of joy when God finally redeems them from their long-standing suffering and despair. This happy event, in turn, follows upon the LORD's astonishing victory over his foes, including death itself, which he destroys "forever," wiping away tears and "put[ting] an end to the reproach of His people" (Isa 25:8). It is possible, of course, to interpret this language of the joyful awakening of the dead and the destruction of death itself as only metaphorical for the restoration of Israel and the establishment of its collective security. Even so, one has to concede that Daniel 12 did not so interpret it, and if the author(s) of Isaiah 24–27 had thought resurrection literally impossible, their choice of it as a metaphor for the national resurrection that they fully expected was highly inappropriate and self-defeating.

In the background of this application of resurrection language to Jewish national restoration lies the idea that the advent and presence of God not only brings about deliverance for his people; it also revitalizes nature, bringing life-giving moisture to desiccated land and fertility to dwindling flocks and herds. As I have noted, the dichotomy of history versus nature is alien to the Israelite worldview and productive of much modern confusion. Thus, a prophet like Hosea (whose oracles influenced Isaiah 24–27), who speaks of God's reviving and raising up those he has punished (Hos 5:14–6:3), can describe Israel after its revival in terms of luxuriant nature. In response to the LORD's life-giving dew, the people blossom like the lily and strike root like a great tree, giving forth a fine fragrance (14:2–9). The new life is not represented as compensation for the suffering they have experienced, since the suffering was deserved and its ultimate cause lay in God's righteous will. Instead, the new life is a correlate of the renewed relationship between God and his people that human repentance and divine grace conjointly bring about. The flourishing of nature (including human vitality) is the normal state of affairs when the people Israel are faithful to the LORD's covenant with them.

Behind all these older biblical antecedents of the prediction of resurrection in Dan 12:1–3 lies, in turn, the momentous Israelite transformation of the myth of the Canaanite god, Baal. In the Canaanite version, Baal dies, a victim of deified Death (Mot), in the hot, dry summer; nature dies with him. But Death is, in turn, killed, Baal lives anew, and nature flourishes and luxuriates in response. Israelite culture (at least as reflected in the Hebrew Bible) adapts this model to a theology centered on the LORD's relation to the people Israel in history. He is the living God and never dies, but the people Israel's own fortunes dwindle and revive in relation to their distance from or nearness to him (which often but not always correlate with their own moral wickedness or goodness, respectively). When they are distant from him, or he from them, they sicken and perish. When they reapproach him in repentance, or he returns to them in deliverance, they revive and flourish. In the vision of texts like Dan 12:1–3, when at last the victorious king arrives to "rule the world justly" (Ps 96:13), the victims of the era of injustice will surely receive their due. But the origin of the idea of God's dramatic intervention and its inversion of the standing world order does not lie simply in the embarrassment caused by the deaths of the holy martyrs.

Each of the several elements that appear in Dan 12:1–3 existed, at least germinally, in earlier stages of the religion of Israel, though their combination and fusion are relatively new and distinctive. They point forward to the Pharisaic and rabbinic doctrine of resurrection (and to their Christian counterpart) as much as they recall their biblical forebears. In addition, however, some scholars have long argued that Zoroastrianism, the religion of the Persian Empire, played a key role in the development of the idea of a resurrection of the dead in Second Temple Judaism.[34] For Zoroastrian theology also spoke of an eschatological victory of truth over falsehood, of light over darkness, and of life over death, the last, importantly, involving a literal reviving of dead bodies. This eschatology has obvious and striking connections with Jewish apocalyptic in general, and with the expectation of resurrection as it appears in Enoch and Daniel in particular. Indeed, since the Persians controlled the Land of Israel from their defeat of the neo-Babylonian Empire in 539 B.C.E. until their own demise at the hands of Alexander the Great two centuries later, it strains credulity to think they exerted no influence at all on Judaism of the period.[35] In the case of resurrection, however, any such influence seems to have been quite distant, a matter of milieu rather than of direct borrowing. For, as John Day points out, the idea that the dead will awaken from their graves is hard to square with the fact that the Zoroastrians neither buried their dead nor spoke of resurrection in the language of waking. These practices, Day stresses, are found in Canaanite tradition, however.[36] It would seem that at most the force of Zoroastrian eschatology nudged Judaism along in its movement toward a belief in the future resurrection of the dead.[37] If Jewish apocalyptic is the mother of the expectation of a general resurrection, then Zoroastrian theology (which probably influenced the development of apocalyptic in Jewish circles) is at best the grandmother. If, however, our argument that the notion of the Divine Warrior is the most important influence on the expectation in question is correct, it would be better to describe Zoroastrian theology as at most a collateral relation whose influence is indirect.

When the belief in resurrection finally makes an unambiguous appearance in Judaism, it is thus both an innovation and a restatement of a tension that had pervaded the religion of Israel from the beginning, the tension between the LORD's promise of life, on the one hand, and the reality of death, on the other. In the case of resurrection, the last word once again lies not with death — undeniably grievous though it is — but with life. Given the reality and potency ascribed to death throughout the Hebrew Bible, what overcomes it is nothing short of the most astonishing miracle, the Divine Warrior's eschatological victory.

Epilogue: The Two Horns of the Ram

Rabbi Ḥananel ben Papa said: "Listen, for I will speak of princely things." Why are the words of the Torah compared to a prince? To tell you that just as a prince has the power to put to death and to grant life, so do words of Torah have the power to put to death and to grant life.
— *Babylonian Talmud* Shabbat 88b

Our exploration into the rabbinic doctrine of resurrection has traced its ultimate origin to the transformation that nature undergoes as a result of the Divine Warrior's astonishing victory. That transformation replaces sterility with fertility, childlessness with new descendants (and the return of lost descendants), hopelessness with a radiant future—death with life. Within the religion of Israel from the earliest time that we can identify it, the hoped-for transformation could not have been thought complete, or even real, without a restoration of the people Israel itself, and this perforce entailed a recovery from humiliation and defeat, a reconstitution of the broken nation, and its rededication to its redeemer and restorer. The affirmation that such a restoration could even bring back the dead was both innovative and deeply conservative. Unfortunately, it is usually only the innovativeness that scholars remark. This is because the innovation is obvious: Israelite tradition had not previously envisioned a single event in which all, or all who were judged worthy, would awaken from their mortal slumber to be awarded life eternal. But the elements of the foundation for such a development had already been laid. For the same tradition had long acclaimed its God as one who "deals death and gives life / Casts down into Sheol and raises up" (1 Sam 2:6), told stories of prophetic miracle workers who had performed individual resurrections in his name, and voiced a communal yearning to experience the "everlasting life" (Ps 133:3) that was a central aspect of the conception of the Temple atop Mount Zion in Jerusalem.

Moreover, Torah traditions already ancient when the expectation of resurrection appeared had conceived of the Israelite nation as the beneficiary of an eternal and indefeasible covenant guaranteeing the people's survival, no matter how grievous their treatment at the hands of oppressors may be or how heinous their own wickedness may prove.[1] Closely associated with this theology were the stories of national beginnings — again, already of venerable antiquity when the belief in a general resurrection appeared — that saw the origin of the people as itself a miraculous reversal of a death-dealing nature that had deprived the covenanted fathers of the futurity that descendants alone represented. In the exile (sixth century B.C.E.), the reversal could be symbolized not only by miraculous replenishment through new births but also by the resurrection of those long dead, their bones dried up and all hope gone. This new image of the restoration of Israel surely marks a major milestone along the way to the doctrine of resurrection that will emerge in full clarity only later.

The expectation of a resurrection in Second Temple Judaism, when it does appear, was thus not a total *novum*. Rather, it was the end product of a centuries-long process by which these old traditions (and others that we have explored but not listed here) coalesced. This fateful coalescence may well have received additional stimulus from the two sources to which scholars often attribute this expectation exhaustively, the indirect influence of Zoroastrianism, which affirmed a future resurrection of the dead, and the immediate trauma of persecution in the days of the Maccabees, when the faithful were put to death precisely for their faithfulness. But, as I have been at pains to argue, these two factors, whether alone or in tandem, cannot account for the shape the belief in resurrection assumes in Judaism. They may have served, in their different ways, as catalysts for that fateful reaction, but they were not themselves the reagents. To concentrate on them alone is to miss both the rich *praeparatio* of antecedent tradition and the complex trajectory that resulted in a belief in resurrection among many Jews of the Second Temple era.

We began our exploration with the rabbis of Talmudic times, and to them we must now return. By their time, the events that we have been tracing lay in the distant past; the biblical texts are remembered and treasured, but the sequences of their composition and their nonbiblical parallels are not. It is too easy to forget that as much time elapsed between the composition of Daniel 12, in which resurrection has become explicit, and the promulgation of the Mishnah, the first great work of rabbinic Judaism, as lies between the Pilgrims of Plymouth Colony and contemporary Americans. As for the belief in a future resurrection of the dead, this was, as we saw in our first two chapters, already a given for the rabbis, so much so that they defined those Jews who disputed it as outside the community and, fittingly, ineligible to benefit from the happy event that they denied. Indeed, belief in the resurrection of the dead had become so essential that many rabbinic texts presented it as the plain meaning of the Written Torah itself and thus the inheritance of all Israel, and not simply as a valid and obligatory item in the Oral Torah peculiar to the rabbis themselves.

This concentration on Torah is a distinguishing characteristic of rabbinic Judaism over against the apocalyptic circles in which the expectation of an eschatological resurrection first emerged. By this, I intend not only the peculiarly rabbinic doctrine of Oral Torah but also the high status that the Written Torah, the Pentateuch, has in rabbinic theology. The Pentateuch is, in fact, the text to which the rabbis devote the most attention, and their tendency is to treat the other books of their Bible as subordinate to it and even as commenting on it. The high status of the Written Torah is the major reason that the rabbis expended so much effort to root the resurrection of the dead therein. To them it was inconceivable that something as central to the relationship of God to humanity as resurrection would have been unknown to Moses or unanticipated at Sinai.

The rabbinic devotion to Torah is itself rooted in certain theological claims that are highly pertinent to our subject. Contrary to a common misperception today, the "people of the book," as Muhammad was later to call the Jews (along with the Christians), did not devote themselves to it purely for intellectual or educational purposes. Rather, given the rabbinic understanding of human nature (and nature in general), the study and practice of Torah is a moral and theological necessity, to which the alternative is nothing less than death, in this world and the next.[2]

Were human nature morally neutral, equally balanced between good and evil, this dire situation might not obtain. In rabbinic thinking, however, human beings are continually assaulted by a formidable innate impulse that the rabbis call the "Inclination" (*yēṣer*) or the "Evil Inclination" (*yēṣer hāra'*).[3] The Gemara quotes an illuminating comment of Rabbi Simon ben Laqish, a sage from the Land of Israel in the early third century C.E.:

> A man's Inclination [*yēṣer*] attacks him every day and seeks to put him to death, as it is said, "The wicked watches for the righteous; / seeking to put him to death" (Ps 37:32), and were it not for the Holy One (blessed be He!), who helps him, he could not withstand it, as it is said, "The LORD will not abandon him to his power; / He will not let him be condemned in judgment" (v 33). (*b. Suk.* 52b)

In this midrash, the "wicked" who is on the lookout for an opportunity to kill the righteous is not another person, as in the verses in the Psalter that serve as the prooftext. Rather, the "wicked" is a person's own nature, continually waging acts of potentially lethal aggression against him. Were persons to rely on their own moral character alone, they would surely perish, since their only ally would in that case also be their assailant. Fortunately, the righteous have a real ally in God, who, protecting them from the powerful enemy within, keeps them alive by enabling them to persevere in their own fragile righteousness. To put the point another way, when God "sustains the living in kindness," as the rabbinic liturgy affirms, he does so in part by protecting the living from their own propensity for conduct that results in death. Were they to rely only upon themselves, the result would be fatal.

In this theology, death is not natural, or at least not altogether so. It results, rather, from human choices, which are themselves partly the consequence of human nature, with its powerful and frighteningly resilient appetite for evil. It thus makes sense that the same Rabbi Simon ben Laqish (whose theology on this is typical) deduces the following three-way equation:

> Satan, the Evil Inclination, and the Angel of Death are all one and the same. (*b. B. Bat.* 16a)

The devil, in sum, kills, but his prey are anything but passive victims. Rather, they are actively complicit in their own demise, choosing the path that leads to death over its life-giving, life-extending alternative. The choice is theirs, but they make it in response to deep God-given promptings within themselves. By failing to check and counteract instincts that they never choose to have in the first place, the wicked do themselves in. Having done so, however, they can still change a death sentence to a decree of new life, if only they choose to walk through the gates of repentance, which are (*mirabile dictu*) always open to them.[4]

Confronted with the knowledge that one carries within oneself a poison as potent as the Evil Inclination, one is quickly predisposed to inquire after the appropriate antidote, and here rabbinic thinking does not disappoint. For the rabbis saw in the Torah itself a prime remedy against the lethal enemy within.[5] Consider the revealing wordplay in the following early midrash:

Our rabbis taught: "Therefore impress" [*wĕśamtem*] [these My words upon your very heart"] (Deut 11:18) — perfect medicine [*sam tam*]. Why is the Torah likened to a life-giving medicine? This can be compared to the case of a man who struck his son with a huge blow and put a compress on his wound. He said to him, "My son, so long as this compress is on your wound, eat whatever you like and drink whatever you like, and bathe in either hot or cold water, and you needn't be afraid. But if you take it off, it will break into ulcers." Thus the Holy One (blessed be He!) said to Israel, "My son, I created the Evil Inclination; I created Torah as its antidote. If you occupy yourselves with Torah, you will not be delivered into its power, as it is said, 'Surely, if you do right, / There is uplift.' But if you do not occupy yourselves with Torah, you will be delivered into its power, as it is said, 'Sin couches at the door.' Not only that: All of its business centers on you, as it is said, 'Its urge is toward you.' But if you want, you can rule over it, as it is said, 'Yet you can be its master'" (Gen 4:7). (*b. Qidd.* 30b)

In this midrash, human beings first discover themselves not in a state of wholeness and health but gravely wounded, wounded, in fact, by their very created nature and thus victims, as it were, of their creator. Perhaps we can detect therein a tinge of resentment against God for having made human beings defective. But if so, the human case is weak, for the victims never existed without the defect, and it is only through the kindness of God that they survive and thrive. Furthermore, as the decoded parable (*nimšāl*) makes clear, the wound is not physical, of course, but moral, its proximate cause being the Evil Inclination. Given how natural the wound is to the patient (for it results, as we have seen, from a constituent element of human nature), it is too much to expect it to be eradicated, at least in this world. In so holding, classical Judaism is vastly more pessimistic (some would say, vastly more realistic) than those streams of modern Western thinking that locate evil in social or economic structures or in learned behaviors that can be just as readily unlearned. In rabbinic thinking, restructuring society in the name of justice — the most instinctive response of modern politics — can never fully achieve the desired goal, for the creators of the new structure are themselves subject to the Evil Inclination, which human beings cannot uproot, just as they did not create it. For that reason alone, the results of the reformers' labor would inevitably be imperfect, fallible, and distorted.

Rather than questing after a final elimination of the poison within, we must, the rabbis thus thought, content ourselves in the here and now with long-term suppressive therapy. A prime form in which this comes is the Torah, which is a medicine so effective that the patient can live a healthy, normal life — so long as he does not forget to take it. By use of Gen 4:7, the rabbis have transformed the LORD's warning to Cain as he seethed with fratricidal jealousy into a commendation of Torah as an antidote to the destructive impulses the first murderer felt. Cain, of course, failed to heed the admonition and became the slave rather than the master of his own sinful urge. The people Israel, by contrast, have an enormous advantage that he lacked. They have the Torah, which is vastly more encompassing and vastly more substantive than any simple admonition. For Torah is a total life practice with which they can occupy themselves communally and individually, mentally and morally. At its best, it serves to distract its practitioners from the thoughts and actions that lead to sin, to habituate them to do the good, and to fortify their will against the wound within that would otherwise break into deadly ulcers.

Like the other modalities of good that God has put at the disposal of human beings, the Torah requires constant vigilance — indeed, the moral equivalent of war — in order to counter the evil within.[6] Another statement in the name of Rabbi Simon ben Laqish puts it well:

> A person should always incite his Good Inclination [yēṣer haṭṭôb] against his Evil Inclination [yēṣer hāraʿ], as it is written, "So tremble, and sin no more." If he is victorious over it, well and good. If not, let him occupy himself with Torah, as it is said, "ponder it." If he is victorious over it, well and good. If not, let him recite the *Shema,* as it is said, "on your bed." If he is victorious over it, well and good. If not, let him remind himself of the day of his death, as it is said, "and be still" (Ps 4:5).[7] (*b. Ber.* 5a)

Here the rabbi interprets the successive phrases of Ps 4:5 in terms of the assaults of the Evil Inclination upon its prey. The countervailing force of the Good Inclination may, with considerable effort, suffice to allow for the desired moral victory. But it may not, and if so, the Torah is the next weapon of choice. Should it fail as well, one must resort to the recitation of the central text of the rabbinic liturgy known (after its first word) as the Shema.[8] If even this fails, then the thought of one's own inevitable death, and the judgment that follows, is the last weapon in the arsenal of moral struggle that the rabbi develops.

The righteous and the repentant, of course, die as well, and the rabbis tend to see their deaths, too, as the result of sin (though this is only a generalization and is sometimes a matter of dispute).[9] A major stream of rabbinic thought makes an important distinction, however, between the death of the righteous and that of the wicked. The demise of the righteous, however deserved it may be in one respect, has positive effects in another respect and is not to be easily equated with punishment. This we see clearly, for example, from a midrash that notices that the report of the death of Miriam (Num 20:1) directly follows the chapter on the "red cow" (Numbers 19), which speaks of a central rite of purification:

> Rabbi Ammi said: Why was the death of Miriam put next to the passage about the red cow? To tell you that just as the red cow effects atonement, so does the death of the righteous effect atonement. (*b. Moʿed Qat.* 28a)

Another midrash makes a related point with reference to the report of Aaron's death in Deut 10:6, which directly follows an elaborate version of the story of the Golden Calf (Deut 9:11–10:5):

> Rabbi Yudan, son of Rabbi Shalom, said: Why did Scripture put the death of Aaron next to the shattering of the tablets [of the Decalogue]? To teach you that the death of the righteous is as hard on the Holy One (blessed be He!) as the shattering of the tablets. (*b. Men.* 91a)

In short, though death is, in one obvious and pedestrian sense, the great equalizer, the fact that everyone dies does not imply that everyone is equally wicked. For just as the lives of the wicked and the righteous are different, so is the effect of their death different, both on their fellow humans and on God. And as we shall see, their ultimate destiny, too, is different, *toto caelo,* for the righteous are promised life in the World-to-Come following their resurrection. In that sense, too, the equalization of destinies that death brings about turns out to be temporary. As in the Hebrew Bible, so in rabbinic literature, the last word lies with life, not with death, with God's transformative and redemptive victory, not with humanity's sordid defeats.

According to a number of rabbinic texts, the human struggle against the Evil Inclination serves the larger purpose of contributing to the ultimate victory of God over human evil. Here, as often in rabbinic thought, the two worlds, This World (*hāʿôlām hazzeh*) and the World-to-Come (*hāʿôlām habbāʾ*), to use the rabbis' terminology, are thus inextricably connected; the rabbinic focus on ethical action in This World hardly bespeaks indifference toward the World-to-Come. One indication of this is the way the rabbis can describe certain practices as evidence that the person performing them is a member of the World-to-Come.[10] Such passages are usually understood as commendations of the practices in question, and this they surely are. But there are other ways to commend a practice, and to limit the meaning of such statements to this one function is to miss the fact that they also serve as characterizations of the World-to-Come, that is, of the nature of life transformed by redemption. The following midrash builds on prophetic promises of the redemption — indeed, the re-creation — of human beings to make the connection of life before redemption and afterward beautifully:

> Israel said to the Holy One (blessed be He!), "Master of the Universe, You know the power of the Evil Inclination, how formidable it is!" The Holy One

(blessed be He!) said to them, "Chip away [*saqqĕlû*] at it a little in this world, and I will remove it from you in the future," as it said, "Build up, build up the highway, / Remove the rocks [*saqqĕlû mēʾeben*]!" (Isa 62:10). Similarly, it says, "Build up, build up a highway! / Clear a road! / Remove all obstacles / From the road of My people!" (Isa 57:14). In the World-to-Come, I will uproot it from you: "I will remove the heart of stone [*ʾeben*] from your body and give [you a heart of flesh]" (Ezek 36:26). (*Num. Rab.* 15:16).

The last verse cited comes from an oracle in which the prophet Ezekiel speaks of God's future repatriation and restoration of Israel. For Ezekiel, however, human nature is so incorrigibly evil that there are no grounds to imagine human beings in the state of righteousness that such a restoration requires.[11] Without such righteousness, the sins that resulted in exile would immediately manifest themselves anew, and the restoration, far from being permanent, as the prophet intends, would be exceedingly short-lived. The answer is nothing short of a re-creation of human beings, in which God replaces their stony hearts with fleshy ones, that is, hearts that are sensitive and obedient to the divine will. The image of removing stones in Ezek 36:26, in turn, recalls the oracles of restoration in Isaiah, which repeatedly speak of the urgency of raising up a highway by clearing out the rocks that obstruct the march of the redeemed back to Zion (Isa 57:14; 62:10). Finally, putting the oracles in the books of Ezekiel and Isaiah together, we must infer that the "obstacles" to be removed from the road of the redeemed are not only literal rocks but meta-phorical ones as well, namely, the moral character of the would-be redeemed themselves, a character marked by the formidable power of the Evil Inclina-tion. The practical counsel of this sophisticated and complex little midrash is that the people Israel should chip away at those rocks as best they can in this world. They should engage in what I earlier termed "long-term suppressive therapy" so that God in his grace may remove the Evil Inclination altogether, endowing them in the World-to-Come with a nature free of the appetite for sin so prominent in This World. Moral victories are possible — indeed, individuals can even train themselves to face a lessened degree of temptation — in the here and now. Human righteousness is not solely a consequence of divine grace; those who would be righteous must do their own part. But the final victory, the one that allows for a life without incessant moral struggle, requires the inter-vention of the Creator to uproot the Evil Inclination that he implanted within us in the beginning.

The notion of a re-creation of human beings to render them fit for life in the World-to-Come naturally calls to mind the resurrection of the dead. For, as we have seen,[12] resurrection, too, is in the nature of a new creation. The logic of resurrection as a form of restoration and purification requires, in fact, that the new persons rise from the dead without the telltale infirmities, moral or bodily, that defined their mortal lives. But here a serious problem presents itself. If the new persons lack the physical characteristics they had in their lifetimes, surely the suspicion will arise that they are not the same persons at all, that a sleight of hand and not the hand of God accounts for their putative return to life.[13] To this problem, too, Rabbi Simon ben Laqish had an answer: "They shall rise with their defects and then be healed" (*b. Sanh.* 91b). Later, Rava made use of a familiar verse to make the same point:

> I deal death and give life;
> I wounded and I will heal. (Deut 32:39)

He reconciled the seeming contradiction thus:

> The Holy One (blessed be He!) said: What I killed I will bring to life, and then what I wounded I will heal. (*b. Sanh.* 91b)

In other words, people will first be resurrected with their infirmities and then healed of them. Just as it would make no sense to enter the World-to-Come with the same flawed moral nature, it would make no sense to enter it with the same flawed physical nature that defines human beings in This World. In Rava's two stages of resurrection, in short, we again see the paradox of the whole idea of resurrection as it has developed. On the one hand, were the dead to come back already healed and transformed, they would no longer be the same persons — the same inextricable combination of body and soul — that they were in this life. On the other hand, were they to come back with their same defective, mortal bodies and morally ambiguous souls, they would be unfit for the eternal life in the World-to-Come for which they are to be resurrected. The schema of two stages — first resurrection, then healing — navigates the paradox brilliantly. It both preserves the continuity of personal identity and subjects the risen dead to a process of re-creation that renders them fit for life after death — a process and a state that are discontinuous with ordinary existence and barely imaginable by those who have not yet undergone them.[14]

The idea that Mosaic revelation presented the people Israel with the choice of life or death was already ancient by the time of the rabbis. "See, I set before you this day life and prosperity, death and adversity," Moses is reported to have admonished Israel just before he died (Deut 30:15), equating life to obedience to the LORD's commandments and laws, and death to defection to other gods. It is significant that some rabbinic texts present these dynamics of life and death as enacted already on Mount Sinai, and not simply spoken of there: the Israelites experience first death, then resurrection even as the Torah is being revealed to them:[15]

> Rabbi Joshua ben Levi said: At every utterance that went out from the mouth of the Holy One (blessed be He!), the souls of Israel went out [of them], as it is said, "My life went away when he spoke" (Song 5:6). Inasmuch as their souls went out [of them] at the first utterance, how did they accept the second utterance? He brought down the dew with which he will resurrect the dead and resurrected them, as it is said, "You released a bountiful rain, O God; / when Your inheritance languished, You sustained it" (Ps 68:10).[16] (*b. Shab.* 88b)

What caused Israel to die with each successive revelation in the Decalogue? The proof text from the Song of Songs suggests one answer: the sheer emotional intensity of hearing God's voice, of standing so close to the ultimate source of all that is, caused Israel to swoon like a lover in the presence of her beloved. But the dual metaphor of medicine and poison that we have seen suggests another possibility (by no means mutually exclusive), that the Torah itself, as Moses' address in Deut 30:15–20 already asserted, has within it potentials both for life and for death, depending on Israel's response to its injunctions. Indeed, on the same page of the Talmud in which we find Rabbi Joshua ben Levi's midrash, we also find this comment about the Torah made by Rava in Babylonia in the fourth century C.E.:

> To those who go to the right side of it, it is a life-giving medicine [*sammā' dĕḥayyê*]. To those who go to the left side of it, it is a deadly poison [*sammā' dĕmûtā'*]. (*b. Shab.* 88b)

This, in turn, is simply another way of saying that if the wounded son (to revert to a midrash we cited earlier) keeps the compress on his injury, he thrives, but if he takes it off, he becomes gravely ill. The Torah offers no unconditional guarantee to any individual; it only presents the choice of two paths, one leading to life and one to death, and urges Israel, in Moses' words, to "choose life" (Deut 30:19). In Rabbi Joshua ben Levi's midrash about Israel's death on Sinai, God's preference for life is so overwhelming that God pre-enacts the eschatological resurrection then and there, with the selfsame agent (the dew) with which he will revive the deceased of all generations at the end of days. At Sinai are both life and death, but at Sinai, too, the last word lies with life.

An augmented version of this same midrash appears in the *Pirké de-Rabbi Eliezer,* an early medieval collection:

> "God spoke all these words, saying, 'I am the LORD your God who brought you. . . .'" (Exod 20:1–2). The first sound went forth, and the heavens and

earth quaked before it, the seas and rivers fled, the mountains and hills tottered, all the trees bent over, and the dead in Sheol came to life and stood up on their feet, as it is said, "[I make this covenant, with its sanctions, not with you alone, but both] with those who are standing here with us this day [before the LORD our God and with those who are not with us here this day]." All those who are destined to be created stood there with them on Mount Sinai, as it is said, "and with those who are not with us here this day" (Deut 29:13–14). And the Israelites who were living fell on their faces and died. A second sound went forth, and they came to life, stood up on their feet, and said to Moses, "Moses our master, if we are able to hear the voice of the Holy One (blessed be He!), we shall die the way we just did, as it is said, 'My life went away when he spoke' (Song 5:6)." (*Pirké de-Rabbi Eliezer* 41)

Here, an artful interpretation of Deut 29:13–14 weaves together the two moments, the Sinaitic and the eschatological, or, if you will, revelation and resurrection, even more tightly. Not only does Israel experience death and resurrection on Sinai, but also those long deceased come back to life, to receive the Torah offered only after their deaths. Indeed, extending the Deuteronomic emphasis on the unending validity of the covenant, this midrash places at Sinai even generations yet to be, as all Israel—the dead, the living, and the unborn alike—face the supreme moment of revelation as one.

In this text, the Sinaitic moment has taken on something of the coloration of the Day of Judgment, as all the generations stand before the incomparable might of God to die or live, as he decrees. The interweaving of the two moments also moves in the opposite direction: The Day of Judgment has acquired some of the coloration of Sinai. For in rabbinic thinking, Sinai, too, is very much a matter of life and death.

The connection of these two moments, growing stronger over the centuries, appears in striking form in a late midrash on the binding of Isaac (or aqedah), another pivotal moment in the history of redemption as the rabbis see it:

The two horns of the ram [that took the place of Isaac according to Gen 22:13] are shofars [i.e., ram's horns blown on important ceremonial occasions]. The left one the Holy One (blessed be He!) sounded on Mount Sinai, as it is said, "The blare of the horn [grew louder and louder. As Moses spoke, God answered him with a sound]" (Exod 19:19). The right one is larger than the left, and it is destined to be sounded at the end-time, when the exiles are gathered in, as it is said, "And in that day, a great ram's horn shall be sounded; [and the strayed who are in the land of Assyria and the expelled who are in the land of Egypt shall come and worship the LORD on the holy mount, in Jerusalem]" (Isa 27:13). (*Pirké de-Rabbi Eliezer* 31)[17]

Here, Sinai has become almost a prototype of the end-time. Its sound comes from the left horn of the ram that took Isaac's place on the altar—the smaller and less significant horn. God holds the larger and more important horn (the right) in reserve for the consummative moment of Israel's restoration, when the exiled and scattered people shall be reassembled around the Temple Mount in Jerusalem. Aiding the latter connection was surely the long-standing Jewish identification of Moriah, the site of the binding of Isaac, with the Temple Mount, an identification that begins already in the book of Chronicles.[18] The first and the last moments of the ram's service take place on the same hallowed ground. Between them falls the second, the revelation of the Torah on Mount Sinai.

We can go further. Each of these three great moments is also, in its own way, an occasion of resurrection.

In considering the first of the three moments, the aqedah, there is little to help us determine precisely when the idea arose that Isaac was actually sacrificed but resurrected afterward. Hints of this appear in relatively early rabbinic sources, but the idea emerges in full clarity only later.[19] An especially apposite example occurs in the same chapter of the *Pirké de-Rabbi Eliezer* as our previous midrash:

> Rabbi Judah says: As soon as the sword reached his throat, Isaac's soul took flight and left. As soon as he [i.e., God] made his voice audible from between the cherubs and said, "Do not raise your hand against the boy" (Gen 22:12), his soul returned to his body. He [i.e., his father Abraham] untied him, and he stood upon his feet. Isaac saw the resurrection of the dead from the Torah, that all the dead are destined to be resurrected. At that moment, he opened his mouth and said, "Blessed are You, O Lord, who revive the dead." (*Pirké de Rabbi Eliezer* 31)

This time, too, Isaac dies, but not because his father has dutifully sacrificed him. Instead, like Israel's death at Sinai (in one interpretation), he dies of the sheer fright of the experience. But, again like Israel at Sinai, Isaac revives — proof positive to him (and the doubting reader) that the resurrection of the dead is not only real but also evidenced in the Torah itself. The risen Isaac thus becomes the first person to recite the closing benediction of *Gevurot* ("Blessed are You, O Lord, who revive the dead"), a central liturgical text of rabbinic Judaism,[20] and the aqedah becomes evidence for a key rabbinic doctrine, that God will raise the dead and the Torah so attests.

We have already seen how the second great moment in the sacred history, too, the Sinaitic moment, became an occasion of resurrection, an earnest of things to come, when "with the dew with which he will resurrect the dead" God resurrected Israel, in the words of Rabbi Joshua ben Levi's midrash quoted above. Here again, a connection to the ram's horn develops. Where the book of Exodus speaks of "the blare of the horn" (20:15) after the revelation of the Decalogue, the Targum Pseudo-Jonathan, a heavily midrashic Aramaic translation of the Torah, cryptically adds "that it was resurrecting the dead."[21] It seems likely that the underlying midrash associates the shofar blown at Sinai with the "great ram's horn" that is to be sounded when the strayed and expelled of Israel are at last regathered on God's holy mountain in Jerusalem (Isa 27:13). Given the multiple associations of the aqedah with resurrection, it was perhaps inevitable that these two horns would be associated not only with each other but eventually with the sacrifice on Mount Moriah as well. For the aqedah had long been interpreted as the act by the grace of which the people Israel had come into being and had been rescued from death,[22] and the expectation of resurrection in Judaism had likewise always been inseparable from the restoration of the ever-dying, ever-reviving people who are the Jews. That those three great moments — the binding of Isaac, the giving of the Torah, and the resurrection of the dead — came to be interfused is itself powerful evidence for the centrality of resurrection in the Judaism that the rabbis bequeathed later generations of Jews.

To the rabbis, resurrection without the restoration of Israel, including its renewed adherence to Torah, was incomprehensible. And without the expectation of resurrection, the restoration of Israel would be something less than what the rabbis thought the Torah had always intended it to be — the ultimate victory of the God of life.

Notes

Chapter One: The Modern Jewish Preference for Immortality

1. A very thorough review of the sources on resurrection in Judaism is Adolf Löwinger, "Die Auferstehung in der jüdischen Tradition," *Jahrbuch für Jüdische Volkskunde* 25 (1923): 23–122.

2. Abba Hillel Silver, *Where Judaism Differed: An Inquiry into the Distinctiveness of Judaism* (New York: Macmillan, 1956), 277, 273, 278. See his entire discussion of immortality and resurrection on pp. 265–84.

3. This line is recited only during the rainy season (i.e., roughly October to April).

4. One could read these verbs as second person. I render them as third because of the third-person form, literally, "and keeps His faith," the pronominal ending of which is unambiguous. The variation of second- and third-person forms in the statements addressed to God in rabbinic liturgy is not unusual.

5. The translation is my own, based on the Hebrew text of the *Daily Prayer Book,* translated and annotated by Philip Birnbaum (New York: Hebrew Publishing, 1949), 83. The variations in wording in the versions of this ancient liturgy are not material to my argument. For a recent discussion of the Palestinian version, see David Instone-Brewer, "The Eighteen Benedictions and the Minim before 70 CE," *JTS* n.s. 54 (2003): 25–44 (the text itself appears on pp. 29–33). For the resonance of the expectation of resurrection throughout the classical Jewish liturgy, see Löwinger, "Die Auferstehung," 116–19.

6. See Jer 23:5; 33:15; and Zech 6:12. Note the use of the root yšʿ in Jer 33:16.

7. See chapters 12 and 13.

8. On this dialectic of the givenness of adversity and evil in this world, on the one

231

hand, and God's reliability to overcome it, on the other, see Jon D. Levenson, *Creation and the Persistence of Evil: The Jewish Drama of Divine Omnipotence,* 2nd ed. (Princeton: Princeton University Press, 1994), esp. chapters 3 and 4.

9. Consider 2 Kgs 4:31, in which *ħēqîṣ,* "to wake up," means to come back from the dead, or, in the Talmud, *b. Ber.* 60b, a passage that has been incorporated into the daily liturgy. It specifies that when Jews awake each morning, they should acclaim God as the one who gives them their soul, takes it from them, and restores it to the dead in the eschatological future. Here, waking up seems to be a miniature resurrection.

10. James Barr, *The Garden of Eden and the Hope of Immortality* (London: SCM, 1992), esp. pp. 45 and 56. See also our chapter 5.

11. See the rabbinic parables about the mutual dependence of body and soul in *b. Sanh.* 91b.

12. A telling example from the Christian side can be found in Peter L. Berger, "Secular Theology and the Rejection of the Supernatural: Reflections on Recent Trends," *TS* 38 (1977): 43. Berger quotes the influential Protestant theologian Shubert Ogden's affirmation that "the promise of faith" means that "we are each embraced in every moment within God's boundless love and thereby have the ultimate destiny of endless life in and through him." "Lest this Pauline prose should rouse false expectations," Berger points out, "Ogden quickly adds, three pages later, that the promise of faith is *not* to be understood as including any kind of personal survival after death." The quote is from Shubert Ogden, *The Reality of God* (New York: Harper and Row, 1966), 226.

13. Milton Steinberg, *Basic Judaism* (New York: Harcourt, Brace and World, 1947), 162–63. Alan F. Segal's claim that the ancient rabbis "are not actually interested in defining the afterlife with the notion of the resurrection of the fleshly body" is overstated. The rabbis believed very much in bodily resurrection and did not see immortality, original or restored, as an adequate substitute for it. Alan F. Segal, *Life after Death: A History of the Afterlife in Western Religion* (New York: Doubleday, 2004), 607. Segal is correct, however, that rabbinic Judaism was willing to entertain the notion that the resurrected body will be "a perfected, spiritual body" (p. 608). See Löwinger, "Die Auferstehung," 66–83.

14. See the discussion of *b. Ber.* 17a later in this chapter and n. 49, below.

15. Steinberg, *Basic Judaism,* 199.

16. See Jakob J. Petuchowski, "'Immortality—Yes; Resurrection—No!' Nineteenth-Century Judaism Struggles with a Traditional Belief," *PAAJR* 50 (1983): 133–47.

17. Neil Gillman, *The Death of Death: Resurrection and Immortality in Jewish Thought* (Woodstock, Vt.: Jewish Lights, 1997), 193.

18. Ibid., 198.

19. Ibid., 198–99.

20. Ibid., 201.

21. But Jakob Petuchowski points out that "the European Liberals and Reformers did not share the strong feelings of their American brethren. (The latter, having made the denial of the Resurrection practically an article of faith, consistently changed the Hebrew text and translated accordingly.) Not a single one of the rituals under consideration here found it necessary to change the Hebrew text, although many of them (but not all!) substituted the concept of Immortality in their vernacular translation or paraphrase."

Jakob J. Petuchowski, *Prayerbook Reform in Europe: The Liturgy of European Liberal and Reform Jews* (New York: World Union for Progressive Judaism, 1968), 215. See also p. 216.

22. *The Union Prayerbook for Jewish Worship* (New York: Central Conference of American Rabbis, 1961), 72.

23. Ibid., 124.

24. *The Gates of Prayer: The New Union Prayer Book* (New York: Central Conference of American Rabbis, 5735/1975), 255–56, and Gillman, *The Death*, 201.

25. Ibid., 206. His reference is to the introduction by Rabbi Robert Gordis to *Sabbath and Festival Prayer Book* (New York: The Rabbinical Assembly of America and the United Synagogue of America, 1946), viii–ix.

26. *Siddur Sim Shalom: For Shabbat and Festivals* (New York: The Rabbinical Assembly and the United Synagogue for Conservative Judaism, 1998), e.g., p. 35a. The first edition of *Sim Shalom* was published in 1985.

27. Gillman, *The Death*, 207.

28. Orthodox prayer books, by definition, retain the traditional rabbinic language. How much reflection contemporary Orthodox Jews, learned and other, give to the doctrine of resurrection — and, indeed, to the theology of the prayer book altogether — is a more complicated matter. In general, Orthodox Jews are more comfortable speaking of the laws of prayer than they are speaking of the content of the prayers. My experience is that among Orthodox Jews, the recitation of liturgical texts affirming resurrection is often seen solely as a fulfillment of halakhic obligation, without concern for the theological character or credibility of the affirmations themselves and that it is not unusual to find Orthodox Jews who privately express attitudes toward the resurrection of the dead similar to those of the non-Orthodox. If I may bring a personal experience to bear, in the summer of 2004, I was privileged to hear a discourse on life after death delivered by an Orthodox rabbi of impeccable credentials and with a long-standing affiliation with one of the premier yeshivot in the world. From his discussion, one would never have guessed that classical rabbinic Judaism affirmed the resurrection of the dead at all, let alone that it emphasized resurrection more than immortality of the soul.

29. See William A. Dembski, "Are We Spiritual Machines?" *First Things* 96 (October 1999): 25–31.

30. Leon R. Kass, *The Hungry Soul: Eating and the Perfection of our Nature* (New York: Free Press, 1994), 34.

31. Reinhold Niebuhr, *The Nature and Destiny of Man* (New York: Charles Scribner's Sons, 1964), 1:48. (The book was originally published in 1941.)

32. Stephen M. Barr, "Theories of Everything," *First Things* 92 (April 1999): 48, 50. For an excellent recent discussion of the inadequacies of materialism, see Mary Midgley, *Science and Poetry* (London and New York: Routledge, 2001).

33. *Union Prayerbook*, 72.

34. Chapter 3.

35. In v 12, read *qibrām*, after several versions.

36. We shall later see that this rather grim view is not the whole story for Psalm 49. Note the psalmist's confidence that God will rescue him from Sheol (v 16). See below, chapter 5. For our purposes here, the point is that the psalmist's postmortem hope is a

hope for *rescue* and not an expectation that some noncorporeal dimension of his self will somehow escape death.

37. *Union Prayerbook*, 72.

38. See *Ancient Near Eastern Texts Relating to the Old Testament*, 3rd edition, ed. James B. Pritchard (Princeton University Press, 1969), 93–95.

39. See Lloyd R. Bailey, Sr., *Biblical Perspectives on Death* (OBT; Philadelphia: Fortress, 1979), 52. On the role descendants play as the functional equivalent of immortality in the Hebrew Bible, see below, chap. 6.

40. Kaufmann Kohler, *Jewish Theology Systematically and Historically Considered* (New York: MacMillan, 1918), 296–97.

41. Ibid., 195–96. See also p. 17, in which Kohler identifies a belief in redemption with a condemnation of earthly life. In fact, the biblical and rabbinic traditions generally affirm both the need for redemption and the dignity and importance of earthly life. The dichotomizing of these two things, unfortunately, played a major role in Jewish apologetics in the twentieth century, with Christianity portrayed as focused on redemption and a renunciation of earthly things and Judaism as the religion of ethics and creative human striving in this world. The outstanding exemplar of this strategy is Leo Baeck's essay "Romantic Religion," originally published in 1922. See *Judaism and Christianity: Essays by Leo Baeck*, translated and introduced by Walter Kaufmann (New York: Atheneum, 1970), 189–292, esp. p. 196.

42. Carol Zaleski, "In Defense of Immortality," *First Things* 105 (August/September 2000): 39. A slightly different version of the same remark appears in Prof. Zaleski's Harvard Divinity School Ingersoll Lecture (2000), "In Defense of Immortality," published in the *Harvard Divinity Bulletin* 29:2 (summer 2000): 16.

43. See Louis Jacobs, *Principles of the Jewish Faith* (New York: Basic Books, 1964), 399–408, and Marc B. Shapiro, *The Limits of Orthodox Theology* (Portland, Ore.: Littmann Library of Jewish Classics, 2004), 149–56. For an account of an early modern reprise of the immortality-resurrection controversy, see David Malkiel, "The Rimini Papers: A Resurrection Controversy in Eighteenth-Century Italy," *Journal of Jewish Thought and Philosophy* 11 (2002): 89–115. Note particularly Malkiel's discussion of the classical sources on pp. 98–103.

44. *Mishneh Torah, Hilkôt Yĕsôdê Hattôrǎ* 4:8–9. See Harry Blumberg, "The Problem of Immortality in Avicenna, Maimonides and St. Thomas Aquinas," in *Harry Austryn Wolfson Jubilee Volume*, ed. Saul Lieberman et al. (Jerusalem: American Academy of Jewish Research, 1965), 2:174–80.

45. *b. Ber.* 17a. The textual variance between Maimonides' version and the one that appears in the Talmud is not significant for our purposes. That the conception of the World-to-Come here is much older than this passage quoted in the name of the early third-century sage, Rav, is easily seen from the synoptic gospels (Mk 12:18–27; Matt 22: 23–33; Luke 20:27–40). Rabbi Joel Poupko has kindly pointed out to me a Tannaitic antecedent to Rav's comment in *Sifre Deut.* 47 as well.

46. *Mishneh Torah, Hilkôt Tĕšûbâ* 8:2.

47. *b. Ket.* 111b. The "clothing" in question may well be their shrouds (I thank my colleague, Professor Bernard Septimus, for confirming this to me). See Jacobs, *Principles*, 401–2.

48. *b. Shab.* 114a; Jacobs, *Principles*, 401.

49. See Daniel Jeremy Silver, "The Resurrection Debate," in *Moses Maimonides' Treatise on Resurrection,* ed. Fred Rosner (New York: KTAV, 1982), 71–102, reprinted from D. J. Silver, *Maimonidean Criticism and the Maimonidean Controversy, 1180–1240* (Leiden: Brill, 1965), 109–35; Jacobs, *Principles,* 401–20; and Shapiro, *Limits,* 149–56.

50. Found in Rosner, *Moses Maimonides',* 21–51. See also Abraham Halkin and David Hartman, *Crisis and Leadership* (Philadelphia: Jewish Publication Society of America, 1985), 209–92.

51. Rosner, *Moses Maimonides',* 35.

52. Albert D. Friedberg, "Maimonides' Reinterpretation of the Thirteenth Article of Faith: Another Look at his *Essay on Resurrection," JSQ* 10 (2003): 1–14, here p. 11. I am indebted to Friedberg for this explanation of the impermanence of resurrection.

53. Ibid., 33.

54. Jacobs points out (*Principles,* 406) that Maimonides seems to have had a predecessor in Abraham ibn Ezra (see the latter's commentary to Dan 12:2).

55. Shapiro (*Limits,* 151–52) notes arguments to the effect that Maimonides understands the term *resurrection (těḥîyat hammētîm)* to mean the disembodied existence of the World-to-Come, thus being able to affirm resurrection without subscribing to its traditional definition.

56. See n 22, above.

57. See the next chapter.

58. Kohler (*Jewish Theology,* 293) points out that "the belief in resurrection had taken too deep a root in the Jewish consciousness and had been too firmly established through the liturgy of the Synagogue for any philosopher to touch it without injuring the very foundations of faith." See David Hartman, *Maimonides: Torah and Philosophic Quest* (Philadelphia: Jewish Publication Society of America, 1976), 250, n. 35: "Resurrection is a miracle which Maimonides accepted simply because the tradition demanded this of him. He did not attempt to explain its significance. His extended treatment of the significance of messianism in his legal writings suggests that messianism (as distinct from resurrection) indeed is essentially related to his philosophy of Judaism." If this is so, it is still a posture very different from that of modern liberal Judaism. Since the latter does not feel bound by tradition to accept a belief in resurrection, it is free to emend the liturgy accordingly.

59. Still another notion that might properly be termed "immortality" has to do with God's rescue of his faithful servant from a very real, very threatening, and eminently irreversible death. See below, chapter 5.

60. Kass, *The Hungry Soul,* p. 34.

61. On this, see Michael Wyschogrod, *The Body of Faith: Judaism as Corporeal Election* (New York: Seabury Press, 1983).

62. This is why Louis Jacobs insists that when resurrection of the body is replaced by immortality of the soul (as he recommends), the latter notion must be qualified so as to include "the state of a soul in eternity with its finite character intact and its finite experiences embraced" (*Principles,* 420). Jacobs's version of immortality is so heavily colored by the traditional doctrine of resurrection that he rejects that one can wonder whether the former would ever have occurred to him if he had not been formed in a tradition that affirmed the latter.

63. Petuchowski, "'Immortality,'" 145.

64. Both were rejected in the famous Pittsburgh Platform (1885). See Petuchowski, " 'Immortality,' " 143–44.

65. Chapters 6, 9, 10, and 12.

Chapter Two: Resurrection in the Torah?

1. Steinberg, *Basic Judaism,* 162–63. The idea is widespread in popular presentations of Judaism and can be found, for example, also in Silver, *Where Judaism Differed,* e.g., 267.

2. See, e.g., the *Mek. de-Rabbi Ishmael,* Běšallaḥ 7 (on Exod 14:31), in which Abraham is said to have "inherited" (*yāraš*) the World-to-Come on the basis of his faith.

3. The exact nature of the act of reading in question is unclear; the reference may be to public, liturgical recitation.

4. E.g., see *t. Sanh.* 13:5. The printed versions of *m. Sanh.* 10:1 tend to include the words "in the Torah," and this has become the best-known reading, whatever its historical authenticity.

5. *m. Abot* 1:3.

6. *Abot R. Nat.* 5.

7. *Ant.* 13:297; 18:17. Note that in the case of the rabbis, some non-Pentateuchal passages are included in the definition of the "Torah" that attests to resurrection. See, e.g., *b. Sanh.* 92a.

8. Note that in some manuscripts the midrash is unattributed. But if "Rabbi" (that is, Judah the Patriarch) did not say it, some other rabbi did.

9. E.g., Num 21:17; Deut 4:41; Josh 8:30; 10:12; 22:1; 1 Kgs 3:16; 8:1.

10. On the exegetical techniques through which interpreters in the Second Temple and rabbinic periods produced a rewritten Bible, see James L. Kugel, *The Bible as It Was* (Cambridge, Mass.: Harvard University Press, 1997).

11. For the relevant rabbinic interpretation of Exod 20:5, see the Targumim and *Mek. de-Rabbi Ishmael,* Baḥōdeš 6. On the contrary biblical thinking, see Joel S. Kaminsky, *Corporate Responsibility in the Hebrew Bible* (Sheffield, U.K.: Sheffield Academic Press, 1995).

12. For reasons of clarity, I have arranged the translation of the Targum in poetic lines that reflect the presentation of the underlying biblical passage in the NJPS and kept the translation of the Targum as close as possible to the NJPS version of the passage as well.

13. See Barr, *The Garden,* 5–6. The parallels with the famed Tablet XI of the Mesopotamian Gilgamesh epic are patent. See the translation by E. A. Speiser in *ANET,* 93–97, esp. p. 96.

14. E.g., Wis 2:23–24 and 4 Ezra 3:7.

15. For others, see Klaus Spronk, *Beatific Afterlife in Ancient Israel and in the Ancient Near East* (AOAT 219; Neukirchen-Vluyn: Neukirchener Verlag, 1986), 156–57.

Chapter 3: Up from Sheol

1. Johannes Pedersen, *Israel: Its Life and Culture,* South Florida Studies in the History of Judaism 28 (Atlanta: Scholars Press, 1991; originally published 1926–40), 461.

2. Ibid., 470. See his whole discussion on pp. 460–70.

3. John Gray, *I and II Kings,* 2nd ed. (London: SCM, 1970), 102.

4. *ANET,* 98–99. The lines are from Tablet XII; the translator is E. A. Speiser.

5. Ibid., 107.

6. Jerrold S. Cooper, "The Fate of Mankind: Death and Afterlife in Ancient Meso-potamia," in *Death and Afterlife: Perspectives of World Religions,* ed. Hiroshi Obayashi (New York: Greenwood Press, 1992), 27. More generally, see *Death in Mesopotamia,* ed. Bendt Alster (Copenhagen: Akademisk Forlag, 1980). For more recent treatments, see Jo Ann Scurlock, "Death and the Afterlife in Ancient Mesopotamian Thought," in *Civiliza-tions of the Ancient Near East,* ed. Jack M. Sasson (New York: Simon and Schuster Macmillan, 1995), 1883–93, and Segal, *Life,* 70–103.

7. Homer, *The Odyssey,* tr. Robert Fitzgerald (Garden City, N.Y.: Doubleday, 1963), 190, rendering *zophon ēeroenta* in 11:155. Fitzgerald's translation seeks to convey not only the murky gloom of the netherworld but also the connotation of *zophos* as the West (related to *Zephuros*), i.e., the furthermost place, just beyond the world-encircling Ocean (*Ōkeanos*).

8. Pedersen, *Israel,* 154.

9. E.g., see Philip S. Johnston, *Shades of Sheol: Death and Afterlife in the Old Testa-ment* (Downers Grove, Ill.: Intervarsity, 2002), 69–124; Theodore J. Lewis, "Dead, Abode of the," *Anchor Bible Dictionary,* ed. David Noel Freedman (New York: Double-day, 1992), 2:101–5; Nicholas J. Tromp, *Primitive Conceptions of Death and the Neth-erworld in the Old Testament,* BO 21 (Rome: Pontifical Biblical Institute, 1969), passim; Christoph Barth, *Die Errettung vom Tode in den individuellen Klage- und Dankliedern des Alten Testaments* (Zurich: Theologischer Verlag, 1987; rpt. from his dissertation of 1948), 76–91; and Pedersen, *Israel,* 460–70.

10. Tromp, *Primitive Conceptions,* 36.

11. Pedersen, *Israel,* 461. In our next chapter, we shall have occasion to note that Sheol and the grave are not always equated.

12. Most commonly, *bôr* and *šaḥat.*

13. The translation of v 2 departs from the NJPS in an effort to capture the pairing of *yôm* and *laylâ.* On Psalm 88, see Bernd Janowski, "Die Toten loben JHWH nicht: Psalm 88 und das alttestamentliche Todesverständnis," in *Auferstehung — Resurrection,* ed. Friedrich Avemarie and Hermann Lichtenberger (Tübingen: Mohr Siebeck, 2001), 3–45.

14. Johnston, *Shades,* 93 (against C. Barth).

15. See Scurlock, "Death," 1892: "Rather than a sudden and complete break, dying [in Mesopotamian culture] involved a shading-off or gradual weakening of connections between the deceased person and the world of the living." See also Hans Hirsch, "Den Toten zu beleben," *AfO* 22 (1968/69): 39–58, where it is shown that the Akkadian expression "to bring the dead back to life" refers to healing the sick.

16. E.g., Pss 30:4; 40:3; Isa 38:18.

17. Cf. Tromp, *Primitive Conceptions,* 137: "The psalmist is in the domain of Death, but by no means in the domain of the dead."

18. Note the similar use of words for "earth" in Sumerian (*ki, kur*) and Akkadian (*erṣetu*). On this, see W. G. Lambert, "Theology of Death," in *Death in Mesopotamia,* 59.

These netherworld connections are defended by Tromp, *Primitive Conceptions,* 23–46. Johnston, *Shades,* 98–114, offers a review of the evidence and an evaluation that is too skeptical, however.

19. E.g., Tromp, *Primitive Conceptions,* 26.

20. Johnston, *Shades,* 108.

21. Tromp (*Primitive Conceptions,* 27) draws attention to Gen 4:11 in this context.

22. Ibid., 37, 39.

23. See the critique in Johnston, *Shades,* 102.

24. He is identified in the superscription (2 Sam 22:1; Ps 18:1) as David after YHWH rescued him from all his enemies, including Saul.

25. The text is closely paralleled, of course, in the variant form of this poem, which is Psalm 18 (vv 5–6).

26. On Belial, see Tromp, *Primitive Conceptions,* 59–66, and Johnston, *Shades,* 114–24.

27. On the Psalm of Jonah and its role in the book, see James A. Ackerman, "Satire and Symbolism in the Song of Jonah," in *Traditions in Transformation: Turning Points in Biblical Faith,* ed. Baruch Halpern and Jon D. Levenson (Winona Lake, Ind.: Eisenbrauns, 1981), 213–46.

28. In v 11, read *wayyēde'* ("he flew") for *wayyērā'* ("he was seen") with several versions and Ps 18:11, for reasons of sense.

29. On the mythic background, see Frank Moore Cross, *Canaanite Myth and Hebrew Epic: Essays in the History of the Religion of Israel* (Cambridge, Mass.: Harvard University Press, 1973), 112–44; and Levenson, *Creation,* 14–50.

30. Johnston insists that "various terms for water, depths and mire are images of and metaphors for the underworld but hardly underworld names" (*Shades,* 123–24). This formulation, though valid, may overestimate the difference between an image or metaphor and a name. Whereas Sheol always *denotes* the underworld, the terms for water and the like can *connote* it just as effectively, even though they, in other contexts, connote other things just as well. The point is context, and the contexts of passages such as those we have been discussing point strongly to an association with the netherworld.

31. Note "the gates of Sheol" in Isa 38:10.

32. On the cosmological issue, see Richard J. Clifford, *The Cosmic Mountain in Canaan and the Old Testament,* HSM 4 (Cambridge, Mass.: Harvard University Press, 1972), esp. 131–60; and Jon D. Levenson, *Sinai and Zion: An Entry into the Jewish Bible* (San Francisco: Harper San Francisco, 1987), 111–37.

33. On Sheol as a city or a prison, see Tromp, *Primitive Conceptions,* 153–56.

34. Gen 1:2. See Levenson, *Creation,* 5.

35. The presence of compound nouns in Ugaritic, however, provides some new evidence for the traditional rendering. See Mitchell Dahood, *Psalms I: 1–50,* AB 16 (Garden City, N.Y.: Doubleday, 1965), 147.

36. Tromp, *Primitive Conceptions,* 36.

37. Janowski ("Die Toten loben," 12–13) argues on the basis of Ugaritic parallels that *ḥopšî* here denotes a discharged soldier and thus draws attention to the inability of the one who is praying to render further service to YHWH.

38. The meaning of the last word (*maḥšāk*) is unclear, and there is versional evidence

to suggest some form of *ḥśk* ("withhold," "deprive") instead. For our purposes, the difference is not essential.

39. On the cult of the dead (broadly conceived), see Klaas Spronk, *Beatific Afterlife*, 28–54; Theodore J. Lewis, *Cults of the Dead in Ancient Israel and Ugarit*, HSM 39 (Atlanta: Scholars Press, 1989); Karel van der Toorn, *Family Religion in Babylonia, Syria and Israel* (Leiden: Brill, 1996), 206–35; and Johnston, *Shades*, 150–95. A more skeptical view can be found in Brian B. Schmidt, *Israel's Beneficent Dead: Ancestor Cult and Necromancy in Ancient Israelite Religion and Tradition*, Forschungen zum Alten Testament 11 (Tübingen: J. C. B. Mohr [Paul Siebeck], 1994).

40. *Maʿăś. Š.* 5:12; *Sifre Deut.* 303. See Rashi to Deut 26:14.

41. E.g., Richard Elliot Friedman and Shawna Dolansky Overton, "Death and Afterlife: The Biblical Silence," in *Judaism in Late Antiquity*, ed. Alan J. Avery-Peck and Jacob Neusner (Leiden: Brill, 2000), 40; Lewis, *Cults*, 102–3. Note, however, Schmidt's skepticism about the feeding of the dead (e.g., *Israel's*, 62, on Ugarit).

42. Jeffrey Tigay, *The JPS Torah Commentary: Deuteronomy* (Philadelphia: Jewish Publication Society, 5756/1996), 244.

43. Thus Herbert Chanan Brichto, "Kin, Cult, Land and Afterlife: A Biblical Complex," *HUCA* 45 (1973): 29; Elizabeth Bloch-Smith, *Judahite Burial Practices and Beliefs about the Dead* (JSOTSS 123; Sheffield, U.K.: Sheffield Academic Press, 1992), 126; Rachel Hallote, *Death, Burial, and Afterlife in the Biblical World: How the Israelites and Their Neighbors Treated the Dead* (Chicago: Ivan R. Dee, 2001), 62.

44. Joseph Blenkinsopp, "Deuteronomy and the Politics of Post Mortem Existence," *VT* 45 (1995): 1–16. Blenkinsopp's claim must be balanced against the more circumspect arguments of Schmidt, *Israel's*, passim.

45. Hallote, *Death*, 36–37.

46. Ibid., 65.

47. See the list of such passages in Spronk, *Beatific*, 39.

48. See Johnston, *Shades*, 181–87; Spronk, *Beatific*, 201, n 3; Marvin H. Pope, *Song of Songs*, AB 7C (Garden City, N.Y.: Doubleday, 1977), 210–29.

49. Dennis Pardee, "Marziḫu, Kispu, and the Ugaritic Funerary Cult," in *Ugarit, Religion and Culture*, ed. Nick Wyatt et al. (Münster: Ugarit Verlag, 1996), 279 (*marziḫu* denotes the Ugaritic cognate of Hebrew *marzēaḥ*). Pardee carefully distinguishes between a "funerary cult," which deals with "the cultic acts associated with burial," and a "mortuary cult," which is "the cult for those who have already passed into the netherworld" (p. 273). The scholars who make so much of the marzēaḥ tend to reconstruct something more like his "mortuary cult."

50. Johnston, *Shades*, 184.

51. In v 7, read *lāhem* as *leḥem* and *'ōtām* as *'ōtô* with the Greek, and *'ēbel* as *'ābēl* with the Vulgate, for evident reasons of sense.

52. For the distinction, see n 49, above.

53. It is true that the MT puts a minor paragraphing sign (*sĕtûmā'*) between v 8 and v 9, but v 9 seems to conclude or comment on v 8, and not to introduce vv 10–13.

54. Note also the finding of John L. McLaughlin, *The Marzēaḥ in the Prophetic Literature* (Leiden: Brill, 2001), who concludes the essential features of the marzēaḥ were "a definite upper-class membership, a religious connection, and alcohol" but not "a

funerary connection" (p. 66). He sees Isa 28:7–8, which he dates "shortly before 700 B.C.E.," as "the first clear connection between a *marzēaḥ* and the cult of the dead" (p. 180). On Amos 6:7 and Jer 16:5, see pp. 80–109 and 185–95, respectively. Even though McLaughlin finds "a funerary setting" (p. 195) in Jer 16:5–9, he does not claim any connection to a cult of the dead.

55. On necromancy, see Josef Tropper, *Nekromantie: Totenbefragung im Alten Orient und Alten Testament,* AOAT (Kevelaer: Butzon and Bercker; Neukirchen-Vluyn: Neukirchener Verlag, 1989); Spronk, *Beatific,* 251–57; Schmidt, *Israel's,* 201–20; Johnston, *Shades,* 150–66; and Segal, *Life,* 124–31.

56. In v 3, read *kĕdāwīd* with the Greek for *kaddûr,* unlike NJPS. In v 4, note chirping as characteristic of dead who are likened to birds. See, e.g., Spronk, *Beatific,* 167, on the fluttering of the Ugaritic *rp'um,* and compare Isa 8:19. In v 5, read *zēdāyik* for *zārāyik* with 1QIs[a].

57. On the complexity of ghostly identity, see Jo Ann Scurlock, "Ghosts in the Ancient Near East: Weak or Powerful?" *HUCA* 68 (1997): 77–96.

58. On the phenomena in question, see Spronk, *Beatific,* 255–56.

59. Studies of this famous and complex event are legion. For an approach to it that focuses on the phenomenon of necromancy, see, e.g., Tropper, *Nekromantie,* 205–27; Johnston, *Shades,* 154–58; and Schmidt, *Israel's,* 201–20. On the literary and theological character of 1 Samuel 28 itself (as opposed to the event it purports to relay), see also Uriel Simon, *Reading Prophetic Narratives,* Indiana Studies in Biblical Literature (Bloomington and Indianapolis: Indiana University Press, 1997), 73–92.

60. What this is precisely is a matter of conjecture and need not occupy us here. Note Exod 28:30, where the Urim aid the high priest in determining *mišpāṭ,* in the sense of a judgment or verdict.

61. P. Kyle McCarter (among others) points out that *rgz* has a technical meaning associated with " 'disturbing, rousing up' the underworld" and points to Isa 14:9 as an analogy. "The Phoenician equivalent of the verb," he writes, "often refers to the violation of tombs in sepulchral inscriptions." See his *I Samuel,* AB 8 (Garden City, N.Y.: Doubleday, 1980), 421.

62. McCarter holds to the position that vv 11–12a are part of a "prophetic reworking of the [original] episode," in which the raised specter was not Samuel at all (*I Samuel,* 421). The position is plausible and intriguing, but the hypothetical original survives in no version, and the passage makes good sense without it. For example, McCarter thinks that "originally it was Saul's imperious tone in v 10 that alerted the woman that her client was not an ordinary man but the king himself" (p. 423). But, given the king's close connection to the prophet who both consecrated him and deposed him — indeed, given the close connection of prophecy and kingship, especially in this period — one would expect Saul more than "an ordinary man" to be raising the ghost of Samuel, and Samuel, in turn, to be more likely to respond to the king than to any "ordinary man." On the same point, there are grounds to doubt McCarter's view that originally it was Saul's "authoritative oath of reassurance" in v 10 that gave away his identity, for "only the king could speak thus" (p. 421). A commoner desperate for a séance could also reassure his necromancer that he would not inform on her in any way. See Johnston, *Shades,* 155. McCarter's view is

followed by the valuable recent study of Bill T. Arnold, "Necromancy and Cleromancy in 1 and 2 Samuel," *CBQ* 66 (2004): 199–213 (on this see p. 206, n 28).

63. Van der Toorn, *Family,* 225. Note that van der Toorn does not consider necromancy to be part of the family religion context in which the ancestor cult found its place (p. 233).

64. Ibid., 230.

65. Ibid.

66. Ibid.

67. *b. Meg.* 13a.

68. See Moshe Garsiel, *Biblical Names: A Literary Study of Midrashic Derivations and Puns* (Ramat Gan: Bar-Ilan University Press, 1991).

69. Van der Toorn, *Family,* 231.

70. *b. Ber* 27b.

71. Van der Toorn, *Family,* 230.

72. Ibid.

73. Particularly important on this general point is the very thorough study by Jeaneane D. Fowler, *Theophoric Names in Ancient Hebrew: A Comparative Study,* JSOTSS 49 (Sheffield, U.K.: Sheffield Academic Press, 1988). Note especially her conclusion that there is "a substantial amount of evidence to suggest that the Hebrew theophoric onomasticon incorporated no thoughts that were incongruous with the mainstream of Israelite religion" (p. 317).

74. See van der Toorn, *Family,* 221–22. On the enormous difficulties involved in this use of the word, see Johnston, *Shades,* 145–46; and Schmidt, *Israel's,* 215–17.

75. Schmidt's challenge to the idea that *ʾĕlōhîm* ever refers to the dead in Syria-Palestine, even in 1 Sam 28:13 (*Israel's,* 215, 217), is not well founded. A particularly good example of the usage can be found in Isa 8:19–20, on which see Lewis, *Cults,* 128–32.

76. On the general issue, see Lewis's conclusion in *Cults,* 49–50, and his comments in "How Far Can Texts Take Us?: Evaluating Textual Sources for Reconstructing Ancient Israelite Beliefs about the Dead," in *Sacred Time, Sacred Space: Archaeology and the Religion of Israel,* ed. Barry M. Gittlen (Winona Lake, Ind.: Eisenbrauns, 2002), 187, n 37, and especially p. 196, where he concludes that "the term is a description of their *preternatural* nature rather than an attempt to deify the dead fully (in the sense of making them equal to the high gods of the pantheon . . .)." For a somewhat different view and a defense of the exalted status of deified patrilinear ancestors, see van der Toorn, *Family,* 206–35, especially pp. 229–31.

77. Bloch-Smith, *Judahite,* 151 (see also p. 123).

78. Brichto, "Kin," 31 (his italics). On the use of the verb *kibbēd* in connection with the treatment of elderly relatives, see Jonas Greenfield, "Adi baltu: Care for the Elderly and Its Rewards," in *Al Kanfei Yonah: Collected Studies of Jonas C. Greenfield on Semitic Philology,* ed. Shalom Paul et al. (Jerusalem: Hebrew University Press, 2001; Leiden: Brill, 2001), 2:912–19, especially p. 914. Greenfield correctly notes (p. 916) the resonance of the ancient Akkadian idiom in rabbinic Judaism (see, e.g., *b. Qidd.* 30b–32a).

79. Van der Toorn, *Family,* 214.

80. Lewis, *Cults,* 43.

81. Hallote, *Death,* 37.

82. See Wayne T. Pitard, "Tombs and Offerings: Archaeological Data and Comparative Methodology in the Study of Death in Israel," in *Sacred Time* (ed. Gittlen), 149. I thank Professor Lawrence Stager for directing me to this article and for his help on the archaeological evidence for Israelite burial practices in general.

83. Hallote, *Death,* 64.

84. See the wise cautions of Pitard in "Tombs," 147, 149.

85. Consider, for example, the likely effect of granting this controversial claim of Schmidt's: "Necromancy and the belief in the supernatural power of the beneficent dead entered Judahite religion and tradition from Mesopotamia in the mid-first millennium" (*Israel's,* 241). A succinct argument that Schmidt's evidence is, however, inconclusive can be found in Johnston, *Shades,* 138–39.

86. B. Halpern, "Jerusalem and the Lineages in the Seventh Century B.C.E.: Kinship and the Rise of Individual Moral Liability," in *Law and Ideology in Monarchic Israel,* JSOTSS 124; ed. Baruch Halpern and Deborah Hobson (Sheffield, U.K.: Sheffield Academic Press, 1991), 71–74.

87. The evidence for the destruction of village culture and its genealogical system of social organization around 700 B.C.E. is, however, weak. See Yigal Levin, "Who Was the Chronicler's Audience?: A Hint from His Genealogies," *JBL* 122 (2003): 229–45. Levin concludes that as late as the fourth century B.C.E. "much of postexilic Judean society — which included both returnees and descendants of those left behind — seems to have retained its 'tribal' character" (p. 242).

88. Halpern, "Jerusalem," 73.

89. Ibid., 71, 72. Joel Kaminsky has rightly pointed out that this kind of formulation underestimates the tenacity and vitality of the traditional corporate structures. See Kaminsky, *Corporate Responsibility,* 120, n 10, and, more generally, pp. 139–78. Kaminsky's strictures against the characteristically modern (and Protestant) notion of increasing individualism and decreasing familial-national identity in ancient Israel need to be more widely taken into account.

90. Blenkinsopp, "Deuteronomy," 1. Others taking this view include Bloch-Smith, *Judahite,* 131; Hallote, *Death,* 62; and Friedman and Overton, "Death," 50.

91. Blenkinsopp, "Death," 8.

92. Hallote, *Death,* 65.

93. *Odyssey* 11:150–224.

94. *Aeneid* 6:680–83, 756–885 (my translation).

95. So Lewis ("How Far," 194) characterizes the background of 2 Sam 18:18 in critique of Schmidt's view that the practice is solely for the purpose of memorialization (Schmidt, *Israel's,* 133; 253 n 510; 257). See below, n 98.

96. If the presentation of Abraham, Isaac, and Jacob as figures in the same genealogy is a later stage in the history of tradition, as many scholars believe, one still has to wonder about the absence of the putatively standard First Temple ancestor cult in these narratives.

97. Van der Toorn, *Family,* 230.

98. On the basis of Mesopotamian and Syrian analogues, some scholars argue that Absalom erected his pillar so that he could be the recipient of the cultic honors that a son was supposed to pay to his deified father after death. See Lewis, *Cults,* 32–33, and van der Toorn, *Family,* 208. The Israelite analogies would suggest, however, that the motivation actually has to do with the remembrance of Absalom's "name" in the absence of a son to carry it on. (On a person's "name" as a kind of placeholder for immortality, see chapter 5, below.) If so, then 2 Sam 18:18 is illuminated less by the interesting non-Israelite parallels than by Israelite texts like Num 27:4; Deut 25:5–10 (especially v 6); and Isa 56:3–5.

99. See Jon D. Levenson, *The Death and Resurrection of the Beloved Son: The Transformation of Child Sacrifice in Judaism and Christianity* (New Haven and London: Yale University Press, 1993), esp. 3–31, 111–42.

100. Bloch-Smith, *Judahite,* 151. Contrast Schmidt, *Israel's,* passim, but especially p.165, where he argues that the Deuteronomistic History presents no polemic against ancestor worship because it is simply unknown to the authors.

101. In recent decades, the dating of Pentateuchal sources has once again become a matter of considerable disagreement, and no consensus is in sight. My comments both here and throughout presuppose the classical view that there were pre-exilic J and E documents that predate D and P and reflect a demonstrable difference in perspective from exilic and Second Temple literature. See Richard Elliott Friedman, "Torah (Pentateuch)," *ABD,* 6:605–22.

102. Deut 18:9–14 prohibits both practitioners but separates the *mĕkaššēp* from the *šō'ēl 'ōb wĕyiddĕ'ōnî wĕdōrēš 'el-hammētîm* in vv 10–11. Could Exod 22:19, which forbids sacrificing to *'ĕlōhîm* and insists that only Yʜᴡʜ is the fit recipient of offerings, have thereby forbidden sacrifices to the dead?

103. On this last point, one of especial importance in the laments and songs of thanksgiving, see Isa 38:18; Pss 6:6; 30:10; 88:11; 115:17; cf. Pss 118:17; 119:175; also Sir 17:27–28. On this, see Hartmut Gese, *Vom Sinai zum Zion,* Beiträge zur evangelischer Theologie 4 (Munich: Chr. Kaiser Verlag, 1974), 191, and Janowski, "Die Toten," 24.

104. See the comment of Johnston (*Shades,* 62): "The deceased was provided with food and drink for the journey to the underworld, but was deemed to have arrived when the corpse had decomposed. Then no further nourishment was provided and the bones could be swept aside with impunity." Here Johnston summarizes the research of R. E. Cooley, "Gathered to His People: A Study of the Dothan Family Tomb," in *The Living and Active Word of God,* ed. M. Inch and R. Youngblood (Winona Lake, Ind.: Eisenbrauns,1983), 47–58.

105. Johnston, *Shades,* 152–53.

106. Schmidt (*Israel's,* 241) argues for a Mesopotamian origin for the practice.

107. Note that, consistent with his argument, Halpern dates J and E to the time of Hezekiah ("Jerusalem," 80). If this dating (or the much later ones that are also current) is accepted, then a major source of our knowledge of Israelite religion in the earlier centuries has disappeared. One can still question, however, whether Hezekian documents would ipso facto be so meticulous as to expunge all memory of practices that were totally unexceptional only a short time before — and so successful in doing so. This is not the case, for example, with building and consecrating shrines other than the royal one in

Jerusalem, as the patriarchs do. As Johnston puts it, "It is unlikely that necromancy was considered so heinous that it was mostly expunged from the records, while many other practices equally condemned by Yahwism were not" (*Shades,* 153–54).

108. Wisdom literature, with its nonhistorical focus, is the exception, but it, too, has no interest in the world of the dead. Note the claim in Job 28:22 that Abaddon (probably a synonym of Sheol) and death do not know where wisdom is to be found.

109. See, e.g., Deut 30:11–14.

110. See Levenson, *Sinai,* 97–101.

Chapter Four: Are Abraham, Moses, and Job in Sheol?

1. *b. B. Bat.* 16a.

2. Rashi ad loc.

3. His comment can be found in Avraham Shoshana, *The Book of Job with the commentaries of RaSHI, Rabbenu Jacob b. Meir Tam, and a disciple of RaSHI* (Hebrew; Jerusalem: Ofeq Institute, 5760/1999), 48. I thank my colleague, Professor Bernard Septimus, for directing me to this volume in particular and for his help with the discussion of Job's supposed denial of resurrection in general.

4. Moshe M. Ahrend, *Rabbi Joseph Kara's Commentary on Job* (Hebrew; Jerusalem: Mossad Harav Kook, 5749/1988), 22.

5. The point is not much affected if we accept the suggestion of BHS to read the second *tiqwātî* as *ṭôbātî* (or the like) on the basis of the Greek.

6. Cooper, "The Fate of Mankind," 27.

7. In v 7, I depart from the NJPS in reading *wĕtakšîlēhû* suggested by the Greek for MT *wĕtašlîkēhû.* In place of "Terror marches him to the king" in v 14, I read *melek ballāhôt* as a construct phrase. On this figure, see Tromp, *Primitive Conceptions,* 119–20.

8. See chapter 3, n 6.

9. For an acutely perceptive and refreshingly sympathetic exploration of the theology of Job's friends, see Carol A. Newsom, *The Book of Job: A Contest of Moral Imaginations* (New York: Oxford University Press, 2003), 90–129.

10. See chapter 3, nn 1 and 3.

11. Johnston, *Shades,* 72. Lewis discounts the telling distribution of the term *Sheol* in his critique of Johnston in "How Far," 188. Lewis prefers a literal reading of the grave-metaphor that Pedersen developed (see above, chapter 3, n 1). "All people are buried; all people go to Sheol," Lewis concludes. But, as we have seen, the application of grave-language to Sheol is not exclusive, and it is misguided to assume that all aspects of burial apply equally to Sheol.

12. Ruth Rosenberg, "The Concept of Sheol within the Context of Ancient Near Eastern Beliefs," dissertation in the Department of Near Eastern Languages and Civilizations, Harvard University (1981), 71. Among her examples of a positive relationship to the grave are Job 5:26; 2 Sam 19:38; Neh 2:3; and 2 Kgs 22:20.

13. Ibid., 163. This is a much more accurate statement than that of Pedersen quoted in chapter 3, n 1.

14. Ibid., 71.

15. Ibid., 85.

16. Note that Rosenberg sometimes employs this more appropriate language herself, e.g., when she writes that "being consigned to the pit does not simply mean to die, but rather to be doomed to die prematurely by divine judgment and wrath" (ibid., 79). A brief but good argument to the effect that death in the Hebrew Bible is never conceived as natural is advanced in Desmond Alexander, "The Old Testament View of Life after Death," *Themelios* 11 (1986): 42. Alexander's idea that "death was perceived by the Hebrews as punishment for man's rebellion against God" (p. 42), however, like his view that "*Sheol* does indeed denote the ultimate abode of the wicked alone" (p. 44), is too sweeping. Unless death is countered by blessing, it is indeed negative, but Sheol is not necessarily punitive. The wicked end up there, but so do the brokenhearted, for example.

17. See chapter 3, n 3.

18. See also Barr, *The Garden,* 29: "Although Sheol is the abode of the dead, it seems to be spoken of mainly in connection with the persons disapproved, the evildoers, the ones who after a rich, powerful and successful life had to be cast down to the lowest of states. . . ."

19. Contra Hallote, *Death, Burial,* 43. Similarly, Eric M. Meyers ("Secondary Burials in Palestine," *BA* 33:1 [Feb. 1970]: 15) sees in the expression "echoes of a time when secondary burial was practiced in pastoral Palestine." But again, if so, the meaning in context is very different. See also his *Jewish Ossuaries: Reburial and Rebirth,* BO 24 (Rome: Biblical Institute Press, 1971). Meyers's insistence there that the idiom indicates that Moses and Aaron were secondarily buried in the promised land (p. 15) is without foundation.

20. Johnston, *Shades,* 34. See the list of passages and the discussion on pp. 33–35.

21. See the list and discussion in Johnston, *Shades,* 34–35.

22. See chapter 7, below.

23. See also Ps 13:4, "lest I sleep the sleep of death" (*pen-ʾîšan hammāwet*).

24. *b. B. Bat.* 57b.

25. See Johnston, *Shades,* 34–35.

26. Examples of passages that seem to regard Sheol as the universal destination are 1 Kgs 2:6; Psalm 49; Job 21:13, and Qoh 9:10. Note also Samuel's prediction to Saul, "Tomorrow your sons and you will be with me" (1 Sam 28:19). Given the violent death predicted for them and, more generally, Yhwh's rejection of Saul, it is reasonable to think the designated locus will be Sheol. It is hard to be certain here, however, since 1 Sam 28:19 never identifies Samuel's subterranean abode as Sheol and gives no clear sense that the deceased prophet is undergoing the deprivations and humiliations that many other texts associate with Sheol. Note also the variant Greek reading "with you," rather than "with me." See McCarter, *I Samuel,* 419. If it is accepted, then Samuel could be predicting Saul and his sons' descent to Sheol without implying that he is there himself. If, on the other hand, we conclude that Samuel was summoned from Sheol in this séance, this hardly establishes the larger claim that all the dead go there. This is so for several reasons, of which the most important is the fact that Samuel may well have died brokenhearted, since his project of anointing a king has so far failed to produce a worthy result and, on the personal level, his sons "did not follow in his ways" but rather became corrupt (1 Sam 8:1–3).

On the understanding of Sheol as the destination of those who die prematurely, violently, punitively, or brokenhearted, Samuel's presence there would thus hardly be surprising. Rosenberg's defense of her understanding of who goes to Sheol can be found in her "Concept," 65–70, 234–45. See also Johnston, *Shades,* 82–84.

27. See Cooper, "Fate," 27, and, more generally, the other works referred to in chapter 3, n 6. For the Ugaritic material, see Baruch Margalit, "Death and Dying in the Ugaritic Epics," in *Death in Mesopotamia,* 243–54.

28. Such as Qoh 9:10. That Qohelet believes that Sheol is the destination of everyone is hardly surprising, since he does not believe in a God who actively intervenes in human destiny at all.

29. One could just as easily call the rabbinic counterpart to "heaven" the "World-to-Come." No judgment is made here about whether assignment to the Garden of Eden was thought to precede or to follow the resurrection of the dead. I simply use Garden of Eden as a cover term to refer to the positive postmortem destination.

30. To be sure, there is room to wonder about where the figures who seem to have escaped death, Enoch (Gen 5:24) and Elijah (2 Kgs 2:11), were taken (*haššāmayîm* in the latter text is best rendered "to the sky," not "to heaven," as in the NJPS). See below, chapter 5. Note, however, that the respective narratives are not interested in this question, unlike the psalms of thanksgiving and those of lament, which are immensely interested in Sheol and provide invaluable information about it. Similarly, there are a few texts in which scholars, with more hope than evidence, find a belief that God will enable the speaker of the prayer to avoid death or to enjoy an Israelite equivalent of Elysium after passing away. See Spronk, *Beatific Afterlife,* 78. Many of these texts are unclear, and all can credibly be interpreted otherwise. See Bruce Vawter, "Intimations of Immortality in the Old Testament," *JBL* 91 (1972): 158–71, and (specifically on Spronk), Karel van der Toorn, "Funerary Rituals and Beatific Afterlife in Ugaritic Texts and in the Bible," *BO* 48:1/2 (1991): 40–66.

31. See chapter 6, below.

32. See Judg 18:30, where the suspended *nûn* in the name of Manasseh suggests the person in question may have been, or was at some point thought to be, Moses' grandson (Exod 2:22).

33. In the Hebrew Bible, that is. In rabbinic literature, "Sheol" has become another name for Gehinnom, the Jewish "hell."

34. See Margalit, "Death," 253.

35. See n 11, above.

36. See n 12, above.

37. James Kugel, "Wisdom and the Anthological Temper," *Prooftexts* 17 (1997): 14–15. I thank my former colleague, Professor Gary A. Anderson, for reminding me of this reflection by our mutual former colleague, Professor James Kugel.

38. This translation departs from the NJPS, which, by rendering *librākâ* "is invoked in blessing," provides more specificity than the words themselves allow, and whose rendering of *šēm* as "fame" seems doubtful, for reasons that will become evident anon.

39. The possibility exists that the Israelite pattern is less innovative than first seems the case. Whether the gloomy underworld was the universal human destination in Mesopotamian and Canaanite cultures is a point that may be open to reexamination. Note this

comment on Mesopotamian conceptions in Lambert, "The Theology," in *Death,* 65: "Thus while both Sumerian and Akkadian had one word and synonyms only for 'death' they do in fact distinguish two kinds: death that comes naturally to mankind at the end of his days, and violent death, from which even the gods were not necessarily exempt. While their literature cannot on a linguistic level distinguish the two, with the result that comment on one can be intertwined with comment on the other, the distinction is a fundamental one without which a grasp of their theology of death will not be attained." Lambert's observation raises the question whether the destinies of both sets of decedents really was identical. Certainly, Mesopotamian culture could generate the idea of a death that is not only natural but also the conclusion of a fortunate, indeed blessed, life. I thank Professor I. Tzvi Abusch for reminding me of "The Mother of Nabonidus," an Akkadian memorial inscription from the sixth century B.C.E., the following excerpt from which strikingly reminds us of the biblical fortunate deaths we have discussed: "My eyesight was good (to the end of my life), my hearing excellent, my hands and feet were sound, my words well chosen, food and drink agreed with me, my health was fine and my mind happy. I saw my great-grandchildren, up to the fourth generation, in good health and (thus) had my fill of old age." The translation is from *ANET,* 561 (the translator is A. Leo Oppenheim). Is there no room to wonder whether Adad-guppi, the woman spoken of here, was thought by the author of the memorial inscription to be in the gloomy, miserable netherworld?

40. Some of the terms of this spurious conclusion have been taken from Pedersen's description of Sheol. See chapter 3, n 2.

41. Cf. Hos 13:14.

42. See the distinction between a "bad" death and a "good" death succinctly made in Bailey, *Biblical,* 48–52.

Chapter 5: *Intimations of Immortality*

In the superscription to this chapter, I have departed from the NJPS translation of Ps 84:5 in order to facilitate the understanding of the midrash quoted in the Talmud.

1. Johnston, *Shades,* 72.

2. The term comes from Spronk, *Beatific Afterlife.* For critiques of it, see Vawter, "Intimations," and van der Toorn, "Funerary Rituals."

3. Rom 5:12–21. On this see, Jon D. Levenson, "Did God Forgive Adam?: An Exercise in Comparative Midrash," in *Jews and Christians: People of God,* ed. Carl E. Braaten and Robert Jenson (Grand Rapids: Eerdmans, 2003), 148–70.

4. The words appear in the blessing to be said at the conclusion of one's being called to the Torah.

5. Much of the oracle is textually difficult. In v 12, read *ḥôtam tabnît.*

6. An assumption defended, for example, by Moshe Greenberg, *Ezekiel 21–37,* AB 22A (New York: Doubleday, 1997), 590. Against this, see John J. Collins, "Before the Fall: The Earliest Interpretations of Adam and Eve," in *The Idea of Biblical Interpretation,* ed. Hindy Najman and Judith H. Newman (Leiden: Brill, 2004), 295–96.

7. See Jon D. Levenson, *Theology of the Program of Restoration of Ezekiel 40–48,* HSM 10 (Missoula: Scholars Press, 1976), 25–36; Manfred Görg, "Wo lag das Para-

dies?" *BN* 2 (1977): 23–33; Lawrence E. Stager, "Jerusalem and the Garden of Eden," *Eretz-Israel* 26 (1999): 184–94; Elizabeth Bloch-Smith, "'Who Is the King of Glory?': Solomon's Temple and Its Symbolism," in *Scripture and Other Artifacts,* ed. Michael D. Coogan et al. (Louisville: Westminster/John Knox, 1994), 18–31; and William P. Brown, *The Ethos of the Cosmos: The Genesis of Moral Imagination in the Bible* (Grand Rapids: Eerdmans, 1999), 248–52.

8. Ibid., 186, 185.

9. Ibid., 187–88.

10. I have found the following comments of Dr. Suzanne Smith helpful in this regard: "Immortality excises the downturn and decline into apparent non-being in the interest of saving (even enshrining) the moment of upspring and incredulity at life entering into greenness and freshness (and their experiential equivalents) out of some lesser, shrunken state. In order to keep that spot of time intact, it has to be figuratively walled off from other moments, and Eden seems, on one level, to be a representation of such a spot of time in space, as does the Temple" (private communication, May 7, 2004).

11. Stager, "Jerusalem," 183–84. On the royal parks and gardens in Jerusalem, see 2 Kgs 25:4; Jer 39:4; 52:7; Qoh 2:5–6; Neh 3:15; and perhaps Song 4:12–16.

12. See Levenson, *Sinai,* 145–76, and, idem, "Zion Traditions," in *ABD,* 6:1098–1102.

13. In v 7, I have altered the NJPS "high mountains" to "mountains of El" in order to capture the likely mythological resonance of the phrase.

14. Clifford, *The Cosmic Mountain,* 37, 48. More generally, see pp. 35–57.

15. In v 8, read *'el-hammayim* with Greek for *'el-hayyāmmâ.* In v 10, read the *kĕtîb, ya'amdû.*

16. See Exod 30:22–30; 37:29.

17. See Clifford, *Cosmic,* 57–79; Levenson, *Sinai,* 145–51.

18. On this, see Gary A. Anderson, *The Genesis of Perfection: Adam and Eve in Jewish and Christian Imagination* (Louisville: Westminster/John Knox, 2001), esp. pp. 46–52.

19. See Jon D. Levenson, "The Jerusalem Temple in Devotional and Visionary Experience," in *Jewish Spirituality from the Bible through the Middle Ages,* World Spirituality 13, ed. Arthur Green (New York: Crossroad, 1986), 39–46.

20. Moshe Weinfeld, "Instructions for Temple Visitors in the Bible and in Ancient Egypt," in *Egyptological Studies,* Scripta Hierosolymitana 28, ed. Sarah Israelite-Groll (Jerusalem: Magnes Press, 1982), 224–50.

21. Cf. Ps 6:6; 30:10; 88:11; 118:17; 119:175; Isa 38:18–20.

22. Ehud Ben Zvi, "Jonah," in *The Jewish Study Bible,* ed. Adele Berlin and Marc Z. Brettler (New York: Oxford University Press, 2004), 1201. On the logic of the placement of the poem in the mouth of Jonah, however, see James S. Ackerman, "Satire and Symbolism in the Song of Jonah," 213–46.

23. But note that the Greek reading *exebalen* would seem to reflect Hebrew *waygāreš.*

24. See Gabriel Barkay, *Ketef Hinnom: A Treasure Facing Jerusalem's Walls* (Jerusalem: The Israel Museum, 1986); Ada Yardeni, "Remarks on the Priestly Blessing on Two Ancient Amulets from Jerusalem," *VT* 41:2 (1991): 176–85; Barkay, "The Priestly Benediction on Silver Plaques from Ketef Hinnom in Jerusalem," *Tel Aviv* 19:2 (1992):

139–94; Erik Waaler, "A Revised Date for Pentateuchal Texts?: Evidence from Ketef Hinnom," *Tyndale Bulletin* 53:1 (2002): 29–55. Barkay dates the script to the second half of the seventh century B.C.E. ("Priestly," 174) and Yardeni (p. 180) to the early sixth, but Waaler seeks an earlier, late eighth- or early seventh-century date (p. 41). The master epigrapher Frank Moore Cross dates it to the mid- to late sixth century. See his *Leaves from an Epigrapher's Notebook,* HSS 51 (Winona Lake, Ind.: Eisenbrauns, 2003), 353, n 24. Johannes Renz advocates an exilic or postexilic date in *Die althebräischen Inschriften* (Darmstadt: Wissenschaftliche Buchgesellschaft, 1995), 1:447–48.

25. Othmar Keel and Christoph Uehlinger, *Göttinnen, Götter, und Gottessymbole,* Quaestiones Disputatae 134 (Freiburg: Herder, 1992), 418. This is from the Ketef Hinnom Silver Amulet Inscription 1, ll. 11–14. Their reading, like all others, is open to considerable doubt. See the variety of opinions in the publications in the previous note.

26. Ibid., 421 (my translation).

27. Christoph Uehlinger, "Gab es eine joschijanische Kultreform?: Plädoyer für ein begrundetes Minimum," in *Jeremia und die deuteronomistische Bewegung,* BBB 98, ed. Walter Groß (Wenheim: Beltz Athenäum, 1993), 68 (my translation).

28. See chapter 7, below. On this narrative, see Armin Schmitt, *Entrückung — Aufnahme — Himmelfahrt: Untersuchungen zu einem Vorstellungsbereich im Alten Testament,* Forschung zur Bibel 10 (Stuttgart: Verlag Katholisches Bibelwerk, 1973), 47–151.

29. E.g., Pss 2:4; 11:4.

30. See Louis Ginzberg, *Legends of the Jews* (Philadelphia: Jewish Publication Society of America, 1913), 4:195–235. Whether already in the Hebrew Bible Elijah was thought to have composed a letter to King Jehoram posthumously, as some have believed, is unclear. See 2 Chr 21:12–15 and Sara Japhet, *I and II Chronicles,* OTL (Louisville: Westminster/John Knox, 1993), 812.

31. E. A. Speiser, *Genesis,* AB 1 (Garden City, N.Y.: Doubleday, 1964), 43. On the Mesopotamian antecedents, see James C. VanderKam, *Enoch: A Man for All Generations* (Columbia: University of South Carolina Press, 1995), 6–14. On the passage in the Bible, see Spronk, *Beatific Afterlife,* 266–67; Schmitt, *Entrückung,* 152–92; and James C. VanderKam, *Enoch and the Growth of an Apocalyptic Tradition,* CBQMS 16 (Washington: Catholic Biblical Association, 1984), 23–51.

32. See Segal, *Life,* 272–81.

33. Rashi to Gen 5:24.

34. Ibn Ezra to Gen 5:24.

35. The translation is by O. S. Wintermute in *The Old Testament Pseudepigrapha,* ed. James H. Charlesworth (Garden City, N.Y.: Doubleday, 1985), 2:62.

36. Artur Weiser, *Psalms* (Philadelphia: Westminster Press, 1962), 385. On the interpretation of these verses, see Spronk, *Beatific,* 327–34, and Schmitt, *Entrückung,* 193–252.

37. See below, chapter 8.

38. See Ps 30:4 and our discussion of it above in chapter 3.

39. In v 24, I have changed "led me toward honor" (NJPS) to "will receive me with glory," for reasons that will become apparent.

40. Schmitt, *Entrückung,* 300, and Dahood, 1:302. On the problem of v 24b in general, see Schmitt, *Entrückung,* 283–302.

41. See Levenson, *Creation*, xvi–xviii.

42. Note the contrast with Psalm 49:18 — "for when he dies he can take (*yiqqaḥ*) none of it along; / his goods (*kĕbôdô*) cannot go down with him (*'aḥărāyw*)" — and Ps 73:24 — "You will receive me (*tiqqāḥēni*) with (*'aḥar*) glory (*kābôd*)." See Spronk, *Beatific*, 327.

43. Spronk, *Beatific*, 327.

44. This use of *lāqaḥ* undermines Alan Segal's conclusion that Enoch and Elijah "are meant to be exceptions; they prove the rule by violating it in such circumstances as to clarify that they are the only two exceptions" (*Life*, 154).

45. Ibid., 345.

46. See chapter 12, below.

47. N. T. Wright, *The Resurrection of the Son of God* (Minneapolis: Fortress Press, 2003), 174. See his important observations on the relationship of immortality to resurrection in the Wisdom of Solomon in general on pp. 162–75.

48. *b. Abod. Zara* 3b. That the children were deceased is evident from the context. See Rashi. In general, see Saul Lieberman, "Some Aspects of After Life in Early Rabbinic Literature," in *Harry Austryn Wolfson Jubilee Volume*, ed. Saul Lieberman et al. (Jerusalem: American Academy for Jewish Research, 1965), 1:495–532.

49. See chapters 12–14.

Chapter 6: Individual Mortality and Familial Resurrection

1. *b. Sanh.* 90b. See chapter 2, above.

2. Barr, *The Garden*, 43.

3. Robert A. Di Vito, "Old Testament Anthropology and the Construction of Personal Identity," *CBQ* 61 (1999): 226–27.

4. It is less clear to me that this is also Di Vito's point. He writes, for example: "The biblical character presents itself to us more as parts than as a whole . . . accordingly, in the OT one searches in vain for anything really corresponding to the Platonic localization of desire and emotion in a central 'locale,' like the 'soul' under the hegemony of reason, a unified and self-contained center from which the individual's activities might flow, a 'self' that might finally assert its control" ("Old Testament Anthropology," 228). On this matter, I have been helped by the following comments of Dr. Suzanne Smith in a private communication (March 31, 2003): "I must say that a self cannot be relatively undefined and permeable (suggesting a sort of liquidity) and readily divisible into discrete parts that are 'almost independent centers' at the same time, unless one envisions the self as something equivalent to molded jello with pieces of fruit suspended in it. Divisibility demands articulated boundaries and a considerable degree of solidity."

5. Di Vito, "Old Testament Anthropology," 227.

6. Aubrey R. Johnson, *The Vitality of the Individual in the Thought of Ancient Israel* (Cardiff: University of Wales Press, 1949), 69, 88.

7. See Pedersen, *Israel*, 172.

8. See Pedersen, *Israel*, 63.

9. Hans Walter Wolff, *Anthropology of the Old Testament* (Philadelphia: Fortress Press, 1974), 20, cited in Di Vito, "Old Testament Anthropology," 218.

10. Johnson, *Vitality*, 66.

11. Ibid., 89.

12. Charles Taylor, *Sources of the Self: The Making of Modern Identity* (Cambridge, Mass.: Harvard University Press, 1989).

13. Di Vito, "Old Testament Anthropology," 220.

14. Ibid., 221.

15. Ibid., 223.

16. See above, chapter 4.

17. See J. Gerald Janzen, "Resurrection and Hermeneutics: On Exodus 3.6 and Mark 12.26," *JSNT* 23 (1985): 43–58, esp. p. 53, where he makes this comment on Rachel's demand of Jacob in Gen 30:1, "Give me children, or I shall die": "If he is not able to give her children, that is an indication . . . that she has not power to give life, her womb is not alive, she is generatively dead. But this means that, for her and in her, the reign of death is virtually absolute."

18. See Levenson, *Death,* 125–42.

19. See, e.g., Rashi to Gen 17:14 and to *b. Shab.* 25b.

20. Donald J. Wold, "The *Kareth* Penalty in P: Rationale and Cases," *SBL Seminar Papers* 1979, vol. 1, ed. Paul J. Achtemeier (Missoula, Mont.: Scholars Press, 1979), 1–45, here p. 15. Note in this context the comment of Rabbah in *b. Yeb.* 55a in regard to punishment with childlessness specified in Lev 20:21: "If he has children, he will bury them; if he does not have children, he will remain childless."

21. Since the deceased kinsman is accounted the father of the child born through levirate marriage (Deut 25:5–10, esp. v 6), Naomi was probably reckoned as the child's grandmother, even though he was born long after both her sons had died.

22. I depart from the NJPS here because I think the last clause is part of Eve's speech.

23. Note that in 1 Chr 4:21, Shelah names his first son "Er," presumably after his deceased oldest brother and probably with the implication that in the end Judah did give Tamar to Shelah (see Gen 38:26).

24. See Levenson, *Death,* 143–69.

25. E.g., see Psalms 6 and 88.

26. See chapter 4.

27. This translation departs from the NJPS, which, by rendering *librākâ* as "is invoked in blessing," provides more specificity than the words themselves allow, and whose rendering of *šēm* as "fame" seems doubtful, for reasons that will become evident anon.

28. William McKane, *Proverbs: A New Approach* (Philadelphia: Westminster Press, 1970), 422–23.

29. See Brichto, "Kin," passim.

30. Though with the later proviso that they must not marry men from outside their own tribe, lest the portion of their own tribe be diminished (Num 36:1–12).

31. On this, see especially Ruth 4:10.

32. See, e.g., P. Kyle McCarter, *II Samuel,* AB 9 (Garden City, N.Y.: Doubleday, 1984), 407–8, and, more recently, van der Toorn, *Family,* 208. Against this, see Schmidt, *Israel's,* passim, esp. p. 253, n 510.

33. Second Sam 18:18 cannot be easily harmonized with 2 Sam 14:27, which records that three sons and one daughter were born to Absalom. If harmonization be sought, the easiest solution is to assume that Absalom's sons had perished (see, e.g, the commentary of Rabbi David Kimchi to 2 Sam 18:18).

34. E.g., Isa 51:4–11 and Ps 74:10–23. See Levenson, *Creation,* 3–25.

Chapter 7: The Man of God Performs a Resurrection

1. See Levenson, *Death,* esp. p. 224.

2. See Michael Fishbane, "Haftarah for Va-Yera," *Etz Hayim: Torah and Commentary,* ed. David L. Lieber (Philadelphia: The Rabbinical Assembly/Jewish Publication Society, 2001), 123.

3. For the translation of *'ednâ* as "fertility" (as opposed to the NJPS's "enjoyment"), see Jonas Greenfield, "A Touch of Eden," in *Al Kanfei Yonah,* ed. Shalom Paul et al., 2:750–55. On p. 754, Greenfield sees the use of the word in Gen 18:12 as denoting, more precisely, "the lubricious quality of the skin due to its being moist and freshened."

4. I have changed the NJPS translation "at the same season next year" in v 14 simply to "next year." On this translation of the elusive phrase *kāʿēt ḥayyâ,* see Mordechai Cogan and Hayim Tadmor, *II Kings,* AB 11 (Garden City, N.Y.: Doubleday, 1988), 57. For our purposes, the important point is that the term is identical in Gen 18:14 and 2 Kgs 4:16 (where the NJPS renders it "at this season next year"), as noted below.

5. Robert L. Cohn, 2 *Kings,* Berit Olam (Collegeville, Minn.: Liturgical Press, 2000), 29.

6. See Levenson, *Death,* 125–42.

7. To be more precise, it ends with the genealogy in which we first hear of Isaac's intended wife, Rebecca, and are thus reassured that the line of Abraham, grievously threatened by the near-sacrifice of his beloved son, will continue (Gen 22:20–24).

8. See, e.g., the use of *lek-lĕkā* ("Go forth") in Gen 12:1 and 22:2, the only occurrences of this phrase in the Hebrew Bible, and note the way 22:15–18 reiterates the language of the early promises to Abraham in 13:16 and 15:5.

9. See Levenson, *Death,* 82–110, and Uriel Simon, *Seek Peace and Pursue It: Topical Issues in the Light of the Bible / The Bible in the Light of Topical Issues* (Hebrew; n.p.: Yedioth Acharonoth and Sifrei Chemed, 2002), 54–57.

10. E.g., Pss 30:4; 34:23; 1 Sam 2:5–6; Ps 113:9. See chapter 3, above.

11. See Levenson, *Death,* 157–64.

12. Note also Gen 37:18–28, where Joseph's brothers resolve first to kill him and then to sell him into slavery.

13. I owe this point about the focus of the stories to Dr. Suzanne Smith.

14. Note the parallel miracles attributed to Elisha's predecessor and master, Elijah (e.g., 1 Kings 17).

15. See chapter 4, above. Commenting on 2 Kgs 4:8–37 and the kindred texts of 1 Kgs 17:17–24 and 2 Kgs 13:20–21, Spronk (*Beatific,* 72) observes that "this revivification of recently deceased persons is more akin to the care of the very ill than to the final resurrection." It may well be that those who died recently were thought to be more susceptible to revivification, but the narrative itself regards the boy as dead and not as "very ill." The critical differences with the "final resurrection" lie elsewhere.

Chapter 8: "Death — Be Broken!"

1. Chapters 6 and 7.

2. E.g., Gen 25:21; 27:41–28:9; 29:31; 30:9–24; 37:18–35; 38:7–10, 27–30.

3. On this danger, see Peter B. Machinist, "The Question of Distinctiveness in Ancient Israel: An Essay," in *Ah, Assyria . . . : Studies in Assyrian History and Ancient Near Eastern Historiography Presented to Hayim Tadmor,* ed. Mordechai Cogan and Israel Ephal (Jerusalem: Magnes Press, 1991), 196–212.

4. For an introduction and translation, see *ANET,* 142–49 (the translator is H. L. Ginsberg). Michael David Coogan, *Stories from Ancient Canaan* (Philadelphia: Westminster Press, 1978), 52–74; and Edward L. Greenstein, "Kirta," in *Ugaritic Narrative Poetry,* ed. Simon Parker (Atlanta: Scholars Press, 1997), 9–48. The vocalization of Ugaritic, in which essentially only consonants were written and there is no subsequent tradition about pronunciation, is notoriously uncertain. Here, I simply follow the forms of the names found in Coogan, *Stories.*

5. See Frank Moore Cross, ʾL, *ʾēl, Theological Dictionary of the Old Testament,* ed. Johannes Botterweck and Helmer Ringgren (Grand Rapids: Eerdmans, 1977), 1:245–48.

6. Coogan, *Stories,* 66.

7. Ibid., 67.

8. Ibid., 69. Ginsberg (*ANET,* 147) and Greenstein (in "Kirta," 31) plausibly render these last lines as a question. How can it be, that is, that a god like Kirta seems to be dying? For our purposes, the sense is not affected.

9. Coogan, *Stories,* 72.

10. See chapter 3, above.

11. For an introduction and translation, see *ANET,* 149–55 (translated by H. L. Ginsberg); Coogan, *Stories,* 27–47; and Parker, "Aqhat," in his *Ugaritic,* 49–80.

12. This English rendering is preferable to "Daniel," which suggests a most unlikely connection with the best-known biblical figure of that name. An allusion to the Danel of Aqhat is more likely, however, in Ezek 14:14, 20 and perhaps 28:3.

13. Coogan, *Stories,* 32–33.

14. Ibid., 33.

15. Ibid., 37.

16. Ibid., 40.

17. Ibid., 41.

18. Ibid., 45.

19. Ibid., 46.

20. Ibid., 33.

21. See William L. Moran, "The Ancient Near Eastern Background of the Love of God in Deuteronomy," *CBQ* 25 (1963): 77–87, rpt. in *The Most Magic Word,* ed. Ronald S. Hendel, CBQMS 35 (Washington: Catholic Biblical Association of America, 2002), 170–81.

Chapter 9: The Widow Re-Wed, Her Children Restored

1. Although essentially only the tribes of the Kingdom of Judah had been exiled, Second Isaiah thinks in terms of the more theologically freighted term, Israel, which refers to the entire chosen people.

2. In v 2, read *ḥaṭṭî* in place of *yaṭṭû,* with various versions.

3. The closest affinity is with the Priestly account of the end of the flood (Gen 9:1–17).

4. In the context of marriage, I use the tetragrammaton rather than the conventional English rendering "LORD" in order to bring out the intensely personal nature of the relationship.

5. Note that Israel and Babylonia now trade places, and the latter, who had afflicted Israel so harshly, loses husband and children even as her erstwhile victim regains them (Isaiah 47).

6. See below, chapter 13.

7. See chapter 7, above.

8. See *ANET,* 131–42; Coogan, *Stories,* 89–115; and Mark S. Smith, "The Baal Cycle," in *Ugaritic,* esp. pp. 135–64. The term "dying-and-rising god" has come under attack of late. See especially Jonathan Z. Smith, *Drudgery Divine: On the Comparison of Early Christianities and the Religions of Late Antiquity* (London: School of Oriental and African Studies; Chicago: University of Chicago Press, 1990), 89–115. In the specific case of Baal, see Mark S. Smith, "The Death of 'Dying and Rising Gods' in the Biblical World," *SJOT* 12 (1998): 257–313. Against this, I find persuasive the argument in Tryggve N. D. Mettinger, *The Riddle of Resurrection: "Dying and Rising Gods" in the Ancient Near East,* CBOTS 50 (Stockholm: Almqvist and Wiksell International, 2001), esp. pp. 57–66. See also John Day, *[YHWH] and the Gods and Goddesses of Canaan,* JSOTSS 265 (Sheffield, U.K.: Sheffield Academic Press, 2000), 117–18. One need not subscribe to the larger claims for a quasi-universal religio-historical category of dying-and-rising god to interpret the story of Baal as that of a deity who has died and risen.

9. See Levenson, *Creation.*

10. See chapter 3, above.

11. See chapter 1, above.

Chapter 10: Israel's Exodus from the Grave

Rabbi Joshua's citation in the superscription to this chapter is 1 Sam 2:6. Rabbi Eliezer's is based on the first half of the same verse but adds words to it in order to justify death and to attribute the resurrection of the dead specifically to God's mercy.

1. See, e.g., Wilhelm Bousset, *Die Religion des Judentums im Späthellenistischen Zeitalter,* 3rd ed., HNT 21 (Tübingen: J. C. B. Mohr/Paul Siebeck, 1926), 506–20, esp. p. 511; Harris Birkeland, "The Belief in the Resurrection of the Dead in the Old Testament," *ST* 3 (1950): 74–77; and Segal, *Life,* 173–203.

2. On the difficulties in the assumption that Israel simply imported the Zoroastrian expectation of resurrection, see also chapter 12.

3. The problem is not unique to this experience but is general in the book of Ezekiel. Cf. Ezekiel 8–11 and 40–48. See Walther Zimmerli, *Ezekiel 2* (Philadelphia: Fortress Press, 1983), 259.

4. *b. Sanh.* 92b.

5. "Breath" may not be the best rendering of *rûaḥ* in this context. Note that the Septuagint reads *rûḥî* ("My breath") in v 6, a version that fits well with even the Masoretic Text of Ezek 36:27. The resurrection, in other words, is effected by God's inspiration of the dead with his own spirit/breath through the medium of the four winds (37:9).

6. John F. Kutsko, *Between Heaven and Earth: Divine Presence and Absence in the*

Book of Ezekiel, Biblical and Judaic Studies from the University of California, San Diego 7 (Winona Lake, Ind.: Eisenbrauns, 2000), 135–37.

7. Ibid., 133.

8. Cf. Ps 139:13–16.

9. Kutsko, *Between Heaven,* 133–34.

10. *b. Sanh.* 91a.

11. E.g., Judg 6:8; 1 Sam 10:18; 12:6; Amos 2:10; 3:1; 9:7; 1 Chr 17:5.

12. Avi Hurvitz, *A Linguistic Study of the Relationship between the Priestly Source and the Book of Ezekiel* (Paris: J. Gabalda, 1982).

13. See chapter 3.

14. See chapter 9.

15. On this, see Cross, *Canaanite Myth,* 112–44.

16. See the fine discussion of this in Baruch J. Schwartz, "Ezekiel's Dim View of Israel's Restoration," in *The Book of Ezekiel: Theological and Anthropological Perspectives,* SBLSS 9, ed. Margaret S. Odell and John T. Strong (Atlanta: Society of Biblical Literature, 2000), 43–67, esp. pp. 53–60.

17. *b. Sanh.* 92b.

18. See above, chapter 7.

19. See Ezekiel 16, 20, 23.

Chapter 11: The Fact of Death and the Promise of Life

1. See Silver, *Where Judaism Differed,* 265–84.

2. Bailey, *Biblical Perspectives,* 38.

3. Di Vito, "Old Testament Anthropology," 221. The words in the single quotes are from John W. Rogerson, "Anthropology and the Old Testament," in *The World of Ancient Israel,* ed. R. E. Clements (Cambridge, U.K.: Cambridge University Press, 1989), 25.

4. On the dating of Pentateuchal sources herein presupposed, see chapter 3, n 101.

5. Note that even in the case of the wise woman of Tekoa, her plea is that David bring back his banished son Absalom, lest the king become like one "without name or remnant upon the earth" (2 Sam 14:7). In other words, she invokes the irreversibility of individual death in defense of intergenerational survival: the survival of the king's identity after his personal death depends on his allowing his son to return. On the intertextual resonance of this, see Larry L. Lyke, *King David and the Wise Woman of Tekoa,* JSOTSS 255 (Sheffield, U.K.: Sheffield Academic Press, 1997).

6. See Barth, *Die Errettung,* 28; and Robert Martin-Achard, *From Death to Life: A Study of the Development of the Doctrine of Resurrection in the Old Testament* (Edinburgh: Oliver and Boyd, 1960), 46.

7. See Barth, *Die Errettung,* 139, where he compares the Akkadian expression *mita bulluṭu,* "to revive the dead," on which see Hirsch, "Den Toten."

8. I have changed the NJPS "past" to "passed," in accordance with proper English grammar.

9. The translation departs from the NJPS in reading *wā'ōmar* or *wā'ômĕrâ* for MT *wĕ'āmar* in v 6, after the Greek and IQIs[a] and in accordance with the situation presup-

posed by the preceding and succeeding verbs. The NJPS translation of v 8b captures the sense in context, though with the larger perspective in mind we can just as readily render the half-line, "But the word of our God stands forever."

10. See Bailey, *Biblical Perspectives,* 48.

11. E.g., Lev 26:9, 22, 29; Deut 28:11, 32, 41, 53–57, 62–63.

12. See Kaminsky, *Corporate Responsibility.*

13. Note also the possibility that "give life" means simply "keep alive" or "sustain in life," as is often the case with the Hebrew verb in question.

14. Johnson, *The Vitality,* 94. See also Martin-Achard, *From Death,* 46, and Barth, *Die Errettung,* 102, 165. I have borrowed the helpful term "biological cessation" from Bailey, *Biblical Perspectives,* 39.

15. The notion that the dead endure, but in a debilitated state that is not "life," seems to apply to those who have experienced the "unfortunate death" of which I have spoken and not to those who die the "fortunate death." Those who endure an unfortunate death are (as Deut 32:39 implies) akin to the ill, whereas those who die a fortunate death end their lives in fulfillment and satisfaction. Until quite late in the Second Temple period, the notion that the latter might long to return to earth is unattested.

16. For the translation of v 5b, which differs from the NJPS, see McCarter, *1 Samuel,* 72.

17. One cannot exclude the possibility that "death" and "Sheol" refer here to the state of deprivation, debility, defeat, and the like, rather than to biological cessation. In other words, it is conceivable that the beneficiaries of God's rescue from Sheol are not "really" dead, as moderns conceive death, but only in a way that appears metaphorical to us. This seems unlikely to me in context, but even if it be so, it does not negate the interpretation that, within the cultural universe of ancient Israel, 1 Sam 2:6 does indeed envision a resurrection of the dead.

18. See chapters 3 and 4, above.

19. See Tromp, *Primitive Conceptions,* 137. There is much room, however, to doubt Tromp's distinction between "the domain of Death" (from which God could save) and the "domain of the dead" (from which there is "no possibility of return"). As we have seen (esp. in chapter 7), it was thought to be possible for a dead person to return from the dead, without reference to Tromp's "domain of Death."

20. 1 Kgs 17:17–24; 2 Kgs 4:8–37. See above, chapter 7. It is less than perfectly clear that the boy whom Elijah revives was, in fact, dead.

21. C. S. Lewis, *Miracles: A Preliminary Study* (New York: Macmillan, 1947), 104.

22. There are reasons to doubt that the disease traditionally translated as "leprosy" was, in fact, the one to which modern clinicians apply the term. Nonetheless, it is clear that Naaman suffered from a chronic and painful skin disorder not easily remedied.

23. See, e.g., Bailey, *Biblical Perspectives,* 4.

24. See below, chapter 13.

25. Di Vito, "Old Testament Anthropology," 221, 200.

26. See my reflections on this phenomenon in Jon D. Levenson, "The Conversion of Abraham to Judaism, Christianity, and Islam," in *The Idea of Biblical Interpretation,* ed. Najman and Newman, 4–7.

27. For illustrations of these last two points, see the references in Brevard S. Childs,

Introduction to the Old Testament as Scripture (Philadelphia: Fortress Press, 1979), 314–16 and 519–20.

28. See the enlightening discussion in Kaminsky, *Corporate Responsibility,* 155–78.

29. 2 Kgs 2:6–12; Gen 5:21–23. See above, chapter 5.

30. 1 Kgs 17:17–24; 2 Kgs 4:8–37; 13:20–21. On 2 Kgs 4:8–37, see above, chapter 7.

31. E.g., Ps 49:6–13; Gen 2:25–3:24; 6:1–4.

Chapter 12: "He Keeps Faith with Those Who Sleep in the Dust"

1. In v 2, note that *'admat 'āpār* ("dust of the earth") may be "a double reading, conflating two synonyms," as John J. Collins puts it in *Daniel,* Hermeneia (Minneapolis: Fortress Press, 1993), 392. Similarly, as often noted (e.g., by BHS), *laḥărāpôt* ("reproaches") may be a gloss on *lĕdir'ôn* ("abhorrence"). Finally, because the NJPS rendering of *maśkîlîm* as "knowledgeable" seems too weak and misleading, I have substituted "wise" in its place throughout. The position of Segal (*Life,* 307) that the term "is actually more causative" and would be better rendered "those who make others wise" is likely but does not make for a felicitous translation. The term *maśkîl* has a rich life in the subsequent history of Judaism. Most relevant to Daniel 12 is its use in the Dead Sea Scrolls. On this, see Carol A. Newsom, "The Sage in the Literature of Qumran: The Functions of the MAŚKÎL," in *The Sage in Israel and the Ancient Near East,* ed. John G. Gammie and Leo G. Perdue (Winona Lake, Ind.: Eisenbrauns, 1990), 373–82.

2. E.g., cf. Judges 4.

3. See George W. E. Nickelsburg, Jr., *Resurrection, Immortality, and Eternal Life in Intertestamental Judaism,* HTS 26 (Cambridge, Mass.: Harvard University Press, 1972), 14, and Collins, *Daniel,* 390.

4. Chapter 11.

5. See Paul D. Hanson, *The Dawn of Apocalyptic: The Historical and Sociological Roots of Jewish Apocalyptic Eschatology,* rev. ed. (Philadelphia: Fortress Press, 1979).

6. This book is not to be identified with others mentioned in Daniel. See Collins, *Daniel,* 391, especially the Qumran parallels adduced there.

7. On the dating, see Brevard S. Childs, *Isaiah,* OTL (Louisville: Westminster/John Knox, 2001), 34–35. Note also the parallel in Mal 3:16–18.

8. See above, chapter 3.

9. Collins, *Daniel,* 392.

10. E.g., 1 Enoch 22.

11. Day, *[YHWH],* 126.

12. On this, see above, chapter 7.

13. See Thomas H. McAlpine, *Sleep, Divine and Human, in the Old Testament,* JSOTSS 38 (Sheffield, U.K.: Sheffield Academic Press, 1987), 15–17. McAlpine puts it nicely on p. 152: "Sleep, then, is a good; but, like most goods, a vulnerable good."

14. *b. B. Bat.* 57b.

15. 2 Kgs 4:1–37; the others are 1 Kgs 17:17–24; 2 Kgs 13:20–21.

16. E.g., Prov 3:15–18; 15:24.

17. See H. L. Ginsberg, "The Oldest Interpretation of the Suffering Servant," *VT* 3 (1953): 400–404, and Nickelsburg, *Resurrection,* 24–26.

18. In v 14, read *ʿālāyw* with the Syriac and Targum. *Yazzeh* in v 15 is very unclear, here translated *ad sensum* and in accordance with the Greek.

19. In Isa 53:10, the NJPS offers as an alternative reading "His arm" (*zĕrôʿô*), on analogy with v 1, understood as a reference to "the vindication which the arm of the LORD effects." This is attractive but lacks versional support. Whether Isa 52:13–53:12 speaks of a death and resurrection is a much-discussed point. See Leonard J. Greenspoon, "The Origin of the Idea of Resurrection," in *Traditions* (ed. Halpern and Levenson), 294–297. In contrast with Greenspoon, Segal (*Life*, 266) maintains that "the most we can say with surety is that the sufferer is brought close to death and then saved by God's will to see his offspring, though he had suffered terribly." But can we not also say that the report of the sufferer's grave (Isa 53:9) makes it likely that he not only came "close to death" but experienced it as well?

20. See Childs, *Introduction*, 314–16.

21. See Collins, *Daniel*, 393, and the references in n 217.

22. Greenspoon, "Origin," 295: "We agree with those who argue that the scene has shifted from the earthly plane, the location of this individual's humiliation, to what we might call the heavenly court, which becomes the location of his exaltation. In other words, God reserved all the rewards due this man until after his death."

23. The translation is the New Revised Standard Version Bible, quoted from *The New Oxford Annotated Bible*, 3rd ed., ed. Michael D. Coogan (Oxford: Oxford University Press, 2001). The translation problems here are severe. See Wright, *The Resurrection*, 347–56, and Dale B. Martin, *The Corinthian Body* (New Haven: Yale University Press, 1995), 123–29.

24. *b. Ber.* 17a.

25. Collins, *Daniel*, 394. See Aristophanes, *Peace*, tr. and ed. Alan H. Sommerstein (Warminster, Wiltshire, U.K.: Aris and Phillips Publishers; Chicago: Bolchazy-Carducci Publishers, 1985), 81. See also Martin, *Corinthian*, 117–20.

26. Contra Segal (*Life*, 291–92), who too readily reads a full-blown angelomorphism into the more restrained simile of Dan 12:3. See the reservations about astral immortality in Wright, *The Resurrection*, 110–12.

27. On the remarkable dependence of Daniel and other late Second Temple compositions on Isaiah 56–66, see, among others, Nickelsburg, *Resurrection*, 20–23, and Segal, *Life*, 263–65.

28. See Nickelsburg, *Resurrection*, 170–73.

29. Like the Song of Hannah. See chapter 11.

30. See Elias Bickerman, "The Maccabean Uprising: An Interpretation," in *The Jewish Expression*, ed. Judah Goldin (New Haven: Yale University Press, 1977), 66–86.

31. Nickelsburg, *Resurrection*, 19.

32. John Day, "The Development of Belief in Life after Death in Ancient Israel," in *After the Exile: Essays in Honour of Rex Mason*, ed. John Barton and David J. Reimer (Macon, Ga.: Mercer University Press, 1996), 248–57. Although Day is here writing about immortality rather than resurrection, his point applies equally well to either.

33. Ahab's punishment is delayed until his son's time because he humbles himself before the LORD (1 Kgs 21:27–29).

34. The notion that God punishes the wicked immediately is especially prominent in Deuteronomy. See Nathan MacDonald, *Deuteronomy and the Meaning of "Monotheism,"* FAT 1, second series (Tübingen: Mohr Siebeck, 2003), 160–62, 165–66.

35. See our discussion of Job's loss and restoration in chapter 6.

36. E.g., Job 23.

37. Wisdom 2.

38. See chapters 1 and 2.

39. The translations from Ben Sira are according to the New Revised Standard Version Bible and again taken from *The New Oxford Annotated Bible.*

40. See the note in *The New Oxford Annotated Bible.*

41. See Wright, *The Resurrection*, 137–40; Segal, *Life,* passim, but esp. pp. 266–69; and Claudia Setzer, *The Resurrection of the Body in Early Judaism and Early Christianity: Doctrine, Community, and Self-Definition* (Leiden: Brill, 2004), esp. pp. 44–52.

42. Dr. Suzanne Smith, private communication. On the problems with the popular deprivation theory of the origins of resurrection, see my review of Segal in *RBL* at http://www.bookreviews.org./bookdetail.asp?TitleId=4277&CodePage=4277 (February 5, 2005).

43. The translation is from Ephraim Isaac, in *The Old Testament Pseudepigrapha,* ed. James H. Charlesworth, 1:24. See Collins, *Daniel,* 395–97, and *The Books of Enoch: Aramaic Fragments of Qumrân Cave 4,* ed. J. T. Milik, with the collaboration of Matthew Black (Oxford: Clarendon Press, 1976), esp. 229–31.

44. Collins, *Daniel,* 395. The passages quoted are from the Book of the Watchers, an originally independent composition that is usually dated to the third century B.C.E.

45. See Hanson, *The Dawn,* esp. pp. 79–208.

46. See chapter 10, above.

47. On the translation "as a corpse," see Philip C. Schmitz, "The Grammar of Resurrection in Isaiah 26:19a–c," *JBL* 122 (2003): 145–49. For *'ôrōt* as "fresh growth," see 2 Kgs 4:39 (where the NJPS renders it "sprouts"). In Isa 26:19, the term may have the more usual meaning, "lights." The translation of the last stich departs from the NJPS, which reads, "You made the land of the shades come to life," apparently on the grounds that *hippîl* has the meaning "to drop young" and thus carries with it a connotation of new life (see *BDB,* 658, and note the use of the *qal* of the same root in v 18). The more usual translation "to make something fall" seems more in order, with "dew" as the understood object.

48. Childs, *Isaiah,* 189.

49. Spronk, *Beatific Afterlife,* 301.

50. On the likely mythological connections of this dew, see Spronk, *Beatific Afterlife,* 304, and Day, *[YHWH],* 120. On the importance of dew in the rabbinic picture of resurrection, see Löwinger, "Die Auferstehung," 66–70.

51. Collins, *Daniel,* 395. So also Day, *[YHWH],* 116. See also his bibliographic references on p. 123, n 86.

52. Robert Martin-Achard, *From Death,* 131.

53. See Theodore J. Lewis, "Mot," *ABD,* 4:922–24.

54. See above, chapter 6.

55. See Childs, *Isaiah,* 191–92.

Chapter 13: God's Ultimate Victory

1. Day, *[YHWH]*, 122.

2. Verse 13b departs from the NJPS and follows instead the translation of Francis I. Andersen and David Noel Freedman, *Hosea*, AB 24 (Garden City, N.Y.: Doubleday, 1980), 625, explained on p. 638.

3. For the translation, see chapter 12, n 47.

4. Reading *wĕyēbôš* as some form of *yābēš*, either *yābēš* itself or *yôbîš*.

5. Day, *[YHWH]*, 122.

6. Ibid., 57–59.

7. Ibid., 122.

8. Ibid., 119–20.

9. Read *yōreh* as *yarweh*, with the Syriac and the Targum. *Malqôš* ("latter rain") probably attracted the change to *yôreh,* which can mean "early rain."

10. See the list in Day, *[YHWH]*, 118, n 76, and note as well Michael Barré, "New Light on the Interpretation of Hosea VI 2," *VT* 28 (1978): 129–41.

11. See chapter 3.

12. Barré, "New Light," 137–38. Oddly, Barré then contradicts himself when he writes that "on its 'primary' level of meaning, Hos vi 2 clearly envisages the recovery of the sick; it has nothing to do with the resurrection of the dead" (p. 140).

13. This departs from the NJPS translation of the first and last verbs as "make whole" and "be whole," respectively, a translation that has been dictated by an interpretation of the verse as having nothing to do with resurrection.

14. Day, *[YHWH]*, 119. The others are Isa 26:14, 19; Job 14:12, 14.

15. E.g., Deut 32:39; 1 Sam 2:6. See above, chapter 11.

16. 1 Kgs 17:17–24; 2 Kgs 4:8–37; 13:20–21. See above, chapter 7.

17. On the issue of the dying and rising god, see chapter 9.

18. Day, *[YHWH]*, 118. Examples of such polemic can be found in Hos 2:10, 15, 18–19; 9:10; 11:2; 13:1–2.

19. On the connection of rainfall to resurrection in rabbinic thought, see Löwinger, "Die Auferstehung," 58–61.

20. E.g., Hos 2:4–25.

21. See Cross, *Canaanite Myth*, 91–111, and Patrick D. Miller, *The Divine Warrior in Early Israel*, HSM 5 (Cambridge, Mass.: Harvard University Press, 1973).

22. Cross, *Canaanite Myth*, 162–63.

23. Contra Lynn White, Jr., "The Historical Roots of Our Ecologic Crisis," in *Ecology and Religion in History,* ed. David and Eileen Spring (New York: Harper and Row, 1974), 15–31. For an effective critique of White, see James Barr, "Man and Nature — The Ecological Controversy and the Old Testament," *BJRL* 55:1 (1972): 9–32.

24. See Moshe Weinfeld, *Justice and Righteousness in Israel and the Nations: Equality and Freedom in Ancient Israel in Light of Social Justice in the Ancient Near East* (Hebrew; Jerusalem: Magnes Press, 1985), esp. pp. 12–56. Essentially the same discussion is elaborated in the English edition, *Social Justice in Ancient Israel and in the Ancient Near East* (Jerusalem: Magnes Press; Minneapolis: Fortress Press, 1995), 25–96.

25. I render *mālāk* in v 1 "has become king" to convey the drama and character of the

event, which are not captured by the NJPS translation "is king." On this, see Sigmund Mowinckel, *The Psalms in Israel's Worship*, 2 vols. (New York: Abingdon, 1967), 1:107–9, and 2:222–24. In v 11, some read "Light shines" (*zrḥ* for *zrʿ*) and *śimḥâ* as the more familiar "joy, happiness" rather than the less known homonym that means "radiance."

26. I owe this formulation to Dr. Suzanne Smith (private communication).

27. Greenspoon, "Origin," 280.

28. Collins, *Daniel*, 395.

29. Cf. Ps 92:10–16.

30. See Cross, *Canaanite Myth*, 164–74. Note that Cross associates Isaiah 34–35 with the work of Second Isaiah (chapters 40–55).

31. The NJPS parenthetical gloss in v 7 derives from the close parallel in Isa 34:13. Note that Isaiah 34 and 35 are but two passages of several in the book of Isaiah that appear to derive from an exilic or early postexilic source associated with Second and Third Isaiah. Segal (*Life*, 202–3) draws justified attention to Isaiah 66, in which one result of the envisioned redemption is that the bones of the redeemed "flourish like grass" (v 14).

32. See the words of Michael Barré cited n 12, above, and our chapter 3.

33. On this notion, see chapter 4.

34. See chapter 10.

35. But note the argument that Jewish apocalyptic eschatology assumed its characteristic shape quite early in the Persian period in Hanson, *Dawn*, esp. pp. 395–401.

36. Day, "The Development," 242.

37. As even Bousset recognizes: "Es gibt überhaupt keine Entlehnung, wenn nicht der Boden dafür irgendwie bereitet ist" (*Die Religion*, 511).

Chapter 14: Epilogue

I have rendered the biblical citation in the superscription (Prov 8:6) differently from the NJPS in order to bring out the sense of the midrash.

1. E.g., Gen 17:7–8; Exod 32:9–14.

2. The majority position that develops in rabbinic tradition maintains that gentiles, who are without Torah, can nonetheless "have a portion in the World-to-Come" if they observe the seven Noahide commandments (see *b. Sanh.* 56a–56b). The question of the stake of gentiles in the Torah was, however, a controversial one among the rabbis. On this, see Marc Hirshman, *Torah for the Entire World* (Hebrew; Tel Aviv: Hakibbutz Hameuchad, 1999).

3. See Solomon Schechter, *Aspects of Rabbinic Theology: Major Concepts of the Talmud* (New York: Schocken, 1961), 242–63. Schechter's study, though first published in 1909, remains highly worthwhile on this and many other points. See also Urbach, *The Sages: Their Concepts and Beliefs* (Cambridge, Mass.: 1975), 471–83. The idea that Judaism teaches that human beings are fundamentally good is a piece of modernist apologetics unsupported by the classical sources. On this, see Joel S. Kaminsky, "Paradise Regained: Rabbinic Reflections on Israel at Sinai," in *Jews, Christians, and the Theology of the Hebrew Scriptures*, ed. Alice Ogden Bellis and Joel S. Kaminsky, SBLSS 8 (Atlanta: Society of Biblical Literature, 2000), 15–43. See also Levenson, "Did God Forgive Adam?"

4. See, e.g., *Pes. R. Kah.* 24:2.

5. See Kaminsky, "Paradise Regained," 35–39.

6. See Schechter, *Aspects*, 264–92.

7. Here, I have rendered the last verb in accordance with the alternative translation in the NJPS note in order to bring out the association with death that the midrash makes.

8. The Shema consists of Deut 6:4–9; 11:13–21; and Num 15:37–41. Its second paragraph focuses on reward and punishment. One of the occasions on which it is recited is at bedtime.

9. E.g., *b. Shab.* 55a–b. I thank Dr. Suzanne Smith for drawing this passage to my attention.

10. E.g, *b. Meg.* 28b: "Anyone who studies halakhot every day is assured that he is a member of the World-to-Come." In this regard, mention should also be made of the Sabbath as an earnest of the coming world (e.g., *m. Tam.* 7:4). Both of these passages eventually came into prayer books and thus have become widely known even among Jews without much rabbinic learning.

11. See Schwartz, "Ezekiel's Dim View."

12. Esp. in chapter 10.

13. See, e.g., *Qoh. Rab.* 1:4:2. On this, see Löwinger, "Die Auferstehung," 74–79.

14. See Janzen, "Resurrection," 49: "One may assume some continuity, some internal and intrinsic connection and identity between the risen life and the historical life which preceded it. In some sense the risen person must be said to be the same person who historically lived and died. But the conditions of the risen life — its modalities — are such as to display aspects of discontinuity. This means, however, that the conditions obtaining in historical existence, while suggestive or adumbrative of the other, cannot entirely control or determine our envisagement of the other."

15. On this, see especially Kaminsky, "Paradise Regained."

16. I have changed the biblical quotes from the NJPS in order to facilitate the understanding of the midrash.

17. Here, too, I have changed the NJPS rendering of Exod 19:19 so as to highlight the connection of the *qôl* of the shofar to God's reply.

18. 2 Chr 3:1. See Levenson, *Death*, 114–24.

19. See Levenson, *Death*, 193–99, and Shalom Spiegel, *The Last Trial* (New York: Behrman House, 1950), passim. Note especially Spiegel's discussion of the connection of the merit accrued in the aqedah to the future resurrection of the dead on pp. 109–13.

20. See chapter 1.

21. On the role of the shofar or trumpet at the resurrection, see Löwinger, "Die Auferstehung," 65. The connection of the horn with resurrection is prerabbinic, as evidenced by 1 Cor 15:52.

22. See R. W. L. Moberly, "The Earliest Commentary on the Akedah," *VT* 38 (1988): 302–23, and Levenson, *Death*, 178–84.

Index of Ancient Sources

Index of Authors